Ethics, Hunger and Globalization

The International Library of Environmental, Agricultural and Food Ethics

VOLUME 12

ETHICS, HUNGER AND GLOBALIZATION

IN SEARCH OF APPROPRIATE POLICIES

Edited by

Per Pinstrup-Andersen
Cornell University
U.S.A.

and

Peter Sandøe
University of Copenhagen
Denmark

 Springer

A C.I.P. Catalogue record for this book is available from the Library of Congress.

ISBN 978-1-4020-6130-1 (HB)
ISBN 978-1-4020-6131-8 (e-book)

Published by Springer,
P.O. Box 17, 3300 AA Dordrecht, The Netherlands.

www.springer.com

Printed on acid-free paper

TABLE OF CONTENTS

SOCIAL JUSTICE, ETHICS, AND HUNGER: WHAT ARE THE KEY MESSAGES?

The international human-rights commitments which the world's governments have accepted over the past half century, if taken seriously as shared values and as legal obligations, are invaluable tools for addressing the inequities of the global economy and the divisions between nations and peoples which are so evident today.

This book will carry that broad theme forward by focusing on one stark reality – millions of men, women, and children on our planet wake up hungry and go to bed hungry each day. The contributors to this book, leading scholars in the fields of ethics, economics, religion, and nutrition, are suggesting a new vision that combines ethics and economics – a vision that recognizes both legitimate national interests and global concerns, and which highlights the connections between ethical principles and law – which for me, of course, centrally includes international human-rights law.

The book seeks to promote concrete policies and practical actions that will reduce poverty, hunger, and malnutrition. As other contributors, notably Professor Asbjørn Eide, have done, I want to reinforce the case for the importance of including a human-rights perspective in efforts to eliminate global hunger. Why? First, because human rights open up new avenues of advocacy and action across a range of areas related to hunger; from agricultural policies and research to technology development, from food production to food safety. Equally important, by embracing a human-rights perspective, we are able to draw on tools of legal accountability which can help push governments and other actors to take appropriate actions to fight hunger and poverty.

THE REALITIES OF GLOBAL HUNGER

It is worth taking a moment to remind ourselves of just what hunger means in human terms. I came face-to-face with the reality of hunger and poverty during my time as President of Ireland and, later, as UN High Commissioner for Human Rights. I remember, as if it were yesterday, my visit to Somalia as President of Ireland. I sat beside women whose children were dying – and children whose mothers were dying. As a mother myself, I felt the sheer horror of that. But as the Head of State of a country that was once devastated by famine while vast quantities of food were shipped abroad, I also felt the terrible and helpless irony that this could actually be

vii

happening again. And, quite frankly, I felt then – and have never lost – a profound sense of anger and outrage and, indeed, self-accusation that we are all participants in that re-enactment.

But if we are to come to terms with the sense that we should be following a different course, and doing more, it is just as important that we also reflect briefly on the almost mind-numbing statistics on world hunger. According to the World Hunger Map, every seven seconds a child under the age of 10 dies – directly or indirectly of hunger – somewhere in the world. The UN's Food and Agricultural Organization (FAO) has recently estimated that the number of undernourished people around the world has increased to 840 million: comprising 799 million in developing countries, 30 million in countries in transition, and 11 million in industrialized countries.

On top of these horrifying statistics, more than 2 billion people around the world suffer from so-called 'hidden hunger' or micronutrient malnutrition, resulting in children who fail to develop their normal physical and intellectual capacities – and will suffer as a result.

We know, too, that the hunger crisis is compounded further by, and interlinked with, other global challenges which must be fought vigorously if we hope to make progress in achieving food security for all. Perhaps the most difficult is the fight against HIV/AIDS. The interconnection between AIDS and hunger can be seen most starkly in Africa, where infection rates are rising among African women. Almost 60% of those living with AIDS in Africa are now women. Women also represent 80% of Africa's small farmers, who have traditionally been able to help their families and communities in times of food crisis. But the toll being taken by AIDS makes this task increasingly difficult.

I learned an important lesson recently about the connections between food security and HIV/AIDS. I was observing the work of a small non-governmental organization (NGO), Mamelani, which provides training and support for a community living in Khayelitsha outside Cape Town. I was reprimanded severely for taking too simplistic an approach to the issue of access to drugs and treatment. 'There are too many voices calling for those who are HIV-positive to have access to antiretroviral drugs, without making it clear that these drugs may be necessary towards the end, but that good nutrition is far more relevant to prolonging life and to the quality of that life,' I was told. My informant continued:

> People who are HIV-positive require greater quantities of vitamins and minerals in order to bolster their immune system and stave off the dire effects of full-blown AIDS. Selenium, vitamin A, and magnesium are particularly crucial. Foods rich in these should be readily available so that the gap period between infection and illness can be widened. With provision comes the need for proper nutritional education to prevent the grave tendency of people falling sick to believe that their only recourse lies in antiretroviral treatment. Indeed, nutrition must be ensured throughout or the benefits of this treatment will be minimal.

The speaker was my 23-year-old son, a volunteer with Mamelani, which teaches appropriate vegetable growing as part of a broader wellness program. The vegetables are grown on plots the size of an average door, which is the space between homes in that part of Khayelitsha.

Unfortunately, the problems don't end with coping with the AIDS pandemic. Lack of access to water supplies, failing local and national markets, inadequate infrastructure, weak national governance, and lack of responsible policy and action by the international community all fuel the food crisis.

Hunger, as we know, is still predominantly a rural problem. Of the 1.2 billion people who suffer from extreme poverty in the world today, 75% live and work in rural areas. The rural poor who suffer from hunger lack access to land resources, are often bound by unjust sharecropping contracts, or cannot grow enough food to feed themselves or their families.

The shocking truth is: We know that hunger is avoidable. There are sufficient food resources in the world to ensure that all the people should have enough to eat. Yet, the reality is that many of the current responses to hunger focus on food production, rather than on food distribution. Without getting into a debate on the efficacy and safety of biotechnology, or the importance of ongoing efforts to enhance agricultural yields, the mere fact that people are starving despite a superabundance of food suggests that we should look harder at how existing food supplies are distributed. Where they are distributed through market mechanisms that are not accessible to those without resources, questions should be asked about agricultural development policies which invest so little in small farmers and local food systems, and which would be more likely to actually feed people who cannot access food through normal market systems.

The bottom line is that we are in desperate need of new approaches, new ideas. We are not progressing at the necessary pace to reach the target originally set in 1996 by the World Food Summit, reiterated in the UN Millennium Declaration in 2000 and at the World Food Summit 2002, of halving the number of hungry people by the year 2015.

The issue we must address is: How could a new framework, based around ethics, social justice, and human rights, make a significant difference in ridding ourselves of hunger now and in the future?

A HUMAN-RIGHTS APPROACH TO FOOD SECURITY

How does a human-rights approach help in addressing the problem of hunger? First, by affirming the equal value and dignity of every individual. By reframing the debate on hunger in terms of rights, it means that taking action is an obligation, not a form of charity. Citizens and civil society groups can use a human-rights approach to put pressure on their national governments, reminding them of their commitments and demanding full civil society participation in the design and implementation of specific reforms.

Since the adoption of the Universal Declaration of Human Rights by the United Nations in 1948, the right to adequate food has been recognized as a central component of the right to an adequate standard of living. This right has also been confirmed in the principal human-rights conventions, in particular, Article 11 of the International Covenant on Economic, Social and Cultural Rights, which has been ratified, and thus accepted as a legal obligation, by the majority of the world's countries.

Most recently, in the Declaration adopted at the Rome World Food Summit in June 2002, the international community reaffirmed 'the right of everyone to have access to safe and nutritious food.'

But what does having this right mean in practice? Essentially, the right to food obligates governments to ensure that adequate food is available, either through domestic production or trade. They must ensure that all people within their jurisdiction have access to food, and that access is not conditional on one's relative wealth, social status, or nationality. As the United Nations Special Rapporteur on the Right to Food, Professor Jean Ziegler, points out in a recent report to the UN Commission on Human Rights, the right to food does not mean simply handing out free food to everyone.

The obligations that this right places on States are best captured in the General Comment, No. 12, adopted by the UN Committee on Economic, Social and Cultural Rights, the expert body mandated to monitor States' compliance with their treaty obligations under the Covenant. As the Committee puts it, the right to adequate food imposes three types of obligations on States: to *respect*, to *protect* and to *fulfill*. The obligation to *respect* requires governments not to take political or other measures that would seriously reduce the availability of food or that would prevent access to adequate food for vulnerable populations. The obligation to *protect* includes the State's responsibility for ensuring that the actions of other governments, private entities or individuals, including transnational corporations over which they exercise jurisdiction, do not threaten the availability of food or deprive individuals of their access to adequate food. The obligation to *fulfill* requires that governments identify vulnerable groups among their populations, such as the physically disabled, children, and victims of natural disasters, and provide food and assistance using strategies that ensure the achievement of a long-term capability of people to feed themselves.

The fulfillment of the right to adequate food requires steps to be taken by all appropriate means, including, in particular, the adoption of legislative measures, supported by the necessary administrative capacity within the public and private sectors where appropriate.

Some 20 countries have adopted constitutions that, in more or less explicit terms, refer to rights concerning food or a related norm. A smaller number have developed legislative means to ensure enjoyment of the right to food in a comprehensive way. But it has become increasingly clear that many governments need additional guidance in taking the steps required to progressively implement the right to adequate food.

MOVING THE RIGHT TO FOOD FORWARD

The World Food Summit in 2002 recommended the elaboration of voluntary guide-lines to support these efforts in the context of national food security. An Inter-governmental Working Group was established to elaborate, over a period of two years, a set of guidelines for this purpose and the FAO Committee on World Food Security has adopted voluntary guidelines to support the progressive realization of the right to adequate food.

The guidelines, although a voluntary instrument, are seen by many as a break-through that will give new energy to efforts to achieve the UN Millennium Goal of halving the number of the world's hungry by 2015. They address the range of actions that governments should take to ensure food security for all at a national level. They provide a new international reference for civil society organizations in scrutinizing governments' performance in defeating hunger and malnutrition around the world. Legal experts will undoubtedly draw on the guidelines in future proceedings involving food security at a national level. I would encourage this book to review these guidelines and consider how they might inform your conclusions and recommendations in the future.

I must be clear in stressing that each country is responsible for ensuring the right to adequate food for its own citizens. But achieving food security for all won't be possible for the poorest people on the planet without more responsible policies and actions on the part of the richest nations.

What would more responsible policies look like in practice? The FAO Panel of Eminent Experts on Ethics in Food and Agriculture has found that, over the past 15 years, aid to agriculture and rural development has declined by nearly half. The Panel also notes that many developed countries have not fulfilled their commitment of contributing 0.7% of their gross national product for development assistance, and have not provided sufficient assistance to the agricultural sector.

The links between adequate food and access to productive resources such as land are also addressed through this analysis. Human-rights standards make it clear that vulnerable people, including landless people, need special attention, and that indigenous peoples and women should be entitled to the right to inheritance and ownership of land. Human-rights standards also emphasize the importance of access to information and scientific knowledge, such as information on nutrition and reform of agrarian systems, in such a way as to achieve the most efficient development and utilization of natural resources.

Clearly, such policies must be changed if rich nations are to play a more constructive role in eliminating hunger. That will require political courage and a greater public awareness of the connections between poverty and global instability which can affect us all.

The FAO Panel rightly observed that:

> Market globalization must be matched by responsible and responsive global governance through institutions capable of ensuring the enjoyment of human rights – including the right to adequate food and

to be free from hunger – to everyone. The international community, through its institutions and organizations, must recognize its duties to offset the negative consequences of globalization on a very un-level playing field, and to advance conditions that generate equal opportunity for all.

The project I now lead – Realizing Rights: The Ethical Globalization Initiative – has been working with the Aspen Institute and the Brookings Institution on precisely this question: How to encourage a more informed and principled approach, here in the United States, to the fight against global poverty. Earlier this year we convened a group of leading experts and policy-makers around the issue of how to influence the USA's policy agenda on poverty. The results of this initial discussion, which will continue next year, are available in a report, *America's Role in the Fight Against Global Poverty*, available on the websites of EGI, the Aspen Institute and the Brookings Institution.

The point is that human-rights standards, together with the international system that has been built up to interpret and support national governments in implementing their treaty obligations, provides important guidance. I wish to stress, however, that human rights alone won't provide all the answers. Some of the dilemmas around hunger that we are facing today present moral and ethical questions that human-rights standards can certainly help to identify but do not always resolve. Consider, for example, the role of the food and agriculture industry. The actors involved in addressing hunger are not only States but also multinational corporations. Every facet and segment of the global food system is increasingly dominated by huge transnational corporations which monopolize the food chain, from the production, trade, and processing, to the marketing and retailing of food. This narrows choices for farmers and consumers. What are the ethical and human-rights responsibilities of this influential industry sector?

According to a recent report, just 10 corporations control one-third of the US$23-billion commercial seed market and 80% of the US$28-billion global pesticide market. Monsanto alone controls 91% of the global market for genetically modified seed. Another 10 corporations, including Cargill, control 57% of the total sales of the world's leading 30 retailers and account for 37% of the revenues earned by the world's top 100 food and beverage companies. In South Africa, Monsanto completely controls the national market for genetically modified seed, 60% of the hybrid maize market, and 90% of the wheat market. Wal-Mart, the world's largest food retailer, is expected to single-handedly control 35% of US food and drug sales by 2007.[1]

Does the current structure of the global food system influence the increasing focus on agricultural yields, and the relative lack of attention paid to how food is distributed locally, nationally and internationally? Some experts contend that the more that companies keep the emphasis on increased yields, the less they have to answer for the distortions caused by their disproportionate market share, and for the social impacts of the agricultural policies they help to advance through their extraordinary influence on the political process.

Due to their size and resources, these corporations can bring increased efficiency to food production – but they can also distort markets, threatening food security and ecosystems. In pointing out that the quest for monopoly profits can lead companies to constrain food access for poor people, Jean Ziegler affirmed last year that 'despite the fact that transnational corporations increasingly control our food system, there are still relatively few mechanisms in place to ensure that they respect standards and do not violate human rights.'[2]

Thus, a new challenge is to ensure that such powerful actors in the globalized economy are accountable for the impact of their policies on human rights, including the right to adequate food. However, most global agri-food companies have yet to sign up to corporate social responsibility initiatives such as the UN Global Compact. Other business sectors, such as the pharmaceutical and IT sectors, which we at EGI are working with through a three-year project – the Business Leaders Initiative on Human Rights – are addressing their respective industry human-rights responsibilities. I would challenge agribusiness to join us in doing the same. These complex issues are effectively dealt with in the various chapters of this book.

What is the significance of the political initiative started on 20 September 2004, when the Presidents of Spain, Brazil, France, and Chile, together with the United Nations Secretary General, presented the idea of a Global Fund Against Hunger and Poverty based on innovative financing mechanisms? I am aware that Oxfam welcomed this initiative as 'an important effort to refocus the priorities of the global agenda,' although it had some reservations. As Honorary President of Oxfam, I am happy to quote them as follows:

> Nevertheless, it is essential to take into account that the 'innovative' mechanisms proposed in the Fund against Hunger will never be an alternative to the principal sources of financing for development. It is these principal sources that will be a measure of the true effort of donor countries: a sustained and ambitious increase in aid flows; effective measures to reduce the foreign debt burden; and fair rules of trade that allow poor countries to take advantage of the opportunities that trade has to offer them. . . .
>
> None of this reduces the importance of finding new ways to finance development. If it achieves adequate backing, the Global Fund against Hunger and Poverty can channel important additional resources through 'innovative financing mechanisms'. In fact, the proposal touches on endemic problems in international development, such as the regulation of tax havens and speculative capital.
>
> The fundamental contribution of the Fund is the political impetus it will give to some initiatives that are already known, among which the following stand out:
>
> • The tax on international financial transactions would not only contribute significant economic resources, but also would help to

stabilize financial markets and alleviate the effects of crises, such as the one suffered by East Asia in the nineties.
- The granting of Special Drawing Rights by the IMF can partly resolve the chronic lack of hard-currency reserves suffered by many developing countries, especially during times of trade and financial crisis.
- The initiative also includes the International Financial Aid Program proposed by the British government two years ago. Despite the fact that there are still many doubts about this instrument, its passage opens the possibility to move forward future commitments in development aid by issuing bonds, backed by donor countries, on the capital market.

CONCLUSION

The message I wish to leave with the reader should come as no surprise: All of us – as individuals, communities, governments, businesses, civil society, and academic institutions – have responsibilities for reducing hunger, here in the United States and around the world.

While national governments have primary responsibility for the protection of human rights, international law also places obligations on States to cooperate and work together in order to create the conditions under which these rights can be realized worldwide. We must prove to people around the world who are denied their fundamental rights that these commitments have meaning, and that we will hold our governments accountable for their actions or inaction.

No one can deny that overcoming global hunger requires better and more responsible governance at all levels. However, it requires the active engagement of the wider society as well. Encouraging such participation is one of the chief strengths of the human-rights approach. The language of rights can be a powerful motivating force that enables members of civil society to mobilize support so they can ensure that the fundamental objective of food security for all is realized. Books such as this one are encouraging because they can provide both grassroots organizations and policy-makers with principled messages that can shape advocacy and legislation in the future.

Making progress in the fight against global hunger will require resources and commitment on an unprecedented scale. It will require that the richest nations see it as part of their long-term national interest to help those governments most in need to strengthen their own systems of governance. This will include rebuilding the capacity of the State to ensure respect for the rule of law and to provide essential public services.

But it will also require us to look beyond immediate responsibilities to our own families, communities, and nations, and to recognize collective responsibilities to our fellow women and men wherever they may be. Perhaps the time has finally come to acknowledge, as the Universal Declaration of Human Rights put it more than half a century ago – 'the inherent dignity and . . . equal and inalienable rights of all members of the human family.'

MARY ROBINSON
Executive Director, Ethical Globalization Initiative

NOTES

[1] *Everyday Low Wages: The Hidden Price We All Pay for Wal-Mart.* A Report by the Democratic Staff of the Committee on Education and the Workforce, US House of Representatives, Representative George Miller (D-CA), Senior Democrat [available at http://www.agribusinessaccountability.org/page/310/1].
[2] *Third Annual Report to the United Nations General Assembly by the United Nations Special Rapporteur on the Right to Food.*

INTRODUCTION AND SUMMARY

The statistics are well known: One-fifth of the world population live in extreme poverty, one in seven is food-insecure, every third preschool child in developing countries does not grow to his or her full potential because of malnutrition, and 10 million of these children die every year of malnutrition, infectious diseases, and other causes that could easily have been avoided. The statistics go on. Why does so much human misery exist in a world that possesses enough resources to assure a healthy and comfortable life for all world citizens? And is it fair? Is it ethical that a small proportion of the world population lives in conditions of material excess, while at the same time so many are unable to meet the most basic needs, such as food, shelter, and clean water?

Whether the current situation is fair or not cannot be answered in an objective, scientific manner. The answer depends on the values of the individual and groups of individuals asked. However, the rhetoric coming from policy-makers is clear: Speech after speech made in national and international fora stress that it is not fair and that something must be done about it. Consider, for example, the Millennium Declaration signed by all world leaders in the year 2000 in which they agreed that 'we will spare no effort to free our fellow men, women, and children from the abject and dehumanizing conditions of extreme poverty, to which more than a billion are subjected.' But most of the rhetoric is not followed up with appropriate action. Is this because policy-makers do not know what action is needed or are they, in all insincerity, simply making what they consider to be politically correct statements with no intention to translate the promises and plans into action? Since the policy-makers are generally well-off and supported by the better-off portion of the population, are they simply unwilling to make the sacrifices they think would be needed to help the less fortunate out of poverty and related misery? Is policy action guided by zero-sum thinking, in which anybody else's gain is my loss, ignoring net social gains from human capital development and improved stability?

How and to what extent do ethical considerations enter into policy decision-making? What are the perceived moral rights and duties of the various population groups? And what are the duties of governments as perceived by policy-makers? Does a desire for social justice play an important role? Economics plays an important role in decision-making but how do ethics and economics interact? What ethical principles should guide policy advice and policy decisions? By tackling these and related questions, this book aims to contribute to our understanding of how ethics and economics interact in policy formulation and to the debate and the design and implementation of policy action to alleviate poverty, hunger, and malnutrition in

1

P. Pinstrup-Andersen and P. Sandøe (eds.), Ethics, Hunger and Globalization: In Search of Appropriate Policies, 1–13.
© 2007 *Springer*.

a rapidly globalizing world. We hope that the book will help develop a shared vision that combines ethics and economics, to counter world poverty, hunger, and malnutrition, and thus contribute to the achievement of the Millennium Development Goals.

Even though ethical thinking may help those in charge to make things happen, ethics also has another role which is less directly related to action. This is to allow those involved in the process of trying to fight poverty and create development to stop and *reflect*. Ethical reflection may be directed at key concepts. Take, for example, equality. Everyone seems to agree that the goal is a more equal world, but what is meant by 'equality'? Is equality a goal in itself and, if so, how is it to be defined? Or is equality a means for future development and poverty alleviation? There is, to take another example, clearly a need to reflect on the relations between means and ends in development. Respect for human rights may be a constraint on the effort to create development – but isn't it also a part of the goal? And, if so, how does the alleviation of poverty weigh relative to the creation of political freedom? And, to mention one last example, how are common values to be found in a climate with growing focus on cultural diversity and respect for local autonomy?

The last question points to a clear role for ethics in development: to assist in finding ways of creating a shared language in which to address the challenges ahead. Here academic ethics may prove useful in at least three ways:
1. by allowing different points of views to be formulated in ethical terms, and to initiate a process of internal reflection relating to these points of view;
2. by showing that there is no external basis for ethics and that it is therefore, in a way, up to the actors to find ways of reconciling potentially conflicting ethical perspectives;
3. ethical thinking may assist in formulating pragmatic goals which may be supported from the different main ethical perspectives.

Clearly, an analysis of ethics which is going to be relevant for a cross-cultural discussion will need to draw on wider resources than those found within academic philosophy. Religion and theology provide another relevant source for ideas. And, of course, disciplines such as economics and developmental studies are also called for. A comprehensive analysis of ethics, economics, and government policy related to poverty and hunger must therefore cut across several disciplines and fields of study, and must involve both scholars and practitioners. The authors of the chapters in this book represent such a diversity of backgrounds.

It is the hope of the editors that the book will prove useful to at least two audiences. Firstly, we hope the book will be of use to people who professionally or otherwise are engaged in development and the fight against hunger and malnutrition and who are interested in viewing these issues from a ethical perspective. For this audience it may be useful to start by reading the final chapter of the book where the attempt is made to give a basic presentation of ethical theory and its relevance to the issues dealt with in this book. Secondly we hope the book will be of interest to people who come from philosophy and ethics and want to read about how the issues are framed in practice.

In the Foreword, the Executive Director of The Ethical Global Initiative, former President of Ireland and former United Nations High Commissioner for Human Rights, Mary Robinson, sets the stage for the book by pointing to the magnitude of the hunger problem, the opportunities and risks presented by globalization, and the human right to freedom from hunger. The message that Mrs. Robinson leaves with us is that all of us, as individuals, communities, governments, businesses, civil societies, and academic institutions, have a responsibility for reducing hunger. She emphasizes that while national governments have a primary responsibility for the protection of human rights, international law places obligations on States to cooperate and to create the conditions under which these rights can be realized. She stresses that there is a need for more responsible governance at all levels, along with a more active engagement of the wider society.

In Chapter Two, Pinstrup-Andersen raises the question of whether the elimination of poverty and hunger is a moral imperative or enlightened self-interest of the non-poor. He makes reference to the very large amount of rhetoric arguing for reduced poverty and hunger, and the subsequent lack of follow-up action. In spite of targets agreed upon at a large number of international conferences, including the World Food Summit and the Millennium Summit, the number of hungry people is roughly the same today as it was 15 years ago. More than half of the developing countries have failed to reduce the number of hungry people since 1990, the first year of the 25-year period during which the Millennium Development Goals should be achieved.

Pinstrup-Andersen then identifies different ethical standards that may be considered in efforts to understand the action or lack of action related to poverty and hunger. One such standard is found in utilitarian ethics. Here it is the outcome that counts. From this perspective, the author raises the question of whether there is a significant ethical difference between the failure to take action which would prevent children from dying, and actively killing those children. The outcome is the same. Few, if any, sane people would argue that it is just as bad not to save a child as it is to actually kill one. Thus, different ethical perspectives seem to be applied in such a case. The author raises the question of whether it is genocide when millions of children die because of neglect by the State. Is failure by governments to take action, as promised on various occasions, a crime against humanity? According to the United Nations and the International Criminal Court, the terms 'genocide' and 'crime against humanity' apply only when certain acts are committed. They do not apply to a situation where there is a lack of action for which resources were available. Recent evidence suggests that 6 million of the 10 million children who die every year of preventable causes could be saved at a very low cost. Yet they are not. Which ethical norm is applied in such a case?

The author proceeds to argue that, in addition to the moral imperative, it is actually enlightened self-interest of the non-poor to help poor people escape poverty and hunger. This is so because the resulting additional economic growth and improved stability would generate social benefits that far exceed the cost of helping the poor.

The chapter concludes with four sets of recommended actions which would combine ethics and economics in appropriate policies.

In Chapter Three, Marinoff places the discussion of ethics and global hunger in the context of the natural world, arguing that moral properties relate exclusively to human beings and that 'nature is amoral to a fault.' The behavior of animals cannot be attributed to moral or immoral behavior except as decided by humans.

Marinoff supports Hume's argument that there is no valid inference from 'what is' to 'what ought to be,' unless a normative premise is introduced into the argument. In other words, one cannot derive normative conclusions from factual premises without introducing a normative premise. And therefore there is a need for ethical thinking to discuss the normative premises underlying policies to fight hunger and poverty. Marinoff then proceeds to discuss four ethics models that may be used by economists in policy analysis: *deontology*, which attempts to present rules for what is 'right' and 'wrong,' including attempts by various religions to develop moral codes; *teleology* or *consequentialism*, including utilitarianism, the most favored ethical foundation for economic analysis; *virtue ethics*, which refer to the 'goodness' or 'badness' of the actor; and *correlative ethics*, which relate to human rights but include the correlative obligations required for the rights to be implemented.

Marinoff is very critical of the Human-Rights Declarations because he sees them as being 'too much wishful thinking or well-intended fantasy' – possibly preventing constructive action from taking place. He argues that the most serious violators of human rights are among the most enthusiastic signatories of Human-Rights Conventions. These same countries fail to meet the obligations necessary to implement the rights. He argues that the behavior of some of its Member Countries makes the United Nations 'a global incubator of acrimony, factionalism, bureaucracy, and hypocrisy.' The noble aspirations as expressed by Member Countries are not supported by the appropriate practices.

Religion plays a critical role in influencing existing ethical standards, including those related to hunger and poverty. In Chapters Four and Five, Marshall and Gilbert analyze how the various world religions address the ethics of hunger and poverty.

On the basis of a review of how several of the world religions treat the ethical dimensions of hunger and poverty, Marshall and Gilbert conclude that organized religion, in both scripture and action, tends to focus on the symptoms of hunger rather than the underlying causes. Marshall divides the efforts of the faith traditions into two areas – feeding people who are in immediate need through such things as soup kitchens, and humanitarian relief and development efforts for people affected by natural and human-made disasters. Gilbert argues that most of the religious rhetoric is directed at the individual rather than toward systematic efforts to assure social justice and equity. Treating symptoms alone is 'like putting Band-Aids on a cancer.' He argues that the world's religions generally do not effectively critique the various systems which produce the chasm between poverty and wealth. The emphasis tends to be on charity instead of justice. Charity is tempting for the non-poor because it gives them a feeling of virtue without making them run the risk of challenging the social and political systems that have enriched the affluent and impoverished the poor.

The two authors agree that organized religion, in many cases, fails to provide a systemic critique of economic and political structures that underlie the existing poverty and hunger. However, both mention a number of exceptions where organized religion as well as faith-based non-governmental organizations (NGOs) have, in fact, attempted to influence these economic and political structures. In spite of this criticism, Marshall claims that it is misleading to make a distinction between development on the one hand, and religion and faith on the other. In fact, she argues that such a distinction is potentially destructive. She would like to see a more creative partnership between development organizations and faith-based organizations, and concludes that 'ending hunger calls for more engagement by a multitude of actors from public and private sectors,' including civil society, 'working together in non-traditional partnerships.' While hunger appeals effectively to compassion, Marshall concludes that 'we have yet to translate this deep human impulse to help into a doable, sound framework for global action to end hunger.'

Both Marshall and Gilbert argue that most faith traditions emphasize compassion and a concern for the less fortunate but, at the same time, many religions seem to involve the perception that poverty and hunger are the norm or inevitable. In Marshall's words, this leads to 'the impulse to alleviate the problem rather than to go for change at the roots.' In four propositions, Gilbert argues that improved equality in income and wealth will result in more freedom in society, in greater equity and fairness, in a stronger sense of community solidarity, and in a greater potential for moral sensitivity and religious meaning.

Statements such as the following, which can be found in UN documents and Declarations agreed upon by most UN members, are quite clear: 'Everyone has the right to a standard of living adequate for the health and well-being of himself and his family, including food,' and 'the States Parties to the present covenant recognize the right of everyone to an adequate standard of living for himself and his family including adequate food,' followed by 'the State's Parties will take appropriate steps to ensure the realization of this right.' However, as pointed out by Marinoff in Chapter Three, rights without obligations or any other means for their enforcement may be of little value.

Since almost all the world's governments have signed these Declarations, they must believe that freedom from hunger is a basic human right. But why, then, are so many people deprived of this right? This, along with suggestions about how to rectify the situation, is discussed by Eide in Chapter Six.

With reference to Sen's theory of entitlements, Eide stresses the importance of the State as a key actor in supporting efforts by individuals to take the necessary action to cover their own needs for food and other basic necessities. While not rejecting Sen's thesis that large-scale famines do not occur in cases of functioning, democratic governments, Eide concludes that even within a functioning democracy, the politically dominant elite is often insensitive to widespread poverty and inequality. He further argues that the news media, while usually alert to sudden catastrophes, whether made by nature or man, can be indifferent to the fate of people suffering from chronic hunger and malnutrition. A better recognition of State responsibility to help individuals fulfill their right to food is called for.

The Rome Declaration on Food Security and the World Food Summit Plan of Action, which were adopted by leaders from 186 countries in 1996, provide a major impetus for greater attention to the right to food by all. Subsequent international efforts by the United Nations Food and Agricultural Organization (FAO), the UN High Commissioner for Human Rights, and a number of other international organizations have achieved only very limited success in altering the behavior of national governments toward a greater emphasis on the achievement of food security at the national and local level. As mentioned by several authors in this book, action or lack of action by national and local governments reveals a rather low relative priority on efforts to assure food security and freedom from hunger for all.

Eide suggests that 'every country should have or develop a national strategy to implement the right to food.' Unfortunately, a very large number of such strategies and plans have been developed over the years with very little impact on action. While the international organizations have made heroic efforts to prioritize action to assure basic human rights, including those related to food and freedom from hunger, their means of implementation are generally voluntary, with little or no power of enforcement and only very limited monitoring and placement of accountability. Thus, the voluntary guidelines to support the realization of the right to food developed by the United Nations in 2004 is not binding for national governments and, although adopted by the UN Committee on Economic, Social and Cultural Rights, appears to have been ignored by most governments. Such guidelines are more likely to be adopted in action by NGOs. In conclusion, Eide calls for action by academic institutions, civil society, and national institutions for human rights to find the most appropriate ways to implement basic human rights, including the right to food.

The Millennium Summit and the resulting Millennium Development Goals were an attempt to place a higher priority on action to reduce poverty, hunger, and related human misery. Unfortunately, once again, rhetoric and promises seem to have exceeded action. In Chapter Seven, Jonsson discusses reasons why such rhetoric and promises regarding hunger alleviation have not been translated into action. The author compares the Millennium Development Goals to a human-rights approach, and concludes that a single-minded focus on the Millennium Development Goals ignores a very large and important part of the Millennium Declaration. The author further argues that basic human rights, including the right to freedom from hunger, can only be implemented alongside democracy. Non-democratic governments may achieve the Millennium Development Goals, but these achievements would be privileges that individuals could lose at any time. Only democracy will assure the rights to freedom from hunger and other basic necessities, according to Jonsson. He concludes that a combination of the human-rights approach and the Millennium Declaration is likely to be preferable to a sole focus on the Millennium Development Goals.

Jonsson then proceeds to make a number of suggestions and recommendations as to how the intent of the Millennium Declaration can be implemented within a human rights approach. He suggests that the gap between rhetoric and action can be reduced or closed by the adoption of a human-rights-based approach to development programming. Such an approach would give equal attention to the achievement of desirable outcomes and the required process. Both would be guided by human rights principles. The fulfillment of specific rights would be achieved through explicit links between those holding the claims and those bearing the duty to fulfill the claims. The use of such an approach to development will, as argued by Jonsson, simultaneously contribute to the reduction of the gap between rhetoric and action and the promotion of democracy.

However, if neither the human-rights approach nor the Millennium Declaration and the Millennium Development Goals are effectively guiding government action toward food security and poverty reduction, what will it take to enable poor people to escape from poverty? In Chapter Eight, Aziz suggests that empowerment of the poor is an essential element of the solution. On the basis of a review of recent trends in world poverty and an analysis of lessons from a number of country case studies, Aziz discusses the imperatives of empowerment and how empowerment can be linked with the human-rights approach.

While agreeing that open trade and well-managed privatization are necessary to stimulate investment and economic growth, Aziz stresses the importance of the State to regulate the market system and to protect various population groups, including the poor. The role of the State in undertaking such activities is fully recognized in high-income countries, while large parts of their globalization efforts emphasize a reduction in the role of the State in every sphere of activity. The result of the failure to recognize the importance of the State, both in low-income countries and internationally, has been harmful to the poor. Similarly, economic adjustment policies advocated or imposed on developing countries from the outside have focused on reducing public expenditure and social services, with adverse affects on employment, income equality, and poverty. While promoting and imposing reductions in subsidies, including those needed to assure access by the poor to basic necessities, high-income countries continue to maintain subsidies for agriculture and a number of other sectors, with the agricultural subsidies alone accounting for more than US$300 billion per year.

Aziz argues that technological and material progress during the twentieth century has been accompanied by a decline in moral concepts and collective responsibility in both poor and rich countries. He suggests that future policy action should be based on a stronger moral base which would include the following arguments: discrimination against the poor and the weak must end; the poor must have fair access to education and health services; and the poor must receive a fair share in the additional resources generated by development in the form of irrigation water, land, credit, and income-generating opportunities. A rights movement must also pursue opportunities for the allocation of 'a larger share of the existing pie' for the poor, including land reform, nationalization of certain industries, and taxation.

Aziz' basic conclusion is clear: 'The lofty goals of human development and human security cannot be reached without the empowerment of the poor.'

On the basis of an analysis of the evolution of development thinking and practice and how it relates to world hunger, Arnold, in Chapter Nine, discusses how NGOs contribute to the global agenda for the alleviation of poverty and hunger, and draws lessons from case studies at the grassroots level. He discusses the distribution of responsibilities between the State and non-governmental organizations (NGOs) and identifies key policy issues, stressing the importance of agricultural and rural development for poverty alleviation. In addition to providing services in response to emergencies, NGOs are of critical importance as collaborators with local partners in development activities, and Arnold argues that the international NGOs have positioned themselves firmly in a global framework for development.

Arnold proposes five interlocking ethical principles to be embodied in NGO activities. These are:

1. To acknowledge suffering and injustice, and to provide a clear moral and ethical dimension to policy debate. He argues that 'the shock of the immoral is a foundational element of all ethics' and that NGOs engage in raising awareness of moral issues, which could otherwise be overlooked, given competing interests.
2. To provide unconditional universal help on the basis of a humanitarian ethics by which NGOs are driven.
3. To target the poorest. This implies a much larger weight being given to benefits obtained by those most in need.
4. To catalyze community-driven development through participatory methods.
5. To promote ethical and political integrity in dialogue with others. Using, as an illustration, critical trade-offs between implementing short-term survival inter-ventions and fostering long-term sustainability, Arnold suggests that NGOs can play an important role in the policy dialogue.

The interaction between ethics and economics in policy formulation and imple-mentation is discussed explicitly in several chapters of this book and is implicit in many places. In Chapter Ten, Thorbecke addresses this interaction explicitly with a focus on the impact of inequalities on economic growth. He discusses equality as an ethical concept and rejects the classical economics notion that increasing inequality is a necessary condition for rapid economic growth at low levels of income. He presents a very convincing case for the argument that, in fact, improved equity promotes economic growth. Six different channels through which this happens are identified and discussed, and the chapter concludes that improved equity is both a means to economic growth and an end in itself. This is an important finding because it removes a potential conflict between ethics and economics. On the basis of this conclusion, the chapter reviews the evidence on changes in equity, both globally and within countries, and concludes that equity among countries, if unweighted by population, has deteriorated dramatically during the past 25 years.

The argument that increasing inequality and poverty today is a precondition for more economic growth and less poverty in the future creates important ethical dilemmas. Is impoverishment of the masses really necessary for the accumulation of an economic surplus to generate future economic growth? If, as argued by Thorbecke, better equality is conducive to economic growth, then improving living conditions for the poor becomes a means toward economic development and future poverty alleviation – and the potential conflict between the ethical objective of egalitarianism and the economic conditions required for growth disappears. It also implies that investment in improving the human capital of the poor, including education and healthcare, will fulfill both humanitarian and long-term economic growth objectives.

As pointed out by Arnold in Chapter Nine, agricultural and rural development are of critical importance in reducing poverty and hunger. However, as stressed by Sen and several authors included in this book, the critical issue in food security is access by individuals and, while the production aspects may play an important role, other aspects of the food and agricultural system are of critical importance. The remaining chapters of this book address specific elements of this system, beginning with von Braun and Mengistu's reflections, in Chapter Eleven, on the ethics and economics of changing behavior in food and agricultural production, consumption, and trade. They first provide a comprehensive analysis of the interaction between ethics and economics in the behavior of various agents in the food system in both developing and developed countries. They then proceed to suggest incentives to induce ethical behavior as well as regulations and activism.

The authors draw heavily on ethical standards from the field of medicine, and propose six areas for action in institutional innovation, and incentives for inducing improved ethical behavior in the food system.

1. The creation of something like a 'Hippocratic oath' for all system actors, and a related set of codes of conduct guiding the food sector.
2. The establishment of food ethics commissions, which would provide a platform for transparent discussion on ethical behavior related to food and agriculture.
3. The removal of harmful incentives such as agricultural subsidies in high-income countries and the introduction of positive incentives for behavioral change, including labeling, increased support to consumer groups, and direct incentives for consumers to improve their diet.
4. The strengthening of ethical considerations as part of the food sector's marketing and business strategies, including the promotion of such things as fair trade and eco-labeling.
5. To encourage consumer activism by ensuring that civil rights are protected and to promote discourse on ethical issues on the basis of a rights-based approach to food security.
6. To promote an ethical environment within which the responsibilities of consumers, producers, NGOs, the news media, national governments, and international organizations are guided.

The authors conclude by suggesting that increased attention to ethics in food and agriculture, along with enhanced political empowerment of the poor, will foster the promotion of ethics in decision-making while increasing and improving the quality of the action needed to end hunger.

Do ethical standards with regard to food production in high-income countries have negative affects on low-income people in developing countries? If so, 'Do wealthy people and their governments have an ethical obligation to moderate qualms or concerns they might have about new agricultural and food technology in virtue of its potential for alleviating hunger and malnutrition?' (Thompson, Ch 13). In other words, should morally compelling benefits to the poor override the less compelling concerns of the non-poor. In Chapter Twelve, Sandøe and Madsen address this question with a specific focus on European resistance to genetically modified crops and existing animal welfare standards in high-income countries. The authors assess the argument that both of these high-income country positions are unethical because they are harmful to poor people in developing countries – an argument that they term 'the poor man's ethics.' They suggest that the argument consists of the following four sequential steps:

1. in response to safety worries or ethical concerns, high-income countries restrict their own agricultural production or trade with the developing countries;
2. the concerns underlying these restrictions are not substantiated by an impartial assessment of the relevant scientific evidence;
3. directly or indirectly, the restrictions have a seriously negative effect on poor people in developing countries;
4. such restrictions are therefore unethical.

The authors suggest that to reach the conclusion that the restrictions are unethical, controversial normative assumptions must be made by proponents of the poor man's ethics. They refer in particular to two such assumptions. First, for ethical concerns to be legitimate, they must be grounded in evidence from natural sciences indicating negative effects on human health or the environment. Second, any remaining ethical concerns should not be acted upon if such actions would have negative effects on people in the developing world. They argue that these two assumptions are not universally accepted. For example, legitimate concerns about distributive justice, such as adverse affects on low-income farmers, cannot be based on evidence from natural sciences. Furthermore the authors argue that some of the factual assumptions typically made by proponents of the poor man's ethics argument are rather dubious. The authors conclude that the arguments in favor of the poor man's ethics, when applied to the cases of genetically engineered food and animal welfare, rely on dubious assumptions.

In Chapter Thirteen, Thompson, on the basis of a review of the main arguments regarding the moral significance of hunger and malnutrition, reviews the arguments behind the concerns that have been expressed about agricultural technology, with emphasis on genetic engineering and its application to food production. He argues that there is a mutually reinforcing feedback loop in which a lack of attention to key ethical issues is seen as evidence of the poor moral character of the supporters of genetic engineering. He concludes that this feedback loop lies at the heart of much of the public resistance to genetically modified organisms (GMOs). Lack of virtue is perceived to be associated with those who develop and promote biotechnology. The presumed weak moral character of the pro-biotechnology camp is perceived by some as evidence of risk, whereby the proponents cannot be trusted. Moral concerns are interpreted as risks and the failure to address those risks is interpreted as a moral problem. Thompson argues that this relationship 'explains the unpredictability, self-righteousness and explosiveness of the opponents' behavior.' Thompson argues that a large share of the blame for the negative public perception of biotechnology rests with the agricultural research community itself – which, he argues, has failed to communicate effectively and respectfully with the general public. The author provides a very rich discussion and analysis of the ethical issues that need to be taken into account in future debates and policy-making regarding the use of modern agricultural technology to alleviate hunger in developing countries.

As mentioned in earlier chapters, actions by high-income countries' governments may affect the well-being of low-income people in developing countries. Previous chapters dealt with this matter as it relates to food safety, modern agricultural technology, and animal welfare. In Chapters Fourteen and Fifteen, Tutwiler, Straub, and Sharma address what is arguably the most important ethical problem of high-income countries' agricultural policies – namely their agricultural subsidies and trade policies. These three authors agree that existing agricultural subsidy and trade policies in the OECD countries are harmful to developing countries and the underprivileged people who live there. Tutwiler and Straub argue that agricultural trade liberalization by OECD countries must be accompanied by trade liberalization by developing countries and improved domestic policies within these countries in order for poor people to derive real benefits. Sharma, on the other hand, argues that developing countries should protect their markets through a food sovereignty approach, while pushing for trade liberalization by OECD countries. On the basis of a number of concrete cases, Sharma shows that the OECD countries are taking advantage of the international trade negotiations undertaken within the World Trade Organization (WTO) to the detriment of low-income countries. He further shows that poor people in developing countries that have opened up for imports of highly subsidized food and agricultural commodities from the OECD countries have been harmed.

The ethical duty of high-income countries to reduce poverty and hunger in developing countries, through direct measures such as financial assistance and food aid, has been supplemented by a more complex concept of a 'duty to dismantle unjust structures and to halt injurious action,' as phrased by Tutwiler and Straub. While the provision of development assistance may entail relatively little, if any, negative economic impact on the donor countries – and in some cases, such as food aid, it may actually provide a benefit through the creation of an outlet for surplus commodities – dismantling existing structures can impose high costs. Furthermore, it may be difficult to agree on a definition of what constitutes unjust structures and injurious actions. Some of the existing structures, including the existing agricultural trade policies by OECD countries, benefit some net food-importing countries while harming others.

The current preferential access to the European sugar market may, in fact, benefit low-income developing countries more than a completely open sugar market without quotas. Middle-income countries with appropriate domestic policies and infrastructure would be likely to benefit from a shift from preferential quotas to a free sugar market. Nevertheless, as pointed out by Tutwiler and Straub, the Millennium Development Goals call for the development of an open trading system with an emphasis on addressing the special needs of the least developed countries, including tariff and quota-free access for their exports. What the Millennium Development Goals apparently fail to stress is the critical importance of appropriate domestic policies, infrastructure, and trade policies by the developing countries themselves if they are to fully benefit from a more open trading system. Tutwiler and Straub go as far as to conclude that the removal of trade-distorting policies in both rich and poor countries is essential to meeting the Millennium Development Goal for poverty and hunger.

Sharma concludes that efforts to achieve an open and ethical global market must begin by a radical restructuring of agriculture in OECD countries. He argues for three sets of action to help remove poverty and hunger.

1. Every country should strive for national food sovereignty, which would protect agriculture and livelihood security of the farming community.
2. Developing countries should be allowed to restore quantitative restrictions and tariffs to protect themselves against highly subsidized food and agricultural commodities from OECD countries. Such quantitative restrictions and tariffs should be removed only as part of the removal of the OECD trade-distorting policies.
3. The international community should develop a multilateral agreement against hunger, based on the principle of the right to food. Such an agreement should form the basis for future negotiations and would ensure that countries have the right to take adequate safeguard measures if their commitment toward the WTO obligations leads to more hunger and poverty.

Like Arnold and other authors of this book, Tutwiler, Straub, and Sharma all stress the importance of agricultural and rural development to achieve the alleviation of poverty and hunger.

The question of whether standards and regulations in high-income countries are unethical for low-income countries is further addressed by Caswell and Friis Bach in Chapter Sixteen with reference to food safety regulations. The question of how behavior and regulations in one country affect another is particularly important as globalization results in stronger links and repercussions among countries. Do the rich set rules that adversely affect the poor? If so, we may have an ethical problem that is brought about by economic interests. The potential and real ethical conflicts between food safety standards in rich and poor countries and their implications for food security and hunger among poor people in developing countries are analyzed. Increasing globalization and trade between developing and developed countries places additional pressures for universal food safety standards reflecting the concerns of high-income consumers in developed countries. Introducing increasingly higher food safety standards in developing countries, however, is likely to increase food prices to the poor – thereby reducing food security and increasing hunger. On the basis of a comprehensive discussion of the various aspects of food safety and hunger, Caswell and Friis Bach argue that the cost of obtaining fairly marginal improvements in food safety in richer countries could instead buy large increases in food safety and food security in poorer countries. They conclude by suggesting a shared vision of moral rights and duties in international negotiations and food safety standards.

Drawing on the context of the whole book, Sandøe, Jensen, and Pinstrup-Andersen in Chapter Seventeen engage in reflections on the role of ethics in the fight against poverty. They begin by trying to pinpoint some of the factors that have led to the growing focus on ethics in relation to development and the fight against poverty and hunger. They then try to clarify the different meanings of the 'ethics' at play in the discussion of ethics and development and they give an overview of the academic discussion of the principles of rightness and fairness. Following this, they try to indicate ways in which academic ethics is relevant to the practical issues raised by development. One conclusion of this discussion is that academic ethics helps to make the ethical concerns at play, and the kinds of priorities and trade-offs that have to be made, more transparent. However, it cannot in itself create a consensus about which ethical concerns are most relevant and the relative importance of these concerns. Therefore, they discuss the sources on which a consensus about ethical assumptions might be based, and they point to international law as a starting point for building an ethical vision that is shared around the globe. Finally, they make some suggestions about how ethical thinking could be used to further global dialogue about development – a dialogue which, ideally, will not only create a better mutual understanding but will also speed up the process of reaching decent minimum goals of development.

ELIMINATING POVERTY AND HUNGER
IN DEVELOPING COUNTRIES: A MORAL
IMPERATIVE OR ENLIGHTENED SELF-INTEREST?

MUCH RHETORIC

Is the elimination of poverty and hunger in developing countries a moral imperative or enlightened self-interest for the non-poor? Countless speeches by leading politicians and others have argued for action to fight poverty, hunger, and related human misery on moral grounds. Gandhi stated many years ago that 'To a people famishing and idle, the only acceptable form in which god can dare appear is work and promise of food and wages' (Fischer 1983). More than 40 years ago, President John F. Kennedy stated at the World Food Congress, 'We have the means, we have the capacity to eliminate hunger from the face of the earth in our lifetime. We need only the will.' In a recent speech, Nelson Mandela (2005) left no doubt about where he stands:

> Like slavery and apartheid, poverty is not natural. It is manmade and it can be overcome and eradicated by the action of human beings. And overcoming poverty is not a gesture of charity. It is an act of justice. It is the protection of a fundamental human right, the right to dignity and a decent life. While poverty persists, there is no true freedom.

President George W. Bush shares the concerns about lack of justice and adds a stability dimension to which I will return later:

> A world where some live in comfort and plenty while half of the human race lives on less than $2 a day is neither just nor stable (White House 2001).

Promises have also been plentiful. Consider, for example, Henry Kissinger's statement at the World Food Conference in 1974: 'Within a decade no man, woman or child will go to bed hungry.' Thirty years have passed and 800 million people go to bed hungry; more than when Kissinger spoke.

These are but a few of thousands of similar statements made throughout the years. Based on the rhetoric, one could easily conclude that the international community agrees that poverty and hunger should be eradicated or at least severely reduced. In fact, governments of virtually every country have agreed to a number of targets and goals to do just that. Recently, in connection with the Millennium Summit, countries

15

P. Pinstrup-Andersen and P. Sandøe (eds.), Ethics, Hunger and Globalization: In Search of Appropriate Policies, 15–27.
© 2007 *Springer.*

agreed to a target of reducing by half the percentage of the world population that suffers from poverty and hunger by the year 2015. The commitment to the target was reaffirmed by all UN members at a UN Summit in 2005. Similarly, at the World Food Summit in 1996, the governments of 186 countries agreed to a goal of reducing by half the number of hungry people between 1990 and 2015. Five years later, at a follow-up conference, the same countries reconfirmed the goal.

LITTLE ACTION

Unfortunately, action has not followed rhetoric. Absolute poverty is estimated to affect about 1.2 billion people, or approximately one-fifth of the world's population (United Nations 2004). The large majority of the poor are found in Asia. About 70% of the poor reside in the rural areas of developing countries, but urban poverty is also increasing rapidly in most regions. Both the number of poor people and their prevalence as a percentage of the total population is decreasing in China and other parts of East and Southeast Asia, while the numbers continue to increase in Sub-Saharan Africa, North Africa, West Asia, and Latin America. During the 1990s the number of absolute poor people in the world decreased by close to 10%. However, if China is excluded from the total, the number actually increased.

Relative income distribution is very skewed and is worsening both internationally and within many countries. The richest 10% of the world population account for 54% of world income (UNDP 2005). The relative income distribution among countries is also getting worse. In 1960, the average per capita incomes in industrialized countries were nine times the average per capita incomes in Sub-Saharan Africa. Today they are more than 20 times greater. Between 1990 and 2000, per capita incomes increased by close to US$5,000 in high-income countries, but by only US$40 in low-income countries. Income inequalities are also increasing within the countries that account for 80% of the world's population (UNDP 2005).

The follow-on consequences of poverty and biased income distribution are severe and widespread. Hunger affects about 800 million people, i.e., about one in six citizens of developing countries. The largest number of hungry people is in Asia, but the number there is decreasing. One in three citizens of Sub-Saharan Africa suffers from hunger, and the number is increasing.

Malnutrition affects about one-fourth of all preschool children in developing countries – or about 135 million. While the number of underweight preschool children is falling, the number of wasted preschool children has not changed during the last 10 years. More than 10 million children die every year; the overwhelming reason is poverty, with more than half dying from hunger and nutrition-related factors.

The difference in preschool child mortality rates between high and low-income countries is astounding and is increasing. Thus, the rate in Sub-Saharan Africa was 18 times the rate in high-income countries in 1990, increasing to 28 times in 2003. In South Asia, the rate was 13 times higher than in high-income countries in 1990, increasing to 16 times in 2003 (UNDP 2005). In 2003, 179 of every 1,000 live-born children in Sub-Saharan Africa died before their fifth birthday. The average mortality rate covers considerable variation among countries and between poor and rich within each country. Thus, more than one-fourth of all live-born children in Sierra Leone die before their fifth birthday, while less than one in 10 die in Lesotho and Eritrea (UNDP 2005). In Mali, 25% of the children born into the poorest sector of the population die before they reach five years of age, compared to 15% for those born into the richest quintile (UNDP 2005). Six of every 1,000 children born in high-income countries die before the age of five years.

A lack of access to clean water, primary healthcare, education, and a variety of goods and service that the non-poor take for granted is commonplace among the poor and disenfranchised.

Poverty is a cause of widespread natural resource degradation. About one-half of the world's poor reside in rural areas that have poor soil, irregular rainfall, poorly functioning markets, and very limited infrastructure and institutions. In their fight for survival, they may have no other option than to participate in the unsustainable use of natural resources, thus causing deforestation, soil erosion, mining of soil nutrients, and reduction of biodiversity. While out-migration from these areas may be the longer-run solution, the sheer magnitude of the numbers of people who live in these areas and the lack of opportunities for them elsewhere mean that out-migration is not a viable short-run solution.

In spite of the targets agreed upon at the World Food Summit and the Millennium Summit, the number of hungry people is roughly the same today as it was in 1990, and with business as usual, extrapolations based on existing data indicate that the number will stay roughly constant between now and 2015. More than half of the developing countries failed to reduce the number of hungry people during the 1990s and if the most successful country, China, is excluded from the statistics, the number of hungry people has risen since 1990 – a trend that appears likely to continue until 2015 (Pinstrup-Andersen 2002). Several international conferences, including the World Food Conference in 1974, the Nutrition Conference in 1990, the World Food Summit in 1996, and the Millennium Summit in 2000, have specified hunger alleviation goals to be achieved within specified time periods. None have been achieved.

The lack of action is accompanied by much rhetoric, plans, targets, and promises. The most cynical of these promises and agreements is undoubtedly the United Nations' Declaration that freedom from hunger is a basic human right. It is cynical because it is not empowered with any means to enforce it. Other recent efforts such as the poverty reduction strategy programs (PRSPs) and the program proposed by the Millennium Development Goals Task Force stress the development of more plans and strategies. So far, the PRSPs have resulted in very little action.

WHAT ETHICAL STANDARDS?

But what ethical or moral perspectives guide the action or lack of action to alleviate hunger and poverty? Four such perspectives are common: *utilitarianism*, *deontological ethics*, *virtue ethics*, and *human-rights ethics*. Utilitarianism is part of the consequentialist school. What counts is the outcome or the consequences of the action taken, not the intent of the action. Whether an action is right or wrong depends on the resulting utility. Deontological ethics, on the other hand, refers to the intent rather than the outcome. The intent may relate to 'doing the right thing' in the context of meeting the motives of society, groups, or individuals, and respecting rules and rights. Virtue ethics also relate to the intent, but differ from deontological ethics by focusing on the actor rather than the action. Doing the right thing makes the actor virtuous. Human-rights ethics prioritize action towards the assurance of specified basic human rights such as freedom from hunger. As further discussed below, the four ethical standards may, but need not, conflict.

The goal of maximizing utility says nothing about whether the gainers deserve the utility, unless, of course, a social-welfare function with assigned differential weights for various population groups is designed and used. For example, a poor person or a child may be more deserving than a non-poor adult. Therefore, a greater weight could be assigned to utility captured by such more-deserving groups. By assigning different weights to income gains obtained by various population groups, we can compare the social net benefit or utility from each policy option. But how do we derive the appropriate weights? Most people would probably agree that a US$1 net gain for the poor carries a higher social benefit than a US$1 net gain for the rich; but how much higher?

Assigning weights to the expected utility of current versus future generations and to humans versus animals present particularly challenging questions. Whose welfare should be maximized and what is a reasonable trade-off between current and future generations, between rich and poor, between two groups of poor people, between people and animals, and between utility maximization and intrinsic values of the natural environment?

Do we explicitly or implicitly subscribe to deontological ethics when deciding among trade-offs? In other words, are there things we do not want to do, even if they are legal and would enhance utility? Yes, of course. Utility maximization takes place within legal as well as ethical constraints. But the ethical trade-offs are sometimes so socially sensitive that we do not make them explicit. For example, most people would probably agree with Singer (1993, p. 229), at least in principle, that 'If it is in our power to prevent something very bad from happening, without thereby sacrificing anything of comparable moral significance, we ought to do it.' But such agreement is not represented in policy action to prevent the annual death of 10 million preschool children of hunger, malnutrition, infectious diseases, and other preventable causes (UNICEF 2002).

A recent study (Bryce et al. 2005) concluded that 6 million of the 10 million child deaths could be avoided by known interventions in each of 42 countries at a recurrent annual cost of US$5.1 billion, or US$1.23 per person living in those countries. Could the richest 10% of the populations of those countries afford to pay US$12.30 annually without sacrificing anything of comparable moral or material significance? Of course they could. Do they? No.

There are several possible explanations for the failure to apply Singer's principle; the obvious one is that we may agree with the principle when it comes to people we know or feel we have something in common with, while the suffering people far away from us – physically and mentally – are of less significance.

But is there a significant ethical difference between the failure to take action which would save children from dying and actively killing children? From a purely utilitarian perspective, the outcome, which is what counts, is the same. From a deontological ethical perspective, however, I can argue that in the case of not taking action, I have done nothing wrong. But killing children is clearly wrong. We can hide behind this argument as long as the children who die are an unseen mass (Singer 1993). But what if my neighbor's child is starving and I could take action to make the child well without sacrificing anything of comparable moral significance? I would presumably subscribe to virtue ethics and do the right thing. Of course, if the well-being of my neighbor's child enters into my utility, utilitarian ethics might lead me to the same action. But what if it is not my neighbor's child but the children of the country for which I am a policy-maker or a food policy analyst?

I agree with Wisman (2003, p. 431), when he states that 'Our potential for happiness is limited by the extent to which we find misery and injustice around us.' The question is whether 'around us' refers to the family, the local community, the country, or the world. Wisman's argument may also explain why governments of some countries forcefully remove poor and starving people from the streets and other public places. Erik Thorbecke (personal communication, 2005) has suggested the hypothesis or conjecture that the welfare weights assigned to individuals are inversely related to the square of the distance between the one who assigns the weights and the one to whom it is assigned; where distance could be geographical or could refer to income level or some other measure of social status.

Is it genocide when millions of children die because of neglect by the State? Is failure by governments to take action, as promised on various occasions, a crime against humanity? Not according to the United Nations and the International Criminal Court. The terms 'genocide' and 'crime against humanity' apply only when certain acts are committed. Failure to act to save lives is not covered, even when States have the means to act (United Nations 1948; International Criminal Court 1999).

Socially sensitive trade-offs are common in economic policy related to the food system. These trade-offs are frequently implicit in the action taken but are not stated. For example, should policies focus on improving the well-being of the poorest children or households even if total utility or social welfare would be maximized by focusing on the less poor? Should public funds be spent on reducing hunger among current children or on prenatal care among pregnant women, which might increase birthweight and prevent many more children from dying in the future?

But even in cases where utility is the appropriate indicator, are incomes a good measure? What about personal freedom and security? China and Vietnam have experienced very impressive reductions in absolute poverty and food insecurity, but personal freedom and democracy are still very limited. In India, personal freedom and democracy are at a high level, but the reductions in poverty and food insecurity are limited.

And how do we deal with corruption? Is this a case where we apply a deontological perspective that it is the wrong thing to do, irrespective of outcome, implying that corruption would be absolutely unacceptable even if it would reduce hunger or if the desired consequence could be obtained only if corruption is an element of the intervention? Should we not consider such policy options? If we do, where do we stop? Do we take a position on what is right or wrong or do we just seek to maximize utility as measured by incomes, irrespective of the source of income? Does legality determine our moral standing? Should we consider policy options in which a corruption element increases utility only in cases and countries where corruption is legal or at least considered acceptable? Should we take a similar position with respect to other actions, such as the production of illegal drugs which, if produced by small farmers, might help millions out of poverty, hunger, and child death? Does legality set absolute ethical limits for policy options, even those that could help millions of poor people out of poverty and hunger? What if millions of child deaths could be avoided at the expense of the lives of thousands of drug addicts? The rational answer is obviously to find alternatives that would save the children without creating drug addicts, but that merely avoids confronting the short-term real ethical trade-off.

A 'right-to-food' ethics is presented in the Universal Declaration of Human Rights: 'Everybody has the right to a standard of living adequate for the health and well-being of himself and his family, including food, clothing, housing and medical care' (United Nations 2004). The International Covenant on Economic, Social and Cultural Rights further states that 'The States Parties to the present Covenant, recognizing the fundamental right of everyone to be free from hunger ... will take appropriate steps to ensure the realization of this right' (Eide 2002).

Although the United Nations Declarations related to food security and freedom from hunger as a human right give the appearance of being legally binding, they are not. Instead of 'right,' a more appropriate term would be privilege or charity, because it is neither an enforceable right nor a claim. It is a privilege that can be granted or, more commonly, not granted. Contrary to enforced rights, privileges or charity can be viewed as an attempt to escape from justice (Kolm 2004); an attempt, such as a transfer program, that can be removed at any time. One could argue that it is a moral right that would be enforced only if those with enforcement power share the underlying moral or ethical standard. Poverty transfer programs are frequently of a short-term nature. Privileges and charity tend to treat symptoms, while efforts to achieve social justice would aim to change underlying causes.

Moral imperatives such as a right to freedom from hunger can be very expensive both in terms of fiscal and economic costs and are very difficult to enforce. Tweeten (2003, p. 19) argues that 'No nation has sufficient resources to honor simultaneously the right to food, shelter, clothing, education and health care for all.' I would argue that few nations can afford a human resource base that lacks any of these basic necessities because of the resulting low labor productivity. Failure to invest in the human resource is not just an ethical problem; it is one of the main reasons for poverty and lack of economic growth in many developing countries – something that nations can ill afford. The widespread recognition that investment in human resources not only helps people out of poverty but also contributes to national economic growth removes a potential conflict between ethics and economics. Another potential conflict is gradually disappearing, as recent evidence which shows that increasing relative inequality is not a precondition for rapid economic growth is accepted (Thorbecke Chapter 10 of this book).

There is no penalty associated with either the failure to protect the right to food or the failure to achieve the goals that countries agreed to as part of international conferences. In fact, accountability is all but absent at both national and international levels. One could argue that the ethical standards and principles to which policy-makers pretend to subscribe are valid for rhetoric but not for action. Although 'The human right to adequate food is recognized in several instruments under international law' (United Nations 1999, p. 1), nobody seems to enforce international law.

Unlike the right to freedom from hunger, property rights are much more likely to be enforced. Furthermore, countries have laws against robbery, fraud, and mistreatment of animals, but public action or inaction resulting in fatal hunger and malnutrition is not unlawful. The existing power structure prioritizes property rights, animal rights, and freedom from fraud and robbery over freedom from hunger. While that should not come as a surprise, it reveals the underlying ethical principles among those in power.

Lack of seriousness in the fight against hunger is also illustrated by international agreements and institutions. We have legally binding international agreements on trade but not on hunger. Under the umbrella of the World Trade Organization, one country can take legal action against another if the latter breaks the rules. But a trade policy that can be demonstrated to cause poverty, hunger, and child malnutrition and death, such as the current agricultural policies in the EU and the USA, is legal. Furthermore, international agencies such as FAO and UNICEF that are concerned about poverty, hunger, and the well-being of children, have no enforcement power over national governments.

SOCIETY VERSUS HOUSEHOLD ETHICS

One of the factors that would make government enforcement of the individual's right to freedom from hunger difficult is that the individual usually resides in a household, and therefore is subject to household decision rules. Government attempts to help individuals achieve their rights may be modified and possibly nullified by household decisions regarding the intra-household allocation of food and other resources that run counter to an absolute priority on achieving freedom from hunger for all household members before any resources are allocated to other needs or wants. Similarly, when transfers are made in kind, e.g., food aid or specific food commodities, households are likely to make counter-adjustments in the overall consumption basket. Thus, good intentions by the public sector, and failure to take into account household decision processes and goals, may add transaction costs without adding benefits.

Low-income households are likely to have several priorities competing for scarce resources. Whether the household decisions are made by a dictatorial household head or through some bargaining process, the hungry and malnourished are usually those in the weakest bargaining position, i.e., preschool children, pregnant women, and breastfeeding mothers.

It is difficult to distinguish between needs and wants. Attempts by government or society to assist households in meeting what society considers as basic needs may run counter to the desires of the head of the household, who may use his or her decision-making power to convert public interventions aimed at meeting needs to meet expenses not considered as basic needs by society. Using food stamps to purchase cigarettes or, if that is not possible, matching the value of the food stamps with equal cuts in food purchases from other income sources, is a case in point. Such conflict between society's attempt to deliver on virtue or deontological ethics and the household head's attempt to maximize his own or his household's utility is typical of transfer programs aimed at improving the nutritional status of preschool children, pregnant women, or other household members perceived to be disadvantaged (Pinstrup-Andersen 1993).

In the context of minimum wages, Finn (2003) suggests that a 'moral consensus that holds society together requires a prosperous nation to guarantee a minimal standard of living to all full-time workers, even if that necessitates a more extensive (and expensive) social safety net for the unemployed.' Could a similar argument be made for poverty and hunger for a prosperous world, in which an international moral consensus would hold the world together, i.e., promote economic growth, social justice, peace, stability, and the absence of terrorism? And why would the argument not be valid for less prosperous nations, particularly middle-income developing countries with an uneven income distribution, such as Brazil, which currently has a president whose top priority is to eliminate hunger?

ENLIGHTENED SELF-INTEREST?

As stated by George W. Bush (White House 2001), 'A world where some live in comfort and plenty while half of the human race lives on less than $2 a day is neither just nor stable.' There is mounting evidence showing a causal link between poverty, hunger, and unequal income distribution, on the one hand, and national instability and poor economic growth, on the other (Messer et al. 1998, 2001; Pinstrup-Andersen 2002, 2003, 2006; Messer and Cohen 2004). While the empirical evidence of a causal link between poverty and international terrorism is weaker than the evidence of a causal link between poverty and national conflict, it is clear that at least some of the people who support or undertake international instability and terrorism find their moral justification in the existence of poverty, hunger, and unnecessary human suffering.

Poor and hungry people are not terrorists, but people with no hope and nothing to lose except their lives and those of their children provide not only a perceived moral justification for terrorism, but also the anger and hatred that drive it. They are susceptible to terrorist appeals. As stated by Jim Wallis in a conversation with President George W. Bush, 'Mr. President, if we don't devote our energy, our focus and our time on also overcoming global poverty and desperation, we will lose not only the war on poverty, but we'll lose the war on terrorism' (*New York Times Magazine*, 17 October 2004, p. 50). In the same article, Mr. Wallis is quoted as saying, 'Unless we drain the swamp of injustice in which the mosquitoes of terrorism breed, we'll never defeat the threat of terrorism.' The Nobel Peace Prize winner, Norman Borlaug, puts it this way: 'We cannot build world peace on empty stomachs' (*World Food Prize Symposium*, Des Moines, Iowa, 14 October 2004).

Failure to deal effectively with perceived and real social injustice will render current military efforts ineffective in dealing with the threat of terrorism. No society – national or international – will be secure when material inequalities and material deprivations are as extreme as they are now. We must try to understand the frustration, hopelessness, and anger of the many millions of people who are poor, hungry, and without the opportunities to escape the human misery they are in. We must then tailor our efforts to assure a socially just, stable, and secure world accordingly. This is our ethical obligation and it is in our own self-interest.

Returning to the question posed in the title of the chapter, I believe that the elimination of poverty, hunger, and associated human suffering is a moral imperative. Is it also a sound economic objective for the non-poor to pursue? For those who subscribe to virtue or deontological ethics, such a question is irrelevant. Elimination of human suffering is simply the right thing to do, irrespective of whether it adds to one's own utility.

Irrespective of the ethical motive, investment in the human resource through food security, education, and primary healthcare has been shown to have a very high economic payoff, not only for the target individuals but also for the non-poor in the societies to which they belong and internationally through mutually beneficial trade expansion and improved national and international stability. Alleviation of poverty and hunger is both a moral imperative and a matter of enlightened self-interest for the non-poor. Failure by the non-poor in developing countries and by the rich countries to prioritize the eradication of poverty and hunger is morally wrong and a danger to their security (Singer 2002). The enlightened self-interest is articulated by the United Nations (2001), as cited in Singer (2002, p. 7) as follows:

> In the global village, someone else's poverty very soon becomes one's own problem: of lack of markets for one's products, illegal immigration, pollution, contagious disease, insecurity, fanaticism, terrorism.

Given the strong ethical, humanitarian, economic, and security reasons for solving poverty and hunger problems, it is puzzling that decision-makers have chosen not to do so. One explanation for the lack of action to commit existing resources to help people out of poverty and related hopelessness is the lack of a shared vision of the moral rights and duties of the various population groups. Another might be that those who have the power to choose either do not expect to benefit from solving the poverty and hunger problems or they do not believe they will be harmed by a continuation of the *status quo*. Given certain social and political constructs they may, of course, be right – at least in the short run.

Some may have a very short time horizon for making choices, and therefore seek immediate results through the application of force instead of the more sustainable but longer-term solution of removing the underlying causes of conflict, namely poverty, hunger, and hopelessness. Furthermore, short time horizons are likely to imply high internal discount rates, making future income gains from investments in human resources less attractive than the immediate extraction of economic surplus through discrimination, exploitation, and force. The short time horizon, together with massive attention by the news media, may also explain why acute hunger problems resulting from natural or human-made disasters are more likely to be solved than the longer-term hunger problem that requires sustainable attention over a long period of time. Lack of understanding of economic relationships and the belief that the economy is a zero-sum game, in which a dollar gained by the poor is a dollar lost by the non-poor, may be other explanations for the lack of action to seek social justice.

WHAT ACTION IS NEEDED?

Efforts to achieve food security for all, or at least meet the World Food Summit goal within a reasonable time-frame, will require action on four fronts:
1. Policies that help the poor gain access to productive resources and markets need to be implemented.
2. Heavy investments must be made in public goods, such as education and healthcare.
3. The poor developing countries, including virtually all African countries and many countries in Asia and Latin America, need to refocus public policies and investment priorities towards agriculture and rural areas. While the specific priorities will vary among countries, heavy investment in rural infrastructure and market structure and performance, agricultural research, primary education, and healthcare are likely to be needed in most of these countries.
4. OECD countries should decouple domestic agricultural subsidies from quantity produced and area used in production, and they should eliminate tariffs and other import restrictions on agricultural commodities, processed foods, and textiles from developing countries. Subsidized exports, including dumping and non-emergency food aid, should also be discontinued.

The four sets of action must be pursued simultaneously. Getting policies and investment priorities right in a low-income developing country which is subjected to an inflow of subsidized exports and closed international markets is unlikely to achieve food security for its citizens. Similarly, the policy changes suggested for OECD countries without appropriate policies in developing countries will primarily benefit high-income countries, including developing countries with appropriate policies and rural infrastructure. Low-income developing countries that fail to pursue domestic policy reform will be left behind.

Globalization, including international trade liberalization, more integrated international capital markets, and a freer flow of labor, information and technology has benefited hundreds of millions of people but many others have been made worse off. Effective food and agricultural policy and institutions are needed to complement and guide globalization to reduce poverty and hunger.

Insufficient access to productive resources and income-earning opportunities by low-income population groups has led to widespread inequality. While attempts to redistribute existing wealth have been unsuccessful in most cases, land reforms in some countries, most notably in South Korea, have been successful. Efforts to give private title to collectively owned and managed land in some African countries such as Somalia and Malawi have had mixed results. It is still too early to judge the impact of ongoing land reforms in Zimbabwe and South Africa and it is not yet clear whether and how the explicitly declared goal by President Lula of Brazil to eliminate hunger in that country will be achieved. It is one of the most refreshing positions taken by any Head of State in recent times and it is my impression that it will be attempted by new investments in public goods of particular importance to the poor along with pro-poor growth and distribution of subsidized food to target groups. Presumably, the approach to pro-poor growth will include expanded access by the poor to productive resources and employment.

Moving beyond Brazil, one of the key questions related to efforts to eliminate food insecurity is whether growth should be pursued independently of its immediate distributional effects or whether pro-poor growth, which may imply a lower overall rate of growth, should be pursued. What is clear is that attempts to redistribute wealth without growth are unlikely to be politically feasible. The existing literature is strong on the importance of economic growth for poverty alleviation but weak on the opportunities for accelerated poverty alleviation through pro-poor growth strategies. However, while some economic trade-offs may embody an ethical dilemma, investment in the human resource through the eradication of poverty, hunger, and malnutrition is likely to achieve both growth and equity goals.

The importance of investments in public goods such as primary education and healthcare to enhance access to remunerative employment and other income-earning opportunities for both growth and equity is widely recognized, along with poor farmers' access to land, credit, appropriate technology, and well-functioning markets for inputs and outputs. While micro-credit programs have been successful in strengthening poor peoples' access to credit in a number of countries, access to credit is still a major bottleneck for smallholder agriculture. Poor infrastructure and related high transportation and transaction costs in the rural areas of most low-income developing countries, along with poorly functioning markets, make it very difficult for the rural poor to benefit from the opportunities embodied in technological developments and globalization. Without expanded investment in rural infrastructure and improved institutions, even those rural poor who have access to land will continue to be marginalized and will remain food-insecure.

CONCLUSION

In conclusion, the global food system, and especially poor people within it, suffers from social injustice and unethical behavior by decision-makers in both low and high-income countries. The gap between rhetoric and action to reduce poverty and hunger by the governments of the majority of the developing countries is particularly worrisome from an ethical point of view. While most of the blame for lack of action rests with developing country governments, several policies in rich countries, some of which are discussed in this book, have severe negative effects on poor countries and people. Failure to explicitly consider such international spillovers from national policies and international institutions slows down globalization and contributes to social injustice and conflict.

REFERENCES

Bryce, J., R.E. Black, N. Walker, Z.A. Bhutta, J.E. Lawn and R.W. Steketee, 2005. Can the world afford to save the lives of six million children each year? *Lancet* 365(9478): 2193–2200.

Eide, A., 2002. The right to food: From vision to substance. In: Borghi M., L.P. Blommestein, eds. *For an Effective Right to Adequate Food*. Switzerland: University Press Fribourg, pp. 27–50.

Finn, D.R., 2003. The moral ecology of markets: On the failure of the amoral defense of markets. *Review of Social Economy* 61(2): 135–162.

Fischer, L., 1983. *The Life of Mahatma Gandhi*. New York: Harper and Row.

International Criminal Court, 1999. *Rome Statute of the International Criminal Court*, Articles 6 and 7 [available at http://www.un.org/law/icc/statute/romefra.htm].

Kolm, S.-C., 2004. *Macrojustice: The Political Economy of Fairness*. Cambridge: Cambridge University Press.

Mandela, N., 2005. *Campaign to End Poverty in the Developing World Speech*. Trafalgar Square, London, 3 February 2005.

Messer, E. and M. Cohen, 2004. Breaking the links between conflict and hunger in Africa. *IFPRI 2020 Africa Conference*, Brief 10.

Messer, E., M. Cohen and J. D'Costa, 1998. Food from peace: Breaking the links between conflict and hunger. *IFPRI Food, Agriculture and the Environment Discussion Paper 24*.

Messer, E., M. Cohen and T. Marchione, 2001. Conflict: A cause and effect of hunger. In: *Environmental Change and Security Project Report No. 7*. Washington, DC: Woodrow Wilson International Center for Scholars, Smithsonian Institution.

Pinstrup-Andersen, P., ed., 1993. *The Political Economy of Food and Nutrition Policies*. Baltimore, MD: Johns Hopkins University.

Pinstrup-Andersen, P., 2002. Food and agricultural policy for a globalizing world: Preparing for the future. *American Journal of Agricultural Economics* 84(5): 1189–1404.

Pinstrup-Andersen, P., 2003. Eradicating poverty and hunger as a national security issue for the United States. In: *Environmental Change and Security Project Report 9*. Washington, DC: Wilson International Center for Scholars, pp. 22–27.

Pinstrup-Andersen, P., 2006. The impact of technological change in agriculture on poverty and armed conflict (Charles Valentine Riley Memorial Lecture). Washington, D.C.: National Agricultural Library, September

Singer, P., 1993. *Practical Ethics*. Cambridge: Cambridge University Press.

Singer, P., 2002. *One World: The Ethics of Globalization*. New Haven: Yale University Press.

Tweeten, L., 2003. *Terrorism, Radicalism, and Populism in Agriculture*. Ames, Iowa: Iowa State Press.

UNDP, 2005. *International Cooperation at a Crossroads: Aid, Trade and Security in an Unequal World. Human Development Report 2005*. New York: United Nations Development Program.

UNICEF [United Nations Children's Fund], 2002. *The State of the World's Children*. New York: UNICEF.

United Nations, 1948. *Convention on the Prevention and Punishment of the Crime of Genocide*. UN General Assembly 260A(III), 9 December [available at http://www.unhchr.ch/html/menu3/b/p_genoci.htm].

United Nations, 1999. *The Right to Adequate Food*. Committee on Economic Social and Cultural Rights, 20th Session, Geneva, 26 April–14 May.

United Nations, 2001. *Report of the High-Level Panel on Financing for Development*. UN General Assembly, 55th Session, Agenda item 101, 26 June [available at http://www.un.org/esa/ffd/a55-1000.pdf].

United Nations, 2004. *Nutrition for Improved Development Outcomes: Fifth Report on the World Nutrition Situation*. Geneva, Switzerland: United Nations System Standing Committee on Nutrition.

White House, 2001. Office of the Press Secretary.

Wisman, J.D., 2003. The scope and promising future of social economics. *Review of Social Economy* 61(4): 425–445.

ETHICS, GLOBALIZATION, AND HUNGER:
AN ETHICIST'S PERSPECTIVE

INTRODUCTION

While the poor have always been with us, and while hunger is a companion to poverty, our globalizing civilization is witnessing unprecedented disparities represented by excessive wealth and massive starvation. We know that half the world's population (mostly Asians) are living on one or two dollars a day, while the middle classes of affluent nations enjoy standards of living that feature – and increasingly revolve around – orgiastic hedonism and consumerism, some of it at the expense of the poorest nations.

Globalization has bought much success to many. Among its fruits are instantaneous mobile data-exchange and allied information technologies, and the shrinkage of space–time via the Internet; the rapid movement of goods and services enabled by complex transportation and communication infrastructures; the transcendence of transnational economic forces over local and even national political constraints; the emancipation and increasing participation of women and members of minority groups across the spectrum of cultural arenas; and an emergent global elite whose members pledge allegiance to planetary management and proudly consider themselves (with some justification) to be 'citizens of the world.'

But on the other side of the digital and global divide, in developing nations as well as in failed States, billions of human beings are caught in terrible poverty traps with little or no hope of extricating themselves, or their children, unaided. Ironically, many forms of so-called 'aid' serve only to exacerbate their suffering. To be sure, the globalized rich are not solely responsible for the plight of the marginalized poor: endemic political and commercial corruption, outdated land and property laws, repressive cultural and religious traditions, lack of fundamental education and healthcare – all these things combine to disenfranchise, impoverish, and starve hundreds of millions of unfortunate souls.

To make matters worse, agricultural subsidies in affluent nations (primarily the USA and the EU) enable the dumping of artificially cheapened produce onto developing markets, effectively shutting out and bankrupting indigenous food producers. This has the secondary effect of driving thousands of destitute farmers and their families from their lands and into appalling shantytown slums surrounding large urban centers, where they and their children will suffer every conceivable misery known to mankind, with little or no hope of improving their lot in life. This is the hideous underbelly of globalization.

P. Pinstrup-Andersen and P. Sandøe (eds.), Ethics, Hunger and Globalization: In Search
of Appropriate Policies, 29–49.
© 2007 Springer.

But since our planet has shrunk so much, at least for those with the means
to traverse it, and is so highly networked by IT and multimedia coverage, at
least for those with the privilege of access, it is impossible to deny or to remain
in blissful ignorance of the large-scale human suffering not solely caused, but
partly perpetuated, by the affluence of the globalizers. Moreover, it is primarily the
affluent who can offer the means of alleviating crushing poverty. Everyone who
benefits from globalization must become aware of the suffering of those who are
marginalized by it; and everyone who is possessed even of the remotest human
sensibility cannot remain morally insensate in the face of so much privation.

World leaders and other key decision-makers have responded in various ways,
which include espousing Millennium Development Goals intended to cut poverty in
half by the year 2015. Although at least some of these goals are being achieved, even
their attainment can backfire in unfortunate ways which worsen poverty for some
while alleviating it for others. Thus the poor are often pitted against one another in
a cruel struggle for survival, a Hobbesian state of economic nature, whose 'victors'
are vaulted across the poverty line into the lower middle classes, with new hope
for themselves and reasonable optimism for their children; but whose 'vanquished'
sink even deeper into the abyss of utter destitution, an economic black hole from
which escape seems impossible.

Economists have developed sophisticated and seemingly accurate models of the
complex dynamics of global hunger and its alleviation, on both macro- and micro-
scales, and are able to propose various remedies to key decision-makers. As social
scientists, economists study phenomena such as poverty and hunger in reasonably
objective and dispassionate ways. As moral human beings, however, they cannot
countenance much of what they have learned in the process of such study. Just as
medical researchers must approach the epidemiology and pathology of diseases as
objectively as possible for the sake of good science, yet as moral beings may be
profoundly moved by what they learn in the context of human suffering imposed
by disease (especially where it is preventable); so economists of good conscience
cannot remain silent in the wake of their discoveries concerning the causes and
effects of widespread global hunger.

Given that their economic prescriptions must therefore be alloyed with normative
ethics, it is only reasonable that economists of conscience would seek to join forces
with moral philosophers – applied ethicists and religionists – who can perhaps
help to locate economic prescriptions in moral frameworks, or ground them in
ethical theories. There is enough food in the world to sustain everyone; what
is lacking is apparently (to revert to a well-worn 'buzzword') the *political will*
to redistribute existing resources more equitably, and to implement policies that
would both institutionalize such redistribution and inculcate sustainable dynamics
of poverty reduction alongside those of wealth creation. Beyond this, perhaps we
need to awaken a *moral will* among the affluent.

This chapter will endeavor to provide some foundational underpinnings to the
undertaking of such a task. Like my economist colleagues, I honor dispassionate
value-neutrality as a desirable perspective from which to assess existing conditions,

causes, and remedies; but am likewise committed to compassionate moral outrage at the deliberate perpetuation of so much human suffering in the world, by forces that wield sufficient might (if insufficient will) to ameliorate the unconscionable horrors of mass deprivation and starvation, in the midst of such plenty.

NON-HUMAN POPULATIONS AND MORAL ANTI-NATURALISM

In the interests of introducing ethics where they are most appropriate, I adopt from the outset a position known to philosophers as 'moral anti-naturalism.' This position asserts that the natural world, exclusive of human beings, embodies no moral properties, and that ascriptions of moral agency, at least on this planet, begin with and apply primarily to humans. While broader views, such as Jainism and Buddhism, extend the doctrine of non-harm (*ahimsa*) to all sentient creatures, such views are exclusively human in their origins, even though other life-forms become their beneficiaries. (Contemporary reformulations of such views, like those espoused by Singer 1975, repose on a different metaphysic.) But the ascription of moral agency, and the fundamental 'right to life' that it entails, regardless of the scope of its beneficence, is a uniquely human invention. There are no ethics in the natural world, and no non-human animal's behaviors can cogently attract the attributes 'moral' or 'immoral.' Nature is amoral to a fault; only humans are capable of imposing (or failing to impose) morality upon themselves.

The biological phenomenon of appetite for food, and its satiation, stem from thermodynamic considerations. Life is improbable, if not anomalous, in that it embodies and sustains negative entropy. While this appears to contradict the second law of thermodynamics, if viewed statistically then life is merely a local, and hence permissible, fluctuation. An ineluctable condition of sustaining negative entropy is the ingestion and digestion of more simple life-forms by more complex ones. This is otherwise termed the 'food chain.'

Schrödinger (1948) was possibly the first to observe that a living organism must feed upon negative entropy, and the essence of metabolism is to free the organism from the (positive) entropy it produces while alive. Specifically, this means that some living matter must deprive other living matter of life in order to live itself. Beyond a certain level of complexity, to be alive entails feeding on other life, sucking order out of the environment and returning disorder to it. This is Darwin's 'struggle for existence.' It is essentially a temporary but ultimately futile resistance against entropy. Standard links in the food chain typically include many varieties of predator–prey relations, modeled mathematically by the Lotke–Volterra equations. These are non-linear but essentially sinusoidal fluctuations of interdependent populations (see Figure 3.1).

The first two of Darwin's (1859) five tenets, which implicate such populations in this context, may be summarized as follows:[1]

1. A struggle for life ensues from an overabundance of reproducing life-forms competing for resources insufficient to sustain them all (from Malthus 1798).

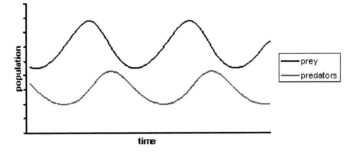

Figure 3.1 Lotke–Volterra equations

2. Of many individuals born, only a small number can survive the struggle long
   enough to reproduce (from observation).

The rediscovery of Mendel's work, and the introduction of the concept of mutation
(by de Vries) and the gene (by Johannsen) heralded the birth of neo-Darwinism,
in which Darwin's brilliant hypothesis of tenet (4) became richly substantiated.
But attempts to extend Darwinian and neo-Darwinian paradigms to the human
species (e.g., Herbert Spencer's social Darwinism, Raymond Cattell's eugenics,
E. O. Wilson's sociobiology) have been hotly contested, and appear woefully
inadequate to the task of accounting for human cultural evolution. Darwin himself
refused Marx's invitation to write the Foreword to *Das Kapital*, and had asserted
to Marx that his (Darwin's) theories pertained only to the animal and vegetable
kingdoms, and not to the realm of human politics.

At the risk of belaboring the point, we make no moral judgments about Darwin's
second tenet. Indeed, we understand that Nature devised or evolved a 'lottery' to
which the progeny of innumerable species are compelled to subscribe. No moral
philosopher bemoans the fate of millions of hatchlings whose 'premature' deaths
sustain the larger food chain, nor praises the 'virtues' of the select few who survive
long enough to reproduce. Even periodic mass extinctions of species (as in the
Jurassic and Late Cretaceous periods) evoke awe without moralization; after all,
95% of all species that ever existed are now extinct. We may lament the loss
of biodiversity, but such sentiment is grounded either in scientific or (at most)
aesthetic regret. We erect no monuments to commemorate the irreversible passing
into oblivion of so many life-forms, nor do we indict Nature for 'crimes against
animality.'

However, the current biological debacle on planet Earth cannot unfold without
attracting moral condemnation, for it is the exclusive handiwork (and latest
foolishness) of *Homo sapiens*. Owing predominantly to the manifold pressures
of unchecked human population growth, to which corporate greed and political
expediency are but willing handmaidens, humans are well-embarked in both the
de-speciation and despoilment of the planet, on extravagant scales. This represents the dark side of globalization. Large-scale human hunger is to some extent

a by-product of an even larger catastrophe, and it is difficult to deplore the part without condemning the whole.

In stark contrast to the Lotke–Volterra equations, the human population curve increases exponentially over time, while natural resources are similarly depleted. Synthetic resources are manufactured or husbanded, but their supply or provision both lags behind demand and lacks sufficiency. This is depicted in Figure 3.2. Billions of people now subsist in poverty and hunger, in the gap between the red and blue curves, and in the region above the black curve. There are insufficient natural resources to sustain them, and insufficient provision of synthetic resources to sustain them.

Before tackling the ethical dimensions of this human-made disaster, let us ask: What faculties has nature bequeathed to other social predators, to prevent them from overexploiting or mal-distributing their food resources to the point of hunger, starvation, or extinction? Owing to the insightful work of Wynne-Edwards (1962), we find a ready reply, which is rooted in territorial imperative. By substituting a parcel of land (or a volume of sea, or air) for the resources it contains, and by establishing an optimal population density for a given species in that territory, nature sets the boundary conditions for an unstable but tenable homeostasis. If the actual population density strays too far from the so-called 'optimum number' (for that species in the given habitat), social behaviors change radically to enable the necessary increase or decrease in numbers, and subsequent regression toward the optimum homeostatic mean.

Table 3.1 depicts some typical optimum numbers of social animals (using data from Pfeiffer 1970 and Forel 1928). Note that in a state of nature, hunting-and-gathering bands of humans maintain roughly the same order of magnitude of population density as wolves. This represents the limits of nature's decree for our population control. Had we remained within them, the terrestrial human population would be not much more than that of wolves and other pack animals. Boasting no masses, we would know no mass starvation either.

Viewed from a neo-Darwinian standpoint alone (thus contrary to Darwin's own prescription about the inapplicability of his thesis to 'political kingdoms'), humankind's survival from the earliest days to the present was, and remains, a

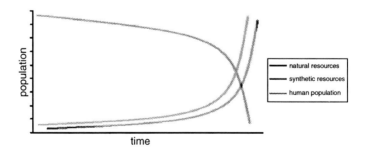

Figure 3.2 Human population dynamics

TABLE 3.1 Typical natural optimum densities

Group type	Typical number	Typical area (sq. miles)	Optimum density
Ant formicary	1,000,000	0.05	20,000,000
Gibbon family	4	0.1	40
Baboon troop	40	15	3.35
Gorilla troop	17	17	1.00
Human band	30	1,000	0.03
Wolf pack	10	1,000	0.01

precarious affair. Each human individual is born an abjectly dependent animal, with an immature nervous system that requires years to develop fully; a defenseless body that protracts juvenility even after years of constant care; and a big brain that requires decades of intensive enculturation to function even at minimal capacity. What is the prognosis for such a creature's survival? By any lights, it is not good. In fact, the fossil record shows that the large primate brain is natural selection's most dubious gambit to date: the bigger the brain, the shorter the life expectancy of the species. Yet this pathetic biped *H. sapiens* has somehow managed to become the planet's top predator, preying not only on every life-form extant (directly or indirectly), and not only on the biosphere itself (e.g., from oceans to oilfields to ozone), but also and most notoriously on our own kind. Political, religious, commercial, social, and sexual predation abound in the human world by default. Morality is a weak and ineffectual brake on human predation.

And therein lays the secret of our 'success,' such as it is. In order not only to survive, but also to emerge as the scourge of the earth's life-nurturing habitat, the feeble and helpless human neonate is vouchsafed a terrible gift: From the first instant to the last, we are self-regarding, short-sighted, and rapacious predators. Congenitally weaponless mankind has no instinctive checks upon the use of any weapons evolved extra-somatically by their big brains: including commercial predation and economic exploitation of their own kind.

In sum, moral codes are tacked on by cultural evolution, as toothless afterthoughts in the teeth of the realization of our terrible predicament. There is nothing in human nature that compels any binding universal morality. Our conceptions of 'good' are mostly congruent with our appetites for power and pleasure, and we form alliances only for the purpose of furthering our own ends. In the absence of an overarching power to keep us all in awe, we will prey on each other incessantly. Nothing save the human predilection for fantasy (bequeathed no doubt to grant us respite from our real condition) gainsays this Hobbesian (1651) vision.

HUMAN POPULATIONS AND THE FOUNDATIONS OF ETHICS

Although nature almost certainly intended that humans should subsist in small hunting-and-gathering bands, and pose no severe threat to any species except perhaps themselves, humans have outwitted nature (temporarily) by learning how to sustain relatively permanent and highly populous settlements. This began in earnest during the Neolithic revolution, which pioneered both the domestication of animals and seasonal agriculture, as well as the tools and weapons necessary for the construction and defense (against less industrious human marauders) of permanent settlements. Thus the Neolithic revolution also marked the conceptualization of goods and chattels, the concomitant replacement of spirituality with materialism, and the beginning of man's separation from nature.

The ongoing invention of tools (e.g., wells and ploughs) and elaboration of symbolic structures (e.g., tribal myths ands legends) afforded both the technological means and the traditional binding forces necessary for the sustenance of increasingly large populations. Since unchecked population growth lies at the heart of both matters (global hunger and planetary despoilment), it is useful to compare human population densities in a 'state of nature' with those sustained by global infrastructures and allied technologies. Tables 3.2 and 3.3 show the results of a mere 14,000 years of cultural evolution – which on a biological time-scale is negligible, but which has nonetheless transformed our species, the planet, and all the natural by-products of eons of geological and biological evolution.

The sustenance of current microstate and metropolitan population densities entails the maintenance and evolution of increasingly complex, multilayered, and fragile networks of technologies dedicated to the production and delivery of goods and services on a massive and historically unprecedented scale. Since the gap between the developed and the developing world has widened in some key respects, and is partly maintained by forces resistant to change, it is increasingly difficult for the least-networked populations to interact with the most-networked ones. Cycles of affluence and cycles of poverty become decoupled; and bimodal distributions of wealth result, which serve only to reinforce the disparities. In terms of food consumption, we see epidemic proportions of obesity at one extreme in the developed world, contrasted with pervasive and severe hunger at the other extreme in the developing world. While the overconsumption of fat- and sugar-laden victuals is a serious problem, symptomatic of a spiritual void that can never be filled (only expanded) by a disposable and instantaneous culture predicated on continuous overdoses of junk goods, junk services, and junk thought, this is simultaneously the lesser of two evils and a contributing cause to the greater evil. That greater evil is acute mass starvation, in contrast with chronic spiritual starvation.

TABLE 3.2 Typical microstate population densities

Microstate	Population	Area (sq. miles)	Density
Liechtenstein	34,000	62	548
San Marino	24,000	29	827
Barbados	180,000	166	1,084
Tuvalu	12,000	9	1,333
Malta	400,000	122	3,278

TABLE 3.3 Typical metropolitan population densities

Metropolis	Population density per sq. mile
London	10,500
Hong Kong	17,333
New York	25,600
Tokyo	34,132
Mumbai	41,984

Why do I call human suffering an evil? I am far from alone in doing so, and my reasons may not be the same as those of many others who utilize such highly charged nomenclature. Yet the fact we do this at all, for whatever reason, is philosophically significant. The human being, alone among myriad other fauna of this earth, is uniquely capable of rendering moral judgments.

Cuckoldry is named after the cuckoo, but this bird is not branded as 'immoral' for having evolved such deceit as its signature survival strategy. The origins of human cuckoldry, among a repertoire of duplicitous behaviors, are observable in chimpanzees and other apes – our closest living relatives. Yet these animals have neither fashioned nor vitiated any moral codes. These complementary moral capacities – nobility and turpitude – reside exclusively within the province of humanity.

While emergent political and social norms (alongside vestiges of sociobiological ones) undoubtedly shaped the ethos of hunting and gathering bands, the transition to permanent settlements – and their inhabitants' conceptualizations of property and all its ramifications – was decisive in the cultural evolution of moral codes. It is no accident that the oldest writings of antiquity (the written tradition representing a cultural breakthrough in the preservation and transmission of symbolic structures) are infused with moral discourse. Nor for that matter is it an accident that all the great world religions share a common core of moral precepts. Among the most ancient sources of axiological guidance, organized religions developed manuals of moral 'best practices,' devised by the shepherds to help maintain and increase their human flocks, but debased or disregarded by the human wolves who prey on them.

To speak of 'the village' (the kind it takes to rear a child in an ideal manner) is to conjure up images of pastoral charm, natural simplicity, and moral decency. One of the last communities to achieve celebrity for philosophical and literary works emanating from such an ethos was that of the New England Idealists. Nowadays, Emerson's (1913) celebration of 'Self-Reliance' and Thoreau's (1854) sojourn on Walden Pond are relics of a bygone age; a scant century and a half in the historical past, but separated from our present by the gulf of globalization, in which virtuality and technology displace mere chronology. The villages of yesteryear were knitted together by the spirit of community. Such villages have all but vanished, transformed out of all recognition in the developed world by successive waves of progress: the Industrial Revolution, utilitarian and democratic reforms, the Golden Age of capitalism, the information revolution, the postmodern exurban sprawl. Community is superseded by technology, and moral consciousness is eroded by technocracy.

In his forthright 1902 rebuttal of social Darwinism, Peter Kropotkin wrote:

> And while in a savage land, among the Hottentots, it would be scandalous to eat without having loudly called out thrice whether there is not somebody wanting to share the food, all that a respectable citizen has to do now is to pay the poor tax and to let the starving starve.

Kropotkin's critique bears substantial weight today, save that our taxes are paid to a more complex array of inefficient, unaccountable, and technocratic governments, while more people than ever starve.

In New York City – the quintessential urban jungle-cum-global village, yet hardly a savage land – the Hottentot custom is all but impossible to practice. Ride the subway system, and you will regularly observe the following sequence of events. First, a charity-worker enters the subway car with a hamper of sandwiches, fruits, and beverages, announces his or her mission, and asks whether anyone is hungry or thirsty. There are no takers, so he or she moves on to the next car. Second, and before long, a beggar enters the car and recites a compulsory tale of woe, often hyperbolically exaggerated because of fierce competition (even in this sector) – 'I am homeless, jobless, HIV-positive, and was shot trying to steal food.' There are no givers, so he or she moves on to the next car. In 10 years of riding the New York subway, I have never seen the food donor and the food seeker in the same car at the same time. Apparently, they have evolved a pattern of perfect mutual avoidance. If the Manhattan chapter of the global village can finesse the Hottentot maxim so deftly, imagine how many more people, across much greater distances, it can also fail to feed.

The inapplicability of the maxim of the Hottentot village to the global village becomes starker in the context of the logic of Emmanuel Levinas' 'other-centered' ethics. Levinas (1974) argues that the very existence of others imposes inescapable moral obligations on us all. He asserts that

> justice remains justice only, in a society where there is no distinction between those close and those far off, but in which there also remains the impossibility of passing by the closest.

To those who sustain virtual selves in that unbounded e-Commons known as cyberspace, the former distinctions of time and space 'between those close and those far off' no longer apply. In principle, any two people anywhere on the planet can communicate instantaneously. But in reality, for instance in the New York subway, there remains a probability approaching certainty of 'passing by the closest,' especially while speaking on a mobile phone to 'those far off.' And if one can so easily 'pass by the closest,' then one can even more easily forget the existence of billions of 'those far off' who have never used phones or e-mail, and who are just as hungry as 'the closest' whom everyone passes by. Levinas would (and did) conclude that such a system is utterly unjust, and that in consequence it is accumulating an incalculable moral debt. The question is: Who will pay?

Moral precepts form no part of the corpus of natural laws (i.e., physical, chemical, biological), and cannot be consistently or coherently grounded in social sciences either (*pace* regnant but naïve and patently falsifiable 'paradigms' like Kohlberg's). Religions have attempted to ordain moral codes as the imperatives of their respective deities; secular philosophers, to ground goodness in universal human contexts; postmodernists, to relativize or deconstruct ethics altogether. It appears that no one can reliably compel anyone to behave morally or immorally, because no one can compel another's choice (that is, cannot curtail another's rapacity). Collectively, we determine what is customary, whereas individually we can follow or flout custom as we wish. Since morals are only customs in the purloined garb of laws, it is empathically moving but empirically dubious to appeal to morality as the slayer of hunger's dragon. Television networks long ago inculcated and then discovered 'compassion fatigue' among their viewers: The sight of too many starving human beings portrayed too graphically for too long does not stimulate prolonged charitable response; it promotes rapid channel-change.

Hume's notorious 'fork' is no dining utensil; rather, a stake in the heart of hopes that moral appeal alone can be decisive in motivating the alleviation of global hunger. For Hume saw most clearly the divide in kind that obtains and persists between matters of fact (that which 'is') and matters of value (that which 'ought to be'). He showed that there is no valid inference from the former to the latter – that is, from factual premises to normative conclusions – unless one smuggles at least one normative premise into the argument. In Hume's (1739) words:

> In every system of morality, which I have hitherto met with, I have always remark'd, that the author proceeds for some time in the ordinary ways of reasoning, and establishes the being of a God, or makes observations concerning human affairs; when of a sudden I am surpriz'd to find, that instead of the usual copulations of propositions, *is*, and *is not*, I meet with no proposition that is not connected with an *ought*, or an *ought not*. This change is imperceptible; but is however, of the last consequence. For as this *ought*, or *ought not*, expresses some new relation or affirmation, 'tis necessary that it shou'd be observ'd and explain'd; and at the same time that a reason should be given; for what seems altogether inconceivable, how this new relation can be a deduction from others, which are entirely different from it.

To illustrate Hume's sharp point with a blunt example, suppose we state the factual premise that millions of children are going to bed hungry tonight. What normative conclusion one validly draws from this depends vitally upon what normative premise one smuggles into the argument. Thus, the following argument is valid:

P1: Millions of children are going to bed hungry.
P2: No child should go to bed hungry.
C: Therefore we should find a way to feed millions of children.

However, changing the normative premise can also change the conclusion radically, and still preserve deductive validity:

P1: Millions of children are going to bed hungry.

P2: No child should be conceived by parents who cannot feed it adequately.

C: Therefore millions of children should not have been conceived.

Many affluent people doubtless withhold help owing to variants of the foregoing argument, which is inhumanly callous yet deductively valid. Even if we wish to assert a universal humanism, with a premise that suffering is wrong, and that wrong should be remedied, we will still encounter difficulties. For example:

P1: Human suffering is wrong.

P2: Wrongs should be remedied.

P3: Millions of people are suffering from hunger.

C: Therefore hunger should be remedied.

I take this to be the central argument of this book, on which there is accord among authors, and for which considerable other support could be garnered. However, if we sharpen our focus on P2, so that it reads 'A wrong should be remedied by those responsible for the wrongdoing,' then to preserve validity we must modify the conclusion to: 'Therefore hunger should be remedied by those responsible for its manifestation and persistence.' But here I suspect there would be less consensus on the critical matter of exactly who are the responsible agents.

If we agree that agricultural subsidies in the USA and the EU are partly responsible, then it would follow that they should be reduced or eliminated. But who is responsible for that? Policy-makers and trade negotiators are appointed by whom? By politicians beholden to agribusiness lobbyists? If so, then the voting public is ultimately responsible for demanding the necessary changes, and the media are responsible for bringing these matters to public attention. Then again, millions of poverty-stricken Indians live in areas that experience some of the world's highest rainfall during monsoons; yet in the dry season clean water has to be trucked in, and purchased by them for 7 rupees per liter. India also has the atomic bomb: Hence one might suppose its engineers more than capable of building reservoirs, cisterns, and irrigation systems. That the Indian government does not undertake such public works is clearly not the fault of millions of obese Americans; nor is it their fault that millions of thirsty but superstitious Indians believe that spells and charms induce the monsoons. India is the world's most populous democracy; its own people and government must be partly accountable for its social ills. Yet it is clear that the democratic political process, governed by short-term interest in re-election, is too myopically self-regarding to effect the necessary changes. And it is also clear that 'media responsibility' is an oxymoron of the first order.

Thus a refusal to be impaled on Hume's fork requires a very careful assessment not only of where responsibility for hunger lies, but also of how it can be meaningfully shouldered. And unlike alleged facts, which are themselves notoriously susceptible to challenge (not only by wholesome skeptics but also by fulsome revisionists and other anti-realists), value-judgments are even more subject to dispute. It is a corollary of Hume's fork that normative premises

themselves do not result from any pristine deduction from fact, and must
emanate from yet other normatives held more primitively to be true. Even among
those most ardently committed to alleviating global hunger, there is bound to
be disagreement on which set of normative claims (if any) will be adopted
as fundamental.

WHICH NORMATIVE ETHICS ARE VIABLE?

As mentioned earlier, economists are seeking viable ethical models in which to
frame or ground their suggested remedies to hunger. I believe this to be a worthwhile endeavor, because the public is much more vulnerable to moral suasion than
are their political and business leaders. Influencing public opinion by means of
consumer sentiment can play a critical role in overcoming political inertia and
corporate indifference alike. Economists tend to see four main 'families' of ethics
as contenders for such models: deontology, teleology, virtue ethics, and correlative
ethics. Let me comment on some strengths and weaknesses of each.

Deontology

This is rule-based morality, epitomized by the Ten Commandments in the Judeo-
Christian tradition and the Eightfold Way in Buddhism. An action is deemed to be
'right' in so far as it conforms to a rule; rules being accorded the moral status of
'good' by default. Deontological justice is therefore attained by mass conformity
to the prevailing dictums, which has a tolerable record in some secular systems but
which is historically inimical to human progress in both totalitarian and theocratic
contexts.

The main advantage of deontology is that it provides a 'rule book' that can
be consulted, in principle, to determine whether a contemplated action is 'right'
or 'wrong.' The main weakness is that there is no consensus about resolving the
inevitable exceptions to the rules. For example, most religious moralities as well
as secular criminal codes contain prohibitions on killing, but quarrels over exceptions to this rule can turn lethal themselves – as in the assassination of abortion-
performing physicians by 'right-to-life' radicals. There is no universal human
consensus about the boundaries of the rule either: Jains and Buddhists teach *ahimsa*,
or non-harm toward all sentient (or even living) beings; whereas Christians preach
brotherly love but may also torture and slaughter animals for mass consumption,
often rearing and force-feeding them under deplorable and ghastly conditions. In
human terms, deontologists also struggle with the moral distinction between killing
and letting die, which is played out in the ongoing and sometimes vituperative
debate between proponents and opponents of passive euthanasia, but which also
has implications for global hunger. For if it is deontologically impermissible to kill
humans to put them out of their 'misery' (as most ethicists assert) but not impermissible to let them die in the interests of preserving their autonomy and dignity
when heroic medical interventions are of dubious merit and would only prolong
suffering (which many ethicists assert), then the danger of transposing this argument

to poverty- and hunger-stricken populations is plain. Swift's (1729) 'Modest Proposal' may be ironically well-named and even tame, if one considers the possibility that some deontologists might sanction the 'letting die' of large populations as the best way to alleviate their suffering and – with inhumane absurdity – to preserve their human dignity. The 1973 movie *Soylent Green*[2] portrays a chilling but eminently foreseeable possible future, and there are ethicists who would endorse it. Thus economists should not look to deontology as the arbiter of global hunger.

In so far as economists identify with secular social science, they may wish to subsume deontology under its celebrated Kantian head. The categorical imperatives, however, are named rather optimistically by Kant (1938), for theycompel no-one who wills to disregard them. Although Kant's attempt to ground morality in a rational framework is perhaps the most objective and noble in the history of Western philosophy, his maxim binds no-one who is unwilling to be bound by it: unlike Newton's laws, among other natural dictates, which have unconditional claim on our assent (i.e., which operate whether we avow them or not).

Teleology

This is outcome-based morality. Formally, an act is defined as 'right' in the case where it produces a balance of good over ill ('act-utilitarianism'); or defined as 'right' if performed in accordance with a rule which, if generally followed, would produce a balance of good over ill ('rule-utilitarianism'). The vernacular slogan was coined by Priestley, but is usually misattributed to Bentham: 'The greatest good for the greatest number.' Although utilitarianism is the best-known form of consequentialism, and was elevated to the status of a credible system of ethics by Bentham (1834) and his protégé, J. S. Mill (1963), it is afflicted with at least three formidable problems, which detract from the theory's universal appeal and applicability.

First, as von Neumann and Morgenstern (1946) pointed out in the introduction to their *Theory of Games and Economic Behavior*, it is impossible to maximize two variables of a given function simultaneously. Thus 'the greatest good for the greatest number' defies our calculus. We can maximize some good, without being able to guarantee its uniform distribution; or we can maximize the number of recipients of some good, without being able to guarantee its greatness.

Second, if anything is clear after 2,500 years of philosophical debate, it is the non-existence and probable non-attainability of a consensus on the meaning of 'good.' Thus, the measurement of any good – and in particular, the greatest good – remains a contentious matter, likely to beget as many moral questions as it is intended to resolve.

Third, a standard criticism of consequentialist ethics in general, and of utilitarianism in particular, is that they fail to take individual rights into account. Indeed, to those who place primary importance on the universality of human rights, utilitarian measures can appear downright immoral. Bent on satisfying the inflamed passions of the greatest number, lynch mobs are utilitarian assemblies, but are hardly exponents of justice. On a grander scale, utopian revolutions are thought to be utilitarian, in the sense of the end presumably justifying the means. But such ratiocinations are fallacious: Ends and means are never independent. Although good can come of ill, ill is not a precondition of goodness. This is a central moral problem that troubles economists, who know for example that we could within a short time feed 90% of the world's starving people. This would be utilitarian, but would also condemn millions of people to death. Doing the 'greatest good for the greatest number' too often entails doing the 'greatest harm to the smallest number.' Utilitarianism is susceptible to intolerable inegalitarianism.

Utilitarian models tend to work well in the medical sphere, from triage to phase-one clinical trials. But this is because some people are dying of injury or illness in any case, and by acknowledging this strategically we can save many other lives. Since injury and illness are inevitable despite our best efforts at prevention, utilitarian criteria seem self-justifying in such contexts. But since there is evidence that our best efforts have not yet been made to alleviate hunger, and moreover that hunger should not be inevitable, utilitarian criteria are less acceptable in this context.

Even from this cursory overview, it is clear that utilitarian ethics are not readily compatible with either rules-based or rights-based systems. Any maxim might be adopted or eschewed in favor of some end, which is anathema to Kantian deontology; while by its very definition, utilitarianism shrinks from a universal (and therefore equal) assertion of human rights.

Virtue Ethics

This ancient and venerable tradition emerged in three different versions, in three great civilizations. Aristotle, Buddha, and Confucius form the 'ABC' of virtue ethics, and their prescriptions are worth heeding. Each of these sages taught that goodness neither inheres in rules, nor obtains as a function of outcomes; rather, is a product of the practice of virtues. The classical Hellenic virtues are courage, temperance, justice, and wisdom; to Aristotle, their practice is conducive to a good life, his *summum bonum*. Buddha's list is encompassed by the Eightfold Path: Right View and Right Intention (the province of wisdom); Right Speech, Right Action, and Right Livelihood (the province of ethical conduct); Right Effort, Right Mindfulness, and Right Concentration (the province of mental development).[3] Buddha's theory and practice is intended to awaken human beings from their deep delusions concerning the nature of self and reality, and raise them to the full potential of their benevolent and compassionate sentience. Confucius is less systematic, but his influence in Asia is even more pervasive than is Aristotle's in the West. Confucius taught that the inculcation and practice of virtues is essential to the balance of the individual, the harmony of the family, and the stability of the State. The five traditional Confucian virtues are humaneness, righteousness, proper deportment, wisdom, and trustworthiness.

Virtue ethics are optimistic, and in their conception of the human nature tend to avoid both religious and political extremes. In rebuttal of conservative views, they conceive the human being neither as a congenitally sinful animal (*qua* Augustine), nor as an irremediably egoistic predator (*qua* Hobbes); but rather as a being that can acquire sinful habits and rehearse egoistic dispositions if unchecked by virtue itself. In rebuttal of liberal views, they conceive the human character neither as a blank slate upon which anything may be imprinted (*qua* Locke), nor as a noble savage corrupted by civilization (*qua* Rousseau); but rather as a partially malleable being who nonetheless admits of some 'hard-wired' traits, ingrained tendencies, and individual idiosyncrasies.

Are there immediate applications of virtue ethics to the problem of hunger? Yes. Let us briefly state one relevant insight from each of the three sages.

Aristotle (1984) claimed that a prosperous middle class is essential to a stable State, and this squares with economists' visions of more normally distributed income curves replacing the bimodal or sawtooth distributions that signal excessive disparities between ultra-poor and ultra-affluent. Indeed, the countries in which hunger is most prevalent are also those with the weakest middle classes. So perhaps Aristotle's *Politics* and *Ethics* should be scanned more closely for advice. Aristotle's 'Golden Mean' represents a moderate and balanced course in all matters, one charted to avoid extremes – including massive poverty and starvation.

Buddha similarly counsels avoidance of both excess and dearth, and cultivation of the 'Middle Way.' The practice of Buddhism as a secular philosophy (not necessarily as a religion) awakens compassion, and with it the mission to help all suffering beings wherever possible. In a very practical sense, some Buddhist precepts, if widely adopted, would make for significant reductions in food consumption (among other things) in the more-affluent nations. The problem of how to translate such putative voluntary reduction into a zero-sum game, such that those who need to consume more could benefit from others consuming less, remains to be solved. Nonetheless, the operative Buddhist maxim – that two-thirds of what one normally consumes is more than sufficient for sustenance – could reduce food consumption (and also obesity and allied problems) significantly in the developed world, and possibly potentiate increased consumption where it is most urgently needed.

Confucian ethics (1989) are also vitally important in his context, although they are at odds with Aristotle and Buddha in certain key respects. In all human societies, there is a constant tension between the claims of the individual on the group, and of the group on the individual. Although individual claims have been considerably furthered in the past century or so, mostly as a consequence of unprecedented dialogues on human rights, the significance of the individual was hardly neglected by ethicists of antiquity. Aristotle's ethics are aimed at leading a fulfilled life, and though fulfillment is by definition an individual matter, it is a developmental process that requires supportive social milieus. Similarly, Buddha's goal of awakening also pertains to the individual, although it cannot be accomplished in the absence of compassion for and from others – hence Buddhism's 'Three Jewels' are Buddha (the potentially awakened one dormant in us all), Dharma (the teachings that conduce to awakening), and Sangha (the community that fosters such teachings). Thus, for Aristotle and Buddha alike, individual development is synonymous with human progress. Confucius differs in the greater weight that he accords to social structures, and to the subordination of the individual to the collective at decisive junctures, in the interests of social stability.

In particular, Confucian ethics recognize a natural authoritarian hierarchy that springs from Tao (the Way), and which is transposable to the human world. In this natural hierarchy, the emperor (i.e., the State) governs subject; husband governs wife; mother governs child. The reciprocity of Chinese metaphysics recognizes that the child needs and desires to be subordinate to the mother; that the wife needs and desires to be subordinate to the husband; and that the citizen needs and desires to be subordinate to political authority. The West has corrupted and reversed this natural order with an excessive focus on individualism, which has undermined the common good to an irreversible and irreparable extent, heralding the ongoing decline and collapse of Western civilization itself.

Confucius asserts that only by acquiescing in our dutiful roles in the natural order of things can we become fully realized as human beings. It is remarkable that, in China and to an extent in Japan (which regards China as the 'parent' culture), the Confucian ethos has prevailed across centuries, surviving wars of dynastic succession, colonialism, communist revolution, cultural revolution, democratization, and now globalization. Moreover, combining the organizational advantages of Confucianism with the developmental potential of capitalistic markets is propelling China to the forefront of global economies.

China is also the first nation to regulate human reproduction as a matter of State policy, in an effort to reduce absolute numbers and thus to mitigate the boundary conditions that drive mass hunger. Only in a Confucian ethos, which entails the subordination of individualism to the larger interests of the collective, could one witness such historical trumping of biological claims by cultural ones. Sexual reproduction is a ubiquitous biological capacity, but not therefore a universal human right. Virtue ethics perennially raises the questions: Which virtues shall be inculcated in the populace, and why?

Correlative Ethics

This is a genuinely new branch of moral discourse, a recent function of the Enlightenment Project and its cognate evolution of human liberties. A salient and pragmatic correlation obtains between rights and duties, because declarations of universal human entitlements do not automatically create or sustain the conditions required for their exercise. In particular, human rights cannot be exercised in a vacuum; their exercise always entails the fulfillment of correlative obligations (or duties) on the part of citizens and organizations alike.

A further distinction is normally drawn between 'positive' and 'negative' rights. A positive right is such that its exercise entails a correlative obligation to provide something; for example, a right to vote cannot be exercised unless candidates and ballots are provided. A negative right is such that its exercise entails a correlative obligation not to interfere; for example, a right to freedom of expression cannot be exercised except in theabsence of censorship. While most people wish to be the beneficiaries of rights, not all wish to fulfill their correlative obligations. This reconstitutes but does not resolve the fundamental tension between individual claims on society versus societal claims on the individual.

But the language of human rights has become so distorted in the West, and public 'rights-consciousness' so pervasive, owing partly to unremitting media oversimplification and partly to political indoctrination in the universities, that many Americans (in particular) inhabit a sublime estate, in which they believe they have rights to everything and obligations to nothing. The distinction between right and privilege has been so conflated, whether innocently or intentionally, that rights are broadly misconstrued as laws of nature that somehow *should* be operative without individual intervention, social cost, or political process. Combined with the postmodern affinity for 'empowerment' – a euphemism for relinquishing power to groups, so that individuals unable to claim or exercise it on their own merits can do so via membership in a newly privileged collective of 'victims' entitled to 'compensation' for the past – the emergence of 'group rights' (a dangerous oxymoron) has made an ironic mockery of the hard-won individual entitlements that form its very foundation.

The brief history of human rights belies such naïve views. Every entitlement hitherto bestowed on humanity has had to be won and maintained by individual intervention, at social cost, and via political process. Those tempted to suppose that rights provide a panacea for the world's ills might think twice, in light of the discrepancy between a right's assertion (which is easy) and its exercise (which can prove difficult or impossible). While the harp of human idealism is soothingly strummed by noble declarations of universal human rights, such as emanate from the precincts of the United Nations, the ears of idealists and realists alike are still pained by cries of human anguish, such as emanate from too many of the nations that glibly espouse but remorselessly violate the said entitlements. Idealists clamor for 'peace and love'; realists reply that peace and love alone could never have de-Nazified Germany, democratized Japan, nor liberated Eastern Europe from the yoke of Soviet totalitarianism.

Even the American Bill of Rights, as laudable a moral document as *Homo politicus* has ever seen fit to ratify and implement, does not accord to anyone a right to food, clothing, shelter, or employment. It merely implies the provision of conditions such that an average person might reasonably suppose, all things being equal in theory but never in practice, that he or she has a decent prospect of securing the necessities of life, and beyond these some luxuries of livelihood, by dint of personal industry and by virtue of political climate. Comprehensive healthcare, quality education, and judicial remedy are not rights in America; one generally gets what one can afford of these, and their price is steep.

The social democracies can, with some justification, claim to have done better than the American Republic in terms of correlative ethics. Social democracies provide the necessities of life as rights, minimally (if all else fails) in the form of a social safety net through whose meshes relatively few citizens slip. However, social democracies operate at a correlative cost: Taxes are graduated to favor a more normal distribution of income, and base taxation rates are sufficiently high (at least by the USA's standards) to subsidize the impecunious, so that the vast majority live above the poverty line. At the same time, economists realize full well that a nexus of boundary conditions has enabled the emergence of these quasi-utopian (but sometimes clandestinely totalitarian) 'nanny States,' a nexus which for a variety of reasons is neither extant nor envisageable in the hungriest parts of the world. Sub-Saharan African and South Asian States are not likely to replicate the political economies of Canada, Denmark, Norway, and Sweden any time soon.

Moreover, even a cursory glance at the normative list of Millennium Development Goals, compared with the appalling facts on the ground in so many signatory nations, compels a shift from idealistic espousals of rights to realistic observations of oppression. Correlative ethics has the smallest purchase in the places that most need it. The most brazen violators of human rights are among the most enthusiastic signatories of Human-Rights Conventions. Notwithstanding its laudable achievements, the UN itself is also a global incubator of acrimony, factionalism, bureaucracy, and hypocrisy. Its collective aspirations for humanity are noble to a fault, but the dehumanizing practices of some of its Member States are debased beyond belief.

So while the language of rights may represent some of humanity's best hopes, it also highlights our worst despair. Do human beings have a 'right' to be born? That question is hardly settled, and co-exists in perpetual tension with woman's emergent right to abortion on demand. Are humans really born free and equal? This reads like Rousseau's (1762) most sophomoric wishful thinking. In fact, humans are born enslaved to their congenital dependencies, to their genes, to their geographies, to their languages, to their cultures, to their religions, to their political economies, and to all the inane prejudices that their parents, teachers, and peers will assiduously and relentlessly instill in them.

Moreover, all humans are born unequal, both to one another and with respect to their own changing states. Individuals differ widely in natural ability and interest; and differ too in acquired expertise and habit. They may be *conceived of* as 'equal' in various abstract senses: e.g., theologically (as children of one God); teleologically (as awakening Buddhas); judicially (as equal before the law); constitutionally (as deserving of equal rights); or humanistically (as entitled to equal opportunity). But natural and acquired inequalities assure that every theoretical, hypothetical, and ideological *conception* of humanity – no matter how egalitarian – will be falsified by the experience of massive and pervasive inequality in practice. So again, the burning question is not whether and according to which criteria we regard people as hypothetically equal; but whether humanity finds ways to constrain the extreme and debilitating inequalities of income and opportunity that cause so much suffering and privation.

Nobody is born free; everybody is born unequal. If high-minded declarations of human rights embody too much wishful thinking or well-intended fantasy at the outset, they may prevent us from confronting the facts in ways that could make a difference.

WHAT SHOULD WE DO?

Globalization is a dynamic phenomenon that depends on evolving and shifting alliances between multinational and transnational business interests on the one hand, and regional, national, and local political interests on the other. The process is also driven by technological innovation, social entrepreneurship, and creative leadership. At its best, globalization denotes a new consciousness of humanity as a whole: as interconnected inhabitants of a single village. In the most salutary sense, planetary managers work daily in a formerly mystical space: Teilhard de Chardin's (1982) *noosphere*, a 'thinking envelope of Earth.' But in the most pejorative sense, globalization is a euphemism for economic feudalism of a kind that engendered the worst horrors of the Industrial Revolution, but on an incomprehensibly larger scale. The gross inequities and grotesque iniquities against which Dickens, Marx, and Mill railed so vociferously in Britain are being repainted on vastly larger canvases throughout the contemporary world.

Pure commercial interests, motivated solely by profit, unchecked by humanitarian concerns, and abetted by entrenched corruption, will always produce inequities; while democratic political interests, motivated mainly by short-term popularity, unable to confront long-term issues, and condemned to ineffectual compromise, will always sustain inequities. At the same time, erosion of public trust in received corporate and political institutions, driven by evidence of unparalleled avarice and ineradicable corruption, alongside the bewildering complexities of postmodernist technocracy, are driving millions of marginalized and disenfranchised souls into the dogmatic arms of proselytizing and often mutually incompatible fundamentalist religions, notably Islam and Christianity, in their most virulently intolerant forms.

Many things need to be done to alleviate global hunger. First, moral force can be brought to bear on corporations and governments, but only if it rises from the grass roots and remains relatively uncorrupted by the interests it must court in order to be heard. Second, if human populations have a 'right' to eat, they also have a correlative obligation not to procreate beyond manageable limits. Third, the husbandry and slaughter of domesticated cattle for flesh is a grossly inefficient and unhealthy way to manage both human diet and terrestrial biomass; while the products of the dairy industry are nothing but toxic waste to human metabolism, a dietary aberration that should likewise be abolished and replaced with wholesome and efficient vegetarian regimes. Fourth, and ultimately, humanity must discover and implement a paradigm that encourages cultural diversity within a unifying human framework; that fosters political, religious, and commercial interests alike, yet that curtails their catalogue of abuses with transcendent and effective moral sanctions.

Having been stimulated to ponder the problem of human hunger, I am not sanguine about the prospect of any of these things being done, or done sufficiently to make a difference. Time and again, natural selection rears its ironic head, and decrees that humans are such fragile and dependent beings at birth, with such slim chances of survival, that they must draw from an seemingly inexhaustible well of self-regarding, rapacious, and myopic egoism, contaminated with xenophobic instincts (that synthetic selection transposes into myths, doctrines, and ideologies) which unfailingly sanctify their own tribe and demonize the adjacent one; and moreover that they shall be possessed of hyperbolic sexuality, such that they will tend to produce progeny in inverse proportion to their material resources.

These tendencies among others, which long ago favored our emergence from caves, abetted our dispersion across the planet, and furthered our adaptation to diverse geographic conditions, now militate decisively against our species. Nietzsche (1891) saw the human being as a parasite on the earth's crust;[4] yet even he forbore from stating the obvious continuation of the analogy: that a wise (or at least a well-adapted) parasite does not kill its host. As top predators, humans have always killed one another along with everything else that moves or breathes; but now we are killing the very planet that once indulged and satiated our rapacious appetites.

If the likes of Dickens, Marx, and Mill were so provoked by the excesses and privations of the Industrial Revolution, what would they have said about the World Wars, revolutionary bloodbaths, genocidal manias, and totalitarian slaughterhouses of the twentieth century? Such mind-bending commentaries were reserved for the generation of Aldous Huxley, Arthur Koestler, George Orwell, and Ayn Rand. Yet the twenty-first century is likely to witness horrors that would make these pale in contrast.

As the exponential curve of human population continues to explode, as natural resources continue to be depleted or despoiled at equally alarming rates, and as dependency on cultural evolution increases accordingly, human populations will be subjected to naturally and synthetically induced catastrophes that will not result in the extinction of hunger or poverty, except via the extinction of our species. The future of moral discourse on these matters appears equally non-Panglossian. Humans excel both in imagining the best of all possible worlds for themselves, while creating the worst.

NOTES

[1] His other main tenets are: (3) A continuous graduation of physical variations between individuals exists, both within and between species (from observation and by hypothesis, respectively); (4) A particular variation, however slight, may be beneficial or detrimental to an individual's survival, relative to its competitors in a given environment. Such variations are inherited by the offspring; they arise, and

are transmitted, in some manner internal to the individual (by hypothesis); (5) The principle 'by which each slight variation, if useful, is preserved' is called 'natural selection' (by definition).

[2] directed by Richard Fleischer, based on a novel by Harry Harrison

[3] See http://www.thebigview.com/buddhism/eightfoldpath.html

[4] "The earth, said he, hath a skin; and this skin hath diseases. One of these diseases, for example, is called 'man.' " Nietzsche, 1891, *Zarathustra's Prologue*.

REFERENCES

Aristotle, 1984. *Nicomachean Ethics, Politics, Economics*, in *The Complete Works of Aristotle, The Revised Oxford Translation*, edited by Jonathan Barnes. Princeton: Princeton University Press, Bollingen Series LXXI.

Bentham, J. 1834. *Deontology*, ed. J. Bowring. Edinburgh, William Tait.

Chardin, P.T. de, 1982. *The Phenomenon of Man*, Glasgow: William Collins Sons & Co.

Darwin, C., 1950 (1859). *On the Origin of Species*. London: Watts & Co. (facsimile of first edition).

Emerson, R., 1913 (1847). *Self-Reliance*, in *The Works of Ralph Waldo Emerson, Essays, First Series*. London: G. Bell and Sons, Ltd.

Forel, A., 1928. *The Social World of the Ants Compared with that of Man*, translated by C. Ogden. London: G.P. Putnam's Sons Ltd.

Hobbes, T., 1957 (1651). *Leviathan*. Oxford: Basil Blackwell.

Hume, D., 1978 (1739). *A Treatise of Human Nature*. Oxford: Clarendon Press.

Kant, I., 1938 (1798). *The Fundamental Principle of the Metaphysics of Ethics*, translated by O. Mantheg-Zorn. New York: D. Appleton-Century Co. Inc.

Kropotkin, P., 1902. *Mutual Aid*. London: William Heinemann.

Levinas, E., 1991 (1974). *Otherwise than Being or Beyond Essence*, translated by A. Lingis. Dordrecht: Kluwer Academic Publishers.

Malthus, T., 1798. *An Essay on the Principle of Population as It Affects the Future Improvement of Society, with Remarks on the Speculations of Mr. Godwin, M. Condorcet, and Other Writers*. London: J. Johnson.

Mill, J., 1907 (1863). *Utilitarianism*. London, New York: Longman's.

Neumann, J. von, &1946 Morgenstern, O., 1946. *Theory of Games and Economic Behavior*. New York: John Wiley & Sons Inc.

Nietzsche, F., 1968 (1891). *Thus Spoke Zarathustra*, in *The Portable Nietzsche*, translated by W. Kaufmann. New York: Viking Press, 1968.

Pfeiffer, J., 1970. *The Emergence of Man*. London: Thomas Nelson & Sons Ltd.

Rousseau, J., 1762. *The Social Contract*. Harmondsworth: Penguin Books.

Schrödinger, E., 1948. *What is Life?*. Cambridge: Cambridge at the University Press.

Singer, P., 1990 (1975). *Animal Liberation*. New York: Avon Books

Swift, J., 1729. *A Modest Proposal*. Dublin: S. Harding.

Thoreau, H., 1965 (1854). *Walden*. New York: Airmont Publishing Company.

Wynne-Edwards, V., 1962. *Animal Dispersion in Relation to Social Behaviour*. Edinburgh: Oliver & Boyd Ltd.

KATHERINE MARSHALL

THE ETHICS OF HUNGER: DEVELOPMENT INSTITUTIONS AND THE WORLD OF RELIGION

THE ARGUMENT

Of the ethical challenges facing humanity in the twenty-first century, none has greater importance than the outrage of global poverty. Of all facets of poverty, none is so stark and so moving as hunger. Images and memories of hunger are embedded in every cultural tradition; the pain and humiliation of hunger is a core theme of many ancient and modern faiths. The call to end hunger thus rallies people from virtually all cultures and traditions. Ending hunger is today enshrined as a paramount objective for the global community, featuring as a Millennium Development Goal to which all nations have subscribed. All partners engaged in the effort called development are committed to bringing hunger to an end.

Against this backdrop, four specific and tightly related imperatives can be defined, with applications ranging from the most global to the most local level.

- The first is the need to understand and affirm the types of path that will lead to an end to hunger at global, national, and community levels: What will it take and how can we get there?
- The second is to understand better why past programs and policies on hunger and food security have succeeded and failed; only thus can we appreciate the very real obstacles in the way, be inspired by real success, and learn from experience.
- The third is to rally and sustain the broad global support for ending hunger that is needed to mobilize energies, resources, and efforts. We need to forge partnerships, many quite new and beyond traditional patterns and expectations, that can translate rhetoric about ending hunger into reality.
- The fourth is to probe more deeply into the reasons why hunger persists, as the basis for dealing with a complex of patterns and issues that promise to remain a continuing challenge for our society into the foreseeable future.

In each of these four areas, ethical issues abound, confronting all partners, including both development and faith institutions among their number.

This chapter explores the intersections of development theory and practice, ethics, and faith, taking hunger as the central theme. It draws three central conclusions.

1. This is an area where there is much common concern and common ground, both among religions and between faith and development institutions. This suggests that there is ample room to work toward better understanding and dialogue among institutions than is presently in evidence.
2. More reflection, and above all dialogue, on the underlying ethical issues arising from faith traditions around hunger and nutrition and the challenges to them

51

P. Pinstrup-Andersen and P. Sandøe (eds.), Ethics, Hunger and Globalization: In Search of Appropriate Policies, 51–70.
© 2007 *Springer*.

from modernity could yield fruitful results. Religions are steeped in teachings and lore about hunger and ways to address it, which have yet to be tapped and reflected upon in a systematic way.
3. Ending hunger calls for more engagement and non-traditional partnerships, both to confront differing perspectives and to benefit from different insights and experience.

POVERTY AND HUNGER

Your hunger is never satiated, your thirst is never quenched; you can never sleep until you are no longer tired. —Senegal 1995
Often she has to decide who will eat, she or her son. —Ukraine 1996
In the mornings, eat sweet potatoes, work
At lunch, go without
In the evenings, eat sweet potatoes, sleep. —Vietnam 1999[1]

It is a great and well-understood irony of our time that while we live in a world with plentiful food supplies, rising food production, and the increasing ability to predict drought, famine, and disasters, millions still go hungry. In 2003, 625 people were killed in terrorist attacks, while some 10 million people died of starvation.[2]

The reasons for persisting hunger are quite well understood. First and foremost, most people need to buy food and many lack the resources to do so, so they go hungry. Poverty and hunger have always gone together and they still do today. Other well-understood problems are the troubling, environment-linked climate events that cause famines and natural disasters in whole regions, and which seem to be on the increase. A particularly troubling contemporary challenge is the vicious cycle clearly seen in the most heavily HIV/AIDS-affected countries, whereby families are too weakened to produce their own food and the effects of droughts are multiplied into chronic famine.

We also understand Amartya K. Sen's brilliant insight into the links between democracy, information, and famine. Sen (1981) has pointed out time and time again that famines do not occur in free societies, because people become aware and compel action in time to prevent disaster. Other dimensions of hunger, though, are more difficult to see and therefore to address. For example, a major cause of hunger, and particularly malnutrition, is ignorance: mothers who are educated feed their children much better. Without education, and especially education for girls, there is no long-term solution to hunger.[3]

This picture underscores clearly a first and central point: the struggle to end hunger is inextricably linked to the struggle to end poverty. An analysis of the causes of persistent hunger, though, drives home the reality that while economic growth is essential to fighting poverty, growth itself, and thus policies to promote growth, are insufficient to address many dimensions of poverty; hunger being prominent among them. The physical, economic, social, and physiological constraints facing poor people also need to be addressed. The solutions, sadly, are far from simple. Many who are hungry are living beyond the reach of markets, at the bottom of the 'poverty trap.' Fighting hunger is thus intimately linked with the complex and much debated challenge of how to address poverty and to assure food security.[4] Bringing an end to hunger involves action across the full spectrum of development issues: education, health services, gender relations, equity in access to services, social safety nets, water supply and housing, and protection of the environment.

It is well known but nonetheless striking (for example, when we witness phenomenal outpourings of sympathy when a famine is brought to light) that little stirs the human heart and passions like hunger. An icon of our time is the horrible images, presented live on television screens, of hungry children in far-off lands with huge eyes and swollen bellies; these images almost invariably evoke an immediate and generous public response. But, we have yet to translate this deep human impulse to help into a durable, sound framework for global action to end hunger. The will is there, but the way is still to be fully defined. Part of the challenge involves doing more and doing it better – bringing food to those who need it in a timely and effective manner. However, there is also a need for quite different kinds of approaches, different policies, and different ethical frameworks. It is sadly still true that traditional humanitarian responses to crises and to great poverty are needed; much of the impetus for such action is a traditional form of 'charity.' However, our analyses of experience over the past 60 years have highlighted the importance of going beyond the impulses and mechanisms of charity and compassion to broader and deeper policy and institutional changes. These alone can address the root causes of problems and change patterns at a more fundamental level. That is what the development challenge today is centrally about.

This brings us to the role of religion and faith. Compassion for fellow human beings, a commitment to human dignity, and concern for the downtrodden and outcast are central tenets of many, if not most, faith traditions. A core teaching of many religions is concern about hunger, and countless traditions call for people who have the means to feed those who are hungry. Other traditions (including fasting, for example) remind those who are sated of what it is like to be hungry and in need. These traditions and the impulses that flow from them have been and remain a vital asset in the global struggle against hunger. They can also, though, be 'part of the problem' in two senses. First, they often involve some sense that poverty and hunger are a norm, or inevitable, and thus speak more to the impulse to alleviate the problem rather than to go for change at the roots. And, second, there can be a tendency to focus on traditions and ancient ideas or wisdom that may not reflect the wisdom of our times and scientific advances. The fight against hunger in 2005 calls for a blend of traditional wisdom and compassion and modern wisdom and compassion informed by what is possible today and our understanding of the contemporary roots of poverty and malnutrition.

MILLENNIUM CHALLENGES, GLOBAL MOBILIZATION

Around the turn of the Millennium in 2000, an important new global consensus about poverty emerged; the first marked global consensus since the end of World War II that saw the creation of the United Nations and agreement on the Universal Declaration of Human Rights. This consensus is most visibly reflected in the Millennium Declaration, a document signed by all world leaders in September 2000 after a great global gathering of the United Nations in New York. In the Declaration, world leaders proclaimed:

> We will spare no effort to free our fellow men, women, and children from the abject and dehumanizing conditions of extreme poverty, to which more than a billion are subjected.

The year 2015 – not very far away from us now – was established as the date at which the global community is committed to judge how well we have done in defeating the ancient scourges of want, ignorance, hunger, and (hopefully) strife.

After the agreement was reached, its essence was articulated in eight specific Millennium Development Goals (MDGs) – designed to be easy to understand and thus act upon, measurable, and monitorable. The MDGs draw heavily on different sources, most notably on a long series of agreements reached at the various UN Conferences held during the 1980s and 1990s; but what is new is the effort at measurement and making the goals amenable to performance-testing. The MDGs are broad but quite straightforward – they include, for example, goals to halve poverty, halt the spread of communicable diseases, ensure that all children go to school and at least finish primary school, and action to protect and improve the environment.[5]

Hunger is at the front and center of the MDG structure.[6] The first MDG calls for eradicating extreme poverty and hunger. The specific text calls for reducing the proportion of people living on less than US$1 a day to half the 1990 level by 2015. The numbers are quite specifically defined, and are based on the 1990 estimate that 28% of all people in low- and middle-income economies fell below the poverty line. Halving this level would bring the total to 14%.[7] The MDG also calls for reducing by half the proportion of people who suffer from hunger, and it places the emphasis both on child hunger and overall levels of hunger (see Figures 4.1 and 4.2).

There was something approaching euphoria in the development community after the MDG framework was established, as it seemed for the first time in history that there was real consensus on what needed to be done to translate decades of rhetoric about global poverty and social justice into action, and to translate commitments (for example to development assistance) into reality. There was talk of a global compact, termed by some a 'covenant,' that committed poor countries to needed efforts, for example to improve governance, and rich countries to reform trade regimes and step up their levels of development assistance. However, progress to date has been patchy and particularly slow in some areas and regions (above all Africa). Specifically, progress to eradicate hunger has been slow, with the

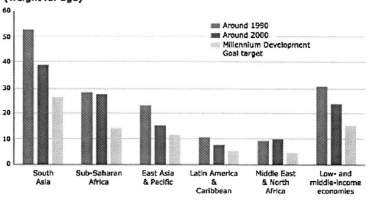

Source: WHO and World Bank staff estimates.

Figure 4.1 Child malnutrition levels in the first and second half of the 1990s. Prevalence rates of underweight children have been falling in most regions, but too slowly to achieve the 2015 target, and in many regions the number of hungry people continues to grow. By 2001, only the East Asia and Pacific and the Latin America and Caribbean regions had fewer undernourished people than 10 years earlier. For prevalence rates of underweight children, progress have been fastest in East Asia and the Pacific, where child malnutrition rates declined by 33%, and South Asia, where rates declined 25%. But many countries, especially in Sub-Saharan Africa, lag behind

Source: http://www.developmentgoals.org/mdgun/5.htm

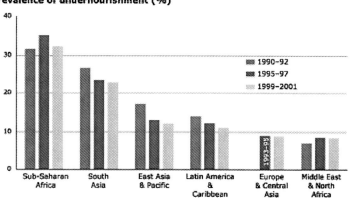

Source: FAO 2003, *The State of Food Insecurity in the World*

Figure 4.2 Change in the proportion of the population consuming too little food to maintain normal levels of activity. Since 1990–1992 the number of undernourished people in developing countries has fallen by 20 million, and the prevalence of undernourishment by 3 percentage points. Regional trends show the greatest progress in East Asia and the Pacific, but the rates of malnutrition remain high in South Asia, and they are rising in Sub-Saharan Africa

situation worsening in some regions. At current rates of improvement, halving child malnutrition by 2015 is *highly unlikely*. This is widely seen as scandalous, given that this goal is technically possible and hunger is preventable.

With a major marker along the trajectory of goals approaching in 2005, an intense process of assessment and reflection took place at a global level during 2004 and 2005, with troubling findings. If projected world income growth remains on track, global poverty rates are projected to fall to less than half the 1990 level – and 360 million more people will no longer face extreme poverty. While poverty would not be eradicated if this goal is fulfilled, it would bring us much closer to the day when we can say that all the world's people have reached a minimally decent standard of living. However, there is great concern that most of the other goals are far from being on the road to realization, with shortfalls already apparent in many areas.

Global campaigns aimed to focus attention on the MDGs during 2005, with a first major UN stocktaking in September. It is striking that many of these campaigns were faith-based and draw specifically on faith traditions.[8] This marked a significant change, as during the first five years of the MDG period many faith institutions were barely aware of the MDGs. At the World Parliament of the Religions meeting at Barcelona in July 2004, the MDGs were added to the program very late in the game and were barely mentioned in plenary sessions (for an audience approaching 9,000 from all over the world). The effort to ensure that the global ethical imperative is integrated with and part of discourse in interfaith and faith institutions can be seen as being at quite an early stage. There are encouraging signs that this is changing, with two of the major global interfaith organizations taking on the MDG challenge as central to their mission (WCRP – Religions for Peace, and the World Parliament of the Religions).

The ethical imperatives facing the global community around poverty, specifically including hunger, have taken a highly visible and new form through the MDGs and the surrounding campaign, and in this forum poverty and hunger are explicitly and tightly linked. One of the central features of the Millennium Declaration and the MDG apparatus is its unambiguous assumption that ending poverty (including hunger) is a responsibility, and indeed is imperative, for the global community. This normative, ethical framework is increasingly part of the global discourse, featuring in UN, G-8, IMF/World Bank and many other meetings. And it is taking on a new tone of concern about, and language of, accountability. The elaborate set of quantitative indicators that has been prepared, the voluminous reports, global as well as country by country, sector by sector, is a new apparatus of benchmarks designed to make progress, or the lack thereof, highly visible and therefore subject to monitoring and pressure. In reflecting on the ethical dimensions of global policy, this framework is an essential backdrop. While religious organizations have not been a core part of this new effort from the outset, they are increasingly seen as critical partners in the overall global effort as well as in regional and country initiatives.

The ethical imperative enshrined in the Millennium Declaration is part of the lineage of a global ethic going back to the Universal Declaration of Human Rights and the Roosevelt Four Freedoms (which includes freedom from want). In that sense, it is part of the large and complex global ethical debate around the respective roles of rights and responsibilities. This is a vast subject on which there is an ample literature, with the works of Hans Kung on the Global Ethic[9] and Liberation Theology from the Catholic Church prominent, but by no means exclusive, examples. These in turn draw in countless and complex ways on the deep wells of traditions of the great religions that call for 'those who have' to help those in want. Here also there is a vast theological literature (for an example, see Sider 1997).

This chapter attempts neither to digest nor to summarize this rich literature. It is worthwhile, nonetheless, to highlight the debates around a 'rights-based' approach to development, which are interwoven throughout with ethical threads. Rights-based approaches tend to draw discussions and action approaches away from the traditional approaches based on charity and toward an ethic based on partnership and mutual responsibilities. This is an area where the literature is much thinner and less explicit; it is also a topic which highlights linkages among the work and debates of faith and development agencies, and which lends itself to practical analysis based on experience on the ground. This framing of issues has many practical applications for issues of hunger.

ENDING HUNGER: A STOCKTAKING

At many levels the issue of hunger is quite straightforward and it is both realistic and reasonable to hope that hunger can be brought to an end. In some writings there is still a lingering residual of the former despairing prognosis epitomized by the writings of Thomas Malthus and encompassing earlier work of the Club of Rome. This suggests that world population will outstrip food supplies and produce a vicious cycle of famine and conflict. This picture seems greatly outmoded today. Today's more hopeful wisdom suggests instead that scientific progress and changing market and production systems offer the prospect, current and projected, of ample aggregate food supplies. Further, we can point to some remarkable progress in fighting hunger. Since 1990–1992, the number of undernourished people in developing countries is estimated to have fallen by some 20 million, and the prevalence of undernourishment by 3 percentage points. Child malnutrition is estimated to have fallen from some 47% in 1970 to 27% in 2000.[10] We know well that famines need not exist today, and many remarkable relief efforts have averted terrible scenarios of hunger and suffering.

That is the 'good news.' The 'bad news' is that hunger lurks in most societies even amidst plenty, and presents particularly grave challenges for the poorest countries and poorest communities. FAO estimates that 852 million people worldwide went hungry in the 2000–2002 period, of which 815 million were in the developing world.[11] Outright hunger is all too common, malnutrition is endemic in many areas, and 'hidden hunger' (including, for example, micronutrient deficiencies) is widespread. An estimated 150 million children under the age of five in developing countries are still malnourished and, by 2020, 140 million children under five in developing countries will still be underweight.[12] Low birth weights are a critical marker of malnutrition, and FAO estimated that 20 million low-birth weight babies were born in the developing world in 2000. WHO estimates that 3.7 million deaths in 2000 could be attributed to underweight.[11] Underweight, the most visible and straightforward aspect of food insecurity is the leading cause of child mortality and a major contributor to both chronic and epidemic disease patterns. Regional trends show the greatest progress in East Asia and the Pacific, but the rates of malnutrition remain particularly high in South Asia;[13] in fact, 46% of South-Asian infants and young children (75.5 million in the age group 0–4 years) are underweight. There are many issues that are linked to the basic problem of hunger. To name two, environmental pressures are aggravated by slash-and-burn agriculture and forest cutting for cultivation, mostly by farmers aiming to produce food; and poor nutrition contributes to the ravages of HIV/AIDS by heightening susceptibility to disease transmission and hastening the onset of full-blown AIDS.

FAITH TRADITIONS, HUNGER, AND MODERN MIRACLES

So what do religious traditions teach us, and what is their role in this global challenge of realizing the potential to prevent famine and hunger? More broadly, what have they to say and teach on the long-term objective of ensuring all people the means to good nutrition?

This is a rich field of inquiry, and the wealth of traditions in different faiths and their keen focus on hunger and feeding the poor explain why, for so many faith traditions, their first engagement with development challenges and institutions is through food and issues of hunger. Many faith traditions have concentrated their explicit efforts to fight hunger in two areas: first, by feeding people who are in need directly (soup kitchens, baskets for poor families, holiday support), and second, through the major role that faith-based non-governmental organizations (FBOs) play in humanitarian relief efforts.

A brief and suggestive set of 'pointers' from different faith traditions is highlighted below. This is an area that deserves both careful reading of the literature and dialogue about its significance for contemporary challenges.

Faith traditions through the ages have responded to poverty in their teachings. Many of the world's faith traditions draw on parables to teach hunger-related ethics, to model how we should respond to the poor among us. Religions, large and small, have rituals around nutrition and sharing food that tell a story of a larger ethic by which their followers should live. The sharing of food, especially with the poor, is a bedrock ritual of most major religions. Some examples:

- Muslims fast during the month of Ramadan, and during this time are expected to show special generosity to the poor, offering food to needy families in their neighborhoods and collecting food for homeless shelters. Those who are permanently exempt from fasting due to medical conditions are required to feed a poor person each day of Ramadan.

- A Jewish tradition calls for reserving a share of crop land specifically to feed the poor. The idea is that God is the real owner of the land and reserves part of it for the poor. 'And when ye reap the harvest of your land, thou shalt not wholly reap the corner of thy field, neither shalt thou gather the gleaning of thy harvest. And thou shalt not glean thy vineyard, neither shalt thou gather the fallen fruit of thy vineyard; thou shalt leave them for the poor and for the stranger; I am the Lord, thy God' (Lev. 19:9–10).
- In Sikhism, the tradition of *langar* is centrally important. After services, a free vegetarian meal is prepared for all, with rich and poor gathering to share a meal. Sharing food is critical for Sikhs, with the Gurus teaching that all Sikhs should share their possessions. The work involved in preparing the food, serving it, and clearing up afterwards is called *seva*, which means voluntary, selfless service.
- In Hinduism, feeding the poor is a central virtue. The poor are to be fed during any special ceremony or occasion. In addition, any poor or pilgrims who come to visit temples are to be fed, for no-one can concentrate on the Almighty with an empty stomach.
- People of the Baha'i faith forgo food and drink from sunrise to sunset every day from 2nd to 21st March, the first day of spring. This cycle is considered a complete month in the Baha'i faith. Fasting is understood to develop self-discipline and an awareness of what it feels like to be poor or hungry.

Religious organizations have through the ages and very much today been among the first to respond in crises, natural disasters, and wars. They have shown a remarkable capacity to mobilize huge networks of support to provide humanitarian aid. Many faith organizations extend their direct support well beyond their own faith membership. They often operate without regard to the religion of those served, and work as partners with both non-religious and other faith organizations. Often when a natural disaster occurs, there is a landscape of humanitarian efforts with leadership shared among a diverse group of faith institutions (the response to the December 2004 tsunami is an example). A small sample of faith-based organizations which operate in the world's poorest and most troubled countries is summarized below by way of example:

- *Christian Aid*, an agency of the churches in the UK and Ireland, works wherever the need is greatest, irrespective of religion. It supports local organizations, which are best placed to understand local needs, and provides help on the ground through 16 overseas offices. An example of their efforts to ease a food crisis followed the scant and erratic rainfall in the Sahelian region in 2000 and a failed harvest. Christian Aid provided funds for the distribution of cereals in the semi-desert province of Oudalan, one of the hardest-hit areas of Burkina Faso. The agency partnered with a Burkinabe non-governmental organization that had worked in Oudalan since 1985, and purchased the cereals to sell on to the communities of the region at a subsidized rate and also maintains stocks to mobilize cereal before the onset of the 'hungry' season around June and July each year.[14]

- *Catholic Agency for Overseas Development (CAFOD)* is inspired by scripture 'to bring good news to the poor' (Luke 4:18) and is funded and supported mainly by the Catholic community in England and Wales to assist poor communities, regardless of creed. During disasters and emergencies, it is usually the poorest that suffer most; hence CAFOD responds on the basis of advice from its partner organizations working with these people. CAFOD is deeply involved in the Darfur province of western Sudan, where we are witnessing one of the world's worst humanitarian crises in over a decade. The Catholic Church in Sudan has joined with other churches to respond to the crises. CAFOD, with 32 years of experience working in Sudan, is co-leading a £14 million joint operation between networks of Catholic and Protestant aid organizations. Together, they are bringing food, safe water, shelter materials, sanitation, and healthcare to half a million displaced men, women, and children. In the longer term, CAFOD has pledged to help refugees by providing seeds and tools to help families replant crops and rebuild their lives.[15]
- *Islamic Relief (IR)*, an international relief and development charity, aims to alleviate the suffering of the world's poorest people. IR develops emergency relief programs to support those seeking aid, as well as promoting sustainable economic and social development by working with local communities, regardless of race, religion, or gender. IR has gained the trust of international organizations such as the World Food Program, the United Nations, the International Red Cross, and other non-governmental organizations. An example of IR's response to a humanitarian crisis followed the war in Bosnia and Herzegovina, where a quarter of a million people were killed, 1.2 million were internally displaced, and some 800,000 were forced to leave the country. IR started its emergency relief program in 1992 by delivering Ramadan food parcels and Qurbani meat to vulnerable sectors of the population.[16]
- *Jewish Coalition for Disaster Relief (JCDR)* brings together the experience, expertise, and resources of Jewish organizations that assist victims of natural or human-made disasters on a non-sectarian basis. In Ethiopia, three consecutive years of persistent drought and poor rainfall, coupled with the effects of armed conflict with Eritrea, devastated Ethiopia's crops and livestock. By June 2000, the food shortage was at its highest level since the famine of 1984/1985, and increasing deaths from starvation were reported.[17] Made up of 29 North-American Jewish organizations, the Jewish Coalition for Aid to Ethiopia collected over US$24,000 for its efforts to address the effects of severe food shortages and drought in East Africa during 2000/2001. Insufficient rainfall over the last several years has resulted in a full-scale food crisis that many experts agree is worse than the one that occurred in 1984 (USAID).[18]

In sum, the gamut of experience of faith organizations in providing relief to hungry people is wide and inspiring.

Many faith traditions have also worked in the wide arena that lies between traditional practices of providing food for those in need and the type of social and economic development programs that aim at more general improvements in welfare. Again, a survey of different faith programs would likely cover every type of development scheme. A feature that is striking in faith commentaries on development imperatives is their focus on interdisciplinary approaches that address all human needs in a coherent manner. Nonetheless, in looking to the problem of hunger, the greatest focus has been at the humanitarian end of the spectrum.

A wise faith leader suggested to me that the ancient parable of the transformation of the loaves and fishes may offer insights into a modern approach to the problem of hunger, indeed offering a model of 'food security.' The story of Jesus and the miracle of the loaves and fishes has traditionally been interpreted as a teaching about feeding the hungry, about generosity to those in need. A different interpretation of the story, in the light of what we know today, suggests that the parable might also tell of a different form of miracle; the start of a process of multiplying food to produce a sustainable development path. In the parable, Jesus took a small stock of bread and fish and, through a miracle, provided enough to feed 5,000 people. The miracle could be seen as an example of using the resources that were available and looking to new ways to multiply them – through new methods of production. The contemporary challenge of food security is about that – holding small stocks but using modern miracles to multiply them so that they are sufficient to satisfy the hunger of those who are in need. The 'green revolution' and other agricultural advances (including a better understanding of nutrition) are seen by some as 'modern miracles' that allow humanity to expand food production to meet its needs.

THE PATH TO HEAVEN AND HELL: LESSONS OF EXPERIENCE

With so much good will and high-level global commitment to ending hunger, symbolized in the MDGs, and with vast contemporary advances in knowledge and technology about food production, why, then, is hunger still widespread? This is indeed the essence of a global ethical challenge, with some facets crystal clear, others far more clouded. Some of the areas of contemporary debate can usefully be highlighted in reflecting on this conundrum. What follows is a rough effort to summarize current consensus on outstanding issues, especially as it reflects links between faith and development communities.

Briefly, six operational challenges and issues can be outlined:

1. The focus has too often been on feeding people rather than addressing the underlying problem that perpetuates or aggravates hunger. Two African proverbs are often invoked to illustrate the challenge. The first calls on us to give needy people a fishing pole and teach them how to fish, rather than giving them fish to eat. The second reminds us that the time to plant a tree that will take a generation to grow is now. Both highlight that long-term perspectives and approaches are essential even in the face of urgent problems. These stories reflect a fundamental and complex challenge: we need to move beyond a concept that focuses simply or primarily on charity and helping those in need out of compassion or obligation.

What we need is a shift of spirit and focus to partnerships with the promise to lead to an equitable and sustainable way of living for all in the future.

2. The boundaries between humanitarian aid and development can be difficult to cross. The challenge arises all too often of how to take an essential relief effort and ensure that it translates well into lasting rehabilitation or a new development path. There is often insufficient dialogue and collaboration among different groups who tend to be involved in these different but intricately related challenges. Financing mechanisms for many agencies reflect a dependence on mechanisms that may not be conducive to encouraging a clear progression from humanitarian relief to longer-term development. Programs that foster dependence on food aid present an all-too-frequent trap. A thorough-going assessment of the humanitarian/development links and issues is called for, with the specific engagement of faith institutions.

3. There is often insufficient appreciation of the cultural dimensions of hunger and food. Food production and marketing are highly culture-specific and this is not always sufficiently appreciated by development specialists and even leading religious figures who come up with solutions and models they see as good and 'normal.' I was trained on a horrific project in Madagascar that sought to introduce Texan and Australian ranching in central Madagascar, including imported Brahman bulls and improved pasture. The project foundered spectacularly as farmers who resented their land being taken burned pastures and stole and butchered the expensive imported cattle. Another common problem is communities whose dependence on markets and purchased food increases when farmers are encouraged to shift from subsistence food production to cash crops; when something goes wrong they are left high and dry, and even in good times gender relations may be altered so that the nutrition of children becomes worse. Changing roles for men and women as production systems are modernized can play both positive and negative roles. Much has been learned about what not to do, but rural development is still hard to do well and countless efforts yield disappointing results. Micro-credit is often hailed as a modern panacea, but even small loans to remarkable women will not yield lasting results in an environment of poor overall policy or destructive social policies. Work in the development arena needs cultural sensitivity, adaptability, creativity, the ability to listen, and a good dose of humility.

4. Malnutrition can be linked to an unwillingness to accept different kinds of food or nutritional patterns, even when food or medication is available. The horrifying and challenging picture of food stocks rotting while people starve, and frequent tensions between givers of yellow versus white maize, and of course the debates over genetically engineered seeds and crops, present a host of ethical issues which often involve faith-based organizations. Active dialogue to address the more contentious issues which resonate in cultural and religious fora are called for.

5. Subsidies and direct safety-net programs have been widely used as instruments for ensuring food at reasonable cost for urban populations and in crisis situations.

Sometimes the costs of such programs have literally crushed government finances, too often with corruption and mismanagement playing a role. The tensions that result from crisis and reform, sometimes taking a form known as structural adjustment, have embroiled many faith leaders in acrimonious debates with governments and development institutions. Dialogue and collaboration have suffered in important, material ways. My experience is that there is a dangerous tendency to oversimplify experience in such areas, both by practitioners and critics, yet the stakes are too high for narrow debate. Much more effort is needed to communicate and understand the policy implications, especially where food issues and security are concerned.[19]

6. The above challenges and issues can all be compounded by insufficient efforts to learn from experience. This applies particularly to the development work of faith-based organizations, which is remarkably poorly documented and analyzed.[20]

Each of these problems is highly complex and involves significant ethical challenges. For example, in Zambia, it has been religious leaders who have taken a lead in resisting the use of genetically modified crops because of real fears that their introduction could undermine the foundations of smallholder farmer agriculture. Yet there are also obvious ethical challenges in allowing hunger to continue when food is to hand in nearby stores. The issues of feeding people versus pushing them toward self-sufficiency involve tough choices. The tension between expediency and mass production and feeding versus sensitivity to local traditions and respecting cultural norms and traditions always presents difficult and complex choices. And thoughtful debate about how government policies can protect those in need (whether through subsidies or food distribution, targeted programs, micro-credit and other means) needs to engage all concerned, reflect consciously about the ethical issues involved, and specifically, engage faith communities thoughtfully, because they are in so many instances central actors.

Perhaps the starkest ethical issue for hunger today, which involves faith communities only indirectly but nonetheless in important roles, is the global challenge of agricultural protection in wealthy countries, specifically the European Community, Japan, and the USA. Widely quoted figures contrast the estimated cost of these subsidies to wealthy-country farmers at around US$350 billion a year, with some US$50–60 billion of development assistance, globally.[21] While there is widespread discussion of reform, the possibility of concrete steps being taken can only be seen dimly on the horizon. This is such a central issue for poor countries (as well as rich ones), and has such a major ethical component, that the engagement of faith leaders in the difficult debate and path of reform seems to be critically needed.

The failure to conquer hunger to date is in part a failure of will, of organization, and of dedication of resources. It is also a reflection that the issues involved are far from simple. In some instances the solutions may be quite technical and lend themselves to classic solutions of agronomy, managerial organization, marketing and distribution. But many of the reasons for continuing problems of hunger are embedded in deep cultural traditions. It is in these areas that the engagement of faith institutions and communities, for example in reflecting on some complex dimensions of nutritional challenges, and in dialogue about some of the underlying issues, has particular importance.

PARTNERSHIPS, ALLIANCES, AND NEW APPROACHES

An underlying conclusion from this analysis is that success in addressing the issues of hunger calls for alliances among different kinds of institutions, often in ways little known or used in the past, and specifically including faith institutions as major partners in many, though not all, cases.

Four areas can be cited:

1. *Advocacy coalitions and efforts to mobilize energy and support for global assistance to end hunger.* Bread for the World and the Micah Challenge are extraordinary examples of such efforts. Many more are needed, as a much deeper appreciation of the imperatives of fighting global hunger among citizens across the world must be developed. At the same time, such advocacy coalitions can encourage thoughtful debate about what is needed to address the ethical issues that arise.

2. *More engagement in dialogue about food policy issues involving ethical questions and engaging faith communities.* At present, the ethical issues involved in food policy are too often little discussed, and many actors involved are often absent from the table. A story of faith group involvement with food security in Ethiopia illustrates the complex relationship between religious groups and bureaucracies even (and perhaps especially) on questions related to basic, very primal, issues of hunger.[22] An initiative in Ethiopia between 1999 and 2001 aimed to engage an interfaith group with international partners and the government, all with a keen interest in food policy. The rationale was that faith groups were deeply involved in a wide variety of food-aid schemes and held strong views (often negative) about government and international community food security policies and approaches. A series of workshops attracted considerable attention and elicited some useful insights and ideas. However, two major obstacles emerged. The first was that the various actors involved understood the concept of food security in entirely different ways, and thus tended toward widely different policy solutions – whether different forms of land reform, credit, and links between smallholder development and agricultural extension. It proved almost impossible to generate a thoughtful, fact-based dialogue about current situations and options. Second, the effort brought into the open the difficulties that faced civil society organizations in general operating in Ethiopia, above all because of their weak capacity and government suspicions of many organizations that impaired their operations. Both factors contributed to a situation where there was little or no good mechanism for interfaith dialogue and action, and still less involving public-sector actors. The upshot was a fizzling out of the effort despite wide agreement that, at a minimum, all concerned should know better what other institutions were doing (this knowledge was and is not available) and

that there was a critical need for dialogue about programs and policies. This kind of effort, despite the difficulties, deserves more investment and support and a good measure of stamina.

3. *Specific partnerships that mobilize the resources and skills of different partners.* In addressing hunger, some of the most exciting successes involve coalitions among private companies, church groups, and community organizations. Many different formulas can be explored and can open new avenues to address the deep-seated obstacles to eliminating hunger. A number of faith-based organizations (World Vision, for example) have been deeply engaged in a wide range of partnerships for decades and already act in a wide range of partnerships. It is worthy of note, however, that these are predominately Christian, and the links of non-Christian organizations (Muslim, Buddhist, etc.) are much less significant at this time, and certainly less clearly defined. The basic point is that there is vast scope for more, better, and different kinds of partnership arrangements.

4. *Pursuing partnerships and dialogue within the international development community on poverty issues, including specifically different dimensions of the challenges of hunger.* The clear (though quite complex) relationship between faith and development might seem self-evident, but that has not been so for the development world, which is only slowly internalizing the need to relate to religious and faith traditions and communities. There is a quite distinct and historic separation and segmentation of the worlds of economic and social development and those of faith and religion, even where the faithful and religious are in fact providing services leading to development. This distinction applies more generally in the overall economic and institutional architecture of our times, with roots above all in the historic separation of Church and State in most Western democracies, but also with ties to the Cold-War period, to the evolution of the economics profession itself, and to international, interdenominational, and national tensions surrounding such issues as women's reproductive health. By tradition, practice, and deliberate decision, the institutions devoted to international development at a global level have seldom interacted with the institutions and issues of religion in a formal way. The guiding principle has been that the State (e.g., public policy and institutions) and Church (e.g., the institutions of faith) remain separate.

This distinction between development, on one hand, and religion and faith, on the other, is misleading and potentially quite destructive. In practice, there is much overlap between the two worlds. Development institutions and most religious traditions and institutions share a deep and fundamental grounding in concern about poverty and poor communities and, thus, their work, ideas, advocacy, and tensions encounter each other at many turns. Distinctions tend to be most marked for the multilateral development banks, which work primarily through ministries of finance and planning. Many other development agencies (bilateral aid agencies, for example, but also some United Nations specialized agencies such as the United Nations Population Fund – UNFPA – and the International Labor Organization – ILO) have long recognized the important roles of faith institutions in achieving results in the areas where they are engaged. The barriers are being called into question but there is still far to go in redefining optimal relationships and ensuring continuing dialogue on critical issues.

The story of the World Bank's engagement with the world of faith and religion over the past eight years is instructive as a reflection of the changing global debates. It illustrates well both the pitfalls and complexities of such dialogue, and its real potential for enhancing the quality of work and partnerships. The World Bank had engaged little with religions except in isolated cases and instances, and in the late 1990s there was considerable tension in relationships, for example in discussions about structural adjustment policies. A small initiative to enhance dialogue was launched in 1998 under the leadership of Lord Carey of Clifton, former Archbishop of Canterbury, and James D. Wolfensohn, President of the World Bank. It initially took the form of two small meetings of global faith and development leaders, but the intention was to create an independent institution, the World Faiths Development Dialogue (WFDD) that would bring the voices and ideas of leaders from the worlds of faith, politics, and economics together in a continuing and dynamic dialogue. The idea was that all would share a commitment to learn from each other and remain open to transformation as a result of greater understanding. Actors from the world of philanthropy, the arts, and the private sector – whether propelled by the horrors of hunger, armed conflict, HIV/AIDS, or child suffering – have also joined this dialogue.

It came as a surprise to those directly concerned when this initiative confronted strong opposition from the governing body of the World Bank, its executive directors. They questioned at a fundamental level whether the dialogue effort should continue at all. While there has been considerable advance, the debate continues and, at this time, the future path of the World Bank work on faith and WFDD are quite uncertain.

What arguments were advanced? The principal concern was what was viewed as the political nature of religion, both in a practical sense, of choosing which leaders to engage, but also more broadly in venturing into the controversial territory of Church–State relations. Another concern and argument related to what was perceived by some as the negative role of religion in the development area, with particular importance for debates on the role of women and reproductive health rights. Finally, there was a set of arguments that essentially saw religion as opposed, in many respects, or even irrelevant to the fundamental goals of development institutions.

At the same time, faith groups themselves have been immensely skeptical about the work of the World Bank and the other international financial institutions (IFIs). If we are to address the critical problems before us, we need to understand better what has led so many preachers, imams, Buddhist monks, Christian congregations, and faith-based organizations to be so vocal in their criticisms of the work of development overall.

In many respects, though, the practical agenda has advanced, and there is an abundance of reflections and dialogue processes under way that engage faith and development institutions in many areas. It can be argued that the dialogue to date has indeed opened new windows to relationships and, above all, insights and ideas, and that these point to a much larger potential in the future. Nonetheless, the sensitivity of and tensions around the discussion of religion and its role in the public policy domain have emerged as a clear lesson and issue for the future.

It might be useful to envisage how a faith and development partnership might work when applied to the twenty-first-century 'Green Revolution for Africa' that United Nations General Secretary Kofi Annan called when he addressed a high level seminar at the time of the African Union Summit in Addis Ababa, Ethiopia, in July 2004. The African Green Revolution, as described by Sachs and Sanchez (2004), requires five science-based components which they note are lacking in Africa today.

- African farmers first need soil nutrients, whether by mineral fertilizers or so-called 'green fertilizers' in the form of manure, nitrogen-fixing trees, and cover crops.
- African farmers need reliable water sources, especially in places where the rains often fail. This must be accomplished through small-scale irrigation and water-harvesting schemes.
- African farmers need improved germplasm – seeds of crop and tree varieties and livestock breeds – all highly productive and well-adapted to local climate and pest constraints.
- African farmers need much more effective agricultural extension services, to help farmers adopt state-of-the-art technologies generated by partnerships between farming communities and a stronger agricultural research system.
- Finally, the most vulnerable groups – pregnant and nursing mothers, children younger than two years old and those at school – should receive supplementary feeding. This must be done with locally purchased foods, thereby increasing market demand while providing balanced diets consisting of foods that villagers like to eat. Shipments of food aid should be limited to emergency starvation situations where local procurement is not possible (see Sachs and Sanchez 2004).

Where there is such a clear vision for what is needed, faith communities have much potential to help governments and international institutions respond to communities in ways that respect their local traditions and answer to their particular needs. Faith communities are important service providers and community leaders and have made remarkable inroads in improving the lives of the poor – the hunger-related ethics in particular deserve our attention and bring great wisdoms to our common work of poverty eradication and development. Listening to this religiously based hunger ethic can help in the vital effort to keep hunger at the very center of our development agenda, and allow all actors to remain poised to respond as effectively and sensitively as possible.

THE CONTINUING CHALLENGE: THE PERSISTENCE OF HUNGER AND POVERTY

Even with the host of complexities we have highlighted here, the basic issues of hunger as it relates to global poverty should be fairly straightforward to resolve. The resources are there, and there are many cases of success to point to, in many different country situations. The basic message on global hunger should be one of imperative need and hope.

It is nonetheless worthwhile to highlight that beyond the basic challenges of fighting hunger lie a host of complex issues that will persist for the foreseeable future. These are evident already in today's ironies of pockets of poverty among plenty, and the epidemic of obesity linked to poverty. Further, we see them in the extraordinary pressures on biodiversity and environment resulting from the hunt for exotic food that wipes out species. The enormous resources dedicated to producing animal protein raise major long-term questions. Will we eat to live or live to eat in postmodern society? Will our descendents revel in a diversity of menu choice or will they live on healthy and environmentally sound diets based on algae? The challenges have barely begun to translate into daily choices.

Once again, the ethical issues and the link to religious traditions are readily apparent. Without entering into detail about specific issues here or proposing any particular path, we can readily argue that dialogue and engagement of a wider range of parties, and more explicit attention to ethical concerns and dimensions of issues, will be essential as we navigate these complex normative and technical waters.

CONCLUDING THOUGHTS

Two overarching conclusions emerge from this discussion. First, we need much more reflection on the underlying ethical issues involving hunger. In this effort, it would be particularly useful to draw, in a more systematic fashion, on the depth of tradition and wisdom of faith traditions and their confrontation with modernity.[23] Second, ending hunger calls for more engagement by a multitude of actors from public and private sectors and civil society, often working together in non-traditional partnerships. This allows them to confront differing perspectives and offer the benefits of different insights and experience.

Theologians from every religion have grappled with the 'whys and hows' of poverty- and hunger-related misery. Many basic issues that are central to the world of development are core issues in all of the major religious traditions, with intellectual, moral, and ethical roots that can be traced back thousands of years. For centuries, faith institutions have played a pivotal role in feeding the hungry, providing services to the poor, and in working to overcome the underlying roots of poverty. In an era of modernization, hunger- and poverty-related ethics have much to teach – of some basic humility, of the importance of sharing and producing without excess waste. Development institutions, academic institutions, and secular research groups too have learned some lessons – of good agricultural practices and technologies, such as weather-systems forecasting, that might help create more effective food systems. They have learned, often the hard way through mistakes, the vital importance of engaging communities and of understanding and sometimes intervening in social patterns of exclusion and gender roles to ensure a more just outcome.

Effective policies to alleviate poverty, hunger, and malnutrition in a rapidly globalizing world will necessarily bring to bear the experience and wisdom of social scientists (including economists), secular researchers, and religiously inspired as well as secular ethicists.

ACKNOWLEDGMENTS

Marisa van Saanen and Olivia Donnelly provided substantial assistance in preparing this chapter and their support is gratefully acknowledged. Helpful comments were received from Per Pinstrup-Andersen and colleagues who participated in the November 2004 Cornell Workshop on "Ethics, Globalization, and Hunger: In Search of Appropriate Policies".

NOTES

[1]   These statements were gathered through the *Voices of the Poor* project, a World Bank exercise that summarized (in three volumes) surveys of over 60,000 poor women and men (see Narayan et al. 2000).

[2]   Figures quoted from the US Embassy to the Vatican (Facts of the Week, *Globalist*, 5 November 2004).

[3]   The benefits of educating girls are well documented (see King and Hill 1993;http://www.ifpri.org/2020/newslet/nv_1299/nv1299a.htm).

[4]   See, for example, Sanchez and Swaminathan (2003) for the UN Millennium Project.

[5]   See http://www.un.org/millenniumgoals/ for more information on the MDGs.

[6]   See http://www.developmentgoals.org/mdgun/5.htm for details on how the goal is formulated, references, periodicity of measurement, etc.

[7]   See http://www.developmentgoals.org/Poverty.htm, which gives a flavor of the detailed framing of goals with regional breakdowns.

[8]   Marshall and Marsh (2003) outline how the MDG challenges specifically apply in the case of faith institutions. The Micah Challenge is an illustration of a faith mobilization effort aimed at global Christian communities (see http://www.micahchallenge.org/global/home/intro.html. A July 2004 meeting of the Vatican's Pontifical Council on Justice and Peace focused on the MDG challenge and its relation to the Church. See also the Bread for the World website (http://www.bread.org/) which offers a 'blueprint' for ending hunger.

[9]   See http://www.cpwr.org/resource/global_ethic.htm for a summary of the Global Ethic as presented to the 1993 World Parliament of the World Religions.

[10]   The FAO annual publication, *The State of Food Insecurity in the World* (SOFI 2004), is an excellent source of data on malnutrition (see also http://www.fao.org/newsroom/en/focus /2004/51786/article_51791en.html).

[11]   See http://www.fao.org/documents/show_cdr.asp?url_file=/docrep/007/y5650e/y5650e00.htm

[12]   See Smith (2000; http://www.ifpri.cgiar.org/2020/briefs/number64.htm).

[13]   Source: Food and Agriculture Organization (2001).

[14]   Accessed from: http://www.christian-aid.org.uk/

[15]   Accessed from: http://www.cafod.org.uk/news_and_events/emergencies/conflict_in_sudan

[16]   Accessed from: http://www.islamic-relief.com/

[17]   *JCDR Final Activities Report*, 21 December 2001.

[18]   Accessed from: http://www.jdc.org/jcdr_main.html

[19]   The debates about structural adjustment are well documented in many analyses and critiques of the World Bank. A prominent example can be found in Daly and Cobb (1989).

[20]   My recent book (Marshall and Keough 2004) is an example of the rich lode of experience of faith development partnerships which has passed virtually undocumented in the development literature.

[21] These figures are cited in many speeches by World Bank President James D. Wolfensohn, based on World Bank research (see, for example, http://web.worldbank.org/WBSITE/EXTERNAL/NEWS/ 0,,contentMDK:20048981~menuPK:34457~pagePK:34370~piPK:34424~theSitePK:4607,00.html).

[22] This case study of Ethiopia is drawn from Marshall and Keough (2004, pp. 90–92). The initiative was launched by the World Faiths Development Dialogue (WFDD) and involved the World Bank.

[23] Comparable efforts include the World Faiths Development Dialogue consultation exercises with a network of faith leaders on, respectively, poverty and social services, and the ILO/World Council of Churches consultation on faith perspectives on decent work.

REFERENCES

Daly, H.E. and J.B. Cobb, Jr, 1989. *For the Common Good: Redirecting the Economy toward Community, the Environment, and a Sustainable Future.* Boston, MA, USA: Beacon Press.

King, E.M. and M.A. Hill, eds, 1993. *Women's Education in Developing Countries.* Baltimore, MD, USA: Johns Hopkins University Press.

Marshall, K. and L. Keough, 2004. *Mind, Heart, and Soul in the Fight against Poverty.* Washington, DC: World Bank.

Marshall, K. and R. Marsh, 2003. *Millennium Challenges for Faith and Development Leaders.* Washington DC: World Bank.

Narayan, D., R. Patel, K. Schafft, A. Rademacher and S. Koch-Schulte, 2000. *Voices of the Poor: Can Anyone Hear Us?* New York: Oxford University Press for the World Bank

Sachs, J.D. and P.A. Sanchez, 2004. We can end world hunger. *World Ark* (Nov/Dec): 10.

Sanchez, P.A. and M.S. Swaminathan, 2003. Hunger in Africa: The link between unhealthy people and unhealthy soils. UN Millennium Project, December 2003. *Lancet* 365: 442–444.

Sen, A.K., 1981. *Poverty and Famines: An Essay on Entitlement and Depression.* New York: Oxford University Press.

Sider, R.J., 1997. *Rich Christians in an Age of Hunger: Moving from Affluence to Generosity.* W Publishing Group.

Smith, L.C. and L.J. Haddad, 2000. *Overcoming Child Malnutrition in Developing Countries: Past Achievements and Future Choices.* IFPRI Discussion Paper 30. Washington DC: International Food Policy Research Institute.

RICHARD S. GILBERT

WHAT HUNGER-RELATED ETHICS LESSONS CAN WE LEARN FROM RELIGION? GLOBALIZATION AND THE WORLD'S RELIGIONS

WHAT IN THE WORLD IS GOING ON?

In a paper entitled "A Parade of Dwarfs (and a Few Giants)", Dutch economist Jan Pen (1973) develops a graphic metaphor to convey the extent of wealth disparity in Western democracies. He asks the reader to imagine a parade of people where everyone's height is proportional to his or her individual wealth. A person of average wealth is represented by a person of average height. The parade begins with the smallest (the poorest) at the front, with the rich bringing up the rear in a one-hour parade. The first marchers are actually buried several feet beneath the ground since they have negative net worth – they owe more wealth than they own. For approximately twenty minutes there are invisible marchers, for they own no wealth. After half an hour there are dwarfs – people about six inches tall, whose wealth is household furniture, a car, and perhaps a small savings account. 'But a surprise awaits us,' writes Pen. 'We keep on seeing dwarfs. Of course they gradually become a little taller, but it's a slow process.' Only at about twelve minutes before the hour do we begin seeing people of average height, for more than three-quarters of the world's population have fewer assets than average. In the last few minutes 'giants loom up ... a lawyer, not exceptionally successful, eighteen feet tall.' In the last few seconds, there are people so tall we cannot even see their heads, the corporate managing directors a hundred yards tall. 'The rear of the parade is brought up by a few participants who are measured in miles ... their heads disappear into the clouds ... The last man, whose back we can see long after the parade has passed by, is John Paul Getty [this was before Bill Gates] ... His height is inconceivable: at least ten miles; perhaps twice as much' (Pen 1980).

This metaphor dramatizes the chasm between rich and poor in a globalized world. Globalization has been defined as

> the broad range of societal transformations that have accompanied the rapid growth in international trade and investment in recent years, as well as the virtual shrinking of the planet due to computers, cell phones, and other accoutrements of the information age (French 2002, p. 174).

It is a commonplace among us, the very context in which we live. As *New York Times* columnist Thomas Friedman puts it, 'Globalization isn't a choice. It's a reality' (Friedman 1999, p. 93).

71

P. Pinstrup-Andersen and P. Sandøe (eds.), Ethics, Hunger and Globalization: In Search of Appropriate Policies, 71–92.
© 2007 *Springer.*

Yet the globalization process, while it has powerfully demonstrated its productive capacity, has a decidedly mixed record of distributing goods and services to the world's people equitably. While some 1.7 billion people (including most Americans) are megaconsumers, there are estimated to be 2.8 billion residing in poverty – which I take to be a surrogate for hunger (Worldwatch Institute 2004, p. xvii). To a disturbing degree the rich get richer and the poor get poorer. According to the *Atlas of Global Inequality*:

> Global income inequality is probably greater now than it has ever been in human history. Currently, the richest 1% of people in the world receives as much as the bottom 57% (University of California 2004).

A study by the Center for Economic and Policy Research (CEPR) reveals that the world's GDP per capita, a measure of income, showed lower growth rates for 1980–2000 than for 1960–1980.[1] Bread for the World, an advocacy organization of religious, labor, and other groups, reports that, while the first half of the 1990s saw hunger cut by 37 million people, the number of the hungry is now rising at a rate of 5 million per year (Bread for the World 2005). The Food and Agricultural Organization of the United Nations (FAO) predicts that the number of hungry people will not be halved until at least 2050 (Bread for the World 2005). As Nobel Prize winning economist Joseph Stiglitz, former chief economist of the World Bank, writes:

> Globalization today is not working for many of the world's poor. It is not working for much of the environment. It is not working for the stability of the world economy. The transition from communism to a market economy has been so badly managed that, with the exception of China, Vietnam, and a few Eastern European countries, poverty has soared as incomes have plummeted (Stiglitz 2002).

On the other hand, Bread for the World also indicates that 'the world as a whole is better off today than it was 30 years ago,' but 'it is little consolation to the nearly 800 million people in the developing countries struggling every day to work, feed and raise their families' (Bread for the World 2005). *New York Times* columnist David Brooks, citing a World Bank study, writes

> I hate to be the bearer of good news...but we're in the 11th month of the most prosperous year in human history...the poorer nations are leading the way ... [this growth] is having a wonderful effect on world poverty ... [and inequality] is shrinking among individuals worldwide (Brooks 2004).

The summary of these disparate accounts, each with a political perspective and interpreting statistics from its own particular bias, is that reduction of poverty and hunger has been extremely uneven and the causes multifaceted. Global resources remain wildly disparate; the United Nations Millennium Development Goals for hunger reduction will probably not be reached; and there seems to be no 'silver bullet' to explain how to do it. To add to the perplexity, the UN Population Division has reported that the world's population will increase by 40% to 9.1 billion in 2050 and virtually all the growth will be in the developing world, particularly in the 50 poorest countries (Lederer 2005). This variegated portrait cannot be viewed with complacency; current trends of the globalized economy do not seem reassuring.

As the United Nations Human Development Report (2003) put it:

> The range of human development in the world is vast and uneven, with astounding progress in some areas amidst stagnation and dismal decline in others. Balance and stability in the world will require the commitment of all nations, rich and poor, and a global development compact to extend the wealth of possibilities to all people.

Normal economic indicators, which we might sometimes call 'misleading economic indicators,' such as gross domestic product (GDP), do not effectively measure the well-being of a people. The UN's Human Life Index, which incorporates data such as life expectancy at birth, GDP per capita, adult literacy rate, and educational enrollment, is a more accurate gauge. In their book, *For the Common Good*, theologian/ethicist, John B. Cobb, Jr., and former World Bank economist, Herman E. Daly, tout the 'Measure of Economic Well Being' as a better metric (Cobb and Daly 1989). Whatever the measurement, it is clear that a world without hunger is a far distant goal.

A GLOBALIZED ETHIC FOR A GLOBALIZED WORLD? WHAT DO THE WORLD'S RELIGIONS SAY?

With all the discussion of the economic dimensions of global life, there is far too little discussion of a globalized morality to deal with problems of such magnitude. There are, of course, two international efforts to establish norms for international development. The 1948 Universal Declaration of Human Rights is a strong statement of criteria for the international order. That document, along with UN Covenants for political and economic rights, has sparked controversy. Articles 3–20 essentially have to do with what are generally called political and civil rights, the so-called 'liberty rights.' Articles 22–27 essentially have to do with social and economic rights. The first set of rights has virtually unanimous approval among the world's nations, but the second is quite controversial due to its designation of economic rights as human rights.

As noted above, the United Nations in September 2000 set Millennium Development Goals, one of which was to 'eradicate extreme poverty and hunger' by 2015, and to 'halve the proportion of people living on less than a dollar a day and those who suffer from hunger.' In January of 2005 a UN blue-ribbon panel presented a comprehensive package of strategies for achieving those goals.

These documents raise the question: What is the purpose of a globalized economy? To benefit individual consumers, to grow corporate profits, to further national interests, or is it to serve the basic human needs of the world's people? Problems of hunger, poverty, and inequity are virtually invisible in discussions of globalization. The particular focus of this chapter, then, is to raise the normative issues – replacing the *what* of economic thought with the *why* of religious perspective. The specific emphasis is on the attitudes and actions of the world's organized religions with respect to poverty – and by implication, to hunger. These perspectives present both promise and peril. Nonetheless, they are essential foundations for understanding the values that both encourage and discourage world economic development which might reduce poverty in the midst of plenty. What has been the response of the world's religions to the distributive injustice that Pen (1980) describes?

Hinduism: Need and Greed

In the classic ancient scripture of Hinduism, the *Upanishads*, we read this about giving and greed: 'There are three branches of the law. Sacrifice, study, and charity are the first' (*Khandogya Upanishad*, 2nd Prapathaka, 23rd Khanda: 1). The *Upanishads*' attitude toward wealth is expressed in these words from the *Kath Upanishad* (1st Adhyaya, 2nd Valli: 104):

> Yea, the wise prefers the good to the pleasant, but the fool chooses the pleasant through greed and avarice. Thou, O Nakiketas, after ordering all pleasures that are or seem delightful, hast dismissed them all. Thou hast not gone into the road that leadeth to wealth, in which many men perish. Wide apart and leading to different points are these two, ignorance and what is known as wisdom.

However, the approach of Hinduism to distributive justice is complicated by its deeply embedded caste system. There are five categories: *Brahmins* (philosophers, priests, and others who perform the function of illuminating the higher truths); *Ksatriyas* (warriors and rulers, entrusted with safeguarding the truth); *Vaisyas* (traders, farmers, and all who have the role of creating wealth and increasing welfare); *Sudras* (workers, charged with supporting all of the above); and finally the *Dalits*, the 'untouchables,' the outcasts of society. The justification for this hierarchical system was challenged in the nineteenth and twentieth centuries by such indigenous reformers such as Rammohan Roy, founder of the Brahmo Samaj movement; Vivekananda, the founder of the Ramakrishna movement; poet Rabadranath Tagore and, of course, Mahatma Gandhi.

Gandhi, though perhaps more a universal prophet than purely Hindu, wrote:

> Men are equal. For, though they are not of the same age, same height, the same skin and the same intellect, these inequalities are temporary and superficial. The soul that is hidden beneath this earthly crust is one and the same for all men and women belonging to all climes ... The word 'inequality' has a bad odour to it, and it has led to arrogance and inhumanities, both in East and West.[2]

In an Eastern *noblesse oblige*, he railed against the wealth and prestige into which he had been born to help create the new India. Writing on the relationship between rich and poor, he expressed a distributive ethic aimed at meeting basic human needs as a priority claim:

> I suggest we are thieves in a way. If I take anything that I do not need for my own immediate use, and keep it, I thieve it from somebody else... In India we have got three millions of people having to be satisfied with one meal a day, and that meal consisting of unleavened bread... and a pinch of salt. You and I have no right to anything that we really have until these three million are clothed and fed better. You and I, who ought to know better, must adjust our wants... in order that they may be nursed, fed and clothed... There is enough wealth to meet everyone's need, but not everyone's greed.[3]

In contemporary Hinduism, this tradition has been met squarely by a capitalistic surge, in part brought on by globalization and the outsourcing phenomenon. The Indian middle classes are prospering through transnational corporations and their need for educated, but in an international context cheap, labor. India is increasing its gross domestic product, but with a very unequal distribution of income and wealth. As Virginia Saldanha, an Indian Christian activist, writes, 'Religion in India had always been considered a private matter' (Saldanha 2003). Thus there seem to be few religious structures to concentrate on issues of economic justice.

Buddhism: Compassion and Right Livelihood

According to tradition, soothsayers informed his father that Siddhartha Gautama would grow up to become either the most powerful king in the world or a poor man who would be a great spiritual teacher. That same tradition indicates that though his father sought to 'protect' him from the world, he did venture forth and beheld the 'four sights': an enfeebled old man, a diseased person, a corpse, and a monk. The Buddha, in a clear rejection of the wealth and privilege to which he had been born, chose the aesthetic life. His life and subsequent Buddhist history are a sharp critique of material acquisition.

The *Dhammapada*, a Buddhist scripture of 423 verses attributed to Buddha, stresses the Middle Path in all matters:

> One road goes to profit, another to Nirvana. Know this, O Bhikku, disciple of Buddha, and struggle for wisdom, not the world's fame.[4]
>
> Fools are not generous: the world of the gods is not for the stingy. Wise men are generous, they find happiness in the next birth.[5]

Buddhist teaching attempts to minimize the desire for self-aggrandizement. Its doctrine of *anatman* breaks out of the shell of preoccupation with one's individual self. The aim in life is not to accumulate that which pleases the self, but to eliminate desire for those things that do not contribute to the spiritual life. The goal of Buddhism is to become a *Bodhisattva*, the truly enlightened being who seeks enlightenment not only for the self, but for others. Bodhisattvas postpone their own entry into Nirvana to instruct others in Buddhist doctrine. Thus Buddhism, economically, is an attack on self-seeking individualism, finding salvation by being bound up with the well-being of others.

The Buddhist critique of global finance, estimated at US$83 billion in capital markets, might be summarized by a Buddhist teacher, Khyentse Rinpoche, who is quoted in a review of the film, *Sandcastles: Buddhism and Global Finance*:

> For his part, Khyentse Rinpoche speaks stirringly of the nature of perception, illusion and enlightenment. When he says, 'Release your attachment to something that is not there in reality, but is a perception,' he could easily be referring to 401(k) investments.[6]

The very non-material emphasis of Buddhism is in itself a critique of globalized economics.

Buddhist economics functions in a more localized economy rather than in a mass-market globalized economy, according to Buddhist scholar Helena Norbert-Hodge, who writes:

> I am convinced that such an examination will engender a desire to oppose actively the trend toward a global economy and to help promote ways of life consistent with Buddhist economics (Norbert-Hodge 1997).

Globalization focuses strictly on material needs, which flies in the face of religious values.

> Significantly, the Western economic system does not set about trying to temper our supposedly self-centered, acquisitive nature, but rather to exploit it: It is believed that an 'invisible hand' will transform the selfish actions of individuals into benefits for society as a whole (Norbert-Hodge 1997).

While Buddhism may seem so spiritualized that it does not attempt social change, there is a movement of 'engaged Buddhism,' personified in the work of the Vietnamese Buddhist monk, Thich Hnat Hanh. Professor Alfred Bloom says:

> Buddhists must make clear the superficiality of contemporary notions of globalism and interdependence and work to rectify injustices created by this process. We must promote equality and support the aspirations for a full life for all people, beyond economic and political power (Bloom 2004).

The British author E.F. Schumacher updates this tendency in his 'Buddhist Economics' essay, claiming that 'right livelihood' requires moderation – the Middle Way – 'to obtain the maximum of well-being with the minimum of consumption' (Schumacher 1973).

Confucianism and Taoism

Confucius, in the *Analects*, also pointed to moderation in wealth and poverty:

> Great Man is conscious only of justice; Petty Man, only of self-interest. ... I have always understood Great Man does everything possible to help the poor but nothing to enrich the rich. ... To centralize wealth is to disperse the people; to distribute wealth is to collect the people. ... Exemplary people understand matters of justice; small people understand matters of profit (1:16). ... If you act on the basis of profit, you will be much resented (4:12). ... I have heard that exemplary people help the needy and do not add to the wealth of the rich (6:4).[7]

And on the potential corruptions of affluence, we read:

> To be poor without bitterness is easy; to be rich without arrogance is hard (14:11).[8]

In China's other great classic, the *Tao Te Ching*, we read:

> Amass a store of gold and jade, and no one can protect it. Claim wealth and titles, and disaster will follow. ... Fame or self: Which matters more? Self or wealth? Which is more precious? Gain or loss: Which is more painful? He who is attached to things will suffer much. He who saves will suffer heavy loss. ... Before receiving there must be giving (36). ... Too much success is not an advantage. Do not tinkle like jade or clatter like stone chimes (39). ... For one gains by losing and loses by gaining (42). ... There is no greater sin than desire, no greater curse than discontent, no greater misfortune than wanting something for oneself (46). ... When the court is arrayed in splendor, the fields are full of weeds, and the granaries are bare. Some wear gorgeous clothes, carry sharp swords, and indulge themselves with food and drink; they have more possessions than they can use. They are the robber barons. This is certainly not the way of the Tao (53). ... The Tao of heaven is to take from those who have too much and give to those who do not have enough.[9]

Very clearly this Middle Way of the Tao is a sharp critique of an uneven distribution of resources; the corruption of both poverty and wealth.

Islam: Zakat, Sadaqah, and Distributive Justice

The *Koran* has a strong egalitarian bent, along with an emphasis on solidarity, kindness and justice (16:90); it condemns hoarders of wealth (3:180); it upholds the virtuous who share it (57:7). *Zakat* is an obligatory act from those with possessions to those without – one of the five pillars of Islamic faith better known as alms-giving. It is essentially a tax on net wealth, a flat rate of 2.5%, and as such underlines the

Koran's proportionate transfer to the poor. The purpose is not to punish productivity but to combine it with a social conscience.

There are two concepts of justice in the *Koran*: *adl* and *ihsan*. Both deal with the concept of balance. The former suggests that justice is the avoiding of excess; hence the use of the scales of justice. The latter goes beyond this concept to refer to the need to restore balance by making up a loss or deficiency. This feeds directly into the concept of *ummah*, the ideal society in which it is recognized that not all are equal and each has different needs. *Ihsan*, then, is the *Koran*'s emphasis on sympathy for the downtrodden and oppressed, an Islamic version of an 'option for the poor.'

A contemporary interpretation of Islamic economics and ethics contends that its goal is to create a social-security system in which every citizen of the country, including especially the unemployed, the old, and the sick, must be guaranteed a reasonable level of income irrespective of the person's ability to earn it. Proportionate payment to the poor and proportionate sacrifice of the rich is a religious obligation. The 'vertical axioms' – unity, equilibrium, free will, and responsibility – combine with the 'horizontal axiom' – social policy.

Zakat is the minimal tax, but also part of a larger voluntary contribution which is *sadaqah*, pious giving. Additional taxes are also permitted, based on the ability to pay. Taxation represents the sharing of a community's income between rich and poor. Social justice implies an equitable distribution of income. Wealth should circulate among the poor and not only among the rich. Rather, wealth which is justly earned is to be regarded as a bounty from God and spent to redress imbalance.

As in all religion, the fundamental teachings of the faith often contradict the reality of the world, as we find huge discrepancies of wealth in many Arab and Islamic nations. In the USA we note with interest that people of Arab descent (not necessarily all Muslims) 'tend to be better educated and wealthier than other Americans,' according to the US Census Bureau. The median Arab family income was reported to be US$52,300; about US$2,300 more than the median income for all US families.[10]

Jewish Teaching: Creation and Covenant

The Jewish biblical heritage is rich in references to economic justice. One of the most notable is the 'Year of Jubilee' concept found in Leviticus 25:10–24 (see also Deuteronomy 15:4). Every 50 years the land was to be returned to its original owners – without compensation. This was a means to equalize land ownership, in those days the primary source of wealth. It grew out of the idea that some had become too rich – some too poor – and Yahweh wanted to level the playing field. However, there is no evidence that the Hebrew people ever followed this imperative from the Book of Leviticus. The concept alone, however, is radical in its redistributive ethic. Even now, religious groups in the USA, along with secular organizations, promote the Jubilee/USA which presses Congress to cancel the foreign debts of the world's poorest countries. The group was highly visible in the November 1999 Seattle World Trade Organization protests and in the April 2000 Washington DC International Monetary Fund and World Bank protests.

The Hebrew prophets clearly proclaimed opposition to great gaps between rich and poor. Isaiah warned:

> Woe to those who join house to house, who add field to field, until there is no more room, and you are made to dwell alone in the midst of the land. The Lord of Hosts has sworn in my hearing: 'Surely many houses shall be desolate, large and beautiful houses, without inhabitant' (5:8–9).

Amos is unparalleled as a prophet for the poor:

> Hear this, you who trample upon the needy, and bring the poor of the land to an end, saying when will the new moon be over ... and the Sabbath ... that we may buy the poor for silver and the needy for a pair of sandals (8:4–6).

From the time of the Hebrew prophets, Jewish concern for inequality and poverty has been divinely mandated. The ethical monotheism of the prophets understood God as Creator of the earth and its inhabitants, a Creator who is not indifferent to the plight of his creatures. Historically, according to S.D. Goitein:

> It should be remembered also that the motivation of charity was largely religious, a duty toward God rather than toward one's fellow man.[11]

This inherent dignity of God's creature carried a vital lesson:

> ...poverty is an affront to the dignity inherent in us as creatures of God. Consequently, those who can are obliged to help others avoid the degradation of poverty.[12]

God as creator leads directly to the Covenant, which is to create a just human community; the only way the Jewish life can be fully lived. Charity is not from one individual to another, but from the community to the poor. The Covenant was made not between individuals and God, but between the Jewish community and God.

Catholic Teaching on Economic Justice

The New Testament is even more explicit in enjoining wealth and championing the cause of the poor. 'Do not lay up for yourselves treasures on earth' (Matthew 6:19). 'For what will it profit a man, if he gains the whole world and forfeits his life?' (Matthew 16–26). The response of Jesus to the rich young man in search of salvation is unequivocal:

> Truly, I say to you, it will be hard for a rich man to enter the Kingdom
> of Heaven. Again I tell you, it is easier for a camel to go through the eye
> of a needle than for a rich man to enter the Kingdom of God (Matthew
> 19:23–24).

In Luke we read, 'Take heed, and beware of all covetousness; for a man's life
does not consist in the abundance of his possessions' (12:15). In Acts there are
several references to the early Christian community holding all goods in common
and sharing as each had need.

> And all who believed were together and had all things in common; and
> they sold their possessions and goods and distributed them to all, as
> any had need (21:44–45; see also 4:32–37).

While these passages from Acts must be understood in the context of the escha-
tological hope of the time that the end of the age was imminent, the point seems
clear. There is a strong Biblical tradition of challenging excess of wealth; at the
same time a 'preferential option for the poor' can be discerned.

The early church carried on this tradition in the writings of St. Jerome and St.
Ambrose. St. Jerome, it was said, would rather store money in the stomachs of the
poor than in a purse. St. Ambrose anticipated Aquinas by indicating that giving
to the poor was not charity, but simply giving that person what was rightfully
deserved. Economic resources were given in common for the use of all people, not
merely the rich.

St. Thomas Aquinas actively engages the distributive justice question in *Summa
Theologica*, as pointed out in a study by Leo S. Schumacher:

> ... all material riches belong in common to the whole human race
> (Schumacher 1949, p. 13).
>   The institution of private property exists for the purpose of
> enabling man to achieve the most effective use of material things
> (Schumacher 1949, p. 17).
>   In the extremes of deprivation one can take and consume another's
> property without violating the seventh commandment:
>   ... whatever certain people have in abundance is due, by natural law,
> to the purpose of succoring the poor (Schumacher 1949, p. 21).

A 'just wage' was not determined by the 'higgling of the market,' but by 'a
considered judgment that looked to the good of the worker and of society as a
whole' (Schumacher 1949, p. 47). Schumacher quotes Kurth Godefroid:

> In the Middle Ages no one dared to hold that a worker's wages need not
> be sufficient to keep himself and his family (Schumacher 1949, p. 47).

Just distribution is according to needs and merits. While there is to be equitable
distribution of public benefits and burdens, this is not absolute equality of distribution.

> Consequently in distributive justice a person receives all the more of
> the common goods, according as he holds a more prominent position
> in the community (Schumacher 1949, p. 59).

However, there is to be both a floor (as we have seen) and a ceiling on the
acquisition of material goods. While practical objections to implementation of such
a goal are formidable, progressive taxation received Aquinas' blessing. Citizens
should be taxed according to their ability to pay.

> Distributive justice would demand a progressive tax rate to equalize the
> sacrifice exacted from the tax payers (Schumacher 1949, p. 60).

The virtuous life requires a sufficiency of goods as opposed to property in the hands
of a few. Wide distribution is therefore required.

The nineteenth-century Papal encyclical *Rerum Novarum*, Father John Ryan's early-
twentieth-century work on living wages and canons of economic distribution, and
the pronouncements of Vatican II in the 1960s indicate an intention to change
public policy regarding poverty. Charles Curran, in a contemporary discussion of
distributive justice and taxation, writes that property rights are limited, not absolute.
The 'goods of creation exist to serve the needs of all' (Curran 1985, p. 121). He
suggests the following formula:

> Goods or advantages are to be distributed according to needs and
> necessities, while burdens should be distributed according to capacities
> (Curran 1985, p. 120).

The Canadian Roman Catholic bishops released a rather radical statement in
December of 1983, entitled *Ethical Choices and Political Challenges*.[13] The spirit
of that document was caught up in Pope John Paul II's September 1984 visit to
Canada:

> The needs of the poor take priority over the desires of the rich; the
> rights of workers over the maximization of profits; the preservation of
> the environment over uncontrolled industrial expansion; production to
> meet social needs over production for military purposes.[14]

In November of 1986 the Roman Catholic Bishops of the United States came
out with their own pastoral letter on economic justice: *Economic Justice for All:
Pastoral Letter on Catholic Social Teaching and the U.S. Economy*. Six years in
the making, the statement is a strong but hardly radical critique of the American
economy. Nevertheless, the letter is an official expression in the tradition of a
'preferential option for the poor.' It emphasizes solidarity or the common good,
and warns against greed, 'the most evident form of moral underdevelopment.'[15]
The bishops condemn a concentration of privilege that results from more than a
mere difference in talent or desire to work, but has systemic causes that must be
examined.

In summary, the bishops assert:

> Distributive justice also calls for the establishment of a floor of material well-being on which all can stand. This is a duty of the whole of society and it creates particular obligations for those with greater resources. This duty calls into question extreme inequalities of income and consumption when so many lack basic necessities. Catholic social teaching does not maintain that a flat, arithmetic equality of income and wealth is a demand of justice, but it does challenge economic arrangements that leave large numbers of people impoverished. Further, it sees extreme inequality as a threat to the solidarity of the human community, for great disparities lead to deep social divisions and conflict.[16]

Christian liberation theology reminds us that traditional theology, like history, is written by the winners. Theology from the 'underside' has its own validity and is, by its very existence, a critique of First-World affluence and the theology it has created. David Hollenbeck, S.J., suggests the use of three ethical principles which give greater articulation to the 'preferential option for the poor':
1. The needs of the poor take priority over the wants of the rich.
2. The freedom of the dominated takes priority over the liberty of the powerful.
3. The participation of marginal groups takes priority over the order that excludes them (Hollenbeck 1979, p. 204).

Protestant Perspectives on Economic Justice

With the rise of the so-called 'Protestant Ethic,' we begin to see a dramatic change in distributive ethics. Prior to the Reformation, the whole range of economic activities had to stand trial at the bar of religion. As the Protestant Ethic and the spirit of capitalism became fused, economics and ethics were segregated. The condemnation of wealth in the Gospels was turned on its head and worldly wealth seemed to become a virtue in the eyes of deity. While the medieval writers understood nature as a moral restraint upon economic self-interest, by the seventeenth century theology had shifted from a concentration on divine ordinance to human appetites, and individualism emerged to give justification as to why self-interest should be given free play (see Weber 1958).

In short, the very qualities of economic gain – ambition, energy, diligence, success – continued to fire the pecuniary spirit long after the religious props had been taken away. So we see the change in attitude toward wealth and poverty. The pursuit of riches, once condemned as the enemy of religion, was now its ally and it would fuel an orgy of materialism.

There is severe Protestant criticism of current patterns in economic distribution. In *The Passion for Equality* Kenneth Cauthen asserts that economic inequality is an offense to justice as well as to charity. This critique faults the American tradition of individualism, a kind of social nominalism in which only individuals are real: as long as the rules are fair and enforced, individuals should get what they can. Moral virtue is thought to reside in self-interest, the happy coincidence of success and virtue. Community as a reality is neglected. This individualism ignores the interdependence that marks modern economic systems and blunts moral perception. He concludes, 'The truth is that we are all in it together' (Cauthen 1987, p. 136).

Mainline denominational bodies, including the United Methodist Church, the Presbyterian Church (USA), and the Episcopal Church, among others, have passed resolutions condemning poverty and supporting anti-poverty programs. As Alexis DeToqueville wrote in the 1830s,

> Religion in America takes no direct part in the government of society, but it must be regarded as the first of their political institutions (DeToqueville 2000).

SYSTEMIC CHANGE: FROM CHARITY TO JUSTICE – A PERSONAL VIEW

The great world faiths have eloquently expressed an historic appeal for economic justice. In general they have warned of the moral corruption of wealth and the injustice of poverty. However, most of this religious rhetoric is directed at the individual adherent. Relatively little of these teachings home in on the structures of power that shape distributive justice. Are the world's religions capable of transforming these noble individualistic teachings into pragmatic social policy? Are they capable of 'speaking truth to power'? Of dropping an ethical plumb-line over globalization? Of calling the rich to account? Of bringing a semblance of economic justice to the poor? Can they move from delivering charity to shaping justice?

There are 358 billionaires in the world who enjoy a net worth of US$760 billion – equal to the net worth of the poorest 2.5 billion of the world's people (Korten 2000, p. 83). As one critic of globalization puts it, 'In the world of big money and multimillion-dollar compensation packages, greed is a worker who wants a living wage' (Korten 2000, p. 231). The global parade metaphor aptly amplifies these striking and disturbing realities.

Another critic, John Berger, describes our predicament in these words:

> The poverty of our century is not as poverty was before, the result of natural scarcity, but of a set of priorities imposed on the rest of the world by the rich. Consequently, the modern poor are not pitied but written off as trash. The ... consumer economy has produced the first culture for which the beggar is a reminder of nothing.[17]

Charity is a tempting option because it leads to feelings of virtue, even self-righteousness, without challenging the systems which have enriched the affluent and impoverished the poor. 'Justice,' as theologian Joseph Sittler once put it, 'is love operating at a distance.'[18] While compassionate love is a personal moral value, justice deals with larger social contexts. It implies a fair distribution of social benefits and burdens. Justice allocates resources based on need, not greed. Of course, we must consider capital formation, profit margins, comparative advantage, return on investment, and all those other powerful abstractions that comprise economic debate. But, for religious critics of globalization, it doesn't stop there.

A *New Yorker* cartoon illustrates our dilemma: It shows three fish swimming, one behind the other. First is a small fish saying, 'There is no justice.' Immediately behind, ready to swallow it, is a larger fish saying, 'There is some justice in the world.' Finally, there is a huge fish about to swallow both saying, 'The world is just.' That is the moral predicament of the prosperous.

Justice, properly understood, is systemic, aiming at the underlying causes of social problems, not at their symptoms. Treating symptoms alone might well be a soporific to cover fundamental injustice; it is like putting a Band-Aid on a cancer. Thus, international relief efforts, however laudable, merely feed the victims of a fundamentally unjust social order instead of rooting out the causes of hunger. A systemic approach challenges the underlying premises and workings of economies which produce 'poverty in the midst of plenty.' A systemic approach deals with policy issues, taxation, government welfare programs, income distribution, and the 'structural adjustment' which world economic bodies impose on developing nations.

We may be persuaded that the world cannot be any other way. Perhaps we should allow the rich to become richer and let the devil take the hindmost. Perhaps social justice is simply inefficient in a global free market. However, it is clear from this brief survey that there is in humanity's ethical tradition, a 'preferential option for the poor,' and a critique of superfluous wealth. The basic tendency is to call for a reduction in inequality of distribution.

While there is an unmistakable criticism of the chasm between poverty and wealth, the world's religions generally do not effectively critique the very systems which produce the chasm. There are exceptions, of course. The differences in response, from charity to justice, seem to follow an East/West division. While the Eastern religions tend to focus on the fate of the individual soul and have a distinctly vertical dimension, humanity's relationship with God; the Western religious traditions – Judaism, Christianity, and Islam – are generally oriented toward history; that is, whatever their belief about the holy and the hereafter, they are determined to transform human history according to their own value systems. They exhibit a more horizontal dimension intersecting the vertical. For example, today's Christian evangelicals, while concerned primarily with individual salvation, have entered the political forum in a powerful way.

Yet, even here, the fundamental tendency of religious organizations is toward direct service to alleviate human needs for food, shelter, and clothing. Religious communities are well known for their domestic soup kitchens and their foreign famine relief programs. Feeding the poor is a non-controversial means of expressing religious faith. However, organized religion, with some important exceptions, does not challenge the fundamental societal structures which allow hunger in the presence of abundant food, poverty in the presence of plenty. By and large the world's religions do not question the fundamental moral premises on which that economy is based. That is often regarded as political, and religious communities believe either that is not their place or perhaps fear controversy in the ranks of their politically pluralistic parishioners. Where organized religion falls short, then, is in a systemic critique of economic and political structures that perpetuate the great economic chasms between people which Jan Pen so graphically describes.

Henry David Thoreau articulates the problem effectively in *Walden.*

> There are a thousand hacking at the branches of evil to one who is striking at the root, and it may be that he who bestows the largest amount of time and money on the needy is doing the most by his mode of life to produce that misery which he strives in vain to relieve. ... Philanthropy is almost the only virtue which is sufficiently appreciated by mankind. Nay, it is greatly overrated and it is our selfishness which overrates it. ... I would not subtract anything from the praise that is due to philanthropy, but merely demand justice for all who by their lives and works are a blessing to mankind.[19]

The Roman Catholic Church, through its Papal encyclicals and its hierarchical power, however, does play a major role in influencing policy. The United States Conference of Catholic Bishops, through the aforementioned pastoral letter on the economy, is an influential force in US domestic and foreign policy. Bread for the World is a church-based Christian organization which advocates for policies more conducive to the transfer of resources and technology from the developed world to the developing world. Most recently the Bread for the World Institute has compiled *Elections Matter: Vote to End Hunger*, citing key issues in the 2004 elections. Executive Director David Beckman claims, 'The federal budget is a moral document, one that affects all of us. God calls us to speak out and help to shape our society' (Beckmann 2004). Later, he writes:

> We join the [Roman Catholic] bishops in calling upon our government to help alleviate global hunger and poverty by increasing development aid to the poorest countries, creating equitable trade policies, and easing the burden of debt and disease (Beckmann 2004).

A World Council of Churches study paper concludes, 'It must be the job of the state to set limits on poverty – but on wealth as well' (Beckmann 2004). In February 2003 the WCC opened conversations with the International Monetary Fund and the World Bank, a promising development. A section on religion has been created within the Bank to explore the role of the world's faiths in development (See *One Country. The online newsletter of the Baha'i International Community.* Volume 10, Issue 4, January- March 1999 for a brief outline of faith statements on development). Mazon (the Hebrew word for 'food') likewise attempts to implement the Jewish tradition of *tikkun olam* – to repair the world – through grants to food providers and advocacy groups. Recently the Ecumenical Patriarch Bartholomew, at the inauguration of the International Interfaith Investment Group (3IG) spoke of *oikologia* (in Greek the maintenance of God's House), and *oikonimia* (in Greek, the principles that govern the house), relating environmental stewardship to economic development.

The work of the Jubilee 2000 organization is indicative of a new approach to the systemic causes of poverty. This coalition of religious and humanitarian groups has worked for the past several years as an advocacy group trying to persuade the USA and the other developed nations of the world to write off the debts owed by poor and developing nations to the institutions of the developed world. That group has now morphed into Jubilee Research,[20] which describes itself as a 'think and do' tank. Their rationale is that many of these debts were the result of economic pressure from developed nations and their institutions and that the debts were often incurred by non-elected leaders of the developing nations who pocketed much of the money for private purposes. Jubilee Research critiques the international financial institutions like the World Bank, the G7, and the International Monetary Fund and advocates for policy-reform favoring the poor in the developing nations.

The Micah Challenge, a project of the World Evangelical Alliance, embracing 3 million local churches in 111 countries, and the Micah Network, was launched in October 2004, in conjunction with the UN ceremony of the International Day for the Eradication of Poverty. The Micah Challenge was created to promote the Millennium Development Goals, basing its mission on the words from the Hebrew prophet Micah, '... what does the Lord require of you but to do justice, and to love kindness, and to walk humbly with your God?' (Micah 6:8) and to 'mobilize Christians against poverty.'[22]

> We exhort Christians to network and to co-operate to face together the challenges of globalization. The church needs a unified global voice to respond to the damage caused by it to both human beings and the environment. Our hope for the Micah Network is that it will foster a movement of resistance to a global system of exploitation.[23]

But, however powerful these religious forces may seem, they have had a limited impact upon the globalization promoted by transnational corporations, the nations and the people who support them. Out of the world's US$24-trillion economy,

> 200 corporations, linked together by strategic alliances and interlocking boards, account for 29% of world economic activity.[24]
> If trade were equally divided, the inhabitants of each square mile would have more than $62,000 in products to trade each year (Bread for the World 1997).

The world's great faiths have not yet gathered around a globalized ethic that can challenge and critique the worship of the capitalist market model and its obsession with profit to the exclusion of all else. And it is sometimes forgotten that originally economics was a subdivision of ethics.

The problem is illustrated by the words of Enrique del Val Blanco, an official of Mexico's Human Services Ministry:

> Everyone feels their life is determined by someone outside, and everyone wants to know who is this person? Who is this force? We

thought that we were on the path of the First World and suddenly something went wrong. One minute the World Bank and IMF were saying Mexico was the best example. Now we are the worst example. What did we do? We are losing control. If we don't find another type of development, we are finished. We surrender (Friedman 1999, p. 114).

Anecdotes such as this personalize what can become an arcane and abstract discussion. We may try to keep hunger above ideology, beyond politics, non-controversial, but that is both impossible and irresponsible. Hunger is not a matter of technical fixes, will-power, or charity. It is more than a humanitarian issue – it has to do with the allocation of power in the world. In the eyes of those who would challenge globalization as it now operates, there is a new Golden Rule: 'Those with the gold make the rules' (Birch and Rasmussen 1978).

At the 1981 Cancun Conference on the North–South dialogue, President Ronald Reagan extolled the free market as the solution to global poverty, citing the Chinese saying about a man who was taught to fish himself instead of relying on being given a fish by others. Nigeria's representative Shagari attached a postscript:

> I agree there is an object lesson here. I must hasten to add, however, that the man has to be supplied with hooks and nets in order to put into practice his invaluable knowledge of fishing.[25]

While democracy enables decisions by majority vote, and while the market allocates resources by what has been called 'the invisible hand,' justice is a virtue that transcends these instrumental ways of making decisions. Justice is like the carpenter's plumb-line that the prophet Amos likened to divine righteousness as the criterion for all human endeavors. The vertical line (justice) intersects the horizontal line (society). Justice can be determined neither by democratic vote nor market machination. It is a transcendent human value that judges all such arrangements.

The Unitarian minister Theodore Parker wrote:

> Yet it seemed to me the money given by public and private charity – two foundations that never fail in Puritanic Boston – was more than sufficient to relieve it all, and gradually remove the deep-seated and unseen cause which, in the hurry of business and money, is not attended to. There is a hole in the dim-lit public bridge, where many fall through and perish. Our mercy pulls a few out of the water; it does not stop the hole, nor light the bridge, nor warn men of the peril! We need the great Charity that palliates effects of wrong, and the greater Justice which removes the Cause (Parker 1859, p. 94).

For prophetic religious communities, compassion is no longer enough, if it ever was enough. Charity without justice, they claim, is like rearranging deckchairs on the *Titanic*.

AN ETHICAL FRAMEWORK: HOW MUCH IS ENOUGH? HOW MUCH DO WE DESERVE?

The religions of the world will continue their fundamental practice of service to the needy, the hungry, and the poor. They will often effectively fill in the gaps left by national and international political and economic entities. A much smaller prophetic group of religious people will become advocates, challenging the 'principalities and powers' of the world to do justice. They will operate in the public square as one of many voluntary associations in democratic dialogue. However, there is yet another level at which they might work, which theologian Paul Tillich called 'silent interpenetration'; the way they shape the individual conscience, and the collective conscience of Nation States, and the international order.

These religious communities have found that large disparities of income and wealth are inherently unjust. Justice is the foundational value in social ethics. It is predicated on the inherent dignity and worth of every human personality. Theologically that has been understood through the phrase 'children of God' in the Jewish and Christian traditions. In more universalistic language it is based on 'reverence for life.' Philosophically understood, it means people are to be treated as ends, not means.

As noted above, the United Nations Universal Declaration of Human Rights, which serves as humanity's ethical charter, specifies not only civil rights but economic rights for the world's people, including the right to a basic food security and freedom from poverty. Of the 30 principles in the Declaration, the first 22 have to do with political freedom – much as are guaranteed in the US Bill of Rights, the first Ten Amendments to the US Constitution. The next several deal with economic rights: the right to social security, the right to desirable work and to join trade unions, the right to rest and leisure, the right to an adequate standard of living, the right to education, the right to participate in the cultural life of a community, the right to social order assuring human rights, the right to safe and fairly compensated work. It is to these universal human rights that the religious communities of humanity need to turn their attention.

But perhaps the most effective way the world's religions can help to alleviate world hunger in the long term is to raise in dramatic and powerful ways the moral foundations of the economic order. I suggest four propositions that argue for the justice of a more equitable distribution of income and wealth. Perhaps a central role of religion is to raise these issues in democratic global discourse. Perhaps it is just as important for the world's religious faiths to ask the right questions as to provide the right answers.

Proposition One

The greater the equality in income and wealth, the more the *freedom* in society. Freedom is understood as the human capacity for self- determination. In economic discussion that value has too often been related solely to the operations of the 'free market.' Freedom in economic terms does contribute to other kinds of freedom – political, religious, social. However, freedom is also a function of the action alternatives from which a person may choose. Freedom from government interference in the market-place needs to be supplemented with freedom for choosing from among viable economic options. Freedom to pursue economic ends is always in tension with the sense of trusteeship – the goods of the earth do not belong to human beings; we are merely their trustees. Nature is not a commodity, but a sacred trust emerging from that creative process of which we are part. Earth's bounties are not private commodities, but the common inheritance of all humankind 'unto the Seventh Generation' in Native American idiom. This tension sets one of the equations of the justice model. Does globalization enhance this broader understanding of human freedom? How can it do so?

Proposition Two

The greater the equality in income and wealth, the greater the *equity (fairness)* in society. A second principle of justice is equity, or fairness, in which each person is entitled to a fair distribution of economic benefits. What is argued for is not absolute equality of results in distribution, but an equity of results which treats people as creatures of human dignity. Equity is in constant tension with efficiency, 'the big trade-off.' What is a just balance between a fair distribution of resources and the incentives stemming from inequality of results? Does globalization promote a fair distribution of resources? What global policies might lead in that direction?

Proposition Three

The greater the equality in income and wealth, the stronger the sense of *community solidarity*. A third principle of justice is community, by which is meant a sense of human solidarity in which voluntary cooperation interacts with humane competition as an ordering principle of justice. Here community is understood as more than the aggregate of the individuals who comprise it, an organic entity whose welfare is of paramount importance, the common good. This common good is neither individualistic nor collectivistic but understands these polarities in creative tension. Community is in constant tension with individualism, a value in which personal uniqueness is honored. In this understanding of community, individuals are not understood as atoms, operating outside any meaningful context. Rather, individuals are members of a human community in which personal self-actualization supplements the obligations and rights of membership. In fact, serving the community becomes one essential source of self-fulfillment. Does globalization encourage creation of solidarity in community, or does it further divide humanity into the 'haves' and the 'have-nots'?

Proposition Four

The greater the equality in income and wealth, the greater the potential for *moral sensitivity* and *religious meaning*. This principle has its roots in the Jewish and Christian traditions of theological covenant – a spiritual compact by which human beings bargain with their experienced universe for justice. The covenant carries an imperative to 'do justice.' It suggests that human interest transcends self-interest. At the same time, it is a pragmatic perspective, taking into account the realities of human nature and society as well as economic problems. Self-interest is inherent in human nature and serves to drive economic activity. The need for solidarity is also inherent in human nature and moves us to compassion.

Economics is more than the calculus of self-interests presumably vectored into some vague common good. Great disparities of income and wealth are spiritually as well as morally debilitating. To paraphrase and expand Lord Acton's famous aphorism:

> Affluence tends to corrupt, spiritually and morally, distancing us from the experience of want and privation. Absolute affluence corrupts absolutely.

As the consumer nations of the world, the USA in particular, battle with obesity and other physical and mental diseases accompanying the narcissistic enjoyment of affluence, billions of the world's people struggle for survival. The graphic reminder of that moral and spiritual corruption is Jan Pen's global parade.

Art Simon, President Emeritus of Bread for the World, has published *How Much Is Enough? Hungering for God in an Affluent Culture.* He makes the spiritual connection between religion and economics by stating, 'We are human beings, not human havings.' One of his chapter headings is indicative of the moral responsibility of the developed nations to the developing countries: 'Living Simply So That Others May Simply Live' (Simon 2003).

The Worldwatch Institute, a highly respected non-profit think tank on world development, concluded its most recent report, *State of the World 2004,* with a chapter entitled, 'Rethinking the Good Life.' The authors, Gary Gardner and Erik Assadourian, quoted the mayor of Bogota, Columbia, as he measured the well-being of his city: 'A city is successful not when it's rich, but when its people are happy' (Gardner and Assadourian 2004). The authors go on to note that the quality of life in the developed nations is deteriorating because of greater stress and time pressures which fracture human relationships and because the natural environment shows more signs of distress. In poor countries quality of life is 'degraded by a failure to meet people's basic needs' (Gardner and Assadourian 2004, p. 165). The authors note that the Canadian Parliament in June of 2003 passed the Canada Well-Being Measurement Act. The *World Values Survey,* conducted between 1999 and 2000 found that income and happiness track well until about US$13,000 of annual income per person, and after that additional income appears to yield only modest additions in self-reported happiness (Gardner and Assadourian 2004, p. 166). They point out that societies scoring highest in the Well-Being Index, especially in Northern Europe, 'also have some of the world's most generous foreign aid programs' (Gardner and Assadourian 2004, p. 179). To the question 'how much is enough,' they quote the Chinese sage Lao Tzu: 'To know when you have enough is to be rich' (Gardner and Assadourian 2004, p. 178).

Robert Heilbroner, in *The Nature and Logic of Capitalism,* provides a sardonic summary of this inquiry:

> If the rich man – or better yet – the rich society – finally wins admission to heaven, I suspect it will be not because capitalists have pure hearts, but because scientists will have succeeded in breeding exceptionally thin and agile camels, and because technology has succeeded in making needles with very large and very wide eyes (Heilbroner 1985, p. 137).

In the words of a Latin-American prayer: 'To those who have hunger, give bread; to those who have bread, give the hunger for justice.'

NOTES

[1] See CEPR website at www.cepr.net/globalization/scorecard_on_globalization.htm.

[2] Attributed to Gandhi.

[3] Attributed to Gandhi.

[4] The *Dhammada*, p. 61.

[5] Ibid., p. 98.

[6] *Sandcastles: Buddhism and Global Finance*: A Film by Alexander Oey. Review in *First Run Icarus Films*, 4 July 2004.

[7] Confucius, *Analects*.

[8] Ibid.

[9] Ibid.

[10] *Ithaca Journal*, 9 March 2005.

[11] *The Poor Among Us: Jewish Tradition and Social Policy*. New York: The American Jewish Committee, 1986, p. 25.

[12] Ibid., p. 28.

[13] *Ethical Choices and Political Challenges: Ethical Reflections on the Future of Canada's Socioeconomic Order*. The Episcopal Commission for Social Affairs, Canadian Conference of Catholic Bishops. Concacan Inc., December 1983.

[14] Address on Christian Unity in a Technological Age [Toronto 14 September 1984]. In: *Origins* 14:16 [4 October 1984], p. 248.

[15] *Economic Justice for All: Pastoral Letter on Catholic Social Teaching and the U.S. Economy*. Washington, DC: National Conference of Catholic Bishops, 1986, p 38 (quoting Pope Paul VI, *On the Development of Peoples*, 1967, p. 19).

[16] Ibid., p. 38.

[17] John Berger in *The Soul and the Operator*, quoted in *The Living Pulpit*, April–June 2001.

[18] Joseph Sittler, source unknown.

[19] Henry David Thoreau, *Walden*, pp. 117–118.

[20] See http://www.jubileeresearch.org/.

[22] See http://www.micahchallenge.org/overview/

[23] Ibid.

[24] *UN Conference on Trade and Development World Investment Report 1996*.

[25] *US News and World Report*, 2 November 1981, p. 32.

REFERENCES

Beckmann, D., 2004. God Calls Us to Shape Our Society. April.

Birch, B.C. and L.S. Rasmussen, 1978. *The Predicament of the Prosperous*. Philadelphia, PA: Westminster Press.

Bloom, A., 2004. Globalization and Buddhism. Shin Dharma Net, website, 4 July 4.

Bread for the World, 1997. *Hunger in a Global Economy: Eighth Annual Report on the State of World Hunger*.

Bread for the World, 2005. *Hunger 2004: Are We on Track to End Hunger?* Bread for the World Background Paper.

Brooks, D., 2004. Good news about poverty. *New York Times*: 27 November.

Cauthen, K., 1987. *The Passion for Equality*. Totoma, New Jersey: Rowman and Littlefield.

Cobb, J.B., Jr and H.E. Daly, 1989. *For the Common Good: Redirecting the Economy Toward Community, the Environment, and a Sustainable Future*. Boston: Beacon Press.

Curran, C., 1985. Just taxes in the Roman Catholic tradition. *Journal of Religious Ethics* (Spring): 121.

DeToqueville, A., 2000. *Democracy in America*. Edited by J. P. Mayer. Translated by George Lawrence. New York: HarperPerennial.

French, H., 2002. Reshaping Global Governance. *State of the World 2002*. The Worldwatch Institute. New York: W.W. Norton.

Friedman, T., 1999. *The Lotus and the Olive Tree*. New York: Farrar. Straus, Giroux.

Gardner, G. and E. Assadourian, 2004. Rethinking the good life. *State of the World 2004*. New York: W.W. Norton & Company.

Heilbroner, R., 1985. *The Nature and Logic of Capitalism*. New York: W.W. Norton.

Hollenbeck, S.J., 1979. Claims in Conflict: Retrieving and Renewing the Catholic Human Rights Tradition. New York: Paulist Press.

Korten, D., 2000. *When Corporations Rule the World*. CoPublications, second edition.

Lederer, E.M., 2005. World Population to Exceed 9 Billion in 2050, U.N. Says. *Business Week* online, 25 February.

Norbert-Hodge, H., 1997. Buddhism in the global economy. *International Society for Ecology and Culture*.

Parker, T., 1859. *Theodore Parker's experience as a minister with some account of his early life*. Boston: Rufus Leighton, Jr.

Pen, J., 1973. A Parade of Dwarfs (and a Few Giants). In: Atkinson A.B., ed. *Wealth, income and inequality*. Middlesex, U.K.: Penguin, pp. 73-82, and second edition, Oxford University Press, 1980

Saldanha, V., 2003. Fundamentalists are not rooted in the truth of their religions. *National Catholic Reporter* (23 April).

Schumacher, E.F., 1973. Buddhist economics. In: *Small Is Beautiful: Economics as if People Mattered*. New York: Harper and Row, Appropriate Technology.

Schumacher, L.S., 1949. *The Philosophy of the Equitable Distribution of Wealth: A Study in Economic Philosophy*. Washington, DC: Catholic University of America Press.

Simon, A., 2003. *How Much Is Enough? Hungering for God in an Affluent Culture*. Baker Book House.

Stiglitz, J., 2002. Single economic model does not suit whole world. *The Times*, 24 July.

UNDP, 2003. *Millennium Development Goals: A compact among nations to end human poverty. Human Development Report 2003*. New York: United Nations Development Program.

University of California, 2004. *UC Atlas of Global Inequality*. Santa Cruz, CA: University of California [available at http://ucatlas.ucsc.edu/].

Weber, M., 1958. *The Protestant Ethic and the Spirit of Capitalism*. New York: Charles Scribner & Son.

Worldwatch Institute, 2004. *State of the World 2004: Special Focus, The Consumer Society*. New York: W.W. Norton & Company.

FREEDOM FROM HUNGER AS A BASIC HUMAN RIGHT: PRINCIPLES AND IMPLEMENTATION

INTRODUCTION: SYNOPSIS

There is in international human rights law a right to food and to be free from hunger. The content of that right, in particular as spelled out by the UN Committee on Economic, Social and Cultural Rights, is preceded by some comments on famine, chronic hunger, and the right to food, drawing in particular on the work by Amartya Sen and emphasizing that the main problem is not lack of food, but of (failed) entitlements and inadequate capacity to take appropriate public action. This is followed by an examination of possible approaches to the implementation of the right to food and to be free from hunger and the current draft of a set of voluntary guidelines, prepared under the auspices of the FAO Council. All of this should be seen in connection with the ongoing debate on rights-based development and on international shared obligations, including the right to development and a possible development compact. Finally, some brief conclusions are drawn.

THE RIGHT TO ADEQUATE FOOD AND TO BE FREE FROM HUNGER: INTERNATIONAL HUMAN RIGHTS LAW

International human rights law is based on the Universal Declaration of Human Rights (UDHR). All subsequent elaborations in international human rights standards, including legally binding international conventions, are built on the Universal Declaration. The conventions of particular significance here are the International Covenant on Economic, Social and Cultural Rights (ICESCR), and the International Convention on the Rights of the Child (ICRC). Important provisions are also found in the International Convention on the Elimination of All Forms of Discrimination against Women (ICEDAW) and the International Convention on the Elimination of All Forms of Racial Discrimination (ICERD). There are many other provisions of relevance for the right to food and to be free from hunger in international law, but these will be only briefly mentioned in this chapter.

The proclamation of the right to food started with the fairly general provision in UDHR Article 25 (para 1), and reads:

> Everyone has the right to a standard of living adequate for the health and well-being of himself and of his family, including food, clothing, housing and medical care and necessary social services, and the right to

P. Pinstrup-Andersen and P. Sandøe (eds.), Ethics, Hunger and Globalization: In Search of Appropriate Policies, 93–109.
© 2007 *Springer.*

security in the event of unemployment, sickness, disability, widowhood, old age or other lack of livelihood in circumstances beyond his control.

A much more detailed elaboration is found in ICESCR Article 11, which reads:

1. The States Parties to the present Covenant recognize the right of everyone to an adequate standard of living for himself and his family, including adequate food, clothing and housing, and to the continuous improvement of living conditions. The States Parties will take appropriate steps to ensure the realization of this right, recognizing to this effect the essential importance of international co-operation based on free consent.

2. The States Parties to the present Covenant, recognizing the fundamental right of everyone to be free from hunger, shall take, individually and through international co-operation, the measures, including specific programmes, which are needed:

   a. To improve methods of production, conservation and distribution of food by making full use of technical and scientific knowledge, by disseminating knowledge of the principles of nutrition and by developing or reforming agrarian systems in such a way as to achieve the most efficient development and utilization of natural resources;

   b. Taking into account the problems of both food-importing and food-exporting countries, to ensure an equitable distribution of world food supplies in relation to need.

Also important is ICRC Articles 24 and 27. Article 24 includes:

1. States Parties recognise the right of the child to the enjoyment of the highest attainable standard of health...

2. States Parties shall pursue full implementation of this right and, in particular, shall take appropriate measures:...

   c. to combat disease and malnutrition.

And Article 27 (in part) reads:

1. States Parties recognise the right of every child to a standard of living adequate for the child's physical, mental, spiritual, moral and social development.

2. States Parties, in accordance with national conditions and within their means, shall take appropriate measures to assist parents and others responsible for the child to implement this right and shall in case of need provide material assistance and support programmes, particularly with regard to nutrition, clothing and housing.

Relevant provisions are also found in ICEDAW, particularly Articles 11 (employment), 12 (healthcare, nutritional rights during pregnancy and lactation), 13 (family benefits), and 14 (special protection of the rights of rural women). ICERD Article 5 obliges States to prevent any discrimination on the grounds of race in the economic life. ILO Convention No. 169 on the Rights of Indigenous and Tribal Peoples also contain relevant provisions of great importance, including land rights. The UN Declaration on the Rights of Persons belonging to National or Ethnic, Religious and Linguistic Minorities contain provisions that have a more indirect relevance to the right to food and to be free from hunger.

More extreme conditions are addressed in the Convention on the Prevention and Punishment of the Crime of Genocide, where one of the prohibited acts is 'deliberately inflicting on the group conditions of life calculated to bring about its physical destruction in whole or in part,' and the prohibition of the use of food as a weapon during armed conflict, as set out in international humanitarian law. This is now also covered by the Statute of the International Criminal Court.

AMARTYA SEN ON FAMINE
AND ENTITLEMENTS – AND HIS CRITICS

Amartya Sen – economist, philosopher, and Nobel laureate – radically changed the way we think about hunger with his studies on starvation. In *Poverty and Famine* he criticized theories that relied on Malthusian ideas about food availability decline, and about climate and mismanagement of resources. While all of these may be relevant factors,

> Starvation is the characteristic of some people not *having* enough food to eat. It is not the characteristic of there *being* not enough to eat. While the latter can be a cause of the former, it is but one of many possible causes. Whether and how starvation relates to food supply is a matter for factual investigation. Food supply statements say things about a commodity (or a group of commodities) considered on its own. Starvation statements are about the relationship of persons to the commodity (or that commodity group) (Sen 1981, p. 1).

He introduced his theory of entitlements, focusing on the ability of people to command food through the legal means available in society, including the use of production possibilities, trade opportunities, entitlements vis-à-vis the State, and other means of acquiring food (Sen 1981, p. 45).

Famines are failures, for some, of their entitlements, or lack of such entitlements. The causes can be human-made, natural, or both. To some extent, they are always human-made; at least by passivity, the lack of a will to intervene through public measures, and failures of governmental or international intervention when entitlements fail. Public action is essential for the prevention of hunger, but this requires recognition of the role of the State as a key actor in redressing negative developments in demand capacity. In our time, where neoliberalism is harking back to the laissez-faire of the nineteenth century, it might be useful to recall the following historic case from the Western world,– namely, the Irish famine of 1845–1849.

There were a number of causes, the most direct being the potato blight. But the famine could have been averted through public action. In her book on the history of the Irish famine, Cecil Woodham-Smith writes:

> Not only were the rights of property sacred; private enterprise was revered and respected and given almost complete liberty, and on this theory, which incidentally gave the employer and the landlord freedom

to exploit his fellow man, the prosperity of nineteenth-century England had unquestioningly been based.

The influence of laissez faire on the treatment of Ireland during the famine is impossible to exaggerate. Almost without exception the high officials and politicians responsible for Ireland were fervent believers in non-interference by Government, and the behaviour of the British authorities only becomes explicable when their fanatic belief in private enterprise and their suspicions of any action which might be considered Government intervention are borne in mind (Woodham-Smith 1961, p. 54).

Subjected to absentee landlords and to this fervent ideology by the government controlling them, the Irish were doomed. The governmental inaction in the economic dynamics, coupled with marginal and misplaced efforts to give some relief, caused 1 million people to die from starvation and related illnesses; nearly 2 million emigrated, a large proportion of them to the USA. Ireland's population dropped from 8 million before the famine to 5 million after it.

On the basis of his studies of famine, Amartya Sen developed and confirmed his famous thesis that large-scale famines do not occur when there are functioning, democratic governments in place in self-governing countries. This is, of course, not because the introduction of self-determination and democracy leads by itself to more food production, but that responsive governments can ensure that food is made accessible to all, provided appropriate public action is taken. The reason why democracy can have this effect is through freedom of speech and active news media and their impact on political decision-making: Governments cannot remain passive when large-scale famines occur.

However, the significance of formal democracy, though important, is not in itself a sufficient guarantee against chronic hunger. Dan Banik, a scholar of Indian descent now located in Norway, has tested Sen in theory and practice. Banik distinguishes between malnutrition, severe malnutrition, famine threat, famine 1 (a community crisis, destitution for large groups), and famine 2 (very high level of excess mortality). Through a very detailed examination of poverty, drought, and malnutrition in Kalanhandi and Purulia in India, and the governmental response, he concludes that while democracy in India has indeed been able to avert massive famine through public action, the Indian democracy has not been able to prevent widespread death by starvation. Increased food availability in India has not improved the health and nutritional status of large sections of the population. Over 200 million men, women, and children suffer from a combination of chronic malnutrition and severe undernutrition, and more than 2.5 million children in India die before they are five years old (Banik 2002, p. 433).

It can now be clearly asserted that the implications of Amartya Sen's conclusions have been blown out of proportion, something with which he himself would probably agree. Democracy and the free press are likely to prevent massive and sudden famines. But, based on the work of Banik (2003) and others, and also on substantial other evidence, it can safely be said that democracy – while important – in itself is not enough to prevent the continuous, silent, and extensive hunger that is so widespread in many countries, including India. The politically dominant elite, even within a functioning democracy, is often quite insensitive to widespread poverty and inequality; the media can also be quite indifferent to the fate of groups traditionally suffering from chronic malnutrition. Only a deliberate rights-based development (as described below), implying a better recognition of State responsibility to respect, protect, and fulfill the right to food, which in no way reduces the need for individuals to take whatever action they can to cover their own needs. Such recognition requires active involvement by critical parts of the civil society in collaboration with international monitoring institutions.

Hunger and poverty cannot be abolished without a clear and deliberate effort to address and remedy the situation of those who are chronically vulnerable. There must be proper management of property, with land reforms where required, proper inheritance arrangements, protection against discrimination on race, caste, gender, and other grounds, taking appropriate public action to facilitate and to fulfill the right to food, as set out in General Comment No. 12 of the UN Committee on Economic, Social and Cultural Rights. Also needed is recognition of an international shared responsibility through the right to development.

RIGHTS AND OBLIGATIONS: FROM THE WORLD FOOD SUMMIT (1996) TO GENERAL COMMENT NO. 12 (1999)

The right to food forms part of the broader right to an adequate standard of living. The right to an adequate standard of living or to livelihood sums up the main concern underlying all economic and social rights, which is to integrate everyone into a humane society. The ultimate purpose of promoting the right to adequate food is to achieve nutritional well-being for each individual child, woman, and man. Human nutritional status is determined by at least three major clusters of conditions that interact in a dynamic fashion, relating to food, health, and care, and with education as a cross-cutting dimension. Food alone is not sufficient to ensure good nutrition for the individual. The right to adequate food is a necessary, but not the only sufficient component of the right to adequate nutrition. The full realization of the latter depends also on parallel achievements in the fields of health, care for the vulnerable, and education. Later instruments, especially the Convention on the Rights of the Child, recognize this broader right to nutrition as well as its cross-cutting nature relative to many other rights, including civil and political rights.

The 1996 World Food Summit

The major breakthrough in international attention to the right to food came with the World Food Summit, held at the invitation of the Food and Agriculture Organization of the United Nations (FAO) in Rome in November 1996.[1] Taking into account that the Rome Declaration on World Food Security and the World Food Summit

Plan of Action were adopted by the Summit and thus by the leaders of the world, the commitments made there must be considered to have overriding legal, political, and moral significance for the world community.

The governments assembled at the Summit declared that they considered it intolerable and unacceptable that more than 800 million people throughout the world, particularly in developing countries, did not have enough food to meet their basic nutritional needs. They recognized that this was not the result of a lack of food supplies, which had increased substantially. The constraints were to be found in the access to food. The problems, they noted, resided in the continuing inadequacy of household incomes to purchase food and the instability of supply and demand, as well as natural and human-made disasters.

They also pointed out that the problems of hunger and food insecurity had global dimensions and were likely to persist and even increase dramatically in some regions unless urgent, determined, and concerted action was taken, especially given the anticipated increase in the world's population and the stress on natural resources. The leaders of the world therefore pledged their political will and their common and national commitment to achieving food security for all and to an ongoing effort to eradicate hunger in all countries, with an immediate view to reducing the number of undernourished people to half the 1996 level no later than the year 2015.

To implement this political will, they made seven commitments spelled out in the World Food Summit Plan of Action. Commitment 7, which deals with implementation, monitoring, and follow-up, is of special importance here. This includes Commitment 7.4:

> To clarify the content of the right to adequate food and the fundamental right of everyone to be free from hunger, as stated in the International Covenant on Economic, Social and Cultural Rights and other relevant international and regional instruments, and to give particular attention to implementation and full and progressive realization of this right as a means of achieving food security for all.

For this purpose, the Summit called on governments, in partnership with all actors of civil society, to make every effort to implement the provisions of Article 11 of the ICESCR; for States that were not yet Parties to the Covenant to adhere to it at the earliest possible time; for the Committee on Economic, Social and Cultural Rights to give particular attention to the Plan of Action in the framework of its activities and to continue to monitor the implementation of the specific measures provided for in Article 11 of the Covenant. The Summit invited the United Nations High Commissioner for Human Rights, in consultation with relevant treaty bodies, and in collaboration with relevant specialized agencies and programs of the United Nations system and appropriate intergovernmental mechanisms, to better define the rights related to food in Article 11 of the Covenant and to propose ways to implement and realize these rights as a means of achieving the commitments and objectives of the World Food Summit, taking into account the possibility of formulating voluntary guidelines for food security for all.

The UN High Commissioner for Human Rights (Mary Robinson at that time) energetically pursued the request of the World Food Summit by organizing a number of consultations with relevant agencies and civil society. One of these was the convening of a Symposium, as part of the annual session of the UN Administrative Committee of Coordination/ Subcommittee on Nutrition (ACC/SCN) on 'The Substance and Politics of a Human Rights Approach to Food and Nutrition Policies and Programmes,' held in Geneva on 12/13 April 1999 and hosted by the High Commissioner for Human Rights. The Symposium was attended by senior officials of several agencies together with their technical focal points, which can be seen as proof of an increasing receptivity to human rights among the development agencies. The Symposium contributed to a better understanding by the agencies of the work of the human-rights institutions as well as their own place in future collaboration with them.

Clarifying the Right to Food: General Comment No. 12 of the Committee
on Economic, Social and Cultural Rights

The most significant milestone was the adoption by the UN Committee on Economic, Social and Cultural Rights of General Comment No. 12 (E/C.12/1999/5) on the right to adequate food (Article 11) on 12 May 1999. That General Comment is of central importance.

The foundation principle of the human-rights system is that everyone is 'born free and equal in dignity and rights and should act towards each other in a spirit of fraternity' (UDHR, Article 1). The Committee affirms in its General Comment (para 4) that

> the right to adequate food is indivisibly linked to the inherent dignity of the human person and is indispensable for the fulfillment of other human rights enshrined in the International Bill of Human Rights. It is also inseparable from social justice, requiring the adoption of appropriate economic, environmental and social policies, at both the national and international levels, oriented to the eradication of poverty and the fulfillment of all human rights for all.

The General Comment expresses the core content of the right to adequate food as follows (para 8):

> The availability of food in a quantity and quality sufficient to satisfy the dietary needs of individuals, free from adverse substances, and acceptable within a given culture; The accessibility of such food in ways that are sustainable and that do not interfere with the enjoyment of other human rights.

The content of 'adequacy' is to some extent determined by prevailing social, economic, cultural, climatic, ecological, and other conditions, but there are some core elements which are applicable under all circumstances and are spelled out in greater detail by the Committee. 'Sustainability' incorporates the notion of long-term availability and accessibility and is intrinsically linked to the notion of adequate food or food security, implying food being accessible for both present and future generations.

In clarifying the content of the term 'adequate,' the General Comment (paras 7–11) lays out in some detail the meaning of the subconcepts of dietary needs, absence of adverse substances, and cultural or consumer acceptability. The concept of 'sustainability' is explained in terms of availability and accessibility – both physical and economic – for different groups of people (paras 12–13). This level of detail is very useful, as it offers an opportunity for more nuanced reporting by States Parties on the realization of the right to adequate food, which only attains full meaning when 'food' also reflects the enjoyment of other rights which will ultimately determine accessibility and constitutes a true carrier of nutritional health.

In general terms, the legal obligations of States Parties to the ICESCR, set out in Article 2 of the Covenant, are clarified in paragraphs 14–16 of the General Comment, based on a study by the present author of a study for the UN Sub-Commission completed in 1987,[2] which was intended as a contribution to the clarification of the nature and levels of State obligations under economic and social rights.

I there introduced an analytical framework under which State obligations can be assessed on three levels: the obligation to respect, the obligation to protect, and the obligation to assist and fulfill human rights. State obligations must be seen in the light of the assumption that human beings, families, or wider groups seek to find their own solutions to their needs. States should, at the primary level, respect the resources owned by the individual, their freedom to find a job of preference, to make optimal use of their own knowledge, and the freedom to take the necessary actions and use the necessary resources – alone or in association with others – to satisfy their own needs.

The State cannot, however, passively leave it at that. Third parties are likely to interfere negatively with the possibilities that individuals or groups otherwise might have had to solve their own problems and meet their own needs. At a secondary level, therefore, State obligations require active protection against other, more assertive or aggressive subjects' more powerful economic interests, such as protection against fraud, against unethical behavior in trade and contractual relations, against the marketing and dumping of hazardous or dangerous products. This protective function of the State is widely used and is the most important aspect of State obligations with regard to economic, social, and cultural rights, similar to the role of the State as protector of civil and political rights.

At the tertiary level, the State has the obligation to facilitate opportunities by which the rights listed can be enjoyed. This takes many forms, some of which are spelled out in the relevant instruments. For example, with regard to the right to food, the State shall, under the International Covenant (Article 11, para 2), take steps to improve measures of production, conservation, and distribution of food by making full use of technical and scientific knowledge and by developing or reforming agrarian systems.

At the fourth and final level, the State has the obligation to fulfill the rights of those who otherwise cannot enjoy their economic, social, and cultural rights. This fourth-level obligation increases in importance with increasing rates of urbanization and the decline of group or family responsibilities. Obligations towards the elderly and disabled, which in traditional agricultural society were taken care of by the family, must increasingly be borne by the State and thus by the national society as a whole.

The Committee generally endorsed this approach in its General Comment No. 12 (para 15).

Economic and social rights, like all other human rights, are often violated, but there has been some controversy over what constitutes a violation of such rights, including the right to food. This is dealt with in the General Comment (paras 17–20). Violations of the Covenant occur when a State fails to ensure the satisfaction of, at the very least, the minimum essential level required to be free from hunger. Resource constraints do not free the government from responsibility; it still has to show that every effort has been made to use all the resources at its disposal in an effort to satisfy, as a matter of priority, those minimum obligations. Any discrimination in access to food, as well as to means and entitlements for its procurement, constitutes a violation of the Covenant. Violations can occur through the direct action of States or other entities insufficiently regulated by States. Non-State actors also have responsibilities, and the State should provide an environment that facilitates implementation of these responsibilities. In regard to the private business sector, whether national or transnational, a code of conduct should be agreed upon and made use of.

STRATEGIES OF IMPLEMENTATION

Conditions differ widely between countries, and the most appropriate ways and means to ensure freedom from hunger and to implement the right to adequate food therefore also varies considerably. If they are true to the commitments, each State Party to the ICESCR and the Convention on the Rights of the Child must nevertheless take the measures required under the particular conditions prevailing in its own country to ensure that everyone is free from hunger, and thereupon move as quickly as possible to a situation where everyone can enjoy their right to adequate food. In so doing, the different levels of State obligations discussed above should be applied, using the particular combination of measures warranted by the national situation.

Every country should therefore have or develop a national strategy to implement the right to food. The first step in any such strategy should be to map the situation for different groups and different regions within the country, taking into account the differences that might exist on the basis of gender, ethnicity, or race, and between rural and urban areas. Such mapping is necessary to identify those who are food-insecure and to develop appropriate responses to food insecurity.

Food security is currently defined as access by all people at all times to the food needed for a healthy and active life. Achieving food security means ensuring that sufficient food is available, that supplies are relatively stable, and that those in need of food can obtain it. National food security would therefore mean that everyone has effective entitlements to adequate food or resources for food and that there is, in principle, enough food to go around. Achieving food security at household level means ensuring that sufficient food is available throughout the territory, that supplies are relatively stable, and that everyone within that territory in need of food has the capacity to obtain it in order to lead a healthy and productive life. Food insecurity is understood as the reverse: where some people at some or all times do not have access to adequate food and therefore cannot lead a healthy and active life.

Food security can therefore be seen as the corollary of the right to food: the State must take the necessary measures to ensure food security for everyone under its jurisdiction. In their national efforts to identify the groups which are food-insecure, States should review – periodically and/or when special circumstances cause significant changes, including serious economic depressions – who is likely to be affected and how different groups may be affected differently on the basis of chronic or transitory vulnerability.

Having identified the groups that are food-insecure, the national strategy should recreate food security for those groups and the population as a whole, formulate policies required for this purpose, and identify the resources available, including human resources that, through self-help, can contribute to meet the goals set. When new and severe resource constraints emerge, caused by a process of economic adjustment, economic recession, climatic conditions, or other factors, measures should be undertaken to ensure, as a minimum, that vulnerable population groups and individuals do not face hunger. This should be achieved through social programs, safety nets, and international assistance.

The realization of the right to food requires full attention also to other human rights. In the elaboration and implementation of the national strategy for the right to food, people's informed participation is essential. Appropriate decentralization can often be required to ensure that the particular conditions in the different regions of the country are taken into account. The central government must at all times remain responsible for ensuring the enjoyment of this and other human rights, i.e., because the dominant groups within particular regions can sometimes be insensitive to pockets of chronic hunger within their part of the territory.

Care must be taken to ensure sustainable management of natural and other resources required for access to food, including the management of land, water, and fishery resources. Furthermore, attention must be given to all aspects of the food chain, from production to consumption. Attention must further be given to the processing of food in order to ensure food safety, to the physical distribution of food in order to enable access for all, and to improving markets, *inter alia* in order to prevent misleading and potentially harmful influences. At the level of the consumer, adequate information is required on the composition of healthy diets. Sanitary conditions and clean water are essential in ensuring that the food actually consumed is safe.

The strategy should give particular attention to the need to prevent discrimination in access to food or resources for food. It should keep in mind the need to give particular attention to vulnerable groups and to the gender situation. Indigenous peoples and some minorities often suffer from more serious malnutrition than the average population, and we have seen that women in many societies face far greater difficulties than men. The strategy should therefore include, *inter alia*: guarantees of full and equal access, particularly for women, to economic resources including the right to inheritance and ownership of land and other property, credit, natural resources, and appropriate technology; measures to respect and protect self-employment and work which provides adequate remuneration to ensure a decent living for wage-earners and their families (as stipulated in Article 7a, para ii, of the ICESCR); maintaining registries on land rights (including forests) and fishing resources important for food production or other means of livelihood in rural areas; special legislation to protect the land rights of indigenous peoples and prevent forced evictions from their land; measures to protect or secure entitlements to land or other sources of livelihood among vulnerable smallholders, landless peasants, and the urban poor without discrimination as to race or ethnicity. It is also essential to ensure access to health, in particular for the child in conformity with Article 24 of the Convention on the Rights of the Child (which through ratifications has become binding on all States with the exception of Somalia and the USA). Also essential in order to avoid malnutrition for children is the necessity to ensure adequate opportunities and time to care for infants and small children.

GUIDELINES TO SUPPORT THE REALIZATION OF THE RIGHT TO FOOD

General Comment No. 12, adopted by the UN Committee on Economic, Social and Cultural Rights, was a major achievement in clarifying the content of the right to food and its corresponding obligations. Nevertheless, its reach is limited; it is only advisory, not binding, and is likely to be read and studied only by a limited circle of persons within the national administration and concerned individuals from academia and relevant non-governmental organizations (NGOs).

The NGOs that took a particular interest in the realization of the right to food and to be free from hunger[3] have, for a long time, advocated that a more operational code of conduct should be developed in order to guide States on how to implement the right to food. They obtained a partial success when, at the 2002 World Food Summit: Five Years Later, the Council of the FAO decided to establish an Intergovernmental Working Group for the Elaboration of a Set of Voluntary Guidelines to support

Member States' efforts to achieve the progressive realization of the right to food in the context of food security.

The Intergovernmental Working Group completed its work in September 2004 and presented the guidelines for the 127 session of the FAO Council, which adopted *'The Voluntary guidelines to support the progressive realization of the right to adequate food in the context of national food security'* in November 2004.[4] The objective of the guidelines is to provide practical guidance to States in the implementation of the right to food. They are based on the legal standards mentioned earlier in this chapter. The following guidelines are listed:

Guideline 1: Democracy, good governance, human rights, and the rule of law
Guideline 2: Economic development policies
Guideline 3: Strategies
Guideline 4: Market systems
Guideline 5: Institutions
Guideline 6: Stakeholders
Guideline 7: Legal framework
Guideline 8: Access to resources and assets (labor, land, water, genetic resources for food and agriculture, sustainability, and services)
Guideline 9: Food safety and consumer protection
Guideline 10: Nutrition
Guideline 11: Education and awareness-raising
Guideline 12: National resources
Guideline 13: Support for vulnerable groups
Guideline 15: Safety nets
Guideline 16: International food aid
Guideline 17: Monitoring, indicators, and benchmarks
Guideline 18: National human-rights institutions
Guideline 19: International dimensions.

It also contains a separate section on international measures, actions and commitments, dealing with international cooperation and unilateral measures, the role of the international community, technical cooperation, international trade, external debt, official development assistance, international food aid, partnerships with NGOs, civil society organizations (CSOs), and the private sector (corporations, enterprises).

The guidelines are likely to increase substantially the awareness of the right to food and to be free from hunger and the corresponding responsibility of States to ensure the enjoyment of that right. It is not possible to enter into a discussion of the different guidelines in this chapter, for reasons of space. It should be pointed out that very cautious language is sometimes used. While many guidelines use the phrase 'States should,' in other cases the phrase 'States may wish' is used. This reflects underlying differences of opinion among the States participating in the drafting. Nevertheless, a great step forward has been made in making the right to food and the freedom from hunger a concrete and operational concern.

ON 'RIGHTS-BASED DEVELOPMENT'

The term 'rights-based development' has appeared with increasing frequency in development discourse and has been taken on board, at least in principle, by several important donor organizations such as DFID, SIDA, and NORAD and by international agencies, funds, and programs such as UNICEF and UNDP (Nyamu-Musembi and Cornwall 2004). The term should be applicable to all countries, however; and human-rights-based approaches ought to become fully integrated into institutional and policy changes in developed countries as well. As defined by the Office of the High Commissioner of Human Rights,

> A rights-based approach to development is a conceptual framework for the process of human development that is normatively based on international human rights standards and operationally directed to promoting and protecting human rights.... It includes the following elements: express linkage to human rights, accountability, empowerment, participation, nondiscrimination and attention to vulnerable groups.[5]

The requirement to base human development on international standards has been repeatedly stressed in international human-rights instruments and in international conferences. It has already started with the obligations undertaken by States when becoming members of the United Nations and thereby becoming bound by the United Nations Charter, where Articles 1, 55, and 56 set the basis for human-rights commitments by States. It was reinforced by the International Bill of Human Rights, in particular, the Universal Declaration of Human Rights Article 28 provides that:

> Everyone is entitled to a social and international order in which the rights and freedoms in this Declaration can be fully realized.

The United Nations Declaration on the Right to Development (1986) proclaims in Article 1 that:

> The right to development is an inalienable human right by virtue of which every human person and all peoples are entitled to participate in, contribute to, and enjoy economic, social, cultural and political development, in which all human rights and fundamental freedoms can be fully realized.

In its Article 2 (para 3), it is stated that:

> States have the right and the duty to formulate appropriate national development policies that aim at the constant improvement of the well-being of the entire population and of all individuals, on the basis of

their active, free and meaningful participation in development and in the fair distribution of the benefits resulting therefrom.

The Vienna Declaration and Programme of Action (UN World Conference on Human Rights 1993), states in Article 1, that:

> The promotion and protection of human rights is the first responsibility of governments.

Since promotion and protection of human rights is the first responsibility of governments, they should be held accountable for their policies of development and change on the basis of human rights. That includes both their internal policies and their policies at the international level. At least, they must be held accountable to ensure that they avoid engaging in any international obligation that undermine their own capability to implement human rights at home. They should also be held accountable to ensure that their policies do not harm the capacity of other States to implement human rights in their society.

The linkage to international human rights standards must be comprehensive, respecting the interdependence and indivisibility of human rights. Economic, social, and cultural rights must be given the same weight and importance as civil and political rights. This is what requires the greatest change as compared to present trends, and which is most strongly resisted by neoliberal ideologies.

ON THE RIGHT TO DEVELOPMENT

Reference has been made above to the Universal Declaration Article 28, which proclaims that everyone has a right to a social and international order in which the human rights can be fully realized. This brings in the question of duties of international cooperation in ensuring human rights, including the right to food and to be free from hunger.

The United Nations Charter Article 1 (para 3) sets out as one of the main purposes of the Organization to achieve international cooperation in solving international problems of an economic, social, cultural, or humanitarian character, and in promoting and encouraging respect for human rights and for fundamental freedoms for all without distinction as to race, sex, language, or religion.

This is further emphasized in Article 55 of the Charter:

> The United Nations shall promote higher standards of living, full employment, and conditions of economic and social progress and development; and solutions of international economic, social, health, and related problems; and international cultural and educational cooperation as well as universal respect for, and observance of, human rights and fundamental freedoms for all without distinction as to race, sex, language, or religion.

Under Article 56, all States Members of the United Nations pledge themselves to take joint and separate action in cooperation with the Organization for the achievement of the purposes set forth in Article 55.

In order for States to have the capacity to pursue a rights-based development, other States and the international community as represented through international organizations should recognize the need for States to have the necessary space to adopt the measures required in line with Article 2 of the Covenant on Economic, Social and Cultural Rights. Under that Article, States have committed themselves to take measures to the maximum of their available resources with a view to achieving progressively the full realization of the rights contained in the Covenant. It is therefore essential that States do not commit themselves to international agreements that reduce that space for States that have difficulties in realizing those rights. This means, above all, that sufficient flexibility must exist in international agreements such as those of the WTO to make it possible for developing countries and countries in transition to take the necessary protective measures where required, while at the same time having full access to the markets of the developed countries, which do not need such protection.

The Declaration on the Right to Development, adopted by the UN General Assembly in 1986, has the following formulation in its Article 4:

> 1. States have the duty to take steps, individually and collectively, to formulate international development policies with a view to facilitating the full realization of the right to development.
> 2. Sustained action is required to promote more rapid development of developing countries. As a complement to the efforts of developing countries, effective international co-operation is essential in providing these countries with appropriate means and facilities to foster their comprehensive development.

Efforts to operationalize the terms of the Declaration on the Right to Development has given rise to considerable controversies within the United Nations, mainly regarding international obligations of assistance. The UN Commission on Human Rights appointed a so-called 'Independent Expert', the Indian professor of economics, Arjun Sengupta, to study the possible mechanisms by which the Declaration could be implemented. One of his proposals has been to adopt what he calls 'development compacts,' which he defines as

> a mechanism for ensuring that all stakeholders recognize the mutuality of obligations, so that the obligations of developing countries to carry out rights-based programmes are matched by reciprocal obligations of the international community to cooperate to enable the implementation of the programmes. The purpose of development compacts is to assure the developing countries that if they fulfil their obligations, the

programme for realizing the right to development will not be disrupted owing to lack of financing.[6]

The process of instituting a development compact involves several steps, which he has spelled out in his *Fifth Report to the UN Commission on Human Rights*. He proposes that initially the focus should be on realizing a few rights, such as the right to food, to health and to education, and to specify the obligations of both the national authorities and the international community.

CONCLUSIONS

An impressive set of legal standards is available. Regrettably, much of it is 'soft law,' at least in the sense that it there are no generally available enforcement mechanisms of these standards. Their impact depends primarily on their recognition and the degree to which they can be brought to influence political choices and legal behavior. This, however, can be much influenced by academics, including research institutions and think-tanks, by NGOs as agents of civil society, and by national institutions for human rights. Thus it is a challenge to us all, and in meeting that challenge we need all the insights we have from our respective academic disciplines and our practical experience, in order to find the optimal ways to move it forward.

Amartya Sen (1999, p. 160) argues in *Development as Freedom* that appropriate polices and actions can indeed eradicate the terrible problems of hunger in the modern world. Based on recent economic, political, and social analysis, it is possible to identify the measures that can bring about the elimination of famines and the abolition of chronic undernourishment.

What is needed is a more thoroughgoing recognition of the responsibility that governments have under international human rights law, and of the commitments undertaken by all members of the international community to ensure the fundamental right of everyone to be free from hunger. This will not only require responsive governments at the national level, making full use of available economic, political, and social tools of public action in line with human rights, but also a corollary duty of outside States and international organizations to assist the affected States in meeting their responsibility, in line with their commitment under the United Nations Charter Articles 55 and 56.

NOTES

[1]   Among the antecedents, mention must also be made of the World Nutrition Conference, held in Rome in 1974, where 'Freedom from Hunger' was explicitly included in the final Declaration.
[2]   UN Doc E/CN.4/Sub.2/1987/23: *The Right to Adequate Food as a Human Right*.
[3]   Prominent among these is FIAN: Food First International Action Network, headquartered in Germany.
[4]   The guidelines can be downloaded from the FAO homepage, http://www.fao.org/docrep/meeting/009/y9825e/y9825e00.htm
[5]   From the Office of the High Commissioner for Human Rights [see www.unhchr.ch/development/approaches.html].

[6] *Fifth Report of the Independent Expert on the Right to Development*; UN doc. E/CN.4/2002/WG.18/6 para 14 [available at http://ods-dds-ny.un.org/doc/UNDOC/GEN/ G02/152/39/PDF/G0215239.pdf? OpenElement].

REFERENCES

Banik, D., 2003. *Democracy, Drought and Starvation in India: Testing Sen in Theory and Practice.* University of Oslo Unipub. ISBN 82-570-4862-3.

Nyamu-Musembi, C. and A.Cornwall,2004. *What is the "rights-based approach" all about? Perspectives from international development agencies* . Sussex: IDS Working Paper 234

Sen, A., 1981. *Poverty and Famines.* Oxford: Clarendon Press.

Sen, A., 1999. *Development as Freedom.* Oxford: Oxford University Press.

Woodham-Smith, C., 1961. *The Great Hunger: Ireland 1845–1849.* London: Penguin Books.

MILLENNIUM DEVELOPMENT GOALS
AND OTHER GOOD INTENTIONS

> On the other hand those sophists who profess to teach politics seem to be very far from actually doing so. They are in fact absolutely ignorant both of the nature of the subject and of the matters with which it deals; otherwise they would not equate it with, or rate it even lower than, rhetoric (Aristotle 1955, p. 341).

During the last two centuries the world has experienced dramatic moral changes. Very few officials today defend colonialism, apartheid, slavery, torture, or genocide. There are more democratic governments than ever before. The world as a whole has never been richer, and the global communication revolution has made almost everybody more aware and informed about the world outside his or her own location. At the same time, however, 2.8 billion people (or 46% of the world's population) live below the US$2 a day poverty line and 1.2 billion people (or 24% of the total) live in extreme poverty (below US$1 a day). Current trends suggest that the number of people living in extreme poverty will increase to 1.44 billion by 2015 (World Bank 2000/2001). Some regions of the world are making progress, while in other regions the poverty situation is getting worse. In 1998, South Asia and Sub-Saharan Africa accounted for 70% of people who are poor; up 10 percentage points since 1987.

After World War II a new 'global ethic' was institutionalized in the creation of the United Nations, with its Charter and the Universal Declaration of Human Rights (UDHR). The Charter states explicitly that the purpose of the United Nations is to promote peace, justice, and human rights. Over the last 50 years, the UN has launched 'development decades,' an almost endless number of initiatives (particularly on Africa), arranged a large number of global conferences and summits, and adopted hundreds of conventions and declarations – all intended to eradicate world poverty. In September 2000, at the largest ever meeting of Heads of States and governments – the Millennium Summit – a broad agenda for change was adopted, including the halving, by the year 2015, of the proportion of people who are poor and who suffer from hunger.

It is already very clear that unless something very dramatic happens, these two development targets will not be achieved by a large number of developing countries, particularly in Sub-Saharan Africa. Are those who prepare these documents and who adopt them so easily a new generation of 'sophists,' who are 'ignorant of the nature of the subject and of the matter with which it deals'? Are these documents

P. Pinstrup-Andersen and P. Sandøe (eds.), Ethics, Hunger and Globalization: In Search of Appropriate Policies, 111–129.
© 2007 *Springer.*

and all the speeches presenting and promoting them just rhetoric, or are there other reasons for the almost permanent gap between what is agreed upon and what is happening in practice?

This chapter attempts to clarify some reasons for this 'gap' and provide some suggestions on how to reduce or close the gap. The Millennium Development Goals (MDGs) will be analyzed as a concrete case. It is clear today that 'business-as-usual' will not achieve, by the year 2015, the MDGs on reduction of poverty and hunger, even if significant new additional funds are made available. What needs to change in order to avoid this continuing global catastrophe?

A conceptual framework for analyzing the rhetoric/action gap will help. Such a framework is presented below

CONCEPTUAL FRAMEWORK

Any problem in society, and possible solution to the problem, has both a scientific and an ethical dimension. Science is based on facts and progresses through observation and experimentation (deduction or induction). Science tells us what is and what can be. Ethics is based on human values and progresses through dialogue and struggle. Ethics tells us what should or ought to be. Science may influence ethics (such as the change in many people's attitude to people living with AIDS when it was made clear that HIV cannot be transmitted through a handshake) and ethics may influence science (such as the prohibition of stem-cell research).

Both science and ethics can be divided into theory and practice. These are dialectically related; one has no full meaning without the other. Theory informs practice and practice informs theory. Or, as Einstein put it, 'There is nothing more practical than a good theory.' A theory determines what we look for (Kuhn 1970). If, for example, the ethical base of a theory excludes human rights, we would hardly look for any human-rights violations.

Figure 7.1 illustrates the different dimensions of a social problem. With this framework, the rhetoric/action gap can be translated into a gap between theory and practice. An objective of this chapter is to examine the role of ethics with regard to this gap.

While scientific discovery normally provides new opportunities for improved practice, changes in ethics may improve or worsen the practice, depending on what ethics dominate. An ethics promoting individualism or egoism will certainly result in a significantly different practice than an ethics promoting communitarianism. The important thing is to fully recognize that all practice has an ethical base.

In order to close the rhetoric/action gap, we need to examine the ethical dimension or base for both the theory (plans, declarations, etc.) and the practice – the resulting actions. The desirable actions are those that contribute to 'development.'

Whatever we may mean by 'development,' it has at least two dimensions. Development requires the satisfaction of at least two conditions: the achievement of a

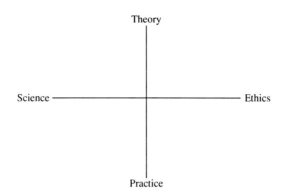

Figure 7.1 The four different dimensions of a social problem

desirable *outcome* and the establishment of an adequate *process* to achieve and sustain that outcome. Most of the MDGs, for example, represent specific, desirable outcomes.

Judging which outcomes are 'desirable' is a result of political processes. There is, however, a surprisingly strong agreement on desirable development outcomes, as manifest by the almost universal agreement on the MDGs. On the other hand, there is considerable disagreement on what constitutes a 'good' process. Most development scholars promote participation, local ownership, empowerment, and sustainability as necessary characteristics of a high-quality process. It will be argued later in this chapter that a human-rights-based approach provides a more clear and useful set of conditions.

Development requires a high-quality process to achieve such outcomes. Participation, local ownership, empowerment, and sustainability are essential characteristics of a high-quality process. Level of outcome and quality of process define a two-dimensional space for social action, as illustrated in Figure 7.2.

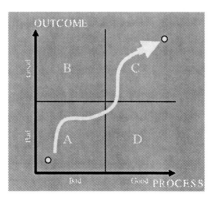

Figure 7.2 Outcome and process in development

Most development starts at A, and the ideal final stage is C. Unfortunately, many development programs move into one of the two areas represented by B or D. The former represents a good outcome at the expense of, for example, sustainability (an aspect of a good process), and is as ineffective as D – a good process without a significant desirable outcome. Some UNICEF-supported immunization programs in the 1980s rapidly moved into B but proved to be unsustainable; while some local, community-oriented programs moved into D but proved impossible to scale up. The ideal path is a progressive achievement of a desirable outcome through the gradual establishment of a 'good' process (the pathway from A to C in Figure 7.2).

In conclusion, the rhetoric/action gap is a gap between theory and practice. As practice is very much a result of the theory adopted, we need to examine current dominant development theories. This chapter will only address the implications of the choice of ethical base for the globalized free-market economic theory, in order to understand the gap between theory and practice.

ECONOMICS AND ETHICS

For a long time, development theory was dominated by neoclassical economists. Gradually, economists started to include non-economic factors, such as health, in their analysis and planning. In most cases, however, the inclusion of these factors was defended for their long-term contribution to economic growth. Development was soon redefined as human development (UNDP 1990), and later as sustainable human development (UNDP 1995).

Almost all of these are 'goal-oriented' or 'outcome-focused,' with limited attention being given to the quality and legitimacy of the process. Sustainability, a process aspect, was seldom implemented in practice. UNDP, the initiator of 'human development,' recognized this weakness in their *Human Development Report* (UNDP 2000):

> Although human development thinking has always insisted on the importance of the process of development, many of the tools developed by the human development approach measure the outcomes of social arrangement in a way that is not sensitive to how these outcomes were brought about.

Current globalization is dominated by the economic globalization based on the theory of free-market economics. Some people claim that the current type of globalized free-market economy is unethical, while others believe that economics and ethics should be kept apart (Langlois 2003). Neither is correct, because all economic theories have an ethical dimension or base, and this dimension cannot be separated from the theory. There is no such thing as value-free economic theory. The issue is therefore not to criticize economics as unethical, but rather to endeavor to achieve a better ethical base. There aremany kinds of 'ethics.' Any textbook on ethics describes different types of ethics, including the ethics of divine command, the ethics of selfishness, the ethics of duty, the ethics of rights, and the ethics of justice (Hinman 2003).

During the last few years, free-market economics is no longer primarily defended for its efficiency, but is instead promoted as an ideology with a very particular ethical base. The statement below, made by a former World Bank economist, illustrates how economics may be determined by a particular ethical position:

> Shouldn't the World Bank be encouraging more migration of the dirty industries to the less developed countries? I think the economic logic behind dumping a load of toxic waste in the lowest-wage country is impeccable and we should face up to that; I have always thought that under-populated countries in Africa are vastly under-polluted (McCorquodale and Fairbrother 1999).

The ethics of current free-market economic theory promotes aggregate economic growth, profit maximization, individualism, non-intervention and minimal intervention, and public expenditure by the State. This ethic includes the realization of civil and political rights through (procedural) democracy, good governance, and the rule of law, but rejects the legitimacy of economic, social, and cultural rights. As mentioned earlier, neoclassical economic theory has dominated economic theory for a long time. An early reaction to the immorality of this theory came from people who developed and promoted *development ethics*.

In conclusion, economic theory, including the currently dominant free-market economics, has, like all social theories, an ethical dimension or ethical base. It is important to understand this base and to challenge its validity. This, however, is not a scientific challenge; it is political, ideological, and ultimately represents a struggle for a more humane ethics.

DEVELOPMENT ETHICS

The push for economic growth dominated development thinking in the 1960s, but there was also growing criticism from those who perceived that even the best-intended policies and programs could have a detrimental impact on people who are poor. These thinkers called for a new focus on development ethics (Crocker 1991). As Denis Goulet, the father of development ethics, stated: 'Development needs to be redefined, demystified and thrust into the area of moral debate' (Goulet 1971, 1980, 1983).

A large number of philosophers, political scientists, and development economists support this position, emphasizing the belief that development should be guided not only by science, but also by ethics. Few of them seem to have recognized that neoclassical economic theory is not value-free; it has, as with all economic theories, a very particular ethical base.

Economists who promoted the economic-growth approach to development gradually responded by shifting attention from the macro to the micro level. The well-being function was extended to include the meeting of 'basic needs,' in addition to per capita real income. This approach was initiated and supported by Robert McNamara, then President of the World Bank, who referred to 'minimum needs,' as well as the 'basic needs' approach put forward by the International Labour Organization (ILO). Paul Streeten and others promoted 'redistribution with economic growth' as a means to satisfying both conditions (Chenery et al. 1974). Amartya Sen, both a philosopher and an economist, went further in promoting a normative approach to development (Chenery et al. 1974). He emphasized the need to develop 'cross-cultural moral minima' and to move from development *economics* to development *ethics*. He argued that development must be about people and must therefore focus on building people's capacities. Amartya Sen is, indeed, the most influential promoter of development ethics (see Sen 1987, 1997).

Amartya Sen and Mahbub ul Haq were both associated with the UNDP's work in the late 1970s and played an important role in the preparation of its first *Human Development Report* in 1990. This report launched, in a most convincing way, the human development approach, which has dominated the work of most UN development agencies since that time. The approach argues that development is about building people's capacities to 'live the life they value.'

It has not been fully recognized that James P. Grant, former Executive Director of UNICEF, was one of the greatest practitioners of development ethics. Without any reference to human rights, he accused the world of being absurd and obscene when millions of young children were dying of easily preventable diseases. He made a very clear distinction between science – which can tell us what is, was, and can be – and ethics, which tells us what ought to be. Many people criticized development ethics as being utopian. Reflecting Kant's famous statement that 'Ought must be preceded by can – it is otherwise Utopia,' Grant developed the concept of 'do-ability.' In trying to realize desirable, ethically defined goals, we can only proceed as fast as possible. UNICEF should thus select 'do-able' interventions.

A very good example of Grant's approach was Andrea Cornia and Richard Jolly's critique of IMF/World-Bank-supported 'structural adjustment programs' in developing countries. Their convincing analysis and forceful promotion of 'structural adjustment with a human face' changed the policies of institutions adopting the Bretton Woods system (Cornia et al. 1987).

Most thinkers and practitioners of development ethics avoided human rights. There were several reasons for that. First, many people equated human rights with civil and political rights, and thought that human rights were too political. Often when human rights were brought up in UNICEF meetings, the response was, 'UNICEF is not Amnesty International.' It is an embarrassing fact that the Convention on the Rights of the Child was not a UNICEF initiative and that UNICEF did not play any active role in the first eight years of its preparation. Second, human rights and human development were seen as very different areas of work. There was only limited contact between development and human-rights organizations, both among UN agencies and international non-governmental organizations (NGOs). Third, most human-rights scholars and activists used a complicated legal language, not understood by anyone except themselves. This language confused, scared, and sometimes threatened people working with development. Fourth, and finally, donor government representatives in the General Assembly and the Boards of the UN funding agencies seldom promoted a human-rights approach themselves, because they did not do that in their own bilateral international assistance agencies.

This all changed with the end of the Cold War, which opened the door for the Secretary-General of the UN to launch his UN Reform. Since then almost all UN agencies and several bilaterals have made strong efforts to translate human rights into an operational program strategy.

In order to better appreciate the fundamental change by the UN Reform, and particularly the Millennium Declaration and the Common Understanding, the human-rights approach adopted by most UN agencies needs to be explained.

A HUMAN-RIGHTS APPROACH[1]

In all cultures, throughout history, every society has had, and still has, a set of norms for what is right and wrong, permissible or not permissible, legitimate and not legitimate. These norms in general regulate the relationships between individuals or actors at different levels of society, including the State. Today only a few States publicly justify systematic denials of recognized human rights (Donnelly 1984). Many people, however, still see a conflict between human rights and development. Donnelly (1984) suggests two possible trade-offs: (1) the equality trade-off (compromising equity in order to allow rapid capital accumulation and economic growth, and (2) the liberty trade-off (denial of some civil and political rights in order first to address underdevelopment). Both of these trade-offs are, of course, unacceptable in a human-rights-based approach.

An easy way to define human rights would be to say that human rights are those entitlements codified in human-rights covenants and conventions. Such a definition, however, is too dogmatic and not very useful for a human-rights-based approach to programming (HRBAP). It would also miss the point that human rights are human constructs, which means that new rights will be constructed and gradually codified. The codification is the end of the process, not the beginning.[2]

Human rights represent a relationship between an individual (*subject* of the right) with a valid claim *and* another individual or group (including the State) with a correlative duty (*object* of the right). A subject of a right becomes a *claim* (or *right*)-*holder*, while the object of the right takes on the role of *duty-bearer*. Further, a human right is both a right *to* something (for example, basic education) and a right *against* somebody (for example, teachers). This is different from an 'entitlement,' which has no correlative duty-bearer.

Most scholars in the area of international human-rights law only recognize obligations on the part of the State. The Convention of the Rights of the Child is an exception, because parents (or other caretakers) are also recognized as duty-bearers. In an HRBAP there is a need to extend the claim–duty relationships to include all relevant subjects and objects at subnational, community, and household levels. It is interesting to note that the Preambles of both the International Covenant of Civil and Political Rights (ICCPR) and the International Covenant on Social, Economic, and Cultural Rights (ICSECR) support such an interpretation, stating:

> Realising that the individual, having duties to other individuals and to the community to which he belongs, is under a responsibility to strive for the promotion and observance of the rights recognised in the present Covenant.

Similarly, Article 29 in the Universal Declaration of Human Rights (UDHR) states that human rights are not limited to the relations between citizens and the State.

It is important to recognize that most individuals enter into the roles of claim-holding and duty-bearing at the same time, but always in relation to actors at different levels of society or in relation to different rights. A teacher, for example, has a duty to children to provide good-quality teaching, and at the same time has a claim against the government to receive a salary.

It is equally important to realize that individuals very often cannot meet their duties because some of their rights have been violated. Parents, for example, have a duty to provide food for their children, but may fail to do so due to the lack of a job or cultivable land. In such cases, parents cannot be held accountable for not providing food for their children.

This system of claim–duty relationships is called the *pattern of rights*, and must be identified and understood in a HRBAP.

The identification of duty-bearers and a determination of the extent of their accountability are crucial to a human-rights-based approach to programming. International human-rights law declares that signatories to a UN Convention have three types of obligations: to respect, protect, and fulfill. The obligation to fulfill includes obligations to 'facilitate' and 'provide.' The duties described below should be equally applied to all duty-bearers (Eide 1989).

- *The Obligation/Duty to Respect* requires the duty-bearer to refrain from interfering directly or indirectly with the enjoyment of the right.
- *The Obligation/Duty to Protect* requires the duty-bearer to take measures that prevent third parties from interfering with the enjoyment of the right.
- *The Obligation/Duty to Fulfill (Facilitate)* requires duty-bearers to adopt appropriate legislative, administrative, budgetary, judicial, promotional, and other measures toward the full realization of the right.
- *The Obligation/Duty to Fulfill (Provide)* requires duty-bearers to directly provide assistance or services for the realization of the right.

Human-rights principles and human-rights standards are important concepts in human-rights work. Over the years, conventions, declarations, and individual scholars have suggested different sets of human-rights principles. There is also confusion about the difference between 'principles' and 'standards.' In order to better clarify the relationship between a human-development and a human-rights-based approach, the following definitions are used. A 'human-rights standard' defines the *minimum acceptable level of an outcome*, while a 'human-rights principle' specifies the criteria for an acceptable process to achieve an outcome. For example a 'standard' in relation to the Right to Food would be: (1) availability and adequacy, (2) accessibility, and (3) stability of food supply. The Office of the High Commissioner on Human Rights (OHCHR) is currently working on a list of human-rights standards. The original core human-rights 'principles' were: respect for human dignity, non-discrimination, right to life, and development, participation, and accountability. The Independent Expert on the Right to Development has suggested the following: equity, non-discrimination, participation, accountability, and transparency (Sengupta 2004). A more complete set, and the one recommended here, was suggested by UNDP (2003) and is defined below.

- Universality and Indivisibility
- Equality and Non-Discrimination
- Participation and Inclusion
- Accountability and Rule of Law

A human-rights approach to development pays equal attention to outcome and process. This is why there is a fundamental difference between the achievement of a *standard* and the realization of a right (*standards* and *principles*). A non-democratic or authoritarian government may very well achieve human-rights standards, but these are, at best, privileges that can be withdrawn at any time by the government. It is most like a form of charity. The realization of human rights requires that the individual is in a position to make demands on others (i.e., duty-bearers); to claim their rights against somebody else. This, however, does not mean that just because an individual cannot claim his or her right that the individual does not have that right. Slaves did have the right to freedom before they were in a position to realize that right.

Similarly, rights are different from promises and entitlements. Neither of these has a correlative duty-bearer or entails any obligation. A human-rights approach provides a transparent pattern of claim–duty relationships which define accountabilities at all levels of society.

After the 'pattern of rights' has been identified and agreed upon, the causes of the non-realization of specific rights need to be identified. Excluding evil behavior, reasons for the non-realization of human rights are: (1) lack of capacity of claimholders to claim their rights, and (2) lack of capacity of duty-bearers to meet their duties. Capacity is broadly defined as: (1) responsibility, (2) authority, (3) access and control of human, economic, and organizational resources, capability to communicate, and capability for rational decision-making. If I accept the responsibility that I *should* act; if I have the authority that I *may* act; and if I have the resources so I *can* act; then I can be held accountable for my action or non-action.

The 'pattern of rights' in society can therefore be translated into a 'pattern of accountabilities.' This pattern builds a link between theory and practice. The actions should all aim at building capacities of claim-holders to claim their rights and of duty-bearers to meet their duties. Capacity and capacity development can be monitored and the latter can be cost-estimated. There will be a clear link between theory and practice. The rhetoric/action gap will be reduced or will disappear. The question then is: Would governments and agencies accept such a clear accountability link and such a transparency?

THE UN REFORM AND THE MILLENNIUM DECLARATION

In 1997 the Secretary-General of the UN launched a program of UN reform with a clear emphasis on human rights. In a statement to the Commission on Human Rights two years later he explained:

> As the Secretary-General of the United Nations I have made human rights a priority in every programme the United Nations launches and in every mission we embark on. I have done so because the promotion and defence of human rights is at the heart of every aspect of our work and every article of our Charter (UN Secretary-General to the Commission on Human Rights 1999).

In September 2000 the largest ever number of Heads of State and Governments gathered at a summit in New York, which ended successfully with the adoption of the Millennium Declaration. The Millennium Declaration (UN General Assembly 2000) represents an agreement among Heads of State and Governments on
1. values and principles
2. peace, security, and disarmament
3. development to end poverty
4. protecting our common environment
5. human rights, democracy, and good governance
6. protecting the vulnerable
7. meeting the special needs of Africa
7. strengthening the United Nations.
It is a comprehensive plan for the further implementation of the UN Charter. If implemented, the world would become 'more peaceful, prosperous, and just.' Most UN agencies and bilaterals, however, have reduced the Millennium Declaration to the 11 development goals (MDGs), defined in two paragraphs of the 32-paragraph-long document. Six of these goals are targeted, all defining desirable outcomes. Of the other five goals, four are related to the process. The Declaration, however, contains 39 additional goals, most of them necessary for a sustainable and acceptable process, many of them referring explicitly to human-rights principles. This was recently stressed by the Secretary-General, as quoted by the UNDP administrator, Mark Malloch Brown, who wrote that Kofi Annan had recently

> chided me and others for concentrating so much on the eight Millennium Development Goals that we forget that they are part of the Millennium Declaration, which calls very strongly for democracy and human rights as the route to achieving the goals (UNDP 2004).

The successful effort by many agencies and governments to separate and focus on the MDGs outside of the overall context of the Millennium Declaration is political in nature.

In September 2001 the UN Secretary-General presented a report to the General Assembly entitled *Road Map Towards the Implementation of the United Nations Millennium Declaration* (UN General Assembly 2001). This 'Road Map' is a 60-page, detailed document outlining strategies for action to meet the goals of the Millennium Declaration. Although it is stated (para 201) that 'Human rights are also a central tenet of the UN Reform, which emphasizes the centrality of human rights in all activities of the system,' this is not reflected in most sections of the report. Section III, 'Development and Poverty Eradication: The Millennium Declaration Goals,' for example, is totally focused on sustainable human development. The use of a human-rights approach is never mentioned.

In conclusion, the Road Map brings up human rights, but by no means emphasizes 'the centrality of human rights in all activities of the system.' The focus is on the MDGs, not on the Millennium Declaration as a whole.

The next step was taken in September 2002, when the General Assembly adopted a Report of the Secretary-General entitled *Strengthening of the United Nations; An Agenda for Change* (UN General Assembly 2002), which recommends 35 key actions to reform the organization. Action 2 is of particular importance for a HRBAP. It states:

> The United Nations High Commissioner for Human Rights will develop and implement a plan, in cooperation with the UNDG and the ECHA, to strengthen human-rights-related United Nations actions at the country level.

The Millennium Declaration had recommended two major objectives: (1) to build strong human-rights institutions at the country level, and (2) to incorporate human rights into country-level analysis, planning, and program implementation.

A three-year Plan of Action has been proposed, with the following three objectives:

1. UN country teams will have internalized the fundamental nature of human rights to their missions as well as its implications for their humanitarian and development work.
2. UN country assistance frameworks in development and humanitarian circumstances will systematically build upon human rights norms and principles in their analysis, programming, and implementation.
3. Observations and recommendations of the treaty-monitoring bodies of human-rights treaties of the United Nations system as well as the special procedures of the Commission on Human Rights will be taken into account by the UN actions at the country level.

Most UN agencies have made serious efforts to operationalize a HRBAP. UNDP and UNICEF have been in the forefront. The work of a UN informal Working Group has been active during the last few years. A meeting was arranged in Princeton in 2002[3] and in Stamford in 2003.[4] At the Stamford meeting an agreement was reached by most participating agencies on a Common Understanding of a HRBAP. This agreement was summarized as follows:

1. All programs of development cooperation, policies and technical assistance should further the realization of human rights as laid down in the Universal Declaration of Human Rights and other human rights instruments.
2. Human rights standards contained in, and principles derived from, the Universal Declaration of Human Rights and other international human rights instruments guide all development cooperation and programming in all sectors and in all phases of the programming process.
3. Development cooperation contributes to the development of capacities of 'duty-bearers' to meet their obligations and/or of 'right-holders' to claim their rights.

The Common Understanding has been endorsed by the United Nations Development Group (UNDG).

It took six years from the launch of the UN Reform, which fully recognized the fundamental role of human rights in the work of the organization, to a consensus on what that should mean for development programming. UNICEF has played an important role in this work and the challenge now is to apply a HRBAP in all Country Programs of Cooperation. The need for a practical method has never been more urgent.

Based on the Common Understanding, participants at the Stamford meeting agreed on a set of necessary, specific, and unique characteristics for a program to qualify for being human-rights based.

1. Assessment and analysis in order to identify the human-rights claims of right-holders and the corresponding human-rights obligations of duty-bearers as well as the immediate, underlying, and structural causes of the non-realization of rights.
2. Programs need to assess the capacity of right-holders to claim their rights and of duty-bearers to fulfill their obligations. They then develop strategies to build these capacities.
3. Programs need to monitor and evaluate both outcomes and processes guided by human-rights standards and principles.
4. Programming is informed by the recommendations of international human-rights bodies and mechanisms.

During the development of HRBAP (both in theory and practice) it became increasingly clear that the many 'good programming practices' from years of learning become obligatory in HRBAP, and are therefore no longer optional (Jonsson 2003).

It is important, however, to recognize that the application of 'good programming practices' does not by itself constitute a HRBAP. They are a necessary, but not sufficient, condition.

When the MDGs are taken out of context we are no longer pursuing a human-rights approach; we no longer base our work on a 'non-ethnocentric global ethic' contained in the system of human rights. We are in danger of repeating the same mistake as that made by UNICEF in the 1990s, when the comprehensive World

Summit for Children's declaration was reduced to a limited number of 'WSC Goals,' reflecting some important human-rights standards. The unsustainability of some early achievements in immunization, particularly in Africa, showed that many young children had merely a short-lived privilege to be vaccinated, not a right.

The adoption of human-rights ethics as the base for development theory will both influence and depend on the future direction and content of the rapid ongoing globalization.

GLOBALIZATION AND ETHICS

There are almost as many definitions of 'globalization' as there are authors on the subject. McCorquodale and Fairbrother define 'globalization' as 'an economic, political, social and ideological phenomenon which carries with it unanticipated, often contradictory and polarizing consequences.' Most people agree that globalization has changed the role of the State from being a provider to ensuring an environment conducive for the adoption of a free market. Some even claim that globalization is threatening the sovereignty of the State. Falk (1994) defines 'globalization-from-above' as 'the collaboration between leading States and the main agencies of capital formation,' and 'globalization-from-below' as 'popular participation at local levels, the building of civil societies and the enhancement of non-governmental organizations.' He, however, incorrectly locates human rights in the second category only. A human-rights approach is both 'top-down' and 'bottom-up.' It is true that, in a human-rights approach, individuals are recognized to have rights (i.e., claims on others, in particular on duty-bearers at higher levels of society), which in turn have their valid claims even higher up in society, until we ultimately reach the obligations (duties) of the State ('bottom-up'). It is, however, equally true that the State has valid claims on duty-bearers at lower level of society, who in turn may have valid claims on duty-bearers at even lower levels ('top-down').The pattern of rights (claim–duty relationships) goes both ways.

It is not fully recognized that the UN system of human rights represents one of the most positive manifestations of the last 50 years of globalization. This is often the case with regard to people who only want to see the negative impact of globalization and therefore cannot see the opportunities a more globalized world can provide for the realization of a human-rights approach. Human rights represent a 'non-ethnocentric global ethic' or 'cross-cultural moral minimums' (Nussbaum and Sen 1989).

McCorquodale and Fairbrother (1999) see a positive relationship between economic globalization and the realization of human rights. This is often used as an argument to promote a strategy to give first priority to rapid economic growth, before doing anything directly for human rights. In most cases this position is the result of limiting human rights to civil and political rights, not recognizing economic, social, and cultural claims as human rights. The World Bank had already realized this in 1992, as stated in their *World Development Report* (World Bank 1996) by stressing 'management, accountability, rule of law, and information and transparency'; all, however, aiming at the creation of a stable and safe business climate.

In conclusion, globalization is too complex a phenomenon to deal with analytically and empirically. Globalization must be disaggregated and contextualized. A global free-market economy may increase the aggregate national economic growth for many countries, although far from all, including many of the poorest countries. Globalization often creates winners and losers, the latter having many of their rights violated. As Olof Palme, a former Prime minister of Sweden, once said

> A country needs economic growth and economic growth needs a 'tiger'; a free market is that 'tiger'; it is important to keep this 'tiger' in a cage – not to small and not too big' (O. Palme, personal communication).

A free market aims at economic efficiency, not social equity or the realization of human rights for all. In order to achieve equity there must be public action orchestrated by the State. Public goods are seldom profitable enough to attract private investment. On the other hand, globalization provides new opportunities for the promotion of a 'global ethics' – as embedded in a human-rights approach to development.

Globalization needs to be 'unpacked'. One useful way of doing that is to analyze the relationships between human rights, development, and democracy.

HUMAN RIGHTS, DEMOCRACY, AND DEVELOPMENT

Human rights, democracy, and development have one thing in common – they all represent unachievable human aspirations (Rescher 1987). There will never be a society in which all human rights are realized for everybody, where full and ideal democracy exists, or where development has reached its final stage. In spite of this, most countries strive towards these unachievable goals. It is therefore important to understand how they relate to each other.

At present all governments promote development, including poverty reduction; most governments officially promote human rights; but far fewer governments are democratic or promote democracy – some are even hostile to democracy. What is behind these differences? Basically, development is the least threatening concept for existing power structures; human rights can be realized progressively; but democracy is threatening too many non-democratic governments. Peace, justice, freedom, and human rights are the pillars in the UN Charter – democracy is never mentioned.

The Universal Declaration of Human Rights (Article 21) states: '... the will of the people shall be the basis of the authority of the government.' Democracy is not explicitly mentioned, and many non-democratic governments claim that they represent 'the will of the people.' The Vienna Declaration (United Nations 1992) is more explicit:

> Democracy is based on the free will of the people to determine their own
> political, economic, social and cultural system and their full participation
> in all aspects of their lives.

In summary, democracy has not had the same ideological standing in the UN as
human rights has.

Even though many countries are still non-democratic, democracy today is seen
as the only acceptable and legitimate form of governance. It is therefore important
to understand the complex relationships between democracy, human rights, and
development – and particularly the relationship between democracy and human
rights.

If 'development' is not tautologically defined to include democracy, democracy
does not seem to be a prerequisite for development. Although democracies tend
to develop more rapidly, this is not universally the case. Some non-democratic
countries have experienced very rapid development, and some poor countries with
insignificant development during the last two decades are, in fact, democracies
(Donnelly 1999).

The key issue is to understand the relationship between democracy and human
rights. Is one a necessary precondition for the other?

First of all, why did so many more countries agree to promote human rights
(by ratifying and signing conventions)? A. J. Langlois points out that 'compared
to democracy, human rights hold a very powerful institutional position in the
international arena,' and that

> the UN, for all its faults, is crucial to the development of international
> human rights law and to the creation of an international milieu in which
> human rights are granted international recognition.

He identifies three reasons for the relative success of human rights:
1. *Recognition*: The fact that so many States *de facto* have ratified so many human-
   rights conventions (all States have ratified at least one convention)
2. *Institutionalization at the global level*: Governments ratify conventions for
   reasons of international legitimacy
3. *International human rights law*: Ratification means not only morally, but *legally*,
   binding agreements monitored by UN treaty bodies.

It thus becomes clear that recognition of human rights – including ratification of
UN conventions – does *not* require democracy. Many non-democratic governments
know that if they did not ratify certain conventions they would not continue to
receive development assistance or full international recognition.

These practices have led to the promotion of a 'separationist thesis,' which
basically argues that: 'Democracy is Western-centric, while human rights are
universal' (Spickard 1999). The progressive realization of human rights and the
promotion of democracy should therefore be separated. Democracy will take time,
while many human rights can be realized in non-democratic countries. Human
rights can be realized without democracy, so why wait? This position rests on

two critical assumptions: (1) Democracy *is* Western-centric, and (2) human rights are *not* Western-centric (Langlois 2003, p. 1004). The supporters of this thesis warn that unless these two issues are separated there will be a 'clash of civilizations' (Huntington 1993). The position that democracy is Western-centric has been particularly common in some Asian countries. The idea is that some human-rights values are not compatible with 'Asian values' and must therefore be rejected (Lawson 1998).

It is important to note that those governments most strongly in favor of a separation usually reject democracy because they claim that democracy is Western-centric, not because democracy would threaten a *status quo* that benefits the elite in the country. It is clear that such a position is not about democracy being Western-centric; it is about 'authoritarian governments using the discussion of cultures to stabilize their own authority' (Langlois 2003, p. 1007).

Langlois suggests five counter-arguments to the separationist thesis:

1. As a matter of fact, both democracy and human rights originate from Western culture. If one of these is Western-centric, the other will be Western-centric as well.
2. The ideas and practices of human rights and democracy are interdependent and linked. Historically the two pursue a common agenda. It is very difficult to see any difference between democratic values and human-rights values.
3. Human rights and democracy share the same origin in Western political liberalism, thus in a fully democratic country all human rights are realized, and if all human rights are realized we have a democracy.
4. There is a very important difference between human-rights standards and human-rights principles. Human-rights standards can be met in a non-democratic country. For example, the human-rights standard of universal primary education can be (and has been) met in some non-democratic countries with benevolent leaders. This, however, does not mean that education is a realized right, but that education is enjoyed as a *privilege*. A privilege cannot be claimed and can be withdrawn at any point in time, and is equivalent to charity (Sumner 1989).
5. Benevolent authoritarianism is undesirable, but it is better than non-benevolent forms of control. The separationist thesis tries to convince non-democratic governments to be benevolent. We should, of course, support that effort, but we should always be aware that such actions do not lead to or mean the realization of human rights, but only to the meeting of human-rights standards.

In conclusion, human-rights standards can be met in any country. As far as children are concerned, human-rights standards and basic needs are more or less the same. Meeting needs or human-rights standards, however, is not the same as realizing human rights. Human rights can only be achieved in a democracy. This is the major reason why efforts to meet the MDGs must be understood in the context of the Millennium Declaration. Implementation of the Millennium Declaration requires both democracy and human rights; the MDGs can be met without democracy, although this is less likely.

At a more conceptual level, democracy and human rights are dialectically related. Each one lacks its full meaning without the other. Democracy requires human rights and human rights require democracy. The achievement of sustainable human development calls for pursuing *both* democracy and human rights.

CONCLUSIONS

There is a significant gap between statements in conventions, declarations, global initiatives, and development plans and the action on the ground to implement them. This is what has been called the 'rhetoric/action gap' and reflects the gap between development theory and development practice. While the scientific aspects of the relationships between theory and practice are often examined and explained, the ethical aspects are seldom recognized or discussed. This has led to some observers demanding a stronger ethical consideration in current development work. Such a position, however, fails to appreciate the fact that current development theory and practice do have an ethical base, at least implicitly.

Neoliberal free-market ideology provides the ethical base for most development work at present. The problem is not the lack of ethics, but that the ethical base is not made explicitly visible and debated. Such a debate would clearly show that this ethical base does not recognize economic and social rights, or the need for public action to provide public goods, and limits democracy to procedural democracy.

The rhetoric/action gap can be reduced or closed by linking the rhetoric, often expressed in human-rights terms, with the action on the ground by adopting a human-rights-based approach to development programming (HRBAP). A HRBAP gives equal attention to the achievement of desirable outcomes and the required process for this achievement. The selection and prioritization of desirable outcomes is guided by human-rights standards, while the process is conditioned by human-rights principles. In a HRBAP, individuals or groups of individuals are explicitly linked in their claim-holding and duty-bearing roles in relation to specific rights. This 'pattern' of rights relationships provides a systematic and explicit base for the identification of accountabilities in development. A program or a project based on HRBAP aims at reducing or closing the capacity gaps of claim-holders to claim their rights and of duty-bearers to meet their duties. This progressively contributes to the respect, protection, and fulfillment of human rights. Monitoring and evaluation similarly need to give equal attention to outcomes and processes.

In a human-rights perspective, MDGs are goals and targets for desirable outcomes, reflecting relevant human-rights standards. The MDGs are important, but form only a small part of the Millennium Declaration. The current mono-focality on the MDGs fails to recognize this fact and could therefore lead to the reduction of the human-rights-based Millennium Declaration to a conventional goal-oriented development effort. The rhetoric/action gap will continue, or even widen.

Human rights and democracy are dialectically related. Real democracy requires the realization of all rights for all people, and the realization of all human rights for all people requires democracy. The promotion and adoption of a human-rights-based approach to development and programming will therefore simultaneously contribute to the reduction of the rhetoric/action gap and the promotion of democracy in society.

NOTES

[1] For a much more detailed presentation, see U. Jonsson, *Human Rights Approach to Development Programming*. UNICEF, Nairobi, 2003.
[2] See also on this topic: Jack Donnelly, *Universal Human Rights in Theory and Practice*, Cornell University Press, 1989; Scott Davidson, *Human Rights*, Open University Press, 1993; L.W. Sumner, *The Moral Foundation of Rights*, Clarendon Press, Oxford, 1989.
[3] UNDP, *Recommendations of Inter-Agency Workshop on Implementing a Human Rights Approach in the Context of the UN Reform*, Princeton, NJ, 24–26 January 2001.
[4] UNDP, *Report from the Second Inter-Agency Workshop on Implementing a Human Rights-Based Approach in the Context of UN Reform*, Stamford, USA, 5–7 May 2003.

REFERENCES

Aristotle, 1955. *Nicomachean Ethics*. Translated by J.A.K. Thompson. London: Penguin Classics.
Chenery, H., M.S. Ahluwalia, C.L.G. Bell, J.H. Duloy and R. Jolly, 1974. *Redistribution with Growth*. Oxford, UK: Oxford University Press.
Cornia, A., R. Jolly and F. Stewart, 1987. *Adjustment with a Human Face*. Oxford, UK: Oxford University Press.
Crocker, D.A., 1991. Toward development ethics. *World Development* 19: 457–483.
Donnelly, J., 1984. Human rights and development: Complementary or competing concerns? *World Politics* 36: 255–283.
Donnelly, J., 1999. Human rights, democracy and development. *Human Rights Quarterly* 21: 608–632.
Eide, A., 1989. *The Right to Adequate Food as a Human Right*. Study prepared for the United Nations Centre for Human Rights, Study Series No. 1. Geneva and New York: United Nations Center for Human Rights.
Falk, R., 1994. The making of global citizenship. In: van Steenborgen, B., ed. *The Condition of Citizenship*. Thousand Oaks, CA: Sage, pp. 127–140.
Goulet, D., 1971. Obstacles to world development: An ethical reflection. *World Development* 11: 609–624.
Goulet, D., 1980. Development experts: The one-eyed giants. *World Development* 8: 481–489.
Goulet, D., 1983. *The Cruel Choice: A New Concept in the Theory of Development*. New York: Atheneum.
Hinman, L.M., 2003. *Ethics: A Pluralistic Approach to Moral Theory*, 3rd edn. Belmont, CA: Wadsworth Publishing Company.
Huntington, S., 1993. The clash of civilizations. *Foreign Affairs* 72: 22–49.
Jonsson, U., 2003. *Human Rights Approach to Development Programming*. UNICEF. Eastern and Southern Africa Regional Office, Nairobi, pp. 38–41.
Kuhn, T., 1970. *The Structure of Scientific Revolutions*, 2nd edn. Chicago, IL: University of Chicago Press.
Langlois, A.J., 2003. Human rights without democracy? A critique of the separationist thesis. *Human Rights Quarterly* 25: 990–1019.
Lawson, S., 1998. Democracy and the problem of cultural relativism: Normative issues for international politics. *Global Society* 12: 251–270.
McCorquodale, R. and R. Fairbrother, 1999. Globalization and human rights. *Human Rights Quarterly* 21: 735–766.

Nussbaum, M.C. and A. Sen, 1989. Internal criticism and Indian rational traditions. In: Krausz, M., ed. *Relativism, Interpretations and Confrontation*. University of Notre Dame Press.

Rescher, N., 1987. *Ethical Idealism: An Inquiry into the Nature and Function of Ideals*. Berkeley and Los Angeles, CA: University of California Press.

Sen, A., 1987. *On Ethics and Economics*. Oxford: Basil Blackwell.

Sen, A., 1997. Human rights and Asian values. *New Republic* 14–21 July: 33–40.

Sengupta, A., 2004. Human right to development. Paper presented at the Nobel Symposium, Oslo, Norway.

Spickard, J.V., 1999. Human Rights, Religious Conflict, and Globalisation. Ultimate Values in a New World **Order**. *International Journal on Multicultural Societies* 1: 2–19.

Sumner, L.W., 1989. *The Moral Foundation of Rights*. Oxford: Clarendon Press, pp. 18–53.

UN General Assembly, 2000. *General Assembly Resolution 55/2, United Nations Millennium Declaration*, 18 September 2000; *General Assembly Resolution 55/162, Follow-up to the Outcome of the Millennium Summit*, 18 September 2000.

UN General Assembly, 2001. *Road Map Towards the Implementation of the United Nations Millennium Declaration*. Report of the Secretary-General, 6 September 2001.

UN General Assembly, 2002. *Strengthening of the United Nations: An Agenda for Change*. Report of the Secretary-General, 9 September 2002.

UN Secretary-General to the Commission on Human Rights, 1999. *Speech*, 7 April 1999.

United Nations, 1992. *The World Conference on Human Rights: Vienna Declaration and Programme of Action*. A/CONF. 157/23.

UNDP, 1990. *Human Development Report*. Oxford University Press.

UNDP, 1995. *Human Development Report*. Oxford University Press.

UNDP, 2000. *Human Development Report*. Oxford University Press, p. 22.

UNDP, 2003. *Poverty Reduction and Human Rights*. UNDP Practice Note.

UNDP, 2004. See http://www.undp.org, accessed June 2004.

World Bank, 1996. *The World Development Report 1996: From Plan to Market*. World Development Report.

World Bank, 2000/2001. *World Development Report 2000/2001: Attacking Poverty*, pp. 21–25.

WHAT WE KNOW ABOUT POVERTY
AND WHAT WE MUST DO: ETHICAL
AND POLITICAL ASPECTS OF EMPOWERMENT

INTRODUCTION

We all know the figures reflecting the gravity and scale of poverty in the world as the most serious moral issues of our time:

- That 1.1 billion people or 28% of the global population are absolutely poor, living on less than US$1 a day.
- Almost half the world population, or 2.7 billion people, are also poor, living on less than US$2 a day. Many of these people slide back into the category of absolutely poor, i.e., those earning less than US$1 a day, in years of bad crops, natural calamities, or economic recession.
- About 40% of the absolute poor (430 million) live in South Asia, 30% (or 316 million) in Sub-Saharan Africa, and about 5% (50 million) in Latin America and the Caribbean.
- At least 140 million children in the developing world are seriously undernourished. The vicious circle of poverty and hunger affects the ability of adults to work and to give birth to healthy children, further crippling the capacity of these children to learn and to lead healthy and productive lives.

We also know that nine years after the 1995 Copenhagen Social Summit, when the target to halve poverty by 2015 was first adopted; eight years after the 1996 World Food Summit, when the target of halving the number of hungry people was accepted; and four years after the Millennium Summit of 2000, the poverty and hunger situation has not improved much, as shown by various independent assessments of the Millennium Development Goals (MDGs):

- In percentage terms, there has been some reduction in the proportion of the global population, living on less than US$1 a day – from 28% in 1990 to 21% in 2001 (see Table 8.1). However, in absolute terms, the number of absolute poor has declined from 1.22 billion only to 1.09 billion, and much of that decrease is because of the sharp decline in the level of poverty in China from 490 million to 88 million. If China is excluded from the global figures, the overall incidence of poverty has in fact increased in the rest of the developing world in the past 10 years.
- The pace of reduction in the proportion of people suffering from hunger is even slower – from 19.8% in 1990 to 17.0% in 2001 (see Table 8.2). The absolute number of undernourished people has declined only marginally from

P. Pinstrup-Andersen and P. Sandøe (eds.), Ethics, Hunger and Globalization: In Search of Appropriate Policies, 131–147.

TABLE 8.1 Trends and forecasts for poverty

<table>
<tr><th></th><th colspan="9">REGION</th></tr>
<tr><th></th><th>East Asia</th><th>of which China</th><th>South Asia</th><th>of which China</th><th>Eastern Europe & Central Asia</th><th>Latin America & the Caribbean</th><th>Middle East & North Africa</th><th>Sub-Saharan Africa</th><th>TOTAL</th></tr>
<tr><td>1990 Number in poverty (millions)</td><td>472.2</td><td>374.8</td><td>462.3</td><td>357.4</td><td>2.3</td><td>49.3</td><td>5.5</td><td>226.8</td><td>1218.5</td></tr>
<tr><td>1990 Proportion in poverty (%)</td><td>29.6</td><td>33.0</td><td>41.3</td><td>42.1</td><td>0.5</td><td>11.3</td><td>2.3</td><td>44.6</td><td>27.9</td></tr>
<tr><td>2001 Number in poverty (millions)</td><td>271.3</td><td>211.6</td><td>431.1</td><td>358.6</td><td>17.6</td><td>49.8</td><td>7.1</td><td>315.8</td><td>1092.7</td></tr>
<tr><td>2001 Proportion in poverty (%)</td><td>14.9</td><td>16.6</td><td>31.3</td><td>34.7</td><td>3.7</td><td>9.5</td><td>2.4</td><td>46.9</td><td>21.1</td></tr>
<tr><td>2015 Forecast number in poverty (millions)</td><td>117.0</td><td>na</td><td>309.0</td><td>na</td><td>19.0</td><td>62.0</td><td>8.0</td><td>398.0</td><td>913.0</td></tr>
<tr><td>2015 Target number needed for MDG (millions)</td><td>301.8</td><td>229.8</td><td>347.7</td><td>258.5</td><td>1.2</td><td>35.0</td><td>4.4</td><td>197.4</td><td>849.4</td></tr>
<tr><td>2015 Forecast proportion in hunger (%)</td><td>5.8</td><td>n.a.</td><td>18.3</td><td>na</td><td>4.0</td><td>10.0</td><td>2.0</td><td>45.0</td><td>15.0</td></tr>
<tr><td>2015 Target proportion needed for MDG (%)</td><td>14.8</td><td>16.5</td><td>20.7</td><td>21.1</td><td>0.3</td><td>5.7</td><td>1.2</td><td>22.3</td><td>14.0</td></tr>
</table>

Notes and sources:

The figures for poverty are not comparable with the figures for hunger at the regional and total level, primarily because the composition of the regions varies between the two sources and because different population projections for 2015 are employed by the two sources.

The World Bank's *Global Economic Prospects 2004*, projects that 41 million people in China will be poor by 2015; however, this poverty forecast is inconsistent with the projections by Chen and Ravallion (2004) due to different underlying assumptions, especially those regarding inequality.

The target number needed to achieve the MDG was realized by applying the proportion needed for the MDG (last row of the table) to the projected population levels of 2015. For comparability, the population projections from Chen and Ravallion (2004) (World Bank population projections) were used.

TABLE 8.2 Trends and forecasts for hunger

| | REGION | | | | | | | |
	East Asia	of which China	South Asia	of which China	Latin America & the Caribbean	Near East & North Africa	Sub-Saharan Africa	TOTAL
1990–1992 Number in hunger (millions)	274.7	193.0	291.1	214.5	59.0	25.3	165.5	816.6
1990-1992 Proportion in hunger (%)	16.3	17.0	26.0	25.0	13.0	8.0	35.0	19.8
1999–2001 Number in hunger (millions)	210.8	135.3	293.1	213.7	53.4	40.9	198.4	797.9
1999–2001 Proportion in hunger (%)	11.6	11.0	22.0	21.0	10.0	10.0	33.0	17.0
2015 Forecast number in hunger (millions)	135	n.a	195	na	40	37	205	601.0
2015 Forecast proportion in hunger (percentage)	6	n.a	12	na	6	7	23	11.0
2015 Target number needed for MDG (millions)	171.5	119.2	219.1	155.8	40.8	20.1	150.0	572.1
2015 Target proportion needed for MDG (%)	8.1	8.5	13.0	12.5	60.5	4.0	17.5	9.9

Notes and Sources:

The figures for poverty are not comparable with the figures for hunger at the regional and total level, primarily because the composition of the regions varies between the two sources and because different population projections for 2015 are employed by the two sources.

The target number needed to achieve the MDG was realized by applying the proportion needed for the MDG (last row of the table) to the projected population levels of 2015. For comparability, the population projections from FAO (2003a) (UN population projections) were used.

816 million to 798 million. Again, if the reduction of 60 million achieved by China is excluded, the number of people suffering from hunger in the rest of the developing world was higher in 2001 than in 1990.

The root causes of poverty are deep and complex, and spring from the basic power structure of a society with its skewed distribution of land and the resultant economic system dominated by feudal, tribal, or ethnic elites. The benefits of economic growth or improvements in agricultural productivity in such a society will inevitably accrue to those who own the land and have access to irrigation water, credit, or markets; with the poor receiving some crumbs in the form of seasonal employment at the time of harvest or in post-harvest activities.

These inherent causes of poverty are further compounded by human-made policies that discriminate against the poor and deny them the opportunity to compensate for their lack of assets or other income-earning opportunities, through the acquisition of education and skills. A much larger proportion of the resources allocated for education and health services in most developing countries are, in practice, pre-empted by expensive schools, colleges, and hospitals in urban areas for the benefit of relatively well-off members of society.

Macro-economic policies in most developing countries have a persistent urban bias as they provide positive incentives and high tariff protection to industry, and negative protection to agriculture to provide cheap raw materials to industry and also to keep wages low through lower food prices. These adverse terms of trade not only affect overall agricultural incentives, but have a devastating effect on the livelihood of small and marginal farmers.

Renewed international concern with poverty reduction in the past decade has coincided with the advent of globalization, with its focus on the free-market philosophy. While an open trade regime and well-managed privatization is necessary for stimulating investment and growth, globalization, with its strong emphasis on reducing the role of the State in every sphere of activity, has not been very helpful in reducing poverty. The driving force of globalization is competition and, by definition, poor people and poor countries are at the lowest rung of the competitive ladder. The inherent limitations of an unregulated market system and the resultant need to protect the consumer, the small businesses, and the underprivileged communities are fully understood in the more advanced societies, leading to large-scale State interventions in different sectors of the economy. But at the global level and in devising policies for the international financial institutions (IFIs), these realities are often ignored.

The adjustment policies being advocated to the developing countries also have a negative impact on the poor. By cutting down public expenditure, reducing subsidies, and raising taxes and utility charges, these policies invariably lead to a bitter mixture of rising unemployment, growing inequality, and shrinking social services. In such conditions, the poor have to bear a disproportionate share of the burden in lean periods caused by an economic slowdown or a natural disaster. At the same time the developed countries do not practice what they preach, and are currently providing over US$300 billion a year as agricultural subsidies. As a result, there is no level playing field for agricultural trade, with adverse consequences for millions of poor farmers in the developing world.

In the face of these overwhelming constraints, the increase in poverty in many countries in the past decade should not come as a surprise. As mentioned earlier, if the Chinese figures are excluded, the overall incidence of poverty in the rest of the developing world has increased in the past 10 years.

If these failures are carefully analyzed, the political and moral dilemmas facing mankind will stare us in the face. We are living in a world in which we constantly produce surplus food but 800 million people remain perpetually hungry. We spend US$900 billion a year on arms and can spare only US$60 billion as development assistance for low-income countries.

LESSONS OF EXPERIENCE

In the past three decades, despite the obstacles listed above, many developing countries have succeeded in reducing hunger and poverty by combining strong economic growth with sustained social progress through a participatory process, and by keeping in view the moral imperatives of social justice, national harmony, and democratic decentralization. The experience of seven countries (China, Korea, Vietnam, Malaysia, Chile, Uganda, and Tunisia) in poverty reduction is briefly described in the Appendix. The lessons emerging from these success stories must be carefully analyzed and replicated by other countries because the primary responsibility for eliminating hunger and poverty must rest with the countries themselves. Some of the lessons can be summarized as follows:

- All the countries that have succeeded in achieving a substantial reduction in the level of poverty have had an average growth rate in per capita income that was at least 3% per annum in the 1990s (8.8% in China, 6% in Vietnam, 4.7% in Korea, 4.1% in Chile, 4% in Malaysia, 3.6% in Uganda, and 3.1% in Tunisia). In most of these countries, 60%–70% of the reduction in poverty can be attributed to the growth in per capita incomes and the rest to social and pro-poor policies.
- The contribution of growth to poverty reduction is greater in countries where agricultural productivity is rising steadily in response to investments in small-scale irrigation, rural infrastructure, and policies to improve the terms of trade for the agriculture sector.
- These countries were able to achieve macro-economic stability through fiscal discipline and utilized the fiscal space thus created to expand public-sector investment in infrastructure and social spending on education and health and for programs to promote employment.
- These countries also achieved social and political harmony by reducing racial, ethnic, or intergroup strife or violence through strong leadership and a commitment to the objective of national unity.
- The hardcore poor communities or less-developed regions were targeted, including welfare assistance to the vulnerable groups.

- Policies for reducing income disparities between different regions or between urban and rural incomes have been less successful but have been initiated in most of these countries as an important component of the anti-poverty programs.
- An important element of the poverty reduction strategies has been democratic decentralization through the transfer of power, resources, and responsibility for development activities to local officials, elected institutions, or community organizations. This approach has produced better results when decentralization was accompanied by the social mobilization of the poor into viable and self-sustaining community organizations, leading to their empowerment.

Many other countries have formulated medium-term poverty reduction strategy papers (PRSPs) with the support of IMF and the World Bank. These strategies have generally been useful in analyzing the extent and causes of poverty and in identifying opportunities for pro-poor investments. But in most cases there is no clear link between poverty analysis and poverty reduction policies, and the focus remains partly on growth strategies that are not pro-poor and partly on macro-economic stability through reductions in public expenditure. This in turn has reduced fiscal space for social spending and for expanding investment and employment. In practice, therefore, the implementation of PRSP has not led to any significant reduction in poverty, particularly in countries where the increase in per capita income is marginal, i.e., less than 2% per annum. In addition to 12 developing countries where per capita GDP growth in the 1990s was more than 3% per annum, it was between 2% and 3% in 25 countries. In the rest, it was below 2%, and in at least 40 developing countries the per capita GDP growth in the 1990s was negative. In such conditions, notwithstanding the scale of anti-poverty policies and programs, poverty is bound to increase.

The development literature has already documented many examples to show that economic growth alone is not enough for poverty reduction. We have scores of examples of jobless growth, in which economic expansion is not accompanied by a corresponding increase in employment opportunities, and of ruthless growth, in which the additional incomes generated do not flow equitably to all sections of the population. The growth process must ensure adequate participation of the poor, safeguard the environment, and take into account the local socio-cultural values.

Imperatives of Empowerment

Anyone making an objective assessment of the obstacles and constraints in reducing poverty will readily recognize that these constraints can not be removed without the empowerment of the poor at all levels – local, national, and international.

In socialist countries where the political power base of those in power springs from the bottom, any effort to organize the poor to demand their share in the resource pool or in the fruits of progress does not pose a challenge. In fact the local layers of the ruling parties stimulate and nurture this process. In countries with mixed economics, the process of empowerment of the poor can be strengthened only through genuine democracy. In the recent Indian elections, for example, there was a pro-poor shift in the political power structure. In countries in which democratic institutions and values are not strong, the political process is generally dominated by the powerful elites or by tribal or feudal interests. Any social movements and organizations representing the poor cannot therefore easily challenge the monopoly of power and resources by these politically dominant groups and the public officials supporting them. In such situations, empowerment of the poor, so necessary for poverty reduction, faces formidable obstacles.

The contrast is clearly reflected in different approaches to poverty reduction in socialist countries and other countries with weak democratic institutions. In comparison with China, which has reduced the level of poverty from 49% to 7% of the population, the poverty reduction strategies so far formulated by many other developing countries have not paid due attention to the political economy of poverty reduction.

Mainstreaming the Right to Development

The ground situation varies enormously from one country to another but the starting point for overcoming the political obstacles to empowerment can be found by gradually evolving a legal and administrative framework for enforcing the concept of 'right to development.'

Article 25(i) of the Universal Declaration of Human Rights reads as follows:

> Everyone has the right to a standard of living adequate for the health and well-being of himself and of his family, including food, housing and medical care and necessary social services and the right to security in the event of unemployment, sickness, disability, widowhood, old age or other lack of livelihood in circumstances beyond his control.

The written constitutions in many developing countries provide for similar rights but these are generally vague and non-enforceable in the legal arena.

The 'rights approach' if carefully evolved and nurtured through a coalition of supportive political parties and civil society organizations, can lead to a coherent framework of laws, rules, standards, and enforcement procedures which is capable of influencing national and international policies and actions.

An important prerequisite for extending the concept of a human rights approach to development is a minimum consensus at the national level on the meaning and scope of development. To start with, however, it should not be difficult to reach a consensus on two rights – the right to food and the right to basic education. Once these two rights are accepted and gradually enforced through a series of policies, structures, and monitoring systems, other elements of the broader concept of human development and human security can be added to the package.

The second prerequisite is a strong coalition of all the stakeholders in support of the poor. Even if relevant laws are promulgated, they would not automatically lead to desired policies and actions without widespread public awareness and sustained public pressure. Policy-makers are generally isolated from reality by their own affluence and their narrow vested interests. They have to be shaken into action by highlighting different facets of poverty and deprivation that afflict their societies.

This has to be accompanied by the power of public pressure from the civil society and, where available, a segment of the political leadership to force the government in power to adopt pro-poor policies. This interaction will also ensure the participation of the poor and, if successful, will lead to their empowerment.

In countries where the political power structure is highly centralized, it will not be easy for civil society organizations to gather enough weight and momentum to make a difference. In such cases, the rights movement will have to follow a decentralized approach based on different issues: lack of good-quality schools in rural areas, non-availability of clean drinking water, high transport costs, price of electricity and gas for poor households, a sudden rise in food prices, unrestricted exploitation of forests or other natural resources in a particular region. Some community organizations might concentrate on the needs and interests of special groups such as minorities and women. Reaching out to the people and the media on these issues and seeking their support will strengthen the rights movement and gradually influence policies in the desired direction. In some cases it may even lead to a change in the political power structure in favor of the poor, as was witnessed in the recent Indian elections.

THE MORAL DIMENSION

The movement for the right to development can draw considerable strength from the moral dimension. Unfortunately in the twentieth century the technological and material progress has been accompanied by a corresponding decline in our moral concepts and collective responsibility, in rich and in poor nations alike. The moral foundations of policies therefore remain weak in the developed and in the developing world. It is therefore necessary to dissect the arguments in support of the right to development into those whose moral basis cannot be questioned from those that may be less convincing.

- The first dimension of the rights movement must be to end the discrimination against the poor and the weak. The poor are too weak in most countries to compete in the labor and product markets. They therefore get low wages for their labor and low prices for the small surpluses they may generate. Any efforts to organize them to compete fairly in these markets and the right of the poor to buy their minimum requirements of food and other essential products at reasonable prices would place them on the high moral ground.
- The second dimension revolves round the rights of the poor to have fair access to education and health services. The poor are chronically deprived because they have limited land or other income-generating assets. The only way they can escape the vicious circle of poverty is to acquire education and skills and enjoy reasonably good health, because sickness of the bread-winner in a family leads to further erosion in the limited assets that poor households possess. Denying poor households the opportunity to educate their children and to learn new skills is to condemn them to perpetual poverty. Acceptance of the right to education for all is therefore a paramount moral imperative for all societies and education is also the most important ladder for empowerment.

- The third plank of the rights movement would be to ensure that the poor receive their due share in the incremental resources generated by development in the form of irrigation water, new land reclaimed, credit and income-generating opportunities. Here also the moral basis of such a demand is very strong and can be sustained through the support of the public and the media.
- Beyond these three dimensions, the rights movement can enter turbulent waters, if it demands for the poor a larger share of the existing pie, through land reforms, nationalization of industries, or massive taxation. The success of the movement in these areas will depend on the strength of its political coalition and not only on moral persuasion.

In the final analysis, the right to development can become a strong platform for popular action, if it is conceived and articulated in a human-development perspective. In such a perspective, increasing the income of the poor is an important initial objective but is, at the same time, only a means to the broader objective of development, namely 'an expansion of human capabilities, a widening of choices, an enhancement of freedoms and a fulfillment of human rights' (UNDP 1996). In its logical evolution, the process of human development will mature into the concept of human security which calls for 'the security of all people everywhere, in their homes, in their jobs, in their streets, in their communities, in their environment. It is security through development not through arms' (UNDP 1994).

These lofty goals of human development and human security cannot be reached without the empowerment of the poor. At the level of the individual, empowerment depends primarily on the level of human development, through education and training. At the community level, empowerment comes from social mobilization through which effective community organizations can create awareness and generate political and moral pressure to protect the rights of the poor and the deprived. At the national level, all the threads of empowerment, if they are strong enough, can converge into a strong coalition in support of the poor, leading to legal and constitutional provisions and higher budgetary allocation to guarantee the right to development or more limited rights like the right to food or the right to education, accompanied by institutions and structures to secure those rights.

THE GLOBAL DIMENSION

As the 1994 *Human Development Report* pointed out,

> The concerns about human security are more globalized today than global trade because poverty and desperation can not be stopped at national borders. Poor people may be stopped but not the tragic consequences of their poverty. They travel without any passport and they travel in unpleasant forms. Drugs, AIDS, pollution and terrorism stop at no national frontier today. They can strike at devastating speed in any corner of the world. In fact, when people travel, they bring much dynamism and creativity with them. When only their poverty travels, it brings nothing but human misery (UNDP 1994).

It is seldom realized that it is easier, more humane, and less costly to deal with the issue of human security upstream rather than downstream. But the world has not learned many lessons on this score. As the recent report of the World Commission on the Social Dimension of Globalization, entitled *A Fair Globalization: Creating Opportunities for All*, emphasizes:

> However, current systems of governance of globalization of national and international levels have not realized their potentials for most of the world's people and in many instances have made matters worse. Seen through the eyes of the vast majority of men and women around the world, globalization has not met their simple aspiration for decent jobs, livelihoods and a better future for their children. In 2003, official figures for global unemployment reached a record high of over 185 million people. Unofficial figures would be much higher, especially if one includes the underemployed and the working poor (World Commission on the Social Dimension of Globalization 2004).

These trends are largely the result of deep-seated and persistent imbalances in the current workings of the global economy which are both ethically unacceptable and politically unsustainable. We have reached a crisis stage in the legitimacy of our political institutions, whether national or international. There is an urgent need to rethink current institutions of global economic governance, whose rules and policies are largely shaped by powerful countries and powerful players. The unfairness of key rules of trade and finance, reflect a serious 'democratic deficit' at the heart of the system. The failure of policies is due to the fact that market-opening measures and financial and economic considerations have consistently predominated over social ones, including measures compatible with the prerogatives of international human rights law and the principles of international solidarity.

The vision put forward by the Summit, co-chaired by the Finnish President Tarja Halonen and Tanzanian Benjamin Mkapa, is to bring into being a system of global governance that is genuinely supportive of and conducive to national development strategies ('there can be no successful globalization without a successful localization'), where powerful actors are held accountable, and where efforts to achieve coherence between economic and social objectives would place the needs and aspirations of ordinary people at the center of rules and policies.

The Commission, which submitted its report at a special Summit organized by the United Nations on 20 September 2004, suggested that taxes be imposed on greenhouse gas emissions, and certain cross-border financial transactions should be put in place to build a US$50-billion fund to fight poverty and achieve the other MDGs.

In 2004, the 56th session of the UN Sub-Commission on Human Rights considered a study on *Mainstreaming the Right to Development into International Trade Law and Policy at the WTO* by the University of Michigan. It assesses trade rules and policies and the issue of reform in WTO architecture and governance and how the interpretation of WTO law could benefit from the right to development perspective.

The reform of the global economic and financial institutions is long overdue. But finally, public opinion across the globe is coming round in favor of more fundamental reforms based on the principle of shared responsibility for global governance. The time therefore seems ripe for some form of international taxation, as recommended by the World Commission on the Social Dimension of Globalization, to supplement resources for achieving the MDG of halving poverty by 2015. But this task will also require policies and institutions that can overcome the political obstacles to the empowerment of the poor.

REFERENCES

UNDP, 1994. *Human Development Report 1994: New Dimensions of Human Security.* New York: United Nations Development Programme.

UNDP, 1996. *Human Development Report 1996: Economic Growth and Human Development.* New York: United Nations Development Programme.

World Commission on the Social Dimension of Globalization, 2004. *A Fair Globalization: Creating Opportunities for All.* Geneva: International Labour Organization.

Chen and Ravallion, 2004. *How Have the World's Poorest Fared Since the Early 1980s?* World Bank. *Global Economics Prospects 2004*, World Bank. *Health, Nutrition and Population Demographic Projections*, http://devdata.worldbank.org/hnpstats/DPselection.asp (accessed 16 Sept 2004).

Population Division of the Department of Economic and Social Affairs of the United Nations Secretariat. *World Population Prospects: The 2002 Revision* and *World Urbanization Prospects: The 2001 Revision*, http://esa.un.org/unpp (accessed 16 Sept 2004).

FAO, 2003a. *The State of Food Insecurity in the World 2003.*

FAO, 2003b. *World Agriculture: Towards 2015/2030. An FAO Perspective.* edited by Jelle Bruinsma.

Millennium Project, 2004. *Interim Report of Task Force 2 on Hunger.*

APPENDIX TO CHAPTER EIGHT

Brief Review of Poverty Reduction Efforts in Seven Countries

China   The most outstanding example of success comes from China, which has already surpassed the Millennium Development Goal of halving poverty, 15 years before the deadline of 2015. According to World Bank figures, the number of poor people living on less than US$1 a day has dropped from 490 million in 1981 to 88 million in 2002, or from 49% to 6.9% of the population. According to official Chinese figures, the number of poor people below the extreme poverty line of annual per capita income of 625 yuan (about US$75) fell from 250 million in 1978 to 29 million or 3% of the rural population in 2003.

A visible change in national priorities to focus on poverty reduction took place in 1977/78 with the emergence of a group of leaders who were firmly committed to pass on the benefits of reforms to the masses. The reforms process for poverty reduction can be divided into four different phases:

• In the first phase, from 1978 to 1985, the focus was on rural reforms through institutional changes in land-holding such as the household responsibility system, liberalizing procurement prices and quotas, and an active research and extension program in support of agriculture. This led to an accelerated pace of development and a sharp reduction in rural poverty from 250 million in 1978 to 125 million in 1985.

- In the second phase, from 1986 to 1993, the focus shifted from rural to urban and industrial growth, especially in the coastal areas. There was a corresponding slow-down in the growth of rural incomes from 12% in 1978–1985 to only 2% in 1986–1993. As a result there was relative stagnation in the level of rural poverty during this period.

- In 1994, the government launched the National Plan for Poverty Reduction to lift the remaining 80 million poor from poverty within seven years (1994–2000); hence the name '8–7 Plan.' It focused on three main programs: subsidized loans, food for work, and government budgetary grants. The subsidized loans (about half the total funds under the Plan) were meant to assist households with land improvements, increased cash and tree crops, livestock production, and small-scale industrial activities. The Food For Work Program (30% of the total outlay) was meant to use surplus farm labor for local infrastructure. Budgetary grants (20% of the total poverty fund) supported investment in poor areas across sectors. Since 1997, funding for poverty reduction has been increasing by 50% in real terms every year and was matched by provincial and local governments. Total central-government funding during 1994–2000 under the 8–7 Plan was 113 billion yuan (about US$13.6 billion) which was about 6% of total government expenditures. As a result, household per capita income in the target counties grew at an annual rate of 12.8%, or 2% higher than the national average during this period.

- Keeping in view the lessons emerging from the 8–7 Plan, the Chinese government has launched a New Century Rural Poverty Alleviation Plan for the period 2001–2010. In addition to poor counties, the new Plan directly targets 50,000 poor villages. This includes poor villages in non-poor counties excluded from the 8–7 Plan. It also emphasizes participatory planning at the village level, and a more flexible multi-sectoral approach according to local conditions. The Plan also accords higher priority to basic health services because sickness has been identified as a major factor in accentuating poverty. Other policies include increased agricultural prices combined with reduced agricultural taxes, and more liberal migration policies, making it easier for people to move to cities and between regions.

- The Chinese poverty reduction strategy has been evolving in the light of actual experience, but a very major factor in its success was rapid economic growth. China's GDP has been growing in real terms at an average of 9.4% in the 25-year period 1978–2003. This, together with a slow down in the rate of population growth, has meant a per capita income growth of 8.2% over this period that is unprecedented in human history.

REPUBLIC OF KOREA

Korea has also been remarkably successful in combining rapid economic growth with a significant reduction in poverty. Between 1975 and 2001, Korea's per capita income has grown at an average of 6.2% per annum, which is the second highest after China. At the same time, Korea's Human Development Index (HDI) has moved up to the 'high' category with a score of 0.879 and 30th position in a group of 175 countries.

Korean achievement is especially significant because less than 25% of the country's land area is cultivable and it also possesses very few natural resources. It compensated for the shortage of cultivable land and natural resources through an active policy of human and skills development under which 99.8% literacy is combined with a 34% enrollment in science, mathematics, and engineering, as a percentage of all tertiary students. It has a sound policy framework to promote growth through the private sector and a comprehensive social program to upgrade the education and living standards of poor families. This Korean model of poverty alleviation is based on a 'productive welfare' approach which seeks

> improvement in the lives of all low income households, promote programs for human development to create opportunities for self reliant development, and guarantee a basic living standard by expanding the coverage of social insurance to all people.

The productive welfare approach has reduced poverty in Korea through (a) the National Basic Livelihood Security Act, (b) expansion in the coverage of social insurance, including two health insurance schemes, (c) human resource development programs to enhance the access of vulnerable groups to the labor market and to protect the rights of irregular employees, (d) extending the policy of minimum wages to all industries. These policies have given Korea a more productive and efficient labor force, increasing its competitive edge in the global markets and stimulating export-led growth in high-value sectors.

A major factor in the reduction of rural poverty in Korea has been the program of land reforms, combined with a policy of higher agriculture prices relative to the prices of agricultural inputs. This has led to increased productivity in the agriculture sector, raising rice yields by 50%, and to higher farm incomes.

After the 1997 economic crises, the Korean Government expanded its anti-poverty programs to ease the impact of mass lay-offs, including temporary livelihood protection for those who had lost their jobs.

VIETNAM

Vietnam is another country that has achieved the Millennium Goal of halving poverty, 15 years ahead of the target. In 1990, Vietnam was in the middle of a multidimensional economic and social crisis, with 70% of its population trapped in absolute poverty, and an inflation rate of 100–200% a year. By successfully implementing its 10-year Strategy for Socio-economic Stabilization and Development for the period 1991–2000, Vietnam succeeded in reducing the poverty level from 70% to 35%, primarily because it achieved, as a result of land reforms and economic liberalization, an average GDP growth of 7.6% per annum, doubling the size of the Vietnam economy. The average rate of industrial growth during the decade was 11.2% and of agriculture 4.2%. Inflation was gradually brought down to 5%. Vietnam's HDI has improved from 0.582 in 1985 to 0.688 in 2001.

In 2002, Vietnam adopted its Poverty Reduction and Growth Strategy as a part of the comprehensive Socio-economic Development Strategy for the period 2001–2010. It also incorporates national MDGs, which in many sectors are more ambitious than the Millennium Development Goals adopted by the Millennium Summit in September 2000. The philosophy of poverty reduction in Vietnam is based on a broader concept of human development that goes beyond incomes, education, health, to enlarging choices and opportunities for the people. This broader concept flows directly from Vietnam's socialist philosophy of 'a rich people, a strong nation, and an equal and civilized nation,' and lays the basis for institutional and governance structures that have broad popular support.

In terms of the future, there are reasonably good prospects that Vietnam will be able to maintain an average GDP growth of 7% in the current decade (2001–2010). But the emphasis of the 10-year strategy is on industrialization and modernization. This could lead to growing inequality between urban and rural areas. As a result, the same pace of growth (7% per annum) will not reduce the level of poverty to the same extent as it did in the 1990s. The real challenge for Vietnam in the coming years will be to preserve the quality of growth to ensure it reaches all segments of society, including minorities and remote communities, and maintains a gender focus in all poverty reduction efforts.

MALAYSIA

Malaysia presents another outstanding example of equitable growth, poverty reduction, and racial harmony. Malaysia achieved a sustained increase of 4.1% in per capita GDP between 1975 and 2001 and improved its HDI rank to 58 and Gender-related Development Index to 53, as a result of a very comprehensive and sound policy framework whose main aim was not maximum growth but national unity.

Malaysia's policy framework for equitable growth and poverty reduction has evolved through three medium-term plans supplemented by a series of sectoral plans, and as a result problems of poverty and hunger have been virtually overcome.

The core policies were incorporated in the New Economic Policy (NEP) for 1970–1990, aimed at national unity through:

• the rapid and continuous economic growth with equitable distribution
• the eradication of poverty
• the restructuring of society.

In 1990, another National Development Policy was announced for the period 1991–2000, along with a more ambitious longer-term perspective called Vision 2020. There were a series of sectoral plans such as the Industrial Master Plan, National Agriculture Policies. and the Privatization Master Plan. In 1998, the National Economic Recovery Plan was formulated to overcome the adverse effects of the 1997 economic crisis.

The main thrust of the poverty reduction strategy of Malaysia was on increasing the productivity of the poor and diversifying the sources of their income by expanding non-agricultural activities for poor households. The income tax rate for the poor was either eliminated or reduced. The private·sector and the civil society played a major role in this effort and particularly in transforming the economy, and that was made possible by the prolonged period of peace and security in the country. Malaysia, a multiracial society, has not had any racial strife since 1969.

This core poverty reduction strategy was supplemented by special programs to target the poor and by providing welfare assistance to the disabled and the handicapped. Every effort was made to maintain stable food prices through government intervention in the production and marketing of essential items.

The main lesson of Malaysia's success in poverty reduction seems to be the importance of overcoming racial or ethnic strife through an active policy of promoting national unity and the adoption of practical strategies for power-sharing and wealth-sharing. In multiracial or multi-ethnic countries, sustained development is not possible if there is racial or intergroup violence over prolonged periods.

Secondly, chronic disparities between different communities and regions can only be narrowed through proactive policies to provide equal opportunities to all and to protect the rights and interests of the weaker segment of society, including women. A free-market-based system without such interventions can widen disparities and lead to social unrest.

Thirdly, a policy framework with active government intervention does not mean that the role of the private sector to expand industries, jobs, and business opportunities should be circumscribed. Malaysia succeeded in evolving a particularly complementary framework for cooperation between the public and the private sectors.

CHILE

Chile presents another interesting case study to show that even high GDP growth without an explicit poverty reduction strategy would not automatically reduce poverty.

Chile went through a serious economic crisis in the early 1980s, when its GDP fell by 16%, unemployment went up to 30%, and half the population went down below the poverty line. At least 30% of the population was affected by extreme poverty.

The Economic Recovery Program launched in 1985 revived the economy and the financial situation, but measures launched to achieve this improvement, like reducing taxes and government spending, also curtailed social spending by as much as 3% of GDP. This had the effect of increasing unemployment, and poverty, and there was a sharp deterioration in the quality of services.

In 1990, the newly elected government accorded high priority to poverty reduction and launched a new 'growth with equity' strategy. In 1994, the National Program of Poverty Eradication was announced.

A tax increase in the early 1990s enabled the government to expand social expenditures by 200% throughout the 1990s, particularly in health and education. But these expenditures were not cost-effective because of highly centralized and bureaucratic controls over public hospital and educational institutions. The approach is now being modified to allow community-based organizations to apply for public funds to develop projects for improving social infrastructure and starting micro-enterprises for the benefit of low-income households. A new Solidarity and Social Investment Fund (FOSIS) has been set up for this purpose.

Under the 1994 Poverty Eradication Program, 80 municipal districts were selected on the basis of their high poverty ratios, and resources were allocated to them to reach the poorest families.

As a result of these programs, Chile has achieved a per capita GDP growth of 4.7% in the 1990s, and the incidence of poverty has been reduced from 40% in 1990 to 17% in 2001. But it has been more difficult to eradicate extreme and chronic poverty. In 2002, a new program, Chile Solidario Program, was initiated to target the extremely poor through a decentralized system. The provision of income support subsidies and public services is monitored by local public officials to ensure effective access. The program also provides assistance to poorer households for finding employment or receiving training. It is too early to judge whether this transition from the traditional method of providing public services or income support to a more integrated community-centered approach will be more effective in reaching the extremely or chronically poor households.

UGANDA

Uganda is one of a few countries in Sub-Saharan Africa to achieve an average growth GDP rate of 6% in the 1990s (3.6% per capita growth) and a single-digit rate of inflation. As a result, the proportion of people living in absolute poverty has also declined from 56% in 1992 to 38% in 2002/03.

The acceleration of growth occurred following the economic reforms in 1992 that included restoration of property rights to return properties confiscated in 1972 and special measures to promote and facilitate new investment. The Uganda Investment Authority was set up in 1991. As confidence improved, total investment jumped from 8% of GDP in 1998 to 21% in 2002/03, laying the basis for a close partnership between the government and the private sector.

A Poverty Eradication Action Plan was launched in 1997 to expand measures to increase incomes for the poor and investments in primary education, healthcare, clean water and sanitation. A Poverty Action Fund was also set up in 1998, to protect poverty-related expenditures from budgetary cuts in years of fiscal squeeze.

Uganda has also been successful in reducing the HIV prevalence rates from 30% in 1986 to 6% in 2002 through its AIDS Control Program and the Uganda AIDS Commission set up in 1990. An active research program and public awareness campaign have been the main features of the AIDS Control Program.

The main lesson of Uganda's experience has been its ability to use poverty reduction as a tool for nation-building and to evolve a decentralized system with enough autonomy to deliver public services to the poor.

TUNISIA

Tunisia has also succeeded in combining a sustained increase of 3.1% per annum in per capita income in the 1990s with low inflation reflected in an average annual increase of only 1.9% in the Consumer Price Index. Tunisia's success in developing its human resources, with an HDI of 0.740 is also accompanied by a sharp reduction in the incidence of poverty from an estimated 22% in 1975 to 4% in 2003.

Tunisia offers an interesting example of poverty reduction in a period of economic liberalization (1987–2002) in which a higher growth rate broadened the fiscal space to permit a major expansion in the education and health sectors. In 1989, the Government launched a major reform of the education system that increased the basic education cycle to nine years and introduced free and compulsory education until the age of 16. Attention was also paid to the quality of teachers by increasing the percentage of teachers with higher degrees from 67% to 78% within five years and providing computers to all schools. These achievements not only helped to create a more productive workforce but also reduced poverty.

The decline in poverty in Tunisia is partly due to the steady increase in national income and partly due to the employment-generating investments in public works such as roads, soil conservation, forestry, and urban infrastructure. Tunisia's efforts in launching special programs for the poor, such as the Food Subsidy Program, have not been very successful, but more recently, it has modified the program to make it more targeted and has also introduced housing finance subsidies for low-income people, and has encouraged civil society organizations to monitor the delivery of public services.

ETHICS AND HUNGER: A NON-GOVERNMENTAL ORGANIZATION (NGO) PERSPECTIVE

INTRODUCTION

The poor you will always have with you (Mark 14:3–9).

Is hunger an inevitable part of the human condition? With 840 million people suffering from hunger across the world, is it fanciful to imagine a scenario where hunger is substantially reduced, or to dream of a day when hunger is eradicated?

In recent years, profound economic and political developments have brought these questions into focus. For many developing countries, strong economic growth has reduced the number living in poverty and driven an overall decline in world hunger from one-fifth to one-sixth of the global population. Elsewhere hunger – the most extreme manifestation of poverty – has persisted. This is most striking in the case of Sub-Saharan Africa, which has been accurately described as being in a 'development crisis' (Sachs et al. 2004). Here the scale of hunger is climbing and is increasingly compounded by conflict, poor governance, and HIV/AIDS. These contrasting fortunes have motivated the international community to reassess its approach to development thinking and practice. A critical response has been to place poverty reduction at the center of the new global agenda for development. At the heart of this agenda lies the Millennium Development Goals (MDGs), which aim to substantially reduce poverty and increase human welfare by 2015.

The purpose of this chapter is to assess how international non-governmental organizations (NGOs) can contribute to this agenda. The chapter focuses on how best to integrate ethical perspectives into food security interventions,[1] paying special attention to the experience of Sub-Saharan Africa. The chapter examines this question by drawing on emerging policy processes that are shaping efforts to increase food security in the world. In particular the chapter draws on the findings of the UN Millennium Project Hunger Task Force.[2]

The chapter also draws on the case-study experiences of Concern Worldwide, an international NGO founded in Ireland in 1968. In the intervening years Concern has worked on many of the large-scale humanitarian disasters and has been engaged in long-term development work. At present, Concern operates in 27 least-developed countries, with programs in livelihoods, health, education, and HIV/AIDS, mainly in Sub-Saharan Africa and in Asia.

The chapter is divided into two main sections. The first section examines key related changes in development thinking and practice in recent years. It focuses on

P. Pinstrup-Andersen and P. Sandøe (eds.), Ethics, Hunger and Globalization: In Search of Appropriate Policies, 149–164.
© 2007 *Springer*.

the role of international NGOs in a changing political landscape, where the responsi-bilities of State and non-State actors are firmly embedded in the Millennium Devel-opment Goals. Here a confluence of conceptual, legal, and political factors is seen to impact upon contemporary approaches to reducing hunger. The emerging policy framework regarding food security is then presented. It is argued that the NGO perspective can add a valuable dimension to this policy framework. In particular the NGO experience can focus on how best to integrate an ethical perspective into food security interventions.

The second half of the chapter explores the NGO perspective in greater detail. The need for civil society space is emphasized, particularly in developing economies where governance and institutions are often weak. Drawing on this proposition, this section outlines what lessons can be applied from the grassroots experience of NGOs to reduce food insecurity. The analysis identifies key policy issues spanning across the main dimensions of NGO work, including emergency response, sustainable development processes, and advocacy. This is supported by case-study evidence from Concern's experience.

DEVELOPMENT THINKING AND PRACTICE:
NGOS AND FOOD SECURITY

Over the past two decades there have been significant advances in development thinking and practice. A confluence of conceptual, legal, and political factors has combined to strongly influence current approaches to food security. These issues shape the context through which the NGO perspective is framed and discussed in this chapter.

NGOs and the Global Agenda for Development

The role of NGOs has substantially changed over the past 20 years,[3] with inter-national NGOs now playing a significant role in the political landscape for devel-opment. The NGO distinctiveness in this arena is driven by grassroots experiences. NGOs play an important role in both bearing witness, particularly in emergencies where human rights may be abused or under threat, and in communicating the realities in developing countries to the decision-makers and public of the developed nations.

The growing influence of international NGOs has been influenced by a combi-nation of political as well as economic factors. According to Lindenberg and Bryant (2001), the growth of the Northern international NGO sector became a torrent in the 1980s and 1990s due to six important factors:
1. The public fiscal crisis which occurred in the early 1980s in the wake of the world recession
2. The collapse of the Soviet Union in the early 1990s, which created a vacuum into which Northern international NGOS were pulled
3. Democratic 'openings,' with some countries moving to elections and a devel-oping democracy

4. Bilateral and multilateral incentives
5. An increase in private giving for humanitarian and development purposes in richer countries
6. The revolution in global communications.

In response, international NGOs have been accorded an increasingly important role in relation to policy influencing, as actors in responding to humanitarian problems, and in working toward long-term development.

This increased responsibility has led to international NGOs operating on a number of different levels and using a number of different methodologies. First, international NGOs continue to be important service-providers in the response to emergencies, particularly in the distribution of food aid alongside other UN agencies. Partnerships with NGOs drive the work of the World Food Program (WFP), which is currently engaged in longer-term strategic planning with civil society. Currently, the WFP works with over 1,000 local NGOs and over 200 international NGOs to complement food aid with technical and non-food inputs.

Second, NGOs are placing more emphasis on working with local partners and developing their capacity, with a consequent reduction in the level of expatriate staff. This emphasis is directly linked to achieving sustainability and involves changing methodologies, such as client participation, e.g., participatory rural appraisal (PRA) techniques. Third, NGOs are increasingly engaging in policy advocacy, drawing on evidence from their field-based experience, as well as a deeper analysis of structural aspects of the world economy.

These changing roles in service delivery, development, and advocacy position the international NGO firmly in a global framework for development. This has also taken place against a backdrop of shifts in thinking about the essence of sovereignty of individual States. In recent decades there has been an increasing focus on the impact of human-rights norms, bringing a shift from a culture of sovereign impunity to one of national and international accountability. The increasing influence of the concept of human security has also played a role; what matters is not just State security but the protection of individuals against threats to life, livelihood, or dignity that can come from within or outside the State. In short, a large and growing gap has been evolving between international behaviors, as articulated by the State-centered UN Charter, and evolving State practices, which highlight the limits of sovereignty (Evans and Sahnoun, 2002).

Inevitably this presents its own unique challenges for international NGOs. For example, NGOs need to strike a balance between their operationality and their role as an advocacy organization. Furthermore, NGOs are subject to increased demands to show their effectiveness and accountability as their legitimacy and credibility is challenged in the public arena.

Food Security: Conceptual, Legal, and Political Context

The experience of international NGOs can be of particular value in identifying appropriate policies in the area of hunger – the most extreme manifestation of poverty. In recent years there have been shifts in the underlying conceptual, legal, and political context addressing food security. These changes, which have conceptu-alized development in terms of human security and poverty, have focused attention on the need for integrated, multi-sectoral responses to hunger. NGO action is one part of this integrated response.

At a theoretical level, the work of Amartya Sen has made a major contribution to the evolution of development theory and practice.[4] Sen's work has been of particular relevance in understanding how food security can be approached from an ethical as well as an economic perspective. Sen's analysis departs from traditional welfare economics and income-based approaches to development. Rather than focusing exclusively on income, growth, and utility, the analysis emphasizes freedoms, rights, capabilities, and entitlements.

A central theme to this analysis identifies poverty as the deprivation of basic capabilities rather than on income alone. While Sen favors the expansion of 'real freedoms' as the principal objective or 'end' of human endeavor, he recognizes that, in today's world, many people suffer a particular form of 'unfreedom.' He equates this 'unfreedom' with three sources, i.e., economic poverty, lack of public facilities, and denial of political and civil liberties by authoritarian regimes.

This approach has a number of far-reaching implications with respect to integrating ethical perspectives into food security. First, in understanding the root causes of food security it requires us to consider an analysis of the entire economic system, rather than an analysis of food output and supply alone. Second, this deter-mines that food security should not be defined in terms of food availability, but rather through the entitlements of individuals and groups. The 'entitlement' that a person enjoys relates to the commodities over which he/she can establish ownership and command. Entitlements are determined by a person's endowment of productive resources, production possibilities, and exchange conditions.

Most significantly, this framework allows us to look at the causation and dynamics of famine and food insecurity in a broad way and not as some mechanical balance between consumption and production. One of Sen's key conclusions is that famines do not occur within democracies and where accountable government systems exist. This thesis is supported in the academic literature. In a review of the linkage between governance and famine, von Braun et al. (1999) note that in the final decades of the twentieth century, no country known to have a strong commitment to democracy was prone to famine, while countries with repeated famines could be categorized as 'authoritarian,' having an 'ambiguous commitment to democracy' or being under 'contested sovereignty.'

From a legal perspective, this analysis has been instrumental in the principle that everyone has a right to adequate food.[5] The formal adoption of this right at the 1996 World Food Summit marked a milestone achievement. Delegates asserted

> the right of everyone to have access to safe and nutritious food, consistent with the right to adequate food and the fundamental right of everyone to be free from hunger.

Delegates further pledged to cut the number of the world's hungry people in half by 2015. This pledge became the basis for the Millennium Development Goal on Hunger.

These conceptual and legal changes have been paralleled by significant shifts in the political landscape for development assistance. In recent years, international institutions and donors have broadened their understanding of poverty from a narrow focus on income and growth to include freedoms, rights, and social interactions. This has been strongly influenced by the 1999 World Bank Comprehensive Development Framework (CDF), which stressed the interdependence of all elements in development, e.g., social, structural, human, governance, environmental, economic, and financial. It may also be asserted that the CDF attempted to learn from some of the policy failures of the international financial institutions (IFIs) in earlier years, including the implementation of Structural Adjustment Programs (Wolfensohn and Bourguignon 2004).

The CDF promoted four principles that appeared to address past shortcomings in development policy. First, development efforts should be rooted in a long-term, holistic vision of a country's needs, not just macroeconomic but also social and structural. Second, it should focus on results rather than inputs. Third, it should be based on country-owned strategies. And fourth, development actors should foster partnerships to support the country-owned strategy. The CDF led to the Poverty Reduction Strategy (PRS) process, a major innovation in aid delivery adopted by the boards of the World Bank and IMF, which provided a basis for expanded debt relief and increased aid funding for countries adopting it.

These political factors have strongly shaped the architecture of international development. The system of international development is now contextualized by a range of interlocking agreements and mechanisms including the Monterrey Declaration (Financing for Development) and the Johannesburg Declaration (Sustainable Development Summit). More recently, the Doha Round of Multilateral Trade Negotiations has added a new dimension, with its stated priority being to promote development, and agricultural reform in particular.

At the heart of this global agenda lie the Millennium Development Goals (MDGs), which aim to substantially reduce poverty and increase human welfare by 2015. The importance of the MDGs go beyond the fact that they are clear, measurable, and time-bound commitments set by the international community; most importantly, they define a set of reciprocal responsibilities for governments in developing and developed countries and development actors, including civil society, if the MDGs are to be achieved. It is in this wide context that the role and perspective of an international NGO is currently conceived. This critical point is further developed in the second half of this chapter.

Emerging Policy Framework for Food Security

The theoretical, legal, and political factors discussed above have all given rise to a deeper analysis of what is needed to achieve greater levels of food security and a reduction in hunger. A key outcome of this has been a changing paradigm in the *modus operandi* of approaching food security. This involves an emerging consensus that national governments and donors must reposition their strategies to explicitly promote agricultural and rural development if hunger is to be reduced.

This consensus marks a turn-around in addressing food security and builds on substantial cross-country experiences that prove the effectiveness of agricultural growth in reducing poverty (Wiggins 2003). There are three important mechanisms through which this can work (Matthews 2003). First, there is the direct impact of agricultural growth on farm incomes. Second, there are numerous rural economy linkages, e.g., off-farm employment. Third, there are positive impacts at the national level of reduced food prices, e.g., to raise the real incomes of the rural poor.

What is distinctive about this emerging framework is that, for the first time, it involves an approach where responsibilities are held by national governments and donors alike. Agricultural interventions have had a poor track record in Sub-Saharan Africa, not for the lack of thought, but rather because of an ineffective approach. For example, the weakness of the African rural economy tells a story of State interference, policy distortion, and domestic policy bias, further compounded by unfavorable macroeconomic factors such as unstable commodity prices and exchange-rate fluctuations. It is against this backdrop that Official Development Assistance (ODA) toward agriculture has been ineffective and is falling. For example, between 1990 and 1999 ODA to agriculture (broadly defined) fell by 31%.[6]

Additionally, the story of African agricultural development cannot be divorced from externally driven factors. The issue of agricultural trade reform for development is a make-or-break issue in the current Doha Round of Multilateral Trade Negotiations (MTNs). The priorities of developing countries can be narrowed down to three areas (FAO 2003):[7]

- First, the reform of tariff structures – including peaks and escalations – which often offset the comparative advantage that should accrue from trade.
- Second, addressing the proliferation of non-tariff barriers, e.g., dumping, import licensing, safety measures.
- Third, promoting the need to support domestic agriculture through coherent development interventions.

The connection between reform of agricultural policy in OECD countries, international agricultural trading arrangements, and development prospects for poorer countries brings into focus the issue of policy coherence for development. The latest World Bank (2003) estimates suggest that full removal of all trade barriers would yield global welfare gains of US $ 400–900 billion, more than half of which would go to developing countries, with agriculture and food accounting for 70% of gains. However, it is also clear that many of the poorer countries that are not integrated into the global economy will not benefit in the short to medium term from agricultural trade liberalization. Creating a more favorable context for development, through both domestic and international policy reform, is crucial for Sub-Saharan Africa where, in many countries, 80% of the population depends on subsistence agriculture.

It is against this backdrop that national governments and donors have started to revise their policy approaches to food security. In 2002, African governments committed themselves to allocate at least 10% of their national budget to agriculture, rural development, and food security within five years.[8] In July 2003, the African Union Summit Declaration on Agriculture and Food Security resolved to implement the Comprehensive Africa Agriculture Development Program (CAADP)[9] to adopt fair policies for agricultural development and commit increased budgetary resources for their implementation. Similarly, there is a growing consensus among institutional donors, including the World Bank, the EU, FAO, IFAD (International Fund for Agricultural Development), regional development banks, and major bilateral agencies that national and global hunger reduction targets will not be met unless policies address measures to stimulate agriculture and the rural sector.

In short, the argument has come full circle. Agriculture and rural development are now on the agenda for reducing hunger and feature prominently as key action areas for achieving the Millennium Development Goals. This is evidenced most strikingly by the emerging policy recommendations advanced by the UN Millennium Project Hunger Task Force (see Table 9.1).

The recommendations of the Task Force place significant emphasis on agriculture and nutrition, together with strategies that stimulate rural economies, generate jobs, and establish social services and safety nets to reach those who need them most. The strategy places agriculture at the center of a broad policy agenda for reform. This includes a focus on investment in public goods for agriculture, such as research, as well as public goods that will stimulate the rural economy, e.g., health and education.

A full discussion on the recommendations of the Task Force is beyond the remit of this chapter. However, what is relevant is the degree to which the Task Force Report reflects and redefines contemporary thinking on food security. The essence of this recommended strategy is that in order to reduce food and nutritional insecurity, it is necessary to increase people's capacity to cope.

NGO Perspective

The emerging policy framework around food security fits squarely with the practical experience of NGOs; in particular, the NGO experience in complex ethical scenarios.

There is no template for arriving at decisions as to what to do, other than a general approach of targeting those in most need and promoting their longer-term needs. However, while applying this general approach and bringing a political judgment on any given situation, there are a number of interlocking ethical principles that we believe arise from an NGO perspective. These include:

1. Acknowledging suffering and injustice
2. Providing unconditional universal help
3. Targeting the most extreme poor
4. Catalyzing community-driven development
5. Promoting ethical and political integrity in dialogue with others.

TABLE 9.1 Millennium Hunger Task Force: Emerging policy recommendations (Hunger Task Force 2005)

#	Level	Recommended action	Key interventions to overcome hunger
1	Global	Move from political commitment to action	1. Advocate political action to meet intergovernmental agreements 2. Strengthen the contributions of donor countries and national governments 3. Improve public awareness
2	National	Reform policy and create enabling environment	1. Promote an integrated policy approach to hunger reduction 2. Restore the budgetary priority of the agricultural and rural sectors 3. Build developing country capacity 4. Link nutritional and agricultural interventions 5. Increase poor people's access to productive resources 6. Empower women and girls 7. Remove internal and regional barriers to agricultural trade
3	Community	Increase agricultural productivity of food-insecure farmers	1. Improve soil health 2. Improve access to better seeds and planting materials 3. Establish effective agricultural extension services
4	Community	Improve Nutrition among Vulnerable Groups	1. Promote mother and infant nutrition 2. Prenatal nutrition and supplementary feeding programs 3. Reduce malnutrition among school-age children and adolescents 4. Reduce infectious diseases that contribute to malnutrition
5	Community	Reduce vulnerability to disasters and shocks	1. Build and strengthen national and local early-warning systems 2. Build and strengthen national and local emergency response systems 3. Invest in productive safety nets
6	Community	Make markets work for the poor and increase income for the food-insecure	1. Invest in and maintain market-related infrastructure 2. Improve access to financial services for the poor and food-insecure 3. Provide and enforce a sound legal and regulatory framework 4. Strengthen labor markets for the rural and urban poor 5. Ensure access to pro-poor market information 6. Promote and strengthen community and farmer associations 7. Promote alternative sources of decent employment and income
7	Community	Restore natural assets for the food-insecure	1. Help communities and households to restore or enhance natural resources 2. Secure local ownership, access, and management rights to natural resources 3. Develop natural-resource-based 'green enterprises' 4. Pay poor rural communities for environmental services

Acknowledging Suffering   Non-governmental organizations (NGOs) provide a clear moral and ethical dimension to policy debate. The shock of the immoral is a foundational element in all ethics. NGOs engage in raising awareness of moral issues, which could otherwise be overlooked, given competing interests.

Unconditional Universal Help   NGOs are also driven by a humanitarian ethic that encapsulates the idea of unconditional universal help. This essentially involves prioritizing human life and the dignity of those in greatest danger. Humanitarian approaches are supported by the underlying principles of humanity, impartiality, neutrality, and independence. For an NGO this gives rise to many operational freedoms and first-hand insights. However, it also yields its own ethical dilemmas such as value clashes, the risk of humanitarian complicity, and the risk of indirectly legitimizing human-rights violations.

Targeting Those Most in Need   The operative ethic of international NGOs is directly connected to targeting the extreme poor. Fundamentally, this is an ethical stance that responds to human suffering as a primary ethical stimulus. For Concern, this policy on targeting is predicated on a belief that more weight needs to be devoted to helping those in extreme need. This contrasts with some of the unweighted, aggregated approaches that continue to influence the policy engagements of bilateral and multilateral donors.

Catalyzing Community-Driven Development   Community-driven development is a fourth dimension to Concern's ethical perspective. This recognizes that those who are suffering most have inherent capabilities for full self-expression but lack the resources to do so. The most effective way to harness this is through participatory methods in vulnerability and risk assessment. This is a variant of utilitarianism that aims at prioritizing the 'greatest good of the greatest number in the longer term.'

Promoting Political and Ethical Integrity in Dialogue with Others   NGOs offer unique experiences in complex ethical scenarios. This often involves critical trade-offs between implementing short-term survival interventions and fostering long-term sustainability. The operative challenge of balancing these interventions can contrast with the challenges encountered by other development actors. In a policy context, both approaches are necessary and should dialogue with each other. This reinforces the underlying importance of policy advocacy.

A PRACTICAL AGENDA FOR DEFEATING HUNGER

Thus far this chapter has focused on the evolution of development thinking and practice and how it relates to the problem of world hunger. I have identified certain advances in the conceptual and legal framework for tackling hunger as well as an apparently increased political commitment to the objective. Within this changing context it was shown that NGOs have a distinct perspective to bring to the debate.

As indicated above, the Hunger Task Force Report provides a full agenda for tackling hunger. The report points to a number of responsibilities for governments in developing countries that will need the support of other actors if they are to be realized. In this context, there is a critical role for civil society, both at a local level and through international NGOs. For the governments of least-developed economies, this raises a number of thorny issues. They need to decide the freedoms and scope within which they wish their civil society to develop. Within whatever framework that space for civil society is defined, the respective roles for domestic civil society and international NGOs also need to be determined.

This analysis recognizes that hunger reduction and development has a political dimension, consistent with the thinking of Amartya Sen discussed earlier, which requires governments to facilitate certain 'freedoms.' In this context, civil society and NGOs have a significant role to play, particularly by integrating ethical principles into practical policy responses. This is the focus for the remainder of the chapter, which highlights key lessons for policy in emergencies, development, and advocacy, drawing on Concern's work and experience.

Emergencies

In any given year, between 5% and 10% of undernutrition can be linked to emergencies arising from drought, conflict, and socio-economic shock. The close link between hunger and disaster makes emergency response a priority for NGOs. Emergency events highlight that vulnerability to disasters and shocks are cross-cutting issues that affect all efforts to reduce food insecurity, which points to the centrality of disaster risk reduction for a sustainable development process.[10]

In short, this points to two key lessons:
1. The need to build in-country emergency response capacity
2. The need to invest in productive safety nets to protect the poorest from short-term shocks and longer-term food insecurity.

This is particularly relevant given the increasing complexity of recurring food crises, where the concentration of growing numbers of vulnerable people in one area raises the risk that a single event can cause massive disruption.

Building Emergency Response Capacity   Developing countries need to build their own humanitarian relief institutions and networks to protect against extreme hunger in a timely manner. For some time, NGOs have been leading actors in developing community-based early-warning systems. However, these systems need to be better linked with contingency planning and with multi-year budgeting of national resources for immediate use during a crisis. A number of developing countries have already made significant progress in this area. For example, Ethiopia, 20 years on from its famine of the mid-1980s, has developed efficient early-warning systems for famine. Bangladesh has also developed good nutritional surveillance programs.

National emergency capacity can address a number of shortcomings in international responses to humanitarian disaster. Too many emergencies seem to take national and international institutions by surprise. Preparedness and early monitoring interventions can address this, especially if supported by pre-crisis investments in community planning and micro-finance programs (which have a potential insurance function). In an emergency situation, this can also increase the potential for food assistance to be derived from local or regional purchases in order to support local and regional agricultural and marketing systems. This feeds into a wider debate regarding the monetization of food aid, which in turn, requires increased donor attention and flexibility. National capacity can also be directed into the pre-locating and financing of humanitarian resources for rapid distribution in times of need.

Risk-Reducing Safety Nets   The second lesson focuses on the need to reduce acute vulnerability through productive safety nets. Formal social security or safety-net concepts reflect the 'protection of last resort' function of governments that has underpinned economic growth in most industrialized countries. In a developing country scenario, such safety nets can make the vital difference between life and death when shocks or disasters occur.

A key dimension in the design of safety nets is to ensure their productive value and link to longer-term food security. As argued by the Hunger Task Force Report, this can often involve investing in community activities such as the creation of grain banks, the rehabilitation of degraded environments (through food-for-work and cash-for-work schemes), and the protection of community natural resources. While these interventions are effective and tend to have wider spillover effects, it is important to note that they may often involve high transaction costs and may not be easily implemented in sparsely populated areas. This raises the risk that safety nets miss out on the most vulnerable.

This risk is particularly significant with respect to HIV/AIDS; DeWaal and Whiteside (2003) argue that the HIV/AIDS pandemic has such far-reaching adverse consequences for food insecurity that we are witnessing a 'new-variant famine.' The key feature of this thesis is that, unlike more traditional famines which typically kill the weaker members of society, e.g., children and the old, HIV/AIDS attacks young productive adult workers, leaving an imbalanced population of orphans and elderly in its wake. This hypothesis helps to explain the reality of food shortages and its specific manifestations, e.g., (1) household-level labor shortages due to adult morbidity and mortality, (2) loss of assets and skills due to adult mortality, (3) the burden of care for sick adults and children orphaned by HIV/AIDS, and (4) the vicious interaction between malnutrition and HIV.

A key implication arising from this is the need to reconsider the importance of welfare provision as a risk-reducing strategy. Much of the rethinking in this area has been led by the World Bank. In 2000, the World Bank Social Protection Strategy Paper (World Bank 2000) highlighted the need to expand the definition of social protection to encompass all public interventions that help individuals, households, and communities to manage risk, or that provide support to the critically poor. It also recommended that social protection programs be embedded in an integrated approach to poverty reduction based on a new framework for social risk management. This continues to be a disputed area amongst development actors.

Sustainable Development

As highlighted previously, a critical dimension of sustainable development is the
need to build local capacity in the face of severe implementation constraints. While
initially popularized by academics such as Chambers and Conway (1991), livelihood
approaches to development have been advanced by development agencies such as
the UK's Department for International Development (DfID) as well as the NGO
sector. Livelihoods approaches complement new approaches to aid by providing
important qualitative perspectives on the needs and opportunities faced by the
poor; identifying entry points and sequences for development interventions and by
providing a reality check on the increasingly macro focus on aid (ODI 2002). They
can also bring into focus the views of the poor on policy implementation, which
help to identify interventions that are robust in the face of chronic implementation
constraints (ODI 2002).

Capacity-Building

A key element of development programming is to build capacity by setting in place
sustainable development, stimulating social entrepreneurship, and linking skills,
institutions, and sectors that would otherwise not happen. A vital component to
this approach is working in partnership with local actors. Once successful programs
are in place, this should allow for the disengagement of an international NGO.
However, by its nature, capacity-building is a slow process.

This illustrates the centrality of institutions and governance in the development
process. A weak public sector and poor absorptive capacity are key mitigating
factors in development planning, and also limit the effectiveness of international
aid. In this context, the systematic investment in local institutions must be seen as
an action area for all donors.

This is particularly relevant with respect to agriculture and food security, since
poor countries tend to have low capacity in these areas and ministries of agriculture
are usually forced to compete with the bigger-spending government departments.
The need for on-the-job training applies across staff in government, NGOs, private
sector and community-based institutions. Such broad-scale training efforts will, over
time, create the absorptive and implementation capacity for larger-scale investments.

Advocacy

The emergency and development work of an international NGO affords important
insights, which if applied to policy advocacy can influence the social, economic,
and political environment which impacts on the poor. Advocacy can connect micro-
level program experience to the macro-level policy environment. For many NGOs
a key aspect to advocacy is that it is premised on well-established relations with
bilateral donors and international institutions, with a focus on lesson-learning and
the value of shared organizational experience.

Advocacy takes place in different arenas and at different levels. For example, one
dimension of advocacy involves awareness-raising and the mobilization of views
amongst the public. Advocacy can also focus on national and local processes in

developing countries. This is influenced by the proliferation of advocacy 'entry points' in some Southern civil societies, e.g., PRSPs, legal-rights-based campaigns, and grassroots networks.

Rights-Based Approach (RBA)

Allied to this is an awareness that advocacy should be connected to rights-based approaches in program interventions. This viewpoint is not without controversy. The current political realities in a number of developing countries are not conducive to an active espousal of a rights-based approach to development. A number of NGOs who have committed themselves to an RBA have found it difficult to operationalize and connect it to their existing programs.

The Overseas Development Institute (ODI 2002) has set out other grounds on which there is debate about a rights-based approach to development. First, to realize citizens' full economic and social rights would require levels of public spending – and institutional capacity – which are not feasible in poor States. Second, the human-rights framework provides little guidance on prioritizing the rights of present and future generations. Third, the emphasis on individual over collective rights, and on rights over responsibilities, is sometimes seen to threaten not only environmental sustainability but also economic stability and social cohesion.

However, the incorporation of a rights-based approach has many attractions. A rights-based approach can afford a deeper analysis of underlying problems, leading to rooted advocacy and capacity-building support for local and Southern organizations to complement equally necessary service-delivery work. While there is no single model of an RBA, such approaches tend to incorporate three underlying principles:

1. *Analyzing root causes of problems:* These causes can be identified as either policies (e.g., lack of national laws or strategies) or practices (e.g., implementation of the law, cultural practice) that need to change if the rights of beneficiaries are to be fulfilled. The changes that need to happen will often be at several levels, ranging from local to national, and sometimes to international levels.
2. *Beneficiaries as primary actors for change:* An RBA has a clear premise of empowering those in extreme poverty and enabling social change through a human-rights lens.
3. *Use of legal frameworks and agreements:* This involves using the existing legal frameworks at international, national, and local levels to ensure change in policy or practice.

The incorporation of a rights-based approach thus raises many possible advantages. There is considerable overlap in the basic principles underpinning livelihoods and rights approaches to poverty reduction. First, rights can provide insights into the distribution of power and represent a possible way of examining the operation of institutions and political process that influence the livelihoods of the poor. Second, sustainable livelihoods analysis offers one way to prioritize efforts to obtain rights for the poor.

CONCLUSIONS

Some 840 million people are hungry in the world today. Although progress has been made in hunger reduction, the scale of hunger in a world of plenty raises profound moral issues for the global community. Apart from the moral issues, the existence of hunger on this scale gives rise to huge economic and social costs in terms of morbidity and mortality, labor efficiency, and reduced economic performance.

Significant progress has, however, been made over the past 10–15 years in deriving a conceptual, political, and policy framework for reducing hunger. Many of the technical approaches to achieve this are known. The Report of the Millennium Project Hunger Task Force provides a comprehensive agenda for achieving the Millennium Development Goal on Hunger by 2015. Translating this agenda into action via political will and consistent policy is the challenge.

This chapter has provided an NGO perspective as to how the MDG on Hunger can be achieved through drawing on the experience of Concern case studies; this NGO experience is seen to bring a distinctive ethical perspective, rooted in a humanitarian ethic and recognizing the importance of agricultural and rural development, in achieving broad-based development.

Governments of developing countries are faced with fundamental choices as to the space they wish to give civil society within the development process. If governments restrict that space, whether for their own civil society or for international NGOs, they are likely to retard development and to negate opportunities for reducing hunger.

International NGOs have a particular role to play as partners to the governments and civil society of developing countries. They need to be able to contribute to innovative approaches to reducing hunger, whether in responding to emergencies, building productive safety nets, or strengthening capacity to improve livelihoods. NGOs can also play a role, through advocacy, in improving policy, both in developing countries and at the international level, aimed at reducing, and ultimately eliminating, hunger.

The overall framework for tackling poverty and hunger should be the MDGs, to which world leaders are committed to achieving by 2015. It is possible to achieve the MDG on Hunger by 2015 but this will require big changes in policy in both developed and developing countries. Such changes demand urgency in tackling hunger that has not been sufficiently evident in many countries or at the international level. It is crucially important that such urgency is reflected in future national and international policies and action. All of us – academics, NGOS, policy professionals, and politicians – have a responsibility to generate that urgency.

NOTES

[1] In its common usage, 'hunger' describes the subjective feeling of discomfort that follows a period without eating. The term used more exactly to describe lack of food is 'food insecurity.' Food insecurity exists when people do not have physical and economic access to sufficient, safe, nutritious, and culturally acceptable food to meet their dietary needs and to lead an active and healthy life. This definition of

food adheres to the principle that everyone has a right to adequate food, and to be free from hunger as enshrined in the International Declaration of Human Rights.

[2] The UN Millennium Hunger Task Force is part of the UN Millennium Project, an independent advisory project consisting of 10 thematically oriented task forces. The Millennium Project is a three-year initiative that will be completed by 30 June 2005. The Millennium Project's research focuses on identifying the priorities, processes, and finances necessary to achieve the Millennium Development Goals. The 10 thematically oriented task forces perform the bulk of the research. They comprise representatives from academia, the public and private sectors, civil society organizations, and UN agencies, with the majority of participants coming from outside the UN system. The UN Millennium Hunger Task Force published its report in January 2005. Their work contributed to an overall Millennium Project synthesis report, entitled '*A Global Plan to Achieve the MDGs?*' The author was a member of the UN Millennium Hunger Task Force.

[3] The main focus of this discussion will be on the role of the international NGOs, although it is clearly acknowledged that the role of civil society within developing countries is of crucial importance in the development process.

[4] The work of Amartya Sen and Mahbub ul Haq was also instrumental in the development of the UNDP Human Development Index.

[5] As proclaimed in the Universal Declaration of Human Rights and the International Covenant on Economic, Social and Cultural Rights of 1966.

[6] Agriculture, broadly defined, includes crop and livestock production, land and water, agricultural inputs and services, fisheries and forestry, as well as research training and extension, manufacturing of agricultural inputs, environmental protection, agro-industries, rural development and infrastructure, and regional and river development.

[7] While these priorities outline general concerns amongst developing countries, they also relate to South–South trade, which is increasingly defined by anti-competitive practices..

[8] More recently NEPAD (New Partnership for Africa's Development) has reinforced this commitment by calling for increased efforts to stimulate an agricultural renaissance in support of food security in Africa. Significantly, NEPAD identified the growing prevalence of the HIV/AIDS pandemic as a critical factor exacerbating food insecurity, with its impact on agriculture likened to that of a natural disaster.

[9] In 2002 the CAADP was launched under the auspices of NEPAD.

[10] In this context, Concern views disaster risk reduction responses as incorporating hazard identification and monitoring, vulnerability analysis, mitigation activities, preparedness planning, and advocacy.

REFERENCES

Chambers, R. and G. Conway, 1991. *Sustainable Rural Livelihoods: Practical Concepts for the 21st Century*. Institute for International Development.

DeWaal, A. and A. Whiteside, 2003. *New Variant Crisis: AIDS and Food Crisis in Southern Africa*. Lancet Publishing Group.

Evans, G. and M. Sahnoun, 2002. *The Responsibility to Protect*. Foreign Affairs.

FAO, 2003*Anti Hunger Programme: A Twin-Track Approach to Hunger Reduction – Priorities for National and International Action*.

Hunger Task Force, 2005. *A Global Plan to Achieve the MDGs?*. New York: Millennium Project.

Lindenberg, M. and C. Bryant, 2001. *Going Global: Transforming Relief and Development NGOs*. Kumarian Press.

Matthews, A., 2003. *Coherence Between Ireland's Official Development Assistance and Agricultural Trade and Support Policies*. Presentation to the Development Forum. Preliminary Draft.

ODI, 2002. *Rights and Livelihood Approaches: Exploring Policy Dimensions*. ODI Briefing Paper.

Sachs, J., et al., 2004. *Ending Africa's Poverty Trap*. Brookings Papers on Economic Activity.

von Braun, J., T. Teklu and P. Webb, 1999. *Famine in Africa: Policies for Relief and Prevention*. Baltimore, MD: Johns Hopkins University Press.

Wiggins, S., 2003. Trade reform, agriculture and poverty in developing countries: A review of the empirical evidence. In: *OECD Agricultural Trade and Poverty: Making Policy Analysis Count.* Paris: OECD.

Wolfensohn, J. and F. Bourguignon, 2004. *Development and Poverty Reduction: Looking Back, Looking Ahead.* Washington DC: World Bank.

World Bank, 2000. Social protection sector strategy: From safety net to springboard. Washington D.C.

World Bank, 2003. Global Economic Prospects 2004, Washington, D.C., World Bank.

ERIK THORBECKE

ECONOMIC DEVELOPMENT, EQUALITY, INCOME DISTRIBUTION, AND ETHICS

ECONOMIC DEVELOPMENT, INCOME DISTRIBUTION, AND POVERTY REDUCTION

The essence and major objective of socio-economic development is raising the standard of living of all individuals and particularly that of the poor. It has become almost universally accepted that, in the setting of low-income developing-world countries, economic growth is a necessary condition to poverty reduction. A crucial issue in this context is whether a relatively unequal income distribution is also a precondition for growth to occur. This was the prevailing view under the 'classical' framework based on the argument that the rich (the capitalists) save a larger proportion of their income than the poor (the workers). Hence, for a given level of total income, a more unequal income distribution would generate a larger flow of aggregate savings that could be channeled into investment to yield a higher growth rate of GDP.

In this sense the desirability of an unequal income distribution could be ratio-nalized on economic grounds, while clashing with the ethical concern for more equality, equity, and egalitarianism. 'More poverty today' was a precondition to more economic growth and less poverty in the future. As the Cambridge School boldly put it; impoverishment of the masses is necessary for the accumulation of a surplus over present consumption.

In contrast, the modern approach to the political economy of development provides support for the contention that relative equality is consistent with growth – as demonstrated, for example, by the phenomenal growth performance of East Asia in the last half century. If, indeed, equality is conducive to growth, then it becomes a *means* toward economic development and future poverty alleviation, and the conflict between the ethical objective (norm) of egalitarianism and the economic conditions required for growth disappears. While it is clear that the relationship between inequality and growth is a very complex one and likely to be charac-terized by non-linearities and threshold effects and strongly influenced by political economy factors and the prevailing institutional framework, a case can be made that, under the proper conditions, equality can be conducive to growth.

The essence of this chapter is that if equality is a means to economic development, it converges with the ethical norm of egalitarianism. One important implication of this convergence is that policies and reforms targeted toward greater equality may become much more attractive and palatable to policy-makers – as the presumed trade-off between equity and efficiency tends to vanish.

P. Pinstrup-Andersen and P. Sandøe (eds.), Ethics, Hunger and Globalization: In Search of Appropriate Policies, 165–179.

It is important to clarify at the outset that what is meant by equality here is 'relative equality,' and that any reference to this concept should be interpreted in a relative sense. Even if one subscribes to the thesis that equality is consistent with future growth and development, it is clear that in a free enterprise, market economy incentives play a crucial role. Entrepreneurs are risk-takers and expect to be rewarded for the creative destruction they perform.

Views regarding the optimal degree of equality (or inequality) considered desirable in a given society to achieve the twin objectives of a fair (and just) society and the incentives and rewards required for growth differ significantly. At one extreme is the belief of Margaret Thatcher (and her followers among the right-wing) that:

> It is our job to glory in inequality and see that talent and abilities are given vent and expression for the benefit of all (quoted in George 1997).

At the other extreme would be the welfare-state model long adopted by governments in Scandinavian countries and among developing countries such as Sri Lanka, for example.

The determination of the optimal societal degree of equality (or inequality) depends crucially on the specific norms prevailing in a specific society and the value placed on (a) present versus future equality, and (b) on the degree of inequality required to provide the necessary incentives to entrepreneurs. In principle one could derive the optimal degree of inequality consistent with those constraints through a computable general equilibrium model – an exercise that would go far beyond the scope of this chapter.

EQUALITY AS AN ETHICAL END OR MEANS?

Over the ages, the principle of equality was adopted by many cultures as an ethical end worthy of pursuing. Most religions advocate equality and poverty reduction – in one form or another – as desirable norms. Christianity emphasizes loving one's neighbor as oneself that, at the limit, implies a high degree of altruism and equality; as individuals are expected to treat others as they treat themselves. This implies that interpersonal effects are given a high weight in each individual welfare (utility) function.

In advocating equality, the key question is equality of what? The most likely candidate is the relative equality of human welfare – a highly multidimensional concept. It includes, among other components, the satisfaction of basic needs (particularly for food), as well as adequate education and health status. In addition, human welfare is enhanced in a society in which justice and fairness prevail. Equality of opportunity and 'procedural justice' (Nozick) as opposed to 'distributive justice' (Rawls) would be favored as alternative candidates by many people. However, equality of opportunity and procedural justice are greatly influenced by the prevailing distribution of income, wealth, and other more intangible factors such as the distribution of power, knowledge, and information – all of which can be subsumed under the heading of human welfare.

Any attempt at measuring welfare is confronted with two major and intractable problems; first, how to make interpersonal welfare comparisons and, second, how to weigh each of the myriad of dimensions constituting welfare. However imperfect, the best proxy for human welfare is a person's income or wealth. As Putterman et al. (1998) argued:

> A person's income may be a good proxy for his level of functioning, resource control, and opportunities: We do not claim it is the best one can do, but it is certainly one of the easiest characteristics of a person to measure, among those that might be appropriate for egalitarian concerns.

In this chapter, it is assumed that the distribution of income is an acceptable proxy for the distribution of human welfare and, in a more general sense, for equality as such. A more equal income distribution connotes a more equal distribution of human welfare and *vice versa*. One important qualification is that ideally one should focus on the secondary income distribution, i.e., the primary income distribution after taxes, corrected for the imputed value of public services (such as educational and health benefits) received by individuals.

How did equality evolve into and become a moral principle embraced by so many cultures and societies? Human beings are born with different genetic characteristics and intellectual potentials. They are also born in different settings and are subject to a myriad of different environments as they grow up. Human beings seem to perceive from a very early age how they differ from others physically, psychologically, and anthropologically.[1]

Traditional societies have tended to be organized on the basis of physical and moral differences among groups and individuals (e.g., serfs and lords, slaves and masters, castes, racial and ethnic groups). The segmentation into groups was internalized within societies. Could it be that at some stage the strife for equality was triggered by a reaction to the inequalities caused by segmenting individuals into iron-clad categories that ruled out any intergroup mobility?

The perception of inequality among individuals does not appear to have prevailed in totally hierarchical societies such as the Incas and the feudal system in Middle-Ages Europe. In such hierarchical societies, individuals accepted without questioning their predetermined socio-economic status.

The search for more equality would appear to come into play only after a society has reached a stage where a minimum degree of individualism and universalism prevails. As the rigid societal ordering starts to weaken, the demand for equality among the more deprived groups starts to express itself. Perhaps the prime historical example is the French Revolution, which called for 'Liberty, Equality, and Fraternity.'

This would suggest that the concept of equality is not innate but rather adopted to improve the functioning of a society. In this context one can hypothesize that those societies that embraced this norm functioned and survived better than those that did not. Cooperative behavior, in contrast with equality, would appear to be innate.

Whereas cooperative behavior brings with it a relatively more equal income distribution, if it goes too far it could conflict with the incentives needed for growth. In contrast, competitive behavior is typically associated with a more uneven income distribution that is called for to elicit innovations and investment – leading to growth. Too much equality and cooperative behavior can lead to stagnation, while too much inequality fed by an overly competitive pattern of behavior can lead to the breakdown of the social order.

So far, the concept of equality has been considered and discussed as an *end* in itself. But, as pointed out in the previous section, the modern approach to the political economy of development argues that an initial relatively equal income distribution is consistent with economic development. If this doctrine is correct, it implies that equality is also a *means* toward socio-economic development, and the conflict vanishes between the desirability of egalitarianism on moral and ethical grounds and the (no longer valid) classical contention that the masses have to be impoverished in order to generate the flow of investment needed for growth. Furthermore, as is discussed in some detail in the next section, greater equality of the income distribution has beneficial effects on education, health, and political and social stability, and is a deterrent to crime.

If equality is both an *end* and a *means*, we have a virtuous convergence.

INTERRELATIONSHIP BETWEEN EQUALITY (OR INEQUALITY) AND SOCIO-ECONOMIC VARIABLES

Inequality and Growth

The rejection of the Kuznets hypothesis of the inverted U-shaped relationship between growth and inequality (as per capita income increases) by a number of empirical studies provided much impetus to the new political economy liter- ature that postulates that high initial inequality is detrimental to economic growth (see, for example, Deininger and Squire 1996). The proponents of this approach, while rejecting the immutability of the Kuznets curve, would argue that growth patterns yielding more inequality in the income distribution would, in turn, engender lower future growth paths. Although country-specific evidence is quite limited and might not be generalizable to other settings, a recent study of the dynamics of inequality and growth in rural China based on the growth experience of villages found a robust statistically significant relationship between inequality and lower growth (Benjamin et al. 2004). The authors suggested that the mechanism by which inequality exerts its negative effect was through its tilting of village economic activity away from higher-growth non-agricultural development, and towards agriculture. It thereby impeded the structural transformation into non-agricultural activities.

The Channels Through Which Inequality Affects Growth

The new political economy theories linking greater inequality to *reduced* growth operate through a number of channels, as shown in Figure 10.1 (adapted from Thorbecke and Charumilind 2002). These channels are:

1. Unproductive rent-seeking activities that reduce the security of property;
2. The diffusion of political and social instability, leading to greater uncertainty and lower investment;
3. Redistributive policies encouraged by income inequality that impose disincentives on the rich to invest and accumulate resources
4. Imperfect credit markets resulting in underinvestment by the poor – particularly in human capital;
5. A relatively small income share accruing to the middle class – implying greater inequality – has a strong positive effect on fertility which, in turn, has a significant and negative impact on growth.[2]

   The nature of technological change is still another conduit through which inequality can affect growth. Changes in agricultural technology provide a good example of this link. The Green Revolution technology was developed in the public domain by international research institutions (e.g., the International Rice Research Institute and the International Maize and Wheat Research Institute). Foreign aid donors and foundations provided the funding for the public goods emanating from these institutions. Since the latter were not bound by the profit motive and property rights, they were able to develop high-yielding varieties that were scale-neutral and benefited small farmers as well as large farmers. In a sense, it could be argued that the secondary (as compared to the primary) world income distribution was made somewhat less unequal by the Green Revolution. The spread and diffusion of this technology was facilitated by being in the public domain and has led to a

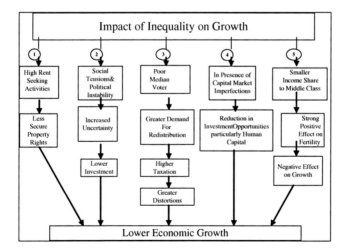

Figure 10.1 Impact of inequality on growth (adapted from Thorbecke and Charumilind 2002)

spectacular acceleration of food production in developing countries and a massive
reduction in food crop prices and world hunger.

In contrast, the present biotechnological revolution is very much in the private
domain. The issues of property rights and royalty payments present obstacles to the
diffusion of this technology to small and poor farmers in the developing world, with
the concomitant risk that the limited growth pattern that will result from adoption
of that technology will be unevenly spread.

In addition to the above channels, some indirect paths (and more circuitous
routes) are likely to exist through which inequality ultimately affects growth. Wide
income and wealth disparities can impact on education, health, and crime through
such manifestations as underinvestment in human capital, malnutrition leading to
low worker productivity, and stress and anxiety. In turn these manifestations may
contribute to lower long-term growth. Both the above channels and additional
indirect paths linking inequality to growth are now discussed in more detail.

We start by describing the causal mechanisms underlying the first two channels
in Figure 10.1, since they are interrelated. The first argument is that a highly
unequal distribution of income and wealth causes social tension and increases
political instability (see channel 2 in Figure 10.1). Greater instability creates more
uncertainty that discourages investment. The political instability, in turn, raises
the risk of the government repudiating contracts, and threatening the security of
property rights, thereby discouraging capital accumulation still further. Moreover,
when the gap between rich and poor widens, the latter presumably have a greater
temptation to engage in rent-seeking or predatory activities at the expense of the
former (channel 1). This increases the number of people who engage in illegal
activities that pose a threat to property rights, thereby lowering economic growth
(Benhabib and Rustichini 1991; Fay 1993). Poor countries may therefore fall into a
vicious cycle of lower investment and reduced growth because they are more likely
to be politically unstable (Alesina and Perotti 1996). Conversely, political stability,
which is enhanced by the presence of a wealthy middle class, has a positive effect
on growth.

The third channel linking inequality to lower economic growth is fiscal in nature
and is based on the work of Persson and Tabellini (1994), who construct a median-
voter model where the political process and economic growth are endogenized. This
channel is based on the effects of inequality on the demand for fiscal redistribution
(Alesina and Rodrik 1994; Bertola 1993; Persson and Tabellini 1994), implying an
inverse relation between inequality and investment in physical capital. An unequal
income distribution implies that the median voter would tend to be poor. In turn,
this would tend to cause a demand for fiscal redistribution financed by taxation.
The taxes would be more distortionary in more unequal societies because the level
of government expenditure and taxation results from a voting process in which
income is the main determinant of a voter's preferences. In particular, in an unequal
society, the poor see large gains from high taxation on the rich. Therefore, the
poorer the median voter in relation to the voter with average income, the higher

the equilibrium tax rate. This in turn leads to an inefficient tax system, distorts economic decisions, and discourages investment and therefore growth.

The fourth channel shown in Figure 10.1 reflects the tendency toward an under-investment in education in the presence of imperfect credit markets. The poor, possessing little or no collateral in the setting of a developing country, are practically sealed off from the formal credit market. Poor households are constrained for cash and, as they are unable to borrow, have a hard time sending their children to school or keeping their children in school. These stylized conditions lead to a vicious cycle where initial inequality and poverty result in underinvestment in education among the poor that further exacerbates inequality. Thus, a more equal income distribution would not only provide collaterals to relatively low-income households but would also tend to reduce credit market imperfections. Parents would have stronger incentives to send their children to school, and thus have a greater demand for more and higher quality education. Their ability and willingness to pay for their children's education would rise, thereby resulting in a higher level of educational attainment in the population.

It has been argued that in a setting characterized by inequality and imperfect capital markets, low-income individuals would tend to underinvest, in general, not just with respect to education. Though the poor and the rich are assumed to possess identical preferences, their savings and investment behavior may differ because they face different institutional constraints and, in particular, credit markets. Redistribution from rich to poor would stimulate growth (Aghion and Bolton 1997; Aghion and Howitt 1998) for the following reasons: (1) large sunk costs preclude the poor from investing in education and entrepreneurial projects, (2) moral hazard occurs because the more the poor must borrow to undertake investment projects, the more they must share their returns with creditors. Incentives to supply the necessary effort to ensure a high return from the investment are therefore low. In this framework, redistribution towards borrowers would result in a favorable incentive effect and, consequently, a positive effect on growth.

The fifth and final channel depicted in Figure 10.1 is based on and reflects a demographic phenomenon (Perotti 1996). Lower-income households tend to have more children than higher-income households. Fertility rates are typically inversely related to household income. Hence, a society characterized by an uneven income distribution would tend to face a higher rate of growth of population than one marked by a more even income distribution. Expressed differently, it means that the smaller the income share accruing to the middle class, the greater its positive impact on fertility and negative impact on economic growth – resulting in a lower average per capita income.[3]

There is at least one more general channel through which inequality affects growth negatively. Since inequality is supposed to affect future growth and the future growth path, it also influences poverty. Cornia (2000) concludes that the widespread increase in inequality has been detrimental to the objective of poverty reduction, because large rises in inequality have stifled growth, and because, for any given growth rate of GDP, poverty falls less rapidly in the case of a more unequal distribution than in the case of a more equitable one. The obvious policy implication which follows from the above causal sequence is that successful poverty alleviation depends not only on favorable changes in average GDP per capita growth but also on favorable changes in income inequality. In short, the study reasserts the contention that the *pattern and structure* of economic growth and development, rather than the rate of growth *per se*, has significant effects on a country's future income distribution and poverty profile.[4]

Impact of Inequality on Education, Health, and Crime

Inequality can entail adverse effects on such socio-economic variables as education, health, and crime, and thus indirectly on growth and development. In addition to the previously discussed impact of inequality on underinvestment in human capital, there are other effects that deserve to be mentioned. The relationship between education and income equality is linked to the economic returns associated with education. Consider the present situation where the nature of technological change and the globalization trend are manifested by a rapidly increasing relative demand for technologically skilled workers. If the demand for unskilled labor is contracting, or growing at a slower rate than the demand for skilled labor, then wage inequalities will increase. The gap between rich and poor will then start to widen. Income inequality will continue to grow until the supply of new college graduates depresses the return on schooling. Moreover, if there is a large disparity in the educational opportunities between the rich and the poor, the benefits of economic growth will be mainly captured by educated workers. This, in turn, would exacerbate income inequality.

Furthermore, as Birdsall (1999) points out:

> When the distribution of income is highly unequal, provision of subsidized basic education to a large segment of the school age population implies a relatively large tax burden on the rich. High- income families are likely to resist. One result can be the under-funding of education – and the decline in quality described above. A second result can be the channeling of public subsidies to higher-education institutions where the children of wealthier families are more likely to be the beneficiaries.

There is a two-way interrelationship between inequality and health. Low income leads to malnutrition, low energy levels, low wages, and back to low income. This vicious cycle dominates poor developing countries. There is overwhelming empirical evidence that poverty drives mortality. Income has a much bigger effect on health at lower rather than higher levels of income. Furthermore, as Deaton (2001) points out:

> income inequality may makes it more difficult for people to agree on the provision of public goods, such as health, water supply, waste disposal, education, and police.

A highly skewed income distribution may reduce the provision of public goods and therefore worsen health.

Moreover, differential access to resources and services, and unequal treatment between the rich and the poor, may result in less effective preventive health care (e.g., childhood vaccinations) and more costly disease control (e.g., tuberculosis treatments). Wilkinson (2000) argues that psychosocial stress (level of depression, isolation, insecurity, and anxiety) is another pathway through which inequality affects health. For all the above reasons, a reduction in deprivation (through, e.g., land ownership, democratic rights, women's agency) might therefore also lead to improved health in the population.

Next, the impact of inequality on crime is explored. Conventional wisdom maintains that income inequality contributes to crime. However, the effects of income inequality on property crime should be distinguished from those on violent crime. The relationship between income inequality and crime can be described by three branches of theories:

1. Becker's (1968) economic theory of crime
2. Merton's (1938) strain theory
3. Shaw and McKay's (1942) social disorganization theory.

Property crime is well explained by Becker's economic theory of crime, while violent crime is explained more by strain and social disorganization theories. Becker's (1968) model was developed further by Ehrlich (1973); the latter argued that payoffs to crime, especially property crime, depend primarily on the 'opportunities provided by potential victims of crime' (Ehrlich 1973, p. 538) as measured by the median income of families in a given community. In other words, the lower the level of legal income expected by an individual to the income level of potential victims, the higher the incentive to commit crimes, particularly crimes against property. Thus, for a given median income, income inequality can be an indication of the differential between the payoffs of legal and illegal activities.

Since incarceration entails loss of income, individuals with low earnings potential have a greater incentive to take the risk of committing burglary; a lower opportunity cost if caught, and a higher utility if successful (Chiu and Madden 1998). The net benefit of contemplated crime for an individual against another person can be modeled as proportional to the income difference between them (Deaton 2001). Moreover, this same model shows how low-income individuals' incentives to commit crime increase if the gap between the rich and the poor is greater.

Income inequality also reduces social capital, e.g., the degree of trust and mutual support among individuals. In a poor developing country, social capital is a crucial element in the functioning of a group and community. The community network constituted by friends (neighbors) and families provides a form of insurance against idiosyncratic shocks (e.g., illness, deaths, crop failure) that otherwise could be devastating to the affected households.

Finally, two sociological theories linking inequality to human welfare are worth mentioning: (1) relative deprivation and (2) role models. Relative deprivation theory holds that high levels of inequality make the poor feel worse off, increasing their alienation and stress (Jencks and Mayer 1990; Mayer 2000). One version of this hypothesis is that children feel deprived when they cannot have the same material possessions as other children in their school or neighborhood. Another version is that relative deprivation makes poorer parents feel stressed and alienated, lowering their expectations for their children or reducing the quality of their parenting (McLoyd 1990). The role-model hypothesis holds that children model their behavior on the behavior of those around them. Inequality tends to exacerbate the impact of negative role models.

In summary, the various channels linking inequality to a worsening in human welfare discussed in some detail in this section imply strongly that a move toward greater equality would be conducive not only to an improvement in welfare today but also to socio-economic growth and economic development in the future.

HOW UNEQUAL ARE GLOBAL AND NATIONAL INCOME DISTRIBUTIONS?

If inequality beyond a certain point worsens human welfare and if, as argued in the preceding section, welfare and economic development can be enhanced through greater equality, a key issue is to determine the actual degree of unevenness in the distribution of welfare. The second section of this chapter showed clearly that welfare is a highly multidimensional concept and, as such, very difficult to measure. Hence income is used as an imperfect proxy for welfare. It will be seen that income is very unevenly distributed worldwide as well as within many countries.

At least three different concepts (types) of income inequality can be identified. The first three concepts listed here were defined by Milanovic (2004). The first concept (*Concept 1*) measures differences in mean incomes between countries (or regions). There is no population weighting and every country counts the same. This concept is useful in determining the extent of convergence or divergence among countries or regions. The second concept (*Concept 2*) takes mean national (or regional) incomes but weights them by countries' (regions') populations. In this case the resulting income distributions will be strongly affected by large countries (e.g., China and India) and regions. The third concept (*Concept 3*) measures interpersonal inequality at the global, national, or regional level. At the global level, this concept yields the world's income distribution.

A crucial question is whether the worldwide income distribution has become more or less even during the recent globalization era. According to Concept 1 (national GDPs per capita with each country weighed equally) there has been an almost continuous and sharply rising divergence over the last half century, with the Gini coefficient rising from around 0.43 in 1950 to 0.53 in 2000. On the other hand, based on Concept 2 (with each country's mean income weighed by population size), worldwide income distribution has become significantly more even with the qualification that this trend is totally driven by China. The bottom graph in Figure 10.2 tracks the evolution of Concept 1 since 1950, while the top panel captures the changes in Concept 2. Figure 10.2 reveals clearly that estimates

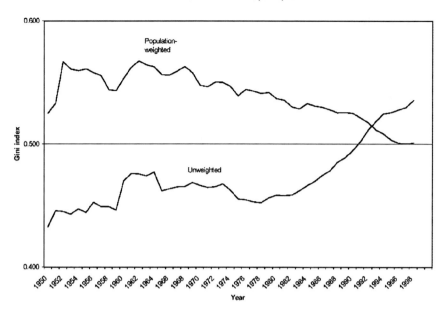

Figure 10.2 Inter-national inequality: unweighted (Concept 1) and population-weighted (Concept 2).
Source: Milanovic (2002b)

of 'between-country' inequality vary widely, depending on whether estimation is made on the basis of use of country weights (Concept 1) or population weights (Concept 2).[5] Note that both of these concepts ignore entirely the distribution of income within countries, and any change over time in those intra-country distributions.

The third concept (Concept 3) captures the inequality across individuals of the world, as it includes the within-country distributions derived from national income and expenditure surveys. In this sense, it is the best measure of world income inequality and its evolution over time. The various attempts to measure it are in general agreement that worldwide inequality is very high (according to Milanovic (2002a), the global Gini coefficient amounted to 0.65 at the end of the 1990s). It rose slightly up to the early 1990s before falling marginally. The extent of inequality can be grasped when it is realized that the richest 1% of people in the world receive as much as the bottom 57%. Alternatively the top 10% of the US population enjoy an aggregate income equal to the total income of the poorest 43% in the world. Or, expressed differently, the total income of the richest 25 million Americans is equal to the total income of almost 2 billion poor (Milanovic, 1999).

Next we explore inequality within countries. The degree of income inequality varies significantly from one country to another. Gini coefficients of intra-country income distributions range between 0.2 and 0.63 (World Bank 2001). The Slovak Republic, Belarus, Austria, and the Scandinavian countries have the most equal income distributions, with Gini coefficients ranging between 0.20 and 0.25. At the opposite end of the spectrum, Sierra Leone, South Africa, Brazil, Guatemala, and Paraguay display the highest Gini coefficients, between 0.60 and 0.65. The US income distribution is relatively less even than in most Western European nations (i.e., a Gini coefficient of 0.41).

In summary, the empirical evidence presented above suggests strongly that both the global income distribution and the within-country income distribution of many countries are very unequal and might thus be an obstacle to achieving the twin objectives of more equality on ethical grounds simultaneously with high growth rates of income. The bulk of world inequality is caused by between-countries' inequality (about 70% of total global income inequality) with the share of within-countries inequality amounting to the remaining 30% of the total. High and rising global inequality of income is likely to worsen inter-country conflicts that could affect global growth.

It is also relevant to note that between-countries inequality has fallen in the last decade because of the excellent growth performance of China and India, which together account for about one-third of the world's population. On the other hand, within-countries inequality has increased in many countries – in particular within China and Eastern Europe. It appears that an important consequence of the globalization forces has been to stimulate the growth of the coastal provinces of China without having a significant impact on the inland provinces.

Finally, of all regions of the world, Africa is by far the worst off in terms of both overall incidence of poverty, extent of inequality, and stagnating growth and development. Of course, poor governance, corruption, geographical factors, and external conditions may be contributing to these three outcomes without necessarily implying any causal connection between inequality and growth. Yet the arguments presented in the third section of this chapter provide some support for this link.

CONCLUSIONS

Equality is a fundamental ethical principle embraced by most cultures and religions. As such it is a desirable norm to achieve and an end in itself. Equality is an all-encompassing concept which presumably can be interpreted as equality of human welfare. In turn, human welfare is multidimensional and very difficult to measure in any objective way. An imperfect, yet acceptable and operationally useful, proxy for human welfare is income. In this sense, equality in terms of the degree of equality in the distribution of human welfare can be approximated by the distribution of income.

In the classical-school paradigm, an unequal income distribution was considered a necessary precondition for growth, economic development, poverty reduction, and a more equitable income distribution in the future, on the grounds that the rich (capitalists) save a larger proportion of their income than the poor (workers).

Hence a more unequal income distribution would generate a larger aggregate flow of savings and investment than a more equal one. This provided a rationale for an initial unequal distribution of income and wealth but created a conflict with the ethical norm of equality as a desirable *end*.

In contrast, the modern approach to the political economy of development identified many channels and paths through which an initially more equal income distribution is consistent with and contributes to growth and socio-economic development. The third section of this chapter discussed in some detail the positive impact of relative income equality on human welfare and, in particular, on political and social stability, education, health, and the deterrence of crime.

Under this new approach, equality was converted into a *means* toward development and poverty alleviation, removing the previous conflict between the desirability of egalitarianism on moral and ethical grounds and the classical view that the masses have to be impoverished in order to generate the flow of investment needed for growth. An important implication of the convergence of equality as both an *end* and as a *means* is that policies and reforms targeted toward improving the education and health of the poor and, in general, reducing large inequities in income and wealth may become politically less difficult to implement.

Underlying a concern for equality is the presumption that income tends to be unequally distributed. The empirical evidence presented in the fourth section of this chapter shows how relatively unevenly world income is distributed and how pronounced the degree of inequality is within many countries. Hence a concern for more equality appears justified – particularly if it does not conflict significantly with efficiency. Clearly the strife for equality should not go so far as to act as a deterrent to the entrepreneurial incentives that are crucial to the functioning of a private enterprise system.

ACKNOWLEDGMENTS

This chapter was prepared for an H. E. Babcock workshop on 'Ethics, Globalization, and Hunger' held at Cornell University on 17–19 November 2004. I owe a debt of gratitude to Alice Sindzingre for extremely useful suggestions in the process of writing of this chapter. The manuscript also benefited from comments by two anonymous referees.

NOTES

[1] John Adams was reputed to have said that 'Inequality of mind and body are so established in the constitution of human nature that no art or policy can ever plane them down to a level.'

[2] See Thorbecke and Charumilind (2002) for a detailed discussion of those channels. The rest of this section draws on this study.

[3] Greater inequality does not necessarily have to imply higher fertility rates. That depends on where the increased dispersion in the income distribution occurs and where and how fast fertility rates change as one moves along the income distribution. For example, if one reduces inequality, but not mean incomes, in a very poor economy, and if fertility rates remain high until one reaches income levels twice the

poverty line – both reasonable conjectures – then fertility would increase with a drop in inequality, not decrease. The basic point made above in the text is, of course, correct but needs to be qualified. I am grateful to a referee for suggesting this qualification.

[4] For a more detailed discussion of the crucial importance of an appropriate pattern of growth and structural transformation on income distribution and the future growth path, see Nissanke and Thorbecke (2004).

[5] Estimates with use of country-weights take each country as one observation, while those with population weights give people equal weights. The merits and demerits of using either method are discussed in detail in Ravallion (2004), who favors some hybrid weighting scheme as a best way of analyzing 'between-country' inequality.

REFERENCES

Aghion, P. and P. Bolton, 1997. A theory of trickle-down growth and development. *Review of Economic Studies* 64: 151–172.

Aghion, P. and P. Howitt, 1998. *Endogenous Growth Theory*. Cambridge, MA and London: MIT Press.

Alesina, A. and R. Perotti, 1996. Income distribution, political instability, and investment. *European Economic Review* 40: 1203–1228.

Alesina, A. and D. Rodrik, 1994. Distributive politics and economic growth. *Quarterly Journal of Economics* 109(2): 465–490.

Becker, G.S., 1968. Crime and punishment: An economic approach. *Journal of Political Economy* 76: 169–217. Reprinted in: *Chicago Studies in Political Economy*, edited by G.J. Stigler. Chicago and London: University of Chicago Press, 1988.

Benhabib, J. and A. Rustichini, 1991. *Social Conflict, Growth and Income Distribution*. New York University, Department of Economics, New York.

Benjamin, D., L. Brandt and J. Giles, 2004. The dynamics of inequality and growth in rural China: Does higher inequality impede growth? Paper presented at a Conference on Inequality in China, Cornell University, October, 2004, mimeo.

Bertola, G., 1993. Market structure and income distribution in endogenous growth models. *American Economic Review* 83: 1184–1199.

Birdsall, N., 1999. *Education: The People's Asset*. Center on Social and Economic Dynamics, Working Paper 5, September 1999.

Chiu, W.H. and P. Madden, 1998. Burglary and income inequality. *Journal of Public Economics* 69: 123–141.

Cornia, A.G., 2000. *Inequality and Poverty in the Era of Liberalisation and Globalisation*. UNU/WIDER Discussion Paper, 2000 (Chapter 1 in: Cornia, G.K. ed. *Inequality, Growth, and Poverty in an Era of Liberalization and Globalization*, Oxford University Press, 2004).

Deaton, A., 2001. *Health, Inequality, and Economic Development*. Cambridge, MA: National Bureau of Economic Research, Working Paper 8318.

Ehrlich, I., 1973. Participation in illegitimate activities: A theoretical and empirical investigation. *Journal of Political Economy* 81: 521–565.

Deininger, L. and L. Squire, 1996. A new data set measuring income inequality. *World Bank Economic Review* 10: 565–591.

Fay, M., 1993. *Illegal activities and income distribution: a model of envy*. New York: Department of Economics, Columbia University.

George, S., 1997. How to win the war of ideas: Lessons from the Gramscian right. *Dissent* 44(30): 47–53.

Jencks, C. and S.E. Mayer, 1990. The social consequences of growing up in a poor neighborhood. In: Lynn, L. and M. McGeary, ed. *Inner-City Poverty in the United States*. Washington DC: National Academy Press.

Mayer, S.E. 2000. How did the increase in economic inequality between 1970 and 1990 affect American children's education attainment? Joint Center for Poverty Research. University of Chicago.

McLoyd, V., 1990. The impact of economic hardship on black families and children: Psychological distress, parenting and socio-emotional Development. *Child Development* 61: 311–346.

Merton, R., 1938. Social structure and anomie. *American Sociological Review* 3: 672–682.

Milanovic, B., 1999. *True World Income Distribution, 1988 and 1993: First Calculation Based on Household Surveys Alone.* World Bank Policy Research Working Papers Series No. 2244, November.

Milanovic, B, 2002a. *Can we Discern the Effect of Globalisation on Income Distribution? Evidence from Household Budget Surveys.* World Bank Policy Research Working Paper 2876. April 2002.

Milanovic, B., 2002b. *The Ricardian Vice: Why Sala-i-Martin's Calculations of World Income Inequality are Wrong.* World Bank, mimeo, November.

Milanovic, B., 2004. *Half a World: Regional Inequality in Five Great Federations.* World Bank and Carnegie Endowment for International Peace, April.

Nissanke, M. and E. Thorbecke, 2004. *The Impact of Globalization on the World's Poor.* UNU/ WIDER Working Paper.

Perotti, R., 1996. Growth, income distribution and democracy: What the data say. *Journal of Economic Growth* 1(June): 149–187.

Persson, T. and Tabellini, G., 1994. Is inequality harmful for growth? *American Economic Review* 84(3): 600–621.

Shaw, C. and H. McKay, 1942. *Juvenile Delinquency and Urban Areas.* Chicago, IL: University of Chicago Press.

Putterman, L., J.E. Roemer and J. Silvestre, 1998. Does egalitarianism have a future? *Journal of Economic Literature* 36: 861–902.

Ravallion, M., 2004. Competing concepts of inequality in the globalization debate. Paper presented at the Brookings Trade Forum, Globalization, Poverty, and Inequality. 13–14 May 2004, Washington DC.

Thorbecke, E. and C. Charumilind, 2002. Economic inequality and its socioeconomic impact. *World Development* 30(9): 1477–1495.

Wilkinson, R.G., 2000. *Mind the Gap: Hierarchies, Health, and Human Evolution.* London: Weidenfield and Nicholson.

World Bank, 2001. *World Development Report.* Washington D.C.

ON THE ETHICS AND ECONOMICS
OF CHANGING BEHAVIOR

INTRODUCTION

The purpose of this chapter is to address the ethics and economics of changing behavior in food and agricultural production, consumption, marketing, and trade. It is important to focus on behavior change because economic outcomes are influenced by individuals' behaviors, which are themselves influenced by evolving social values and ethics. But changing behaviors entail benefits and costs, and thus economic considerations are relevant, even if ethics has intrinsic characteristics. As the world becomes more densely populated and the food chain becomes longer and more complex, some ethical questions have become more important than others.

By 'ethics,' in this chapter, we refer to the principles of conduct that govern an individual, a group, or a profession. Nevertheless, in order to provide more insight into these principles of conduct, we also make reference to 'ethics' as a sub-discipline of philosophy, which deals with what is wrong and right, and with issues of moral obligations and duty.

The largest ethical issue of food production, consumption, and trade is the persistence of hunger. Under no ethical concept is hunger acceptable; comprehensive sets of policies and programs exist to address the problem; yet hunger still persists (von Braun 2003). The setting of goals has so far not had strong effects on cutting hunger at an accelerated rate. We may ask what fresh approaches for strengthening ethical foundations and rights may facilitate behavior that contributes to reducing hunger.

A second related ethical issue arises around the behavior that determines the means of poor people's access to food. Production technology, property rights (including land and intellectual property rights), and access to markets are part of this. Implicit and explicit hindrances of production possibilities result from ethics of technology pessimism among those who could facilitate progress (biotechnology is one example), from over- regulated or ill-designed intellectual property rights (preventing fast access by poor nations), and from trade protection (von Braun and Brown 2003).

Another ethical issue has to do with consumers' lack of trust in food safety. Use of pesticides on produce, genetically modified foods, and spillovers from animal diseases to humans, have made consumers apprehensive about the impacts of food on human health. Also, the ethical externalities of production processes, such as animal welfare and environmental concerns, have become more relevant to consumers, especially in high-income countries.

P. Pinstrup-Andersen and P. Sandøe (eds.), Ethics, Hunger and Globalization: In Search of Appropriate Policies, 181–200.
© 2007 *Springer.*

A growing issue is the perceived deepening of information asymmetries between producers and consumers. Since agricultural research is increasingly being conducted by scientists affiliated to private corporations, consumer groups are suspicious of research outcomes, which they feel are geared more toward profit maximization rather than toward enhancing consumers' interests. Related to this is the concern about increasing concentration in the food industry that may enable producers and retailers to transmit information selectively, thus infringing on consumers' sovereignty to make informed decisions with regard to food consumption.

Lastly, there are ethical issues arising from externalities of behavior and from new ethics itself. For instance, consumer behaviors such as unhealthy diets can be carried over to the next generation; ethically founded production and trade regulations may adversely impact others through price and income effects, in that the enhanced moral well-being of some (rich) consumers may have negative repercussions on other (poor) producers and consumers.

The questions we set out to reflect on here are:

- *Incentives for ethics:* What kind of incentives can induce behavior change from stakeholders in order to address the issues mentioned above? Are such incentives 'ethical'?
- *Regulation for ethics:* To what extent can ethical principles be used to establish institutions and organizations that uphold ethics in the food and agricultural sector? What is the role of regulations and restrictions for that?
- *Activism for ethics:* What kind of interventions can induce positive ethical activism and consumer strengthening on food ethics?
- *Distribution of ethics:* Whose ethics determine the shape of the food system? And how will ethical behavior related to production, consumption, and trade impact on the poor?

While food consumption is conditioned by hugely diverse habits and tastes around the world, and production is partly a function of agro-ecologies, again of huge diversity, the food system is driven by economics and not by an ethical value system. Increasingly, however, the links of the food system to human health come to the forefront. When the food system is understood as part of, or as closely linked to, the health production system, the ethics of the medical profession may shape the future food system ethics.[1] One hypothesis that drives our reflection below is that the ethics of economics and the ethics of the medical profession are conflicting over the design of food and agricultural policies; the risk is high that incoherent, unfair, and inefficient policies will result from that. The potential for a 'healthy' new ethics of food, however, also exists. We will draw on both professions' ethical principles in an attempt to relate them to the ethics and economics of changing behavior in agricultural production, consumption, marketing, and trade. This is addressed in the first part of the chapter.

In a second part of the chapter, we look at the current dynamics of the food systems, first concentrating on changing consumer behavior. Second, we examine the resulting changes in producer behavior and also the role of the information industry in influencing behavior. We then explore the implications of increasing trade on both consumer and producer behavior. Finally, we reflect on 'what to do' in practical terms.

ETHICAL PRINCIPLES IN ECONOMICS AND THE MEDICAL FIELD

Whose Ethics?

According to James (2002), there are two types of ethical problems in the food and agricultural sector. The first type (type I) occurs when there is no general understanding of what is ethical, while the second type (type II) arises when there are recognized ethical principles that are violated because of existing negative incentives for economic agents to act in an unethical manner. Type I problems can usually be resolved through ethical discourse, while the resolution of type II problems require changes at the institutional level to remove harmful incentives.

For type I problems, evaluating whether a deed is ethical is not always a straightforward task. Although some virtues, such as courage and wisdom, are universal, there is considerable disagreement on how exactly one should define ethical behavior.

In philosophy, there are two main opposing schools of thought (see Thompson 2000). On one side, consequentialism, to which the utilitarian school belongs, argues that a deed's ethical value should be defined based on the consequences it brings, with the ultimate objective being the maximization of welfare (i.e., happiness) for all stakeholders. Thus, in practice, consequentialists concentrate on predicting and evaluating possible consequences. On the other side, (neo-)Kantian philosophers argue that an action is ethical if the individual feels he/she has the right or duty to execute such an action. This view inspires itself from Kant's 'categorical imperative,' which defines an ethical action 'as objectively necessary in itself, without reference to another end' (Kant 1785). In practice, this school of thought emphasizes obligation, duty, and rules.

Other approaches to the definition of ethical behavior exist. For instance, virtue ethics emphasizes the character of the individual rather than the action itself. Virtue ethics maintains that individuals make ethical decisions with the pursuit of 'a particular kind of excellence' (Dobson 2004). This approach bases itself on the importance of the generally accepted values of 'courage, wisdom, temperance, fairness, integrity, and consistency' for individuals who find themselves within strong moral communities that promote these virtues. Some of civil society's group or individual actions' attractiveness for larger society derives from this thinking.

The lack of ethical perspective in food and agricultural policies results partly from the neglect of ethics in mainstream economic theory. In this first part of the chapter we investigate this shortfall and see how that reflects on economic policies related to food and agriculture. We will then look into the medical field for inspiration on creating institutions and organizations that would encourage ethical behavior in the food and agricultural sector.

The medical field has potentially similar ethical issues as in the food system in that information asymmetries between physicians and patients exist and the field has experienced a number of scientific and technological advances for which the long-term impacts are unknown. But, unlike the food and agricultural sector, the medical field has enjoyed a dynamic tradition of ethical dialogue since the days of Hippocrates (Beauchamp and Childress 1994; Nicholson 1997). This long tradition of ethical discourse has enabled the creation of institutional mechanisms to mitigate the associated externalities of change and technological advancement (Arrow 1963; Stiglitz 2000).

Ethical Perspectives in Economics

Although the economics profession originates from both ethics and engineering, it has evolved by concentrating heavily on the engineering approach (Sen 1987). Thus, the profession has tackled 'logistical' issues such as how to increase wealth, while neglecting questions of ultimate motivation and purpose (Sen 1987). One manifestation of this narrow view is that in modeling human behavior, economic theory has relied on the assumption that human beings act in a rational manner and are guided by self-interest with the objective of maximizing their utility/profit (Sen 1987). However, not all modeling of human behavior makes such assumptions. For instance, the rational choice model enables economists to consider objectives beyond profit maximization, and some have used it to consider issues such as ethical behavior (e.g., Zusman 1993). Nevertheless, most applications of economic theory eliminate moral considerations in human behavior. In effect, the influences of social institutions such as community, culture, and religion are excluded as explanatory factors of human behavior (Gowdy and Walton 2003). In reality, however, individual preferences and tastes are socially determined and influenced: as stated by Veblen

> the type of temperament belonging to the dominant ethnic element in any community will go far to decide what will be the scope and form of expression of the community's habitual life process (Veblen 1899).

Furthermore, economic theory largely ignores the environmental and social limitations that humans face (Barham 2002).

Another manifestation of the limited role of ethics in economics is the preference for a 'positive' economic analysis over a 'normative' one, even though the difference between the two perspectives is not clear-cut. A 'value-free' analysis is difficult to make in any circumstance because, in the end, an economist uses some of his/her profoundly held values in the choice of research themes over the alternatives and also to promote a certain idea. Indeed

> to understand the moral relevance of positive economics requires an understanding of the moral principles that determine this relevance (Hausman and McPherson 1993).

In addition, it is important for the economist to make his/her underlying value judgments (or 'point of view') apparent and clear in order to make them the subject of discussion. As stated by Weber:

> in the method of investigation, the guiding 'point of view' is of great importance for the construction of the conceptual scheme which will be used in the investigation (Weber 1897).

Further, in welfare economics, where the economist is trying to determine what is best for society, it is impossible to move away from a normative analysis because the economist is essentially judging social achievements (Sen 1987). While the fundamental theorems of welfare economics contain a 'do no harm' principle, they also distance welfare economics from ethics. The Pareto principle states that society as a whole is better off if one person is made better off without making anyone else worse off, assuming that all individuals act in self-interest to maximize their utility (happiness or well-being) (Sen 1987). The problem here is three-fold: First, the Pareto principle assumes that an individual's motivation is purely selfish; second, it assumes that the only things of value for a society is individuals' utilities; and, third, Pareto optimality does not contain any distributional considerations (Sen 1987).[2]

The direct result of this narrow perspective in economic theory is that economic policies have ignored human motivations such as 'goodwill,' 'duty,' 'altruism,' and 'loyalty,' as well as the role of many social institutions, such as community groups, cooperatives, and faith-based organizations, in influencing behavior (Sen 1987; Marshall 2004). Some economists, such as Oded Stark, have attempted to take these human motivations into consideration in their analysis. They start from the position that humans possess varying degrees of 'altruism,' inherited through genetics and/or cultural practices, which may be a strong human motivation in human behavior (Stark and Bergstrom 1993). Altruistic behavior is in a sense the creation of 'mutually beneficial' and 'self-enforcing' agreements between individuals. For Stark, altruistic behavior starts at the family level, within parent – child relationships and sibling relations, and can expand throughout a society through other human relationships, thus creating 'altruistically linked groupings' (Stark 1989).

As for institutions that have a significant impact on human behavior, religious institutions have been especially predominant. Indeed, religions have always provided moral guidelines and frameworks for human behavior (Stephens 1995). They have also promoted altruistic behavior as well as ideas of social justice, compassion, and concern for the disadvantaged (Stark 1989; Marshall and Keough 2004). Further, beyond giving spiritual guidance, religious institutions get involved at the community level by providing basic services such as food, healthcare, and education to the needy (Marshall and Keough 2004). In Africa, for instance, close to half of all social services are being provided by faith-based organizations (Sarbib 2004).

Hence, the neglect of some human motivations such as altruism, and the inattention given to important actors such as religious institutions, are some of the reasons that economic policies have not been effective in the battle against hunger and malnutrition, or in mitigating the negative externalities of uncertainties and information asymmetries in the food system. In *Towards a Hunger Free World*, Swaminathan et al. (2004) articulate the need for an 'ethical revolution,' where the relationships between 'rational' and 'spiritual' qualities of human behavior would be explored. The basic principles embodied in this 'revolution' would be 'diversity, equity, justice, and moral leadership,' and the most efficient way of inducing this revolution would be to integrate these principles into the 'ongoing sustainable development process at the local, national, regional, and global levels' (Swaminathan et al. 2004).

The medical system, through organizational structure along with institutional mechanisms, has been able to address emerging ethical issues and also to encourage ethical behavior from stakeholders. It may thus serve as a model for the food and agricultural system.

Lessons from the Medical Field to Promote Ethical Behavior in Food and Agriculture

In the medical field, in contrast with economics, ethics is institutionalized. A number of medical associations exist at every level whose main purpose is to promote ethical behavior among physicians and to discuss health issues.[3]

Although ethical economic associations such as the Association for Social Economics (ASE)[4] exist, such organizations are not as widespread as in the medical field, and thus do not play a central role in the economics profession. However, these types of organizations are important because they enable the creation of an institutional base for ethical conduct and also permit a group of individuals with similar interests to have a voice in the policy arena.

In the medical field, professional organizations have played a key role in stimulating high moral aspirations from medical professionals. On their own accord, prospective doctors at the end of their medical education typically swear an Oath to uphold high ethical standards in their work.[5] In addition, when joining a professional medical association, they are required to pledge to endorse the association's code of ethics (AMA 2004). The code of ethics, usually inspired by the Hippocratic Oath,[6] contains prescriptions on how the professional should act and what he or she should aim for. In the case of non-compliance, a set of sanctions as severe as expulsion from the association can be applied (AMA 2004).

The rationale behind a code of ethics is two-fold; first, it serves to express a group's adherence to a certain standard of conduct and, second, it increases the likelihood that a person within that group will behave according to that code of conduct (Lichtenberg 1996).

The idea of a code of ethics in the food and agricultural sector may have some advantage in that it would provide the definition of a clear universal guideline of what is acceptable and what is not in food production processes. It would also promote consumer trust in the industry by adding human well-being as another criterion for corporate decisions (Garland 2003). However, instituting a code of ethics in food and agriculture is not as straightforward as in the medical field because the stakeholders in the food and agricultural system do not have personalized relationships such as the one a doctor has with his or her patients, and therefore no party feels a direct responsibility for the other (Garland 2003). Moreover, in the food and agricultural system, because of the complexity of the food chain, it is not clear who would adhere to a code of ethics; would it have to be the scientists affiliated to the big corporations producing food, or the CEOs of these companies, or all the employees? (Garland 2003).

Nevertheless, in recent years, several attempts to implement a code of ethics in the food industry have been made. At the industry level, for instance, in view of the fact that, in developing countries, pesticide poisoning affects between 1 million and 5 million cases every year and that the long-term effects of exposure to pesticides can cause chronic illnesses such as cancer (WHO, FAO, and UNEP 2004), the Food and Agriculture Organization (FAO) devised the voluntary International Code of Conduct in the Distribution and the Use of Pesticides in 1985 (amended in 1989 and revised in 2002). This code of conduct has been accepted by most of the industry and the NGO community, as well as most national governments, and has translated into significant progress in pesticide legislation and regulations. However, little progress has been made in implementation efforts (Dinham 1995).

Another example on the global scale was the drafting of an International Code of Conduct on the Human Right to Adequate Food in 1997 by a group of non-governmental organizations (NGOs) as a follow-up to the World Food Summit (Robinson 2002). The purpose of this code was to define more precisely the State's obligations in providing equal access to food. Initially, this code of conduct had little impact on countries' legislations; many countries' constitutions referred to the right to food but only few had legislation associated with it (Robinson 2002). But, in 2004, this Code of Conduct advanced to voluntary guidelines accepted by most nations. It may thus have a potentially far-reaching impact for food policy.[7]

Apart from the medical professionals' pledge to uphold a certain level of moral standards, the medical field has a set of more restrictive requirements that further strengthen the trust and confidence that patients invest in their physicians. Indeed, entry to the medical field is exclusive and, while in school, the demands in regard to educational standards are very high (Arrow 1963). Scholars of food production and marketing do not have to go through such rigorous training programs.

One way to forge better consumer trust in food producers is more stringent labeling requirements (Barham 2002). Labels focusing on food quality and production processes would enable consumers to make informed decisions on what they are consuming, and in so doing increase their trust in food producers (Barham 2002; Clegg 2003). Commercial brand names can work in similar ways.

CHANGES IN FOOD SYSTEMS AND ETHICAL IMPLICATIONS

The food system is rapidly globalizing. But institutions for globally accepted ethical foundations of the food system are only slowly evolving (codes of conduct, right to food, etc.). The food system has experienced a wide range of changes since the 1980s.

For example, consumers have become a driving force to changes in the food system (see Figure 11.1). Through organized consumer and public-interest groups, especially in industrialized countries, consumers are being more vocal and specific in their demands with regard to the quality and safety of foods available to them, and are also questioning the long-term impacts of current food production processes. This has induced important changes in the agricultural sector (Lang 2004; Variyam and Golan 2002). Indeed, producers who had previously concentrated solely on productivity and efficiency gains are changing their production paradigm in response to consumer demands. To that effect, producers are increasingly forming complex partnerships and are also using technological innovations (Lang 2004). In addition, the food chain is increasingly being accompanied by an information chain, at least in industrialized countries, in internationally traded foods and foods in the supermarket systems of the world. Also, the whole food system has become more research-based.

The current trend of trade liberalization also has important implications for both producers and consumers, as food producers in developing countries become more connected to producers and consumers in developed countries. This has meant that producers in the South are also undergoing change in order to satisfy the demands of consumers in the North (Kirsten and Sartorius 2002).

Trends in Consumer Behavior

Social institutions such as culture, religion, and community heavily influence individual consumer behavior. In the current global setting there appears to be a convergence in consumer preferences across countries and culture; brands names such as Coca Cola and McDonalds are commonplace across the globe as a result of globalization and the revolutionary advances in global telecommunications (Firat 1995). However, this convergence is largely 'superficial,' and consumers remain a non-homogeneous group. Indeed, consumer preferences vary widely across lifestyles, cultures, and economic levels (Venkatesh 1995). Still, a fast-growing global retail food system (i.e., supermarkets) is the dominant feature of the changing food system.

In the developed world, consumers have witnessed a decline in the percentage of total household expenditure allocated to food, along with a greater variety and

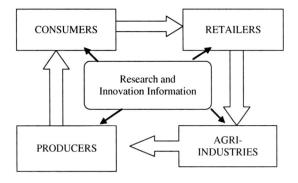

Figure 11.1 Consumer-driven food systems

greater choice in food products. However, despite these improvements, since the early 1980s consumers have increasingly expressed their concern with food safety issues and the long-term impacts of current food production processes on biodiversity and the environment (Lang 2004).

Europeans, having experienced more food-related scares such as 'mad-cow disease,' tend to be more sensitive to issues of food safety. They are therefore more risk-averse and cautious about accepting new technologically engineered food products (Ansell and Vogel 2005). As a result, the demand for alternative agricultural products (e.g., organic produce) has increased dramatically in the last two decades (Wegener 2002).

In the USA, the rise of obesity and related illnesses (such as heart disease) and the advent of scientific evidence linking health to diet, have induced anxiety about the health effects of foods consumed (Variyam and Golan 2002). And, similarly to the European case, this has translated into increased demand for organic food products. From 1999 to 2000 alone, the demand in such foods increased by 20% (Davis and Stewart 2002).

In most developing countries, the push toward urbanization among the young population has translated into an increased demand for processed foods (FAO 2003). However, large segments of the world's poor population, especially in rural areas, remain outside the globalized retail food system and lack access to healthy diets due to poverty.

Trends in Producer Behavior and Trade

On the supply side, the agricultural sector is changing both in developing and developed countries. The world's agriculture sector is characterized by bifurcation. About 85% of the world's farms are smaller than 2 ha and in most low-income countries the farms are still smaller, while large farms in OECD countries expand in size. The uncertain future of millions of smallholder businesses is a large development issue and management of the transformation of this small-farm sector raises ethical issues.

The current WTO negotiations aim for a 'Development Round.' This aim is basically driven by ethical concerns, but is also a matter of efficient use of global agricultural resources, currently misused due to distorting government interventions. A rule-based trade system, where rules are fair and co-owned by both rich and poor countries, is a fundamental element of an ethical food system.

With increasing trade liberalization, a recurrent issue is the need for a universal set of quality standards for agricultural produce. In 1963, a joint WHO/FAO effort established the Codex Alimentarius Commission in order to outline such standards (WHO/FAO 2004). With the creation of the World Trade Organization (WTO), these Codex standards have become an important assessment tool of whether national food safety standards constitute non-tariff barriers in dispute settlements within the WTO. However, the demand for high-quality produce from consumers in developed countries may be marginalizing small producers and exporters in developing countries.

Another issue present notably in Europe is the public's sense of loss of control of some cultural patrimony with regard to food products (Ansell and Vogel 2005). Indeed, with increased trade, more cheaply produced products are increasingly being imported from other countries and regions, thus competing with local produce.

A strong trend has been the vertical integration of producers and marketers, which has led to the concentration of the agricultural and food processing sector (FAO 2003). This trend has also affected farmers in developing countries, with liberalization of trade facilitating the alignment of some small-scale farmers from the South with larger producers from the North. In particular, the growth of alternative agricultural production, which is relatively labor-intensive, has increased these types of partnerships with mechanisms such as contract farming (Kirsten and Sartorius 2002).

Longer, more complex, food chains and fiscal constraints have reduced States' capacity to insure food safety and have relegated the responsibility to large corporations (Lang 2004). These corporations have increasingly taken on this responsibility in order to differentiate themselves from competitors and to protect their brands (FAO 2003). The problem here is that the 'privatization' of quality control and safety insurance may have negative distributional effects in that only consumers with adequate economic resources would have access to safe foods (FAO 2003). Further, on the supply side, although the new partnerships between big corporations and small farmers in developing countries have created opportunities for some small farmers, others who do not have the resources to meet the necessary quality standards are left marginalized from the production chain (Kirsten and Sartorius 2002). Also, the farmers who are able to align themselves with large corporations become dependent on these corporations for input supplies such as capital goods, seeds, fertilizers, and pesticides (FAO 2003). Finally, increased concentration in the agricultural sector has meant greater power for large producers in the provision of food-related information; a point that we will come back to in the next subsection.

The Role of the Information Industry

Information and the capacity to process and respond to it are central for forming behavior. Food-related behaviors are, however, formed early in life and adjust slowly. Still, the recent change in consumer behavior is due in part to better health and diet information dissemination through government educational programs, nutrition food labels, the media, and producers' health claims. But despite this, especially in high-income countries, among 'informed populations' there is a high level of consumer mistrust of agricultural produce (Variyam and Golan 2002).

A problem in the food information industry is that the available information on quality and safety is often biased. For instance, it has been established that consumers' perceptions of the safety of food from organic production is very different from what can be proven scientifically (Wegener 2002). Consumers may also choose to be imperfectly informed if the price of the news story is high relative to the marginal benefit it brings. Moreover, consumers may find that the opportunity cost of processing further information is too high compared with income growth, and therefore decide to remain uniformed (Swinnen et al. 2003).

There are three major sources of information for consumers: the 'popular media,' producers' advertising and marketing campaigns, and public education programs from government and consumer/public-interest groups (Lang 2004; Wade and Conley 2000). The biggest source of information is the popular media; 90% of consumers in the developed world get their information about food mainly through the press and television (Swinnen et al. 2003). The reason why the media has become such an important source of information is that urbanization has detached the bulk of consumers from farmers (Wade and Conley 2000). There are major inbuilt biases with the media's reporting on food-safety issues. For instance, massive media coverage of a particular food scare can cause a heightened perception of risk, which can impact demand negatively and in turn severely affect production of a particular food. In addition, many media organizations adhere to a certain ideology and tend to promote this ideology in the way they report stories. Further, there is a general tendency in the media to report more widely on bad news because that is what consumers find interesting (Swinnen et al. 2003).

Producers' marketing and advertising campaigns can have profound impacts on consumer behavior. Galbraith points out that consumers living in 'affluent societies' are more susceptible to advertising because they have passed the stage where their basic needs are met (Galbraith 1958).

In contrast to producers, consumer and public-interest groups have small budgets for advertising and marketing; therefore, their information flow is not as continuous (Lang 2004). Nevertheless, in recent years, consumer-interest groups have been effective in insisting on the right to information and also in inducing changes in producer behavior (Lang 2004). The issue of labeling GMO foods is a case in point.

REFLECTIONS ON WHAT TO DO

In the previous sections of the chapter we have shown how the current policy arena connects to ethical perspectives and have described the trends in the food system from the consumer's and producer's perspectives. The purpose of this section is to look at what can be done from a policy angle to promote fair and efficient ethical behavior in food and agriculture. We look at six areas of action in institutional innovation and incentives for inducing behavior change.

Codes of Conduct for the Food Industry and Civil Society Organizations

In adopting institutional mechanisms from the health profession a basic code of conduct could form a basis. A type of 'Hippocratic Oath' for all food system actors may be a Utopian suggestion, but should be considered. On the producer side, because of the rise in consumer activism in demanding better food safety requirements and less negative externalities on the environment and biodiversity emanating from production processes, companies have become more sensitive to such issues (De Masy 2003). The movement for corporate social responsibility has gained momentum, with an increasing number of companies that are recognizing a wide range of ethical responsibilities as well as working with a variety of stakeholders (Sustain Ability and Global Compact 2004). However, these initiatives often remain disconnected from companies' core business activities and their long-term strategies.

There are two basic approaches to promoting ethical behavior in the corporate world: the action-based approach and the agent-based approach (Dobson 2004). The action-based approach entails developing rules or guidelines to restrict management's actions through corporate codes of conduct. In the agent-based approach, individuals in management are encouraged to rationally pursue moral excellence as a goal in itself. A mix of action-based and agent-based approaches can be used for effective change on the producer side.

Just as in the medical field, it is first important to stress the concept of individual responsibility on the part of corporate professionals. In recent years, following major scandals of misconduct in the corporate world, there has been a lot of positive progress in that respect. Indeed, many business schools have now integrated ethics courses into their curricula. Agricultural faculties should also follow suit and include 'food and agricultural ethics' in the curriculum (De Masy 2003). The challenge is to integrate ethics within the core of business activity and long-term business strategies.

Codes of conduct at the industry level may be an effective way of doing this. In a similar way to the medical field, producer associations can play a key role in creating such codes of conduct as well as enforcing them. For instance, in Europe, environmental consciousness within the corporate world in the mid-1980s led some companies to adopt 'eco-auditing' schemes. Eco-audits are essentially evaluation programs that look into the environmental practices of companies with the purpose of improving environmental management in different spheres of business activity, including research and development (R&D), production, distribution, waste management, and procurement (European Commission 1999).

Codes of conduct should also be established for non-governmental organizations (NGOs). Indeed, civil society organizations are playing an increasing role in influencing policy nationally and internationally. It is therefore important for them to function in a transparent and accountable manner in order to increase their legitimacy and credibility. A code of conduct can thus serve as a foundation to promote good management practices within these organizations and, in so doing, increase partnership opportunities with governments and other stakeholders in forming policies.

Establishing 'Food Ethics Commissions'

The diversity of positions when it comes to determining 'what is ethical' points to the importance of discourse in ethics. As emphasized in the first section of this chapter, formal and informal institutions play a significant role in providing a platform for such discourse. Increasingly, aspects of societal decision-preparation (not decision-making, which is the domain of elected representatives), such as in the fields of new medical science and genetics, are today handed to 'Ethics Commissions.' This concept could be considered for food issues as well. In the food and agricultural system, because of the variety of actors and ethical issues, ethics commissions appointed by elected bodies, where all actors would be represented, might be a first step. These commissions could provide the arena for transparent discourse on what food-related ethical behavior is most appropriate in the context of a nation's culture and economic system. National 'Food and Agricultural Ethics Commissions' alone, however, may be problematic, as national sovereignty of food ethics might not internalize externalities. With globalization, there is an increased need for cooperation on a global scale in order to forge ethical principles that consider external effects of changed food ethics, especially impacts on the poor. To this effect, international organizations have a role to play in encouraging multilateral platforms that would address and define international ethical principles around food and agriculture policy issues.

Incentives for Behavior Change

For type II problems (i.e., violation of recognized ethical principles) there is a need for intervention and enforcement at the institutional level to remove incentives that result in adverse effects. Indeed, some government programs have inbuilt incentives for unethical behavior. Badly designed agricultural subsidies can be one such example. In the context of globalization, subsidies present an unfair competitive element for low-income countries. This in turn has a negative impact on poor farmers residing in those countries, as they are unable to compete. But simply removing harmful incentives in the food and agriculture sector is not enough to resolve the existing ethical problems. Active intervention in the form of positive incentives is necessary in order to promote ethical behavior.

On the consumer side, there is a need for a better understanding of food production processes in order for consumers to make informed decisions (Esterson 1996). Thus, the information industry needs incentives to provide sound information to consumers. One way of doing this would be to allocate public resources to science communication and to require producers to provide better information regarding their produce by introducing restrictions on false advertising and by introducing accurate labeling requirements. Such policies are currently lacking enforcement in most low-income countries. Further, more direct incentives could be given to consumers in the form of direct subsidies for healthy foods.

Ethics for Business

A market-based approach is to use ethical considerations as a marketing and business strategy. Since consumers are often concerned about current food production processes, they are usually willing to pay a relatively higher price for a product that does not violate their ethical principles (Basu et al. 2003). The successes of 'eco-labeling' and 'fair trade' (also known as 'alternative trade') initiatives in recent years are examples of this. Indeed, eco-labeling, which started in Germany in the late 1970s, is a voluntary labeling program whose purpose is to provide information to consumers about an environmentally friendly product, thus selling 'feel-good effects.' Since the early 1990s, the program has expanded tremendously in both developing and developed countries (Basu et al. 2003). As for 'fair trade' initiatives, they began in the 1950s in Europe and the USA with the purpose of helping poor farmers in developing countries obtain a 'just price' for their produce by putting them in direct contact with consumers and distributors in developed countries and cutting out the middle-men (Ericson 2002). In the 1990s, fair trade initiatives expanded considerably in European markets for tea, coffee, and chocolate, and started taking hold in the USA in the late 1990s, especially in the coffee market (Moskin 2004). Additionally, 'fair trade' initiatives are being expanded to other products such as bananas and pineapples (Moskin 2004). Many of these initiatives are, at least initially, not sustainable without subsidies. To the extent that they are adding positive societal externalities, this may be justified.

The Ethics of Food Governance and Rights

The current focus on ethics in the food and agricultural sector is mostly driven by consumer and public-interest group activism. In order to keep the discussion of ethics in food and agriculture dynamic, governments must be open to consumers' expressed concerns with regard to the food system. Thus, the basic framework of protecting civil rights and political freedoms and facilitating public debates and discussions is critical in setting a nation's ethical goals (Sen 1999). Where this type of framework does not exist, governments have the primary responsibility to promote such discourse by ensuring transparency and ensuring the right to information and education (FAO 2001). The State also has to encourage the most vulnerable groups in society to participate in the discussions by protecting their freedom of association, expression, and organization (Bhardwaj 2003). A rights-based approach to food security is part of institutional innovations that can contribute to strengthen the actors and advance the judiciary as new actors to end hunger. And, in fact this approach has been gaining support in recent years with the wide acceptance of a set of voluntary guidelines to the right to food (FAO 2004; von Braun 2004). Further, in the international arena, many ethical concerns are shared between countries as a result of globalization. Thus, 'a minimal basic consensus relating to binding values, irrevocable standards and moral attitudes' is essential to building a world order with an ethical foundation (Küng 2005).[8]

Providing an Ethical Environment and Strengthening Roles of Actors

Beyond this basic framework, the different stakeholders (i.e., consumers, civil society, producers, the media, governments, and international organizations) within the food system have to recognize their respective responsibilities in providing a conducive ethical environment. Indeed, consumers, at the individual level, have a responsibility for their own diet and therefore need to educate themselves on the health benefits and risks of different food types (Esterson 1996). The education system must lay the foundations for that capacity in conjunction with the family, and possibly civil society organizations. At the community level, consumers and civil society groups have to exercise their social rights and freedoms by staying informed about food production processes and by continuing to push for better ethical behavior from producers. In so doing, these groups will ensure that ethical issues stay on the policy agenda and that producers are made socially, as well as environmentally, accountable.

As for producers, they have a responsibility toward consumers in terms of supplying accurate information about their produce and their production processes. Further, producers have a responsibility toward future generations; they have to ensure that their current production methods do not have a negative impact on future production capabilities and thus on future food security. Market-based incentives and regulations are the instruments for that.

The media, on its side, has the responsibility of providing accurate information with regard to food. Thus, media groups need to prevent problems such as false reporting, which can have negative impacts in the form of provoking a sense of panic among consumers as well as damaging a producer's reputation (Swinnen et al. 2003).

At the national level, governments have a central role, as they have the responsibility to promote ethical behavior from all the stakeholders in the food and agricultural system. The recent World Health Organization (WHO) Global Strategy on Diet and Health adopted in May 2004 outlines government responsibilities in the health sector, which are also relevant to the food and agricultural sector.[9]

In terms of implementation strategy, at the international level the WHO strategy could be used as a model for action. This strategy first delineates the challenges faced in terms of global diet and health, then states the goals and objectives of the strategy, and subsequently outlines the principles for action. The strategy also outlines the respective responsibilities of involved actors, including the international community, national governments, civil society, and non-governmental organizations, and also the private sector when it comes to promoting good diet and health decisions. The actors in the food and agricultural sector can use these basic guidelines to forge a strategy for action.[10]

In conclusion, we hint at a few research issues. While we suggest the adoption of principles from the medical profession for food and agriculture related ethics beyond the 'do no harm' principles, it is also desirable that the agricultural profession relates more to the ethics profession for jointly defining relevant concepts, issues, and coherent actions. The above-mentioned action areas will probably have little impact if pursued in isolation, but need to be considered as a comprehensive package – but this is a research issue as well.

Furthermore, 'getting more ethical' does not necessarily result in 'getting things done' with respect to ending hunger. The ethical focus may well be on marginal improvements, rather than on the necessary scaling-up of actions to end hunger.

Also, there can be too much of a good thing: pitfalls such as ethical over-regulation must not be ignored. In some cases, market mechanisms work well in giving incentives for ethical behavior. For instance, since companies have to earn the trust of consumers, competition can actually serve ethics.

Our hope is that enhanced political empowerment and political will is fostered by the promotion of ethics. This again, may be addressed as a research issue. If increased attention to ethics in food and agriculture was able to facilitate the needed scaling-up and improved quality of actions to end hunger, an investment in ethics may actually yield high returns.

NOTES

[1]   The medical profession has deep-rooted ethical considerations embodied in the Hippocratic Oath. In medicine, there is a certain 'covenant' between the patient and the physician that encourages ethical behavior on both sides.

[2]   In *On Ethics and Economics*, Sen (1987) offers an alternative to the traditional focus of Pareto optimality on utility maximization. He argues that there is an intrinsic value to rights and freedoms, and that welfare economics needs to pay more attention to the fulfillment of these rights and freedoms, as opposed to just concentrating on utility maximization.

[3]   For instance, the World Medical Association (WMA) is an international organization that brings together physicians from all over the world with the purpose of serving

> humanity by endeavoring to achieve the highest international standards in Medical Education, Medical Science, Medical Art and Medical Ethics, and Health Care for all people in the world (WMA 2004).

Similar professional associations exist at the national and regional levels in many countries. Furthermore, professional medical associations exist by medical specialization, and at the more community level, by hospital or medical center.

[4]   The purpose of the Association for Social Economics is to:

> explore ethical foundations and implications of economic analysis, along with the individual and social dimensions of economic problems, and to help shape economic policy that is consistent with the integral values of the person and a humane community (ASE 2004).

[5]   At the end of medical school, doctors have the option of swearing the Hippocratic Oath or some more modern adaptation of it, such as the Declaration of Geneva or the International Code of Ethics. It is a declaration of physicians' dedication to the humanitarian goals of medicine.

[6]   *The Hippocratic Oath* (translated by Francis Adams):

> I SWEAR by Apollo the physician, and Aesculapius, and Health, and All-heal, and all the gods and goddesses, that, according to my ability and judgment, I will keep this Oath and this stipulation – to reckon him who taught me this Art equally dear to me as my parents, to share my substance with him, and relieve his necessities if required; to look upon his offspring in the same footing as my own brothers, and to teach them this art, if they shall wish to learn it, without fee or stipulation; and that by precept, lecture, and every other mode of instruction, I will impart a knowledge of the Art to my own sons, and those of my teachers, and to disciples bound by a stipulation and oath according to the law of medicine, but to none others. I will follow that system of regimen that, according to my ability and judgment, I consider for the benefit of my patients, and abstain from

whatever is deleterious and mischievous. I will give no deadly medicine to any one if asked, nor suggest any such counsel; and in like manner I will not give to a woman a pessary to produce abortion.

With purity and with holiness I will pass my life and practice my Art. I will not cut persons laboring under the stone, but will leave this to be done by men who are practitioners of this work. Into whatever houses I enter, I will go into them for the benefit of the sick, and will abstain from every voluntary act of mischief and corruption; and, further from the seduction of females or males, of freemen and slaves. Whatever, in connection with my professional practice or not, in connection with it, I see or hear, in the life of men, which ought not to be spoken of abroad, I will not divulge, as reckoning that all such should be kept secret. While I continue to keep this Oath unviolated, may it be granted to me to enjoy life and the practice of the art, respected by all men, in all times! But should I trespass and violate this Oath, may the reverse be my lot!

[7] See *Final Report to the Chair by the Intergovernmental Working Group for the Elaboration of a Set of Voluntary Guidelines to Support the Progressive Realization of the Right to Adequate Food in the Context of National Food Security*, Rome, 23 September 2004 [available at http://www.fao.org/docrep/meeting/008/J3345e/j3345e01.htm].

[8] In *Global Responsibility: In Search of a New World Ethic*, Hans Küng demonstrates that different societies' ethical norms share a common foundation. He finds that the following four basic principles are shared among many religions, traditions, and societies: (1) respect for life, (2) deal honestly and fairly, (3) speak and act truthfully, and (4) respect and love one another (Küng 1991). These basic principles can serve as a foundation for building a 'world ethic,' i.e., a 'minimum of shared ethical values, basic attitudes and criteria to which all regions, nations and interest groups can commit themselves' (Küng 2005).

[9] These responsibilities include:
- Providing accurate and balanced information through education and public awareness programs, as well as adult literacy and education programs;
- Monitoring and evaluating producer health claims and marketing strategies, as well as evaluating whether appropriate labeling is being used;
- Investing in research and evaluation;
- Taking healthy nutrition into consideration in agricultural policies;
- Providing resources to populations with special needs in order to enable them to purchase nutritious food (WHO 2004).

[10] The Food and Agriculture Organization of the United Nations (FAO) started this process in 2000 with a series of expert consultations on ethical issues arising in food and agriculture. So far, this panel has met twice (in 2000 and 2002) and has outlined in detail the current ethical issues facing the food and agricultural sector, and is expected to come up with a tentative guidelines on how to resolve these issues in a third session (FAO 2003).

REFERENCES

AMA [American Medical Association], 2004. *Frequently Asked Questions in Ethics* [available at http://www.ama-assn.org/ama/pub/category/5105.html#oath_oblig (accessed 15 October 2004)].

Ansell, C. and D. Vogel, eds., 2005. *Why the Beef? The Contested Governance of European Food Safety.* Cambridge, MA: MIT Press.

Arrow, K.J., 1963. Uncertainty and the welfare economics of medical care. *American Economic Review* 53(5): 941–973.

ASE [Association for Social Economics], 2004. *Purpose of the Association for Social Economics* [available at http://www.socialeconomics.org/ (accessed 1 November 2004)].

Barham, E., 2002. Towards a theory of values-based labeling. *Agriculture and Human Values* 19: 349–360.

Basu, A.K., N.H. Chau and U. Grote, 2003. Eco-labeling and stages of development. *Review of Development Economics* 7(2): 228–247.

Beauchamp, T.L. and J.F. Childress, 1994. *Principles of Biomedical Ethics,* 4th edn. New York: Oxford University Press.

Bhardwaj, M., 2003. Developing countries' participation in the global governance of biotechnology. In: Song, S.Y., Y.M. Koo and D.R.J. Macer Eubios, eds. *Bioethics in Asia in the 21st Century.* Ethics Institute.

Clegg, A., 2003. You say potato, I say potato: An ethical perspective on the 'right to know'. *BioTeach Journal* 1.

Davis, D.E. and H. Stewart, 2002. Changing consumer demands creates opportunities for U.S. food system. *FoodReview* 25(1).

De Masy, R., 2003. *Introducing 'a Dialogue on Ethics and Responsibility in Agribusiness Education and Practice'.* 13th Annual World Food and Agribusiness Forum and Symposium. Cancun, Mexico: International Food and Agribusiness Management Association.

Dinham, B., 1995. 10 years of FAO Code fails to reduce hazard problems. *Pesticides News* 28: 6–7.

Dobson, J., 2004. Applying virtue ethics to business: The agent-based approach. *Electronic Journal of Business Ethics and Organization Studies (EJBO).*

Ericson, B., 2002. The conscious consumer: Promoting economic justice through fair trade. *The Conscious Consumer.*

Esterson, E., 1996. Taking the links out of the food chain: How to return to a more holistic way of eating. *Conscious Choice* (March).

European Commission, 1999. *ESTO EMAS: The Impact of the EU Eco-audit Regulation (EMAS) on Innovation in Europe.* Milan: Fondazione Eni Enrico Mattei.

FAO [Food and Agriculture Organization], 2001. *Ethical Issues in Food and Agriculture.* FAO Ethics Series No. 1. Rome: Food and Agriculture Organization of the United Nations.

FAO [Food and Agriculture Organization], 2003. *FAO Expert Consultation on Food Safety: Science and Ethics.* Proceedings from Expert Consultation. Rome, 3–5 September 2002.

FAO [Food and Agriculture Organization], 2004. *Intergovernmental Working Group for the Elaboration of a Set of Voluntary Guidelines to Support the Progressive Realization of the Right to Adequate Food in the Context of National Food Security.* Final Report to the Chair, 23 September 2004. Rome: Food and Agriculture Organization of the United Nations.

Firat, A., 1995. Consumer culture or culture consumed? In: Costa, J.A. and G.J. Bamossy, eds. *Marketing in a Multicultural World.* Thousand Oaks, CA: Sage Publications.

Galbraith, J.K., 1958. *The Affluent Society.* Boston, MA: Houghton Mifflin.

Garland, C., 2003. A system of ethics for food? The precautionary principle [available at http://www.ethics.ucsd.edu/seminars (accessed 18 October 2004)].

Gowdy, J.M. and M.L. Walton, 2003. Consumer sovereignty, economic efficiency and the trade liberalisation debate. *Global Environmental Issues* 3(1).

Hausman, D.M. and M.S. McPherson, 1993. Taking ethics seriously: Economics and contemporary moral philosophy. *Journal of Economic Literature* 31(2): 671–731.

Hippocrates, 400 BC. The Oath. Translated by Francis Adams [available at http://classics.mit.edu//Hippocrates/hippooath.html (accessed 6 October 2004)].

James, H.S., 2002. *Finding Solutions to Ethical Problems in Agriculture.* Department of Agricultural Economics Working Paper AEWP 2002-04, University of Missouri, USA.

Kant, I., 1785. *Fundamental Principles of the Metaphysic of Morals.* Translated by Thomas Kingsmill Abbott [available at http://etext.library.adelaide.edu.au/k/kant/immanuel/k16prm/].

Kirsten, J. and K. Sartorius, 2002. *Linking Agribusiness and Small-scale Farmers in Developing Countries: Is there a New Role for Contract Farming?* University of Pretoria Department of Agricultural Economics Working Paper 13.

Küng, H., 1991. *Global Responsibility: In Search of a New World Ethic.* New York: Crossroad.

Küng, H., 2005. *Global Ethic and Human Responsibility.* Markkula Center for Applied Ethics. Submitted to the High-level Expert Group Meeting on 'Human Rights and Human Responsibilities in the Age of Terrorism', Santa Clara University, 1–2 April 2005.

Lang, T., 2004. *Food and Health Wars: A Modern Drama of Consumer Sovereignty.* Cultures of Consumption Working Paper Series No. 14. Birkbeck College, London: Cultures of Consumption, and ESRC-AHRB Research Programme.

Lichtenberg, J., 1996. What are codes of ethics for? In: Coady, M. and S. Block, eds. *Codes of Ethics and the Professions.* Melbourne: Melbourne University Press.

Marshall, K., 2004. Book launch: '*Mind, Heart and Soul in the Fight Against Poverty*'. Washington DC: World Bank, 22 October 2002.

Marshall, K. and L. Keough, 2004. *Mind, Heart, and Soul in the Fight Against Poverty.* Washington, DC: International Bank for Reconstruction and Development/World Bank.

Moskin, J., 2004. Helping third world one banana at a time. *New York Times,* 5 May.

Nicholson, R., 1997. Medical ethics in Europe: A short history. *NIRA Review* (Spring).

Robinson, M., 2002. *The Right to Food: Achievements and Challenges.* World Food Summit: 5 Years Later. Rome: Food and Agriculture Organization.

Sarbib, J.-L., 2004. Book launch: '*Mind, Heart and Soul in the Fight Against Poverty*'. Washington DC: World Bank, 22 October 2002.

Sen, A., 1987. *On Ethics and Economics.* New York: Basil Blackwell.

Sen, A., 1999. *Development as Freedom.* New York: Alfred A. Knopf.

Stark, O., 1989. Altruism and the quality of life. *American Economic Review* 79(2): 86–90.

Stark, O. and T.C. Bergstrom, 1993. How altruism can prevail in an evolutionary environment. *American Economic Review* 83(2): 149–155.

Stephens, A., 1995. *Gender Issues in Agricultural and Rural Development Policy in Asia and the Pacific.* Bangkok: Regional Office for Asia and the Pacific (RAPA) / Food and Agriculture Organization of the United Nations.

Stiglitz, J.E., 2000. *Ethics, Economic Advice and Economic Policy.* Digital Library of the Inter-American Initiative on social Capital, Ethics and Development. Washington, DC: Interamerican Development Bank.

SustainAbility and Global Compact, 2004. *Gearing Up: From Corporate Responsibility to Good Governance and Scalable Solutions.* London: SustainAbility.

Swaminathan, M.S., P. Medrano and R.V. Bhavani, 2004. *Towards a Hunger-free World: The Ethical Dimensions.* Bangalore, India: East West Books (Madras) Pvt. Ltd.

Swinnen, J.F.M., J. McCluskey and N. Francken, 2003. Food safety, the media and the information market. Paper prepared for presentation at the IAAE Conference in Durban, South Africa, 16–23 August.

Thompson, P., 2000. *Food and Agriculture Biotechnology: Incorporating Ethical Considerations.* West Lafayette, Indiana: Department of Philosophy, Purdue University. Prepared for the Canadian Biotechnology Advisory Committee.

Variyam, J.N. and E. Golan, 2002. New health information is reshaping food choices. *FoodReview* 25(1).

Veblen, T., 1899. *Theory of the Leisure Class: An Economic Study of Institutions.* New York: Macmillan Company.

Venkatesh, A., 1995. Ethnoconsumerism: A new paradigm to study cultural and cross-cultural consumer behavior. In: Costa, J.A. and G.J. Bamossy, eds. *Marketing in a Multicultural World: Ethnicity, Nationalism and Cultural Identity.* Thousand Oaks, CA: Sage Publications.

von Braun, J., 2003. *Overview of the World Food Situation – Food Security: New Risks and New Opportunities.* Brief prepared for the Annual General Meeting of the Consultative Group on International Agricultural Research, Nairobi, 29 October 2003.

von Braun, J., 2004. *Ethics and the Global Food System.* IFPRI Forum- Commentary. Washington, DC: International Food Policy Research Institute.

von Braun, J. and M.A. Brown, 2003. Ethical questions of equitable worldwide food production systems. *Plant Physiology* (133): 1–6.

Wade, M.A. and D. Conley, 2000. Assessing informational bias and food safety: A matrix method approach. Paper presented at the World Food and Agribusiness Congress, Chicago, IL, 24–28 June: International food and Agribusiness Association (IAMA).

Weber, M., 1897. *Sociological Writings. Vol. 60.* Heydebrand, W., ed. (1994). London, UK and New York, NY: Continuum Publishing.

Wegener, H.C., 2002. Is alternative food production safe? *EurSafe Newsletter* 4(4).

WMA [World Medical Association], 2004. About the World Medical Association [available at http://www.wma.net/e/about/index.htm#mission (accessed 15 October 2004)].

WHO [World Health Organization], 2004. *Global strategy on Diet, Physical Activity and Health.* Geneva: World Health Organization.

WHO/FAO [World Health Organization and Food and Agriculture Organization], 2004. *Codex Alimentarius Commission* [available at http://www.codexalimentarius.net/web/index_en.jsp (accessed 1 November 2004)].

WHO, FAO, and UNEP [World Health Organization, Food and Agriculture Organization, and United Nations Environmental Program], 2004. Joint note for the media: 'Children are facing high risks from pesticide poisoning' [available at http://www.who.int/mediacentre/news/notes/2004/np19/en/ (accessed 18 October 2004)].

Zusman, P., 1993. Participants' ethical attitudes and organizational structure and performance. In: Csaki, C. and J. Kislev, eds. *Agricultural Cooperatives in Transition.* Boulder, CO: Westview Press.

PETER SANDØE AND KATHRINE HAUGE MADSEN

AGRICULTURAL AND FOOD ETHICS IN THE WESTERN WORLD: A CASE OF ETHICAL IMPERIALISM?

INTRODUCTION

The great advantages of biotechnology have yet to reach developing nations in Africa and other lands where these innovations are now most needed. Acting on unfounded, unscientific fears, many European governments have blocked the import of all new biotech crops. Because of these artificial obstacles many African nations avoid investing in biotechnology, worried that their products will be shut out of important European markets. For the sake of a continent threatened by famine I urge the European governments to end their opposition to biotechnology. We should encourage the spread of safe, effective biotechnology to win the fight against global hunger (White House 2003).

These remarks, which were made in a speech given by US President George W. Bush at the 2003 BIO Conference, are addressed to European governments. Considerable public opposition to genetically modified crops (to which we take Bush to be referring when he speaks of 'biotech crops') exists in Europe. But, according to Bush, European governments should 'end their opposition' to such crops and allow them freely to enter the EU market. In the passage quoted, Bush supports this view with three claims.

- *First*, European opposition to GM crops is based on concerns that are unfounded, and in particular unscientific.
- *Second*, the European ban on imports of GM crops is discouraging African nations from making use of GM crops to improve their agricultural production.
- *Third*, GM crops can play a significant role in alleviating famine in Africa.

To assess Bush's position, we need to examine the plausibility of these claims. We need to ask whether public opposition to GM crops is entirely unscientific – and indeed whether legitimate concerns must be supported by scientific risk assessments anyway. We need to ask whether European opposition to GM crops is a significant factor in the African policy of rejecting gene technology. And we need to ask just how likely it is that GM technology will be a decisive factor in fighting famine in Africa.

These questions receive attention below. However, we shall not confine the discussion to GM crops, for Bush's argument for free trade in those crops is just one of a group of arguments all of which build a case against ethical or safety-based restrictions in the rich world by pointing to undesirable consequences for the poor

P. Pinstrup-Andersen and P. Sandøe (eds.), Ethics, Hunger and Globalization: In Search of Appropriate Policies, 201–214.

world. These arguments – we might call them 'Poor Man's Ethics' arguments – have the following structure:

1. In response to safety worries or ethical concerns, wealthy nations place restrictions on their own agriculture or food production or on trade with the developing world.
2. The relevant worries and concerns are not substantiated by an impartial assessment of the relevant scientific evidence.
3. Directly or indirectly, the restrictions have a serious negative effect on poor people in the developing world.
4. Therefore, such restrictions are unethical.

In this chapter, we do not propose to discuss premise (1); and we will turn directly to (2) and (3). About these premises, which will in effect be the focus for much of what follows, we wish to make two general observations. The first is that, in the case of any particular ethical worry or concern about safety, (2) and (3) will, like most factual claims, be disputable. Hence, in a Poor Man's Ethics argument, it is necessary to show that claims of types (2) and (3) are empirically plausible. As we say, a good deal of the discussion in the main sections of this chapter is about precisely this kind of plausibility.

The second observation is this. It is apparent that the move from (1) to (3) to the conclusion in (4) involves assumptions of a more normative nature. We therefore suggest that these assumptions are implicit in the thinking of George W. Bush and other proponents of Poor Man's Ethics arguments. The assumptions can be expressed as follows:

5. If an anxiety about agriculture or food production is to be the cause of legitimate concern, it must be grounded in evidence, from natural science, indicating negative effects on human health or the environment.
6. The remaining ethical concerns should not be acted on if this will have a negative effect on people in the developing world.

Clearly, claims (5) and (6) are not self-evident. Indeed it is easy to describe counterexamples to them. Against (5) it can be pointed out that it is perfectly possible to have legitimate concerns about distributive justice – i.e., about the division of duties and benefits among citizens. For example, it may be said that certain approaches to agricultural development will put small, low-income farmers out of business. However, the validity of this kind of concern cannot be decided on the basis of evidence from natural science (which is not, of course, to deny that such evidence may be relevant to questions about distributive justice).

Equally, human rights cast doubt on (6). Concerns about human rights are unlikely to be based on scientific evidence indicating negative effects on human health or the environment, so they seem to be remaining ethical concerns of the kind mentioned in (6). However, it would be strange to suggest that such rights should be ignored where their being respected would have a negative effect on people in the developing world. In support of (6) it may be suggested that human rights violations are justified where they are necessary to prevent poverty. It may be said, for example, that although China's one-child policy contravenes widely acknowledged standards of human rights, it is justified by its positive effect on population growth and the consequent eradication of poverty and hunger. However, this suggestion is highly controversial. It certainly does not look like a line of thinking that Bush would endorse, given his stance on human rights; and this revives doubts about (6).

These brief comments on (5) and (6) suggest that Poor Man's Ethics arguments may well fail to carry conviction in certain cases. They do not show, however, that this kind of argument cannot ever be successfully made. We now propose, therefore, to look closely at two specific applications of the Poor Man's Ethics argument. The first is the argument that animal welfare standards in the developed world are unethical because, indirectly, they impose an attitude to animal welfare on people in the developing world which those people do not at present share. We call this the argument against 'Animal Welfare Imperialism.' The second application, which is essentially the Bush case already described, will be called the 'Pro-GM Crops' argument.

For each argument, we first describe the social and political background against which the relevant governments in the developed world, and in particular Europe, take the stance they do on farm animal welfare and GM crops. We then try to spell out the case that can be made against those stances using Poor Man's Ethics arguments. Finally, we try to evaluate the arguments, attending to both their factual and ethical premises. It is our belief that there is an important and unavoidable respect in which the arguments are incompatible. We conclude by explaining this belief.

THE CASE AGAINST 'ANIMAL WELFARE IMPERIALISM'

Animal production in developed countries has changed considerably over the last 50 years. In Europe, this change was driven by public policies and consumer demand favoring more abundant and cheaper food. As a result of these drivers, animal production has become much more efficient, as measured by the cost of producing each egg, or kilogram of meat, or liter of milk. Pressure to be more efficient is now market-driven, with competition between producers, and between retailers, to sell food as cheaply as possible. The process has acquired its own momentum. In many ways this can be viewed as a success story. Thus consumers in these countries are able to buy animal products at prices that are low relative to those of the past. In the 1950s it was typical for people in northern Europe to spend between one-quarter and one-third of their income on food. Now about 10% is usual. The fall in the price of some individual animal products has been even more striking. At the same time, farmers and farm workers, while declining in number, have been able to maintain an income that generally matches similar types of work in society as a whole.

Efficiency has also been achieved through intensification. Farms have increased in size and now keep more animals per unit area, either in housing or on pasture. The methods used on farms have come to involve increasing levels of automation, together with techniques and routines that reduce the labor needed for each animal – for example, cages and other types of housing that control the behavior of the animals and thus make them easier to manage. Animals have also been bred to produce meat, milk, and eggs faster and with less feed. However, these changes in agriculture have come at a price, and to a great extent that price has been paid by the animals. They typically get less space per individual than they did previously, and many live in barren environments that do not allow them to exercise their normal range of behavior. Genetic selection has also introduced a range of production-related diseases (Webster 1994). Profits from increased efficiency are generally short-term, as they are regularly pared away by competition to reduce selling prices; and some of the changes by which efficiency has been increased – for example, reductions in space allowance – have had harmful long-term effects on the animals.

Over the last 20 years or so there has been a growing public awareness of what is done to farm animals in intensive animal production (Appleby 1999), and this has led to various initiatives for change going under the banner of 'animal welfare,' Since the 1970s, research relating to farm animal production has taken a greater interest in welfare. Again, legislation on animal welfare in a number of countries, especially in northern Europe, has had a significant effect on livestock farming and slaughter practices. Some countries have banned egg production in battery cages. Others require pregnant sows to be loose-housed. The EU has steadily introduced regulations on animal welfare to ensure that competition within the common market does not take place at the cost of the well-being of the animals. This regulation covers the transport and slaughter of animals. There is also EU legislation setting minimum standards for the way in which a number of farm animals, including pigs, calves, and laying hens are kept. It should here be mentioned that within the EU there are controversies between countries about how far to go regarding common animal welfare legislation. Finally, initiatives designed to raise animal welfare around the world have recently been made by organizations like OIE (World Organisation for Animal Health) and the WTO (World Trade Organization). Admittedly these initiatives are at present in their infancy.

In connection with animal welfare, there is therefore little doubt that a premise of the kind set out in (1) is correct. But does animal welfare regulation in the Western world have an adverse effect on the developing world? That is, is a premise of type (3) correct here? That depends on how one defines these 'worlds.'

For example, arguments have been going on for many years between the EU and countries covering northern or Arctic areas where a significant number of people make a livelihood from trapping wild fur animals (although recently these arguments were settled when standards for traps were adopted in the relevant countries and across the EU). Another recent example centers on the production of cat fur in China. A broadcast in which it was shown that fur cats were raised in China under extremely cruel conditions led to reactions in a number of rich countries, and Denmark, for example, has since made it illegal to import and make products from fur originating from the domestic cat.

In the future, concerns about animal welfare in the rich world could affect animal production in the developing world in three ways. First, through bodies such as the WTO and OIE, international agreements may be made which outlaw the trading of animal products which do not satisfy certain minimal welfare standards. However, experience within the EU suggests that any such standards will be limited and difficult to enforce.

Second, companies in wealthy parts of the world which import animal products from the developing world might have their own animal welfare standards. These might appear as part of a product specification. However, substantial sanitary standards already cover animal products being exported from a country in the developing world into Western countries, and in reality animal welfare standards are likely to amount to, at most, a small part of a product's specifications.

Third, in several ways, requirements on animal welfare might come to be tied up with *aid* to the developing world. This is most likely to happen if a project funded by aid involves animal use or production. Suppose it were to emerge, for example, in the Western media, that (what by our standards counts as) severe cruelty to animals was taking place in a project financed by Western taxpayers' money. This would probably lead to a public and political outcry, and this in turn could have a negative impact on aid to the developing world in general.

Even if pragmatic observations such as these are realistic, it makes sense to ask whether it is acceptable for wealthy citizens in the Western world to impose their own standards of animal welfare on people who do not share them in the developing world. This question has recently been addressed in a paper by Doerfler and Peters (2006):

> The introduction of European ethical standards in tropical livestock agriculture is critical because it ignores existing moral standards in other cultures that constitute the individual and social identity of human beings in those cultures. Natural conditions widely determine decisions in animal agriculture and animal treatment. The magnitude of human intervention within the production system and the level of economic/technological development have an influence on ethical queries.

In this quotation, and in the paper from which it originates, two lines of argument run in parallel. According to the first line, it is wrong for people in the developed world to impose particular standards of animal welfare on people in less wealthy countries if the latter do not have the ethical concerns that support those standards as part of their cultural identity. As a matter of fact, people in less wealthy countries do not share our ethical concerns, and hence by imposing our standards we show a lack of respect for their cultural values.

The second line of argument alleges that the way animals are kept in parts of the developing world reflects local conditions and cannot be changed. Thus, for example, where animal production is extensively based on pasture, it is inevitable that the animals will at times suffer as a consequence of food shortage owing to dry weather. Animals will suffer – as will humans – but this is due to natural and not human limitations.

So far as this second line of argument is concerned, it is our clear impression that few, if any, observers living in the developed world will complain about animal hardships elsewhere if they are convinced that the suffering reflects inescapable local conditions and goes hand in hand with human misery. However, there will probably be disagreement if the claim is made that just because people live in poor conditions they need to not treat their animals well. And controversy will arise if alternative approaches to animal production are available but are being resisted for cultural reasons. But this returns us to the first line of argument, which seems to raise the key issue, namely: may we impose our standards of animal welfare on people who do not share our culturally formed perspective on animal ethics?

Earlier we drew attention to human rights to cast doubt on the assumption underlying the Poor Man's Ethics argument that ethical concerns should not be acted on if they have negative effects on people in the developing world. Thus the *general* claim that we are not entitled to impose ethical standards on people who do not share them is far from uncontroversial. When it comes to issues of human rights, the dominant view now seems to be just the opposite: it is not just acceptable but desirable – and indeed many would say that we have a duty – to ensure that such rights are respected everywhere. Let us ask, then, whether animal welfare requirements are similar to human rights.

One obvious difference here emerges in international law. Human rights are underwritten by international conventions, which have been signed by a sufficient number of nations to be elevated to the status of international law. In reality, and in particular, politically, this makes a huge difference. However, it must be borne in mind that there was a time when human rights were not underwritten by international law. The question therefore is: Would it have been acceptable for developed countries to impose respect for human rights on less developed countries through trade restrictions and the like at that time? Many commentators would say 'Yes': they would insist that human rights are part of international law because they are universally valid, and not the other way round.

Is it then acceptable to impose, on other countries, animal welfare requirements before their incorporation in international law – as it seems to be with human rights? It might be said that the parallel is at odds with the following, reasonable, principle of tolerance: Except in cases where human rights (or entitlements of similar moral significance) are involved, people should be allowed to decide for themselves about ethical issues. Obviously, however, advocates of the animal cause will want to insist that animal welfare requirements *are* of similar moral significance to human rights. This, they might point out, is precisely why richer countries tend to have rather stringent animal welfare legislation. It is also why, with the Treaty of Amsterdam in 1997, 'respect for the welfare of animals as sentient beings' was written into the EU treaty.

The people who hold these views may be a minority. But most people would probably agree nonetheless that it is reasonable to require that certain minimum standards of animal welfare are met in livestock projects paid for by taxpayers in the developed world.

On balance, the argument against Animal Welfare Imperialism seems less than fully persuasive. It seems reasonable to insist that moderate standards of animal welfare are maintained in developing countries, not least when aid is involved. However, it must also be recognized that the conditions under which animals are kept in some countries may introduce very real mitigating circumstances.

THE 'PRO-GM CROPS' CASE

Bush was right to say that many European governments have opposed the introduction of GM crops in Europe. Within the EU there was a *de facto* moratorium on the release of GM crops between 1998/99 and 2004. And even though the legislation that should make room for the introduction of GM crops on a greater scale in Europe is now in place, GM crop proposals are still not embraced with enthusiasm by most European governments. However, it is also fair to say that opposition to GM crops does not come from the politicians themselves. On the contrary, the EU Commission and many national governments in Europe have invested heavily in plant biotechnology research. The political resistance that exists reflects a lack of *popular* support for GM technology that emerged, or first became fully apparent, in the mid-1990s.

European public attitudes to biotechnology have been well documented, not least in so-called Eurobarometer surveys. These surveys, of countries which are part of, or attached to, the EU, have been conducted every three years since 1991. The latest, from 2002, shows that after a decade of decline, public optimism about biotechnology has increased to levels last seen in the early 1990s. Considerable support for most medical applications of new biotechnology – e.g., genetic testing for inherited diseases and the cloning of human cells and tissues – can be found in each of the 15 EU Member States. For GM crops and food specifically, support seems to have stabilized across Europe between 1999 and 2002. The picture is that the majority of Europeans still do not support GM foods, and this is largely because such foods are not felt to be useful and yet are felt to present risks. For GM crops (exemplified with an insect-resistant crop, which, in the Eurobarometer questionnaire, constitutes a separate category) support is lukewarm. While they are judged to be moderately useful, they are also considered almost as risky as GM foods. Majority support for GM foods is seen in only four countries: Spain, Portugal, Ireland, and Finland (Gaskell et al. 2003).

It is an important finding of the Eurobarometer surveys that it is *not* gene technology, as such, that causes public opposition but some of its applications, such as in food production. Focus group interviews conducted in Denmark supply more detail here. They suggest that the issues to which GM foods give rise include freedom of consumer choice, respect for nature, and democratic control over the development and application of technology (Lassen et al. 2002).

Lack of support for GM crops is not solely a European phenomenon, although it has undoubtedly been strongest here. In North America, certain crops are not grown in GM varieties despite their availability. This has happened with sugar beet, for example, where it seems that the concerns of large producers of soft drinks and candy have acted as an obstacle (Madsen et al. 2005). Something similar has occurred with GM potatoes (Walgate 2003). The opposition to labeling of GM foods by the US food industry also seems to reflect that the there may be some latent opposition to GM foods among US consumers.

However, there is no empirical evidence to suggest, as Bush does in the quotation at the beginning of this chapter, that European resistance to GM crops is motivated mainly by fear. Rather it is the combined effect of perceived risk and perceived lack of benefit that explains public reservations. This is in keeping with a general finding that perceived benefits determine the acceptance of new technologies – as long as the perceived risks are not so large as to be intolerable (Frewer et al. 1998). Perceived benefit is therefore a key prerequisite of the acceptance of gene technology. It should also be noticed that, for many people, risk covers more that what is documented by scientific risk assessments. It also includes uncertainties relating to the existing knowledge in the area. Here the public view may also find some support from the side of science (see, e.g., Wolfenbarger and Phifer (2000), who found that key experiments on both the environmental risk and benefit assessment were lacking).

A GM crop can be beneficial, or have a positive impact, in (at least) two distinct ways: by being commercially advantageous to the producer, or by fulfilling important societal needs (Madsen et al. 2005). The latest global figures record that 90 million hectares are now sown with GM crops, with approximately 38% of these in the developing world. In view of this, it can hardly be denied that GM crops benefit the farmers growing them in developed and developing countries around the world (James 2005).

However, when members of the public in Europe express the opinion that GM crops must be beneficial, they appear, typically, to have the second definition in mind: they are interested in societal needs (Madsen et al. 2005).

It might be said that both kinds of benefit are involved when it comes to GM crops and assistance for the developing world. At any rate, the Danish focus group interviews revealed that the argument in favor of GM crops felt to be most persuasive was their potential to improve the situation in the developing world. However, even this argument failed to persuade many interviewees, who seemed to be suspicious that the claims made about the benefits for poor people in the developing world were exaggerated, with the aim of promoting biotechnology in the developed world (Lassen et al. 2002).

Looking at the present state of the technology, one can understand why some people doubt that GM crops will help to solve food problems in the developing world: For one thing, genetic manipulation is just one of a number of technologies that may help to solve food supply problems and increase earnings in the developing world; in the short and medium term none of these technologies should be thought of as a 'miracle solution' (Teknologirådet 2003). There are a number of interesting new crops under development, e.g., rice with tolerance to insects or enriched in vitamin A content (golden rice), wheat with drought tolerance or tolerance to aluminum.[1] However, at least up to now, the crops available would not directly alleviate hunger in the developing world, because they are intended for animal feed or industrial fiber production. The effect on hunger is at best indirect: By being able to produce cash crops like cotton more efficiently, farmers may become better off and thereby become able to buy more food.

Respected sources also suggest that, even if GM crops that would directly improve food security in the developing world were to become available, we should be cautious about the improvements these will bring. Thus a recent report prepared by the Nuffield Council on Bioethics (2003) concludes that the

> possible costs, benefits and risks associated with particular GM crops can be assessed only on a case by case basis. Any such assessment needs to take into account a variety of factors, such as the gene, or combination of genes, being inserted, and the nature of the target crop. Local agricultural practices, agro-ecological conditions and trade policies of the developing country in which GM crops might be grown are also important. We therefore recommend that in considering whether GM crops should be used or not, it is essential to focus on the specific situation in a particular country, asking the question: 'How does the use of a GM crop compare to other alternatives?' All possible paths of action must be compared, including inaction, in respect of improving, in a cost-effective and environmentally sustainable way, human health, nutrition, and the ability to afford an adequate diet....
>
> The improvement of agriculture and food security depends on several factors. These include stable political environments, appropriate infrastructures, fair international and national agricultural policies, access to land and water, and improved crop varieties, which are suited to local conditions. In focusing on current and potential uses of GM crops we therefore consider only part, albeit an important one, of a large and complex picture. However, we are clear that in particular cases, GM crops can contribute to substantial progress in improving agriculture, in parallel to the (usually slow) changes at the socio-political level.

If this is a reasonable and balanced account of the present situation, the public are entitled to react skeptically when scientists and biotech companies link biotechnology with easy solutions to food problems in the developing world.

Although the first evaluation of smallholders' adoption and benefits from specific GM crops in the developing world looks promising for reducing poverty among these small-scale farmers, concerns have also been raised. In Argentina, glyphosate-resistant soybean was approved in 1996, but by 1997 Lehman and Pengue had already criticized glyphosate-resistant soybeans for permitting intensive cropping of the Pampas, and as a side-effect bringing about a decline in soil fertility, which resulted in increased herbicide use. Recent publications show that the introduction of GM soybean has been associated with some negative effects such as increased herbicide use and cultivation of new lands (previously left as pastures or bush lands), although the net environmental impact is not easily assessed and may in fact be positive (Qaim and Traxler 2005). There is, however, disagreement as to whether or not GM soybean favors smallholder farmers or not. According to Qaim and Traxler (2005), small farms are favored more by the GM soybean technology than large farms are, but according to Joensen and Semino (2004), small farmers cannot afford the machinery for implementing the direct seeding technique that is associated with harvesting the benefits from using Roundup soybean.

In China, insect-resistant (Bt) cotton has been highly successful, now covering 66% of the Chinese cotton area and resulting in increased earnings for small-scale farmers (James 2004). Since its introduction in 1997, it has been estimated that cotton farmers have reduced pesticide use by an average of 13 sprayings per hectare per season. This may have resulted in many fewer poisonings due to toxic pesticides and reduced labor costs (Huang et al. 2002). The smaller number of sprayings has furthermore resulted in less resistance in cotton bollworm to the currently used insecticides (Wu et al. 2005). However, under severe densities of cotton bollworm, the larvae may still damage the crop and there are numerous other insect pests which cause damage to cotton. Therefore Bt cotton may still need to be sprayed with pesticides (Men et al. 2004, 2005; Wu et al. 2005). Interviews with 92 cotton farmers in northern China showed that pesticides were actually sprayed intensively on Bt cotton, with an average of 12.7 sprayings per season; which was, however, attributed to lack of ecological knowledge. The authors suggested further training of farmers in basic ecology and integrated pest management strategies to ensure sustainable production of Bt cotton. A further concern is that resistance towards the Bt toxin, which has been predicted for years, may develop in the cotton bollworm (Wu et al. 2005; Yang et al. 2005). Fortunately resistance has not yet occurred, probably in part because of a successful refuge strategy delaying the development of resistance (Tabashnik 2005), but should such resistance occur and become widespread, then the Bt cotton varieties may lose their efficacy for a period of time.

Insect-protected GM rice – a genuine food crop – is on the threshold of commercialization in China. A study of farm-level preproduction trials indicates that farmers may reduce pesticide use in this crop by nearly 80%, with a resulting decrease in pesticide poisonings. Furthermore, yields were 9% higher than in the non-GM varieties (Huang et al. 2005). However, similar concerns as seen in cotton regarding other pests reducing yields and the development of resistance in the target pest may be to some extent be valid for insect resistant rice too.

Concerns have also been voiced about the sustainability of GM herbicide-resistant rice. With this kind of rice, gene flow, the development of resistant volunteers, and consequent weed control problems for farmers, are all genuine worries (Olofdotter et al. 2000; Madsen et al. 2002).

These points amount to a reply to Bush's assumption that GM crops will guarantee a long-term solution to the problem of hunger in the developing world. A credible version of the Pro-GM Crops argument must resist the temptation to represent GM crops as a simple panacea. We believe that this temptation is successfully resisted in a more modest version of the Pro-GM Crops argument presented by Per Pinstrup-Andersen:

> The problem with the European debate is that it affects the situation in Africa – partly because the Africans hear about the debate and conclude that if the Europeans think that genetic engineering is dangerous, then it is probably also dangerous for us, and therefore we had better say 'no'; and partly because several African countries fear that it could have consequences for their export opportunities to the European market if they open up to genetically modified crops.[2]

It can be argued that this more modest worry was shown to be correct in 2002, when Zambia refused to receive unmilled GM grain, primarily from the USA, as food aid.[3] Zambia and some of its neighbors were, among other things, concerned that imported food containing GM grain might lead to cases of unintended germination and the contamination of domestic crops; and that this might in turn present a barrier to exports to Europe. It is important to note, however, that Zambia was at the time completely unprepared for the introduction of GM crops. In view of this, it is perhaps unfair to conclude from this incident that European skepticism will prevent properly planned and well-considered introductions of GM crops taking place.

Per Pinstrup-Andersen's version of the Pro-GM Crops argument draws attention to two ways in which the European GM debate might be expected to affect the situation in Africa and other poor countries. First, fears might spread from Europe to Africa. Second, exports to Europe, which for many African countries are vital, might fall. But both of these expectations can be questioned. People who anticipate African adoption of European fears need to be reminded that, for the most part, reservations about GM crops in Europe are *not* based on fear – at any rate, there is little evidence that the European public take GM crops to be dangerous. Rather, as explained above, the European reaction is based on a perception of the balance of risks and benefits. Moreover, even if Europeans overestimate the risks and underestimate the benefits of GM crops, their underlying attitude does seem to be in harmony with the sort of approach that Per Pinstrup-Andersen advocates.

There are a number of GM crops with different traits (primarily insect and virus resistance) under development in Africa (Sithole-Niang et al. 2004), and there is no reason to believe that these genetically modified crops, if they were to be grown in a certain African country, would have an adverse effect on exports – not least when it comes to crops that are not used for export. For food crops which are grown for export to Europe, it may be important to think twice before allowing genetically modified varieties of the crops to be grown.

At present, then, there seems to be no good reason to suppose that European resistance to gene technology will have a negative impact on efforts to alleviate hunger and poverty in Africa and other parts of the developing world; and a key premise of the Poor Man's Ethics argument therefore turns out to be suspect.

What will, potentially, have a negative effect is the heavy regulatory burden and extensive risk assessment that must normally be undertaken by a country when it introduces a GM crop. These preliminaries are bound to impose heavy costs on poor countries. However, the costs can only partly be blamed on the skeptical European public. The bulk of EU legislation on release and marketing came into force in 1990, 5–6 years before the debate escalated, and in many respects it is similar to the US regulations, which are also being criticized for limiting commercialization of transgenic crops to a few multinational biotechnology companies (Bradford et al. 2005).

We need, finally, to discuss the ethical outlook that underpins the Pro-GM Crops argument. The argument rests on the premise that more well-off people have an obligation to do whatever they can to help people who are really in need of help. Given their relative wealth, this seems to imply that rich countries should do whatever they can to help the developing world, even to the extent of limiting the right of their citizens to choose what they think is best for themselves. The fact that we do not like the prospect of eating GM food is of no importance, if our refusal to eat such food will effectively prevent impoverished nations from benefiting from biotechnology.

One may agree or disagree with this line of thought. It is clear, however, that if such thinking was genuinely accepted in the developed world, there would be no problem in finding the resources to alleviate hunger and poverty elsewhere. As is spelled out in the chapter by Per Pinstrup-Andersen in this volume, the real problem is that it is very difficult to ensure that governments in rich countries make even the modest sacrifices required to fulfill agreed targets (e.g., the Millennium Development Goals).

In reality, then, as many people have said before, the problem is one of lack of political will. In this context, one cannot help thinking that the question of whether, to alleviate poverty in the developing world, we should give up the right to choose the kind of food we think is best for ourselves, is rather academic.

DISCUSSION

In this chapter we have sought to evaluate two Poor Man's Ethics arguments. We have set out some considerations that suggest that both arguments are weak. The arguments rely on assumptions about the way in which moral standards in the rich world (regarding animal welfare or the use of gene technology in food production) may have negative effects on the livelihood of people in the poor parts of the world. In each case, these assumptions turn out to be dubious.

The Poor Man's Ethics arguments we have examined in the two previous sections rely on a pair of broadly specified ethical principles or assumptions. The first – the argument against Animal Welfare Imperialism – involves the individualist assumption that, as a matter of principle, each person has the right to decide his or her own values. It is concluded from this assumption that to impose Western standards of animal welfare on people in the developing world is to interfere with the latter's rights. The second – the Pro-GM Crops argument – rests on the principle that we should do what we can to help the developing world in order to prevent suffering across the globe. It is concluded from this principle that we should limit our own right to choose what we think is best for us in order to benefit poor and undernourished people in the developing world.

The problem here, as is perhaps already apparent, is that we cannot have it both ways. The individualist assumption that we ought to respect each person's right to decide his or her own values undermines the Pro-GM Crops argument. The principle that we should do what will be most effective in preventing suffering in the world undermines the argument against Animal Welfare Imperialism. So it turns out that the arguments are grounded in ethical outlooks that clearly pull in different directions.

One, very sensible, way forward would be to limit the relative scope of one of the underlying ethical premises. Thus one could say that the right for each individual to decide for him/herself in matters involving values is only valid when this is not done at the cost of preventing suffering to others. However, in the case of alleged Animal Welfare Imperialism, those in favor of animal welfare will certainly argue that they are trying to prevent suffering in others (the animals).

On the other hand, if it really could be argued that wide acceptance of GM crops was *the way* to help starving people in the developing world, then probably the resistance against GM crops would dwindle. However, the real problem, of course, is that there are a lot of other much more obvious ways in which we, at small costs to ourselves, can prevent the suffering of poor people living in the developing world. Maybe it is time to change our focus to these other ways.

NOTES

[1] See http://www.isaaa.org/kc/
[2] Per Pinstrup-Andersen, interviewed by Helle Hartmann-Madsen [see http://www.biotekcenter.dk/].
[3] See http://news.bbc.co.uk/1/hi/world/africa/2459903.stm

REFERENCES

Appleby, M.C., 1999. *What Should We Do About Animal Welfare?* Oxford, UK: Blackwell.
Bradford, K.J., A. Van Deynze, N. Gutterson, W. Parrott and S,H. Strauss, 2005. Regulating transgenic crops sensibly: Lessons from plant breeding, biotechnology and genomics. *Nature Biotechnology* 23(4): 439–444.
Doerfler, R.L. and K.J. Peters, 2006. The relativity of ethical issues in animal agriculture related to different cultures and production conditions. *Livestock Production Science* 103: 257–262.
Frewer, L.J., C. Howard and R. Shepherd, 1998. Understanding public attitudes to technology. *Journal of Risk Research* 1(3): 221–235.
Gaskell, G., N. Allum and S. Stares, 2003. Europeans and biotechnology in 2002. *Eurobarometer 58.0* (2nd edn: 21 March 2003). Report to the EC Directorate General for Research from the project 'Life Sciences in European Society' QLG7CT-1999-00286. http://europa.eu.int/comm/public_opinion/archives/eb_special.htm
Huang, J., S. Rozelle, C. Pray and Q. Wang, 2002. Plant biotechnology in China. *Science* 295: 674–677.
Huang, J., R. Hu, S. Rozelle and C. Pray, 2005. Insect-resistant GM rice in farmers' fields: Assessing productivity and health effects in China. *Science* 308: 688–690.
James, C., 2004. Preview: Global status of commercialized biotech/GM crops 2004. *ISAAA Briefs* 32. Ithaca, NY: ISAAA.
James, C., 2005. Executive summary of global status of commercialized biotech/GM crops: 2005. *ISAAA Briefs* No. 34. ISAAA: Ithaca, NY.

Joensen, L. and S. Semino, 2004. Argentina's torrid love affair with the soybean. *Seedling* Oct 2004: 5–10.

Lassen, J., K.H. Madsen and P. Sandøe, 2002. Ethics and genetic engineering: Lessons to be learned from GM foods. *Bioprocess Biosystems Engineering* 24(5): 263–271.

Lehman, V. and W.A. Pengue, 1997. Herbicide tolerant soybean: Just another step in a technology treadmill? *Biotechnology and Development Monitor* 43: 11–14.

Madsen, K.H., B.E. Valverde and J.E. Jensen, 2002. Risk assessment of herbicide resistant crops: A Latin American perspective using rice (*Oryza sativa*) as a model. *Weed Technology* 16(1): 215–223.

Madsen, K.H., J.N. Thomsen, B. Strandberg and P. Sandøe, 2005. GM sugar beet – What are the concerns? *Advances in Sugar Beet Research* 6. IIRB (Institut International de Recherches Betterav-ières), Bruxelles, Belgium. Pp 25-44.

Men, X., F. Ge, C.A. Edwards and E.N. Yardim, 2004. Influence of pesticide applications on pests and predatory arthropods associated with transgenic Bt cotton and nontransgenic cotton plants. *Phytoparasitica* 32(3): 246–254.

Men, X., F. Ge, C.A. Edwards and E.N. Yardim, 2005. The influence of pesticide applications on *Helicoverpa armigera* Hübner and sucking pests in transgenic Bt cotton and non-transgenic cotton in China. *Crop Protection* 24: 319–324.

Nuffield Council on Bioethics, 2003. *The Use of Genetically Modified Crops in Developing Countries: A Follow Up Discussion Paper* [available at http://www.nuffieldbioethics.org/fileLibrary/pdf/GM_Crops_Discussion_Paper_2004.pdf].

Olofdotter, M., B.E. Valverde and K.H. Madsen, 2000. Herbicide resistant rice (*Oryza sativa* L.) in a global perspective: Implications for weed management. *Annals of Applied Biology* 137: 279–295.

Qaim, M. and G. Traxler, 2005. Roundup Ready soybeans in Argentina: Farm level and aggregate welfare effects. *Agricultural Economics* 32: 73–86.

Sithole-Niang, I., J. Cohen and P. Zambrano, 2004. Putting GM technologies to work: Public research pipelines in selected African countries. *African Journal of Biotechnology* 3(11): 564–571.

Tabashnik, B., 2005. Refuges in India and delayed resistance to Bt crops. *Nature Biotechnology* 23: 414.

Teknologirådet, 2003. *Genmodificerede afgrøder i udviklingslande – udfordringer for udviklingshjælpen.* En rapport fra en arbejdsgruppe nedsat af Teknologirådet. Teknologirådets Rapporter 2003/4.

Walgate, R., 2003. *Genetically Modified Food: The American Experience.* Summary of a Conference organized by the Danish Centre for Bioethics and Risk Assessment and the BioTIK Secretariat, Copenhagen 11–12 June 2003.

Webster, A.J.F., 1994. *Animal Welfare: A Cool Eye Towards Eden.* Oxford, UK: Blackwell.

White House, 2003. *President Bush Urges Congress to Pass BioShield Legislation.* Remarks by the President at the Bio 2003 Convention Center and Exhibition, Washington Convention, Center [available at http://www.whitehouse.gov/news/releases/2003/06/20030623-2.html].

Wolfenbarger, L.L. and P.R. Phifer, 2000. The ecological risks and benefits of genetically engineered plants. *Science* 290: 2088–2093.

Wu, K., W. Mu, G. Liang and Y. Guo, 2005. Regional reversion of insecticide resistance in *Helicoverpa armigera* (Lepidoptera:Noctuidae) is associated with the use of Bt cotton in northern China. *Pest Management Science* 61: 491–498.

Yang, P., M. Iles, S. Yan and F. Jolliffe, 2005. Farmers' knowledge, perceptions and practices in transgenic Bt cotton in small producer systems in Northern China. *Crop Protection* 24: 229–239.

PAUL B. THOMPSON

ETHICS, HUNGER, AND THE CASE
FOR GENETICALLY MODIFIED (GM) CROPS

INTRODUCTION

Do wealthy people and their governments have an ethical obligation to moderate qualms or concerns they might have about new agricultural or food technology in virtue of its potential for alleviating hunger and malnutrition? There have already been a surprising number of specific policy issues in which contradictory answers to this apparently arcane question have been at the core of disagreement. So-called GM (or genetically modified) foods have been developed through recombinant DNA techniques for introducing new traits into plants, microbes, and animals. I will use terminology such as 'GM,' 'GMO,' and 'agricultural biotechnology,' to refer broadly to plants, animals, or microbes that have been transformed using recombinant DNA. These terms are clearly imprecise and could be construed as misleading. In one sense, all agricultural plants and animals are 'genetically modified.' In other contexts finer grained distinctions (such as whether transgenes were derived from the same or a different species, or whether the term 'biotechnology' should include adult-cell mammalian clones) would be relevant. In the present context, the discussion primarily concerns agricultural food crops, and the terminology used here has been widely (even if in some cases grudgingly) accepted.

Several applications of this technology (notably herbicide resistance genes and genes for the *Bacillus thuringiensis* (Bt) toxin) have been incorporated into food and fiber crops that are grown by farmers in the USA, Argentina, and a number of other food-exporting nations. Yet the technology sparked a firestorm of controversy in the late 1990s (see Pinstrup-Andersen and Schiøler 2000; Bauer and Gaskell 2002). Biotechnology's potential to address food shortages and nutritional deficiencies became a frequent talking point among its advocates, especially in debates over proposed shipments of GM maize for use as food aid, and over the prospects for addressing vitamin-A deficiencies with a genetically modified variety popularly known as 'golden rice.' Michael Ruse and David Castle (2002) have edited a collection of essays that presents a useful sample of the 'pro' and 'con' positions, but the details of this debate will not be discussed here.

Although GM crops represent a recent and important instance in which concerns about new technology are countered with an argument stressing the technology's potential for alleviating a morally compelling need, this pattern of moral argument is far from unique. Within agriculture, similar arguments were used in debates over Green Revolution projects that introduced chemical fertilizers and pesticides into

P. Pinstrup-Andersen and P. Sandøe (eds.), Ethics, Hunger and Globalization: In Search of Appropriate Policies, 215–235.

the developing world. Nobel Laureate Norman Borlaug has been a particularly vocal and prominent defender of both the Green Revolution and GM crops. Borlaug's views have been aired on at least one television broadcast (Bill Moyers' NOW, October 2002) and published in a number of outlets, including an editorial in the 6 February 2000 *Wall Street Journal* ('We need biotech to feed the world') and a longer article published simultaneously in *Plant Physiology* (Borlaug 2001), and also in the *Transactions* of the Wisconsin Academy of Arts and Sciences. Borlaug has thus spoken out on this issue and he has not hesitated to suggest that those who voice concerns about agricultural biotechnology act immorally because the needs of the hungry override the concerns of the wealthy.

   Beyond issues of food and hunger, advocates of stem-cell research cite its potential to be used in therapies for devastating diseases as a counter-argument to those who have qualms. Indeed, this general pattern of argument may be so common as to constitute a problem of general interest in the ethics of technology: Does the potential for morally compelling benefits to the needy override less compelling concerns expressed by people who do not share this need? I will not, however, address the question in its most general form, nor do I suggest that an analysis focused on hunger and biotechnology will necessarily be generalizable to other issues in technological ethics. In keeping with a focus on hunger, I will briefly review some of the main arguments that are used to characterize the moral signif-icance of hunger and malnutrition as global problems. While sages, moralists, and philosophers have long pondered the virtue of extending aid to the needy, the needy in question were generally presumed to be members of one's local community. The ethics of world hunger is thus a philosophical problem of comparatively recent origin. I will also make a selective review of some arguments behind qualms that have been expressed about GM food. I will then connect the two lines of argument in which the claims of hunger are pitted against those of the queasy, concluding with a brief discussion of the practical implications for ongoing debates.

THE ETHICS OF WORLD HUNGER

Although global hunger has, in some sense, been a topic of philosophical reflection at least since Thomas Malthus' *Essay on a Principle of Population* in 1798, it is really a topic of the last 40 years. Philosophers began to write on the basis for global obligations to ensure that the world's hungry are fed in response to a rising general awareness of hunger that had multiple sources and themes. One theme was certainly the Green Revolution itself, which in the early years was presented to the public as a technological fix for hunger. Another was the political debate over foreign aid, and especially in connection with US Public Law 480, which established the program for concessionary sales of US grain to countries experiencing food deficits. Private charitable appeals served as a third source of public awareness about the hunger of distant peoples. Children in the 1950s and 1960s were encouraged to 'Trick or Treat for UNICEF,' and organizations dedicated specifically to hunger relief began to solicit funds. All of these sources suggested, at least implicitly, that addressing distant hunger was a morally good thing to do, though they did not examine the ethical basis for this suggestion.

The most enduring philosophical account of the morality of world hunger has been Peter Singer's 1972 article 'Famine, affluence and morality,' in which he argued that even moderately well-off people have a moral duty to limit their consumption of 'luxuries and frills,' so that they may devote their discretionary income to 'those in dire need,' or more specifically famine relief. The key moral premise in Singer's argument held that

> If it is in our power to prevent something very bad from happening, without thereby sacrificing anything else morally significant, we ought, morally, to do so.

Singer himself believed that the key moral premise not only could be deduced from virtually any moral theory, but also stood as a widely accepted moral intuition based on common sense (Singer 1972). Singer's work appeared in conjunction with a broader discussion in which non-philosophers were active participants. Ethicist Joseph Fletcher collaborated with ecologist Garrett Hardin on an argument intended to show why it would be ethically justifiable to stifle the impulse to feed the hungry in a world of unchecked population growth (Lucas and Ogletree 1976). Articles by Singer and by Hardin or Fletcher were reprinted widely in formats that suggested a debate in which Singer argued for famine relief, while the Hardin/Fletcher position was against it.

Aside from Peter Unger's *Living High and Letting Die* (1996), which is an extended reprise of Singer's original 1972 argument, Singer's article itself has had two main types of response. First, some are impressed by the way that Singer's argument calls for radical self-sacrifices that reduce people to lifestyles that, though hardly ascetic by historical standards, are far, far less consumptive than those lived by virtually everyone in developed industrial economies. As such, there are a number of attempts to moderate the argument, bringing it more in line with common-sense moral intuitions. It is notable that even these attempts typically acknowledge that people have ethical obligations to bring aid, even if these obligations are not as radical as Singer's argument would suggest (see Miller 2004). A more widespread (and not mutually exclusive) reaction has been to interpret the radical and surprising nature of Singer's prescription as a consequence of historical changes that have in fact made ordinary common-sense moral intuitions obsolete, or at least inapplicable to the problems of world hunger (Aiken and LaFollette 1977). Although diverse in their particulars, arguments developing this interpretation take global famine and malnutrition to be a consequence of factors such as the end of the colonial era and the wealthy nations' subsequent exploitation of weaker and poorer peoples through inequitable trade, despoliation of the global environmental commons, and alliances of convenience with repressive and corrupt political regimes. What is more, the ease of international trade, travel, and communication can be seen as bringing once strange and distant peoples into the circle of one's moral community. One source for this line of thought can be found in Thomas Nagel's contribution to Peter

Brown and Henry Shue's *Food Policy* (1977), and more extended developments have been made by Shue himself (1980), Onora O'Neill (1986), and most recently by Thomas Pogge (2002). Pogge represents a new generation of philosophers (in which I include myself) who have been impressed by the work of Amartya Sen, and who tend to address hunger as one component in a larger complex of economic and political issues. Thompson (1992) provides a more detailed discussion of the various philosophical positions on hunger than I am offering here, including the differences between consequentialist viewpoints, such as those of Singer or Unger, and neo-Kantian views such as those of Shue, who expresses the morality of hunger in terms of rights, or O'Neill, who utilizes a logic of duties following from the characteristics of agency.

While their theoretical lines of argument differ substantially, most of these philosophical authors see the moral imperatives of hunger as duties arising from the need to remedy inequities and injustices associated with globalization. Such duties did not exist in a world where moral and political relationships were understood as coinciding with national borders, hence there is a genuine need to reconstruct the terms of common-sense morality. Because it is not possible to understand our world as one in which the significance of our daily activities is limited to our local communities or national States, it is incumbent upon citizens from wealthy nations to think of themselves as morally obligated to redress global famine and malnourishment. However, philosophers have never been especially clear on the particular way in which these obligations are to be discharged. Many follow Singer's lead in focusing on personal gifts of money to various relief organizations, though others single out government-to-government aid programs.

I believe that we do no injustice to other authors on world hunger when we construe the recommendation favoring a personal contribution for famine relief as an example or archetype for a more general prescription to support a wide variety of activities intended to promote poverty alleviation and economic development among people less fortunate than the middle classes of the industrialized West. We may also assume that the prescription is limited to activities that are effective in achieving this aim. Philosophers are understandably wary about straying too far into empirical matters that distinguish effective and ineffective forms of assistance, yet evidence about what works is clearly relevant to the conversion of general norms into prescriptions for action. Supporting agricultural research intended to increase or stabilize crop yields is seldom mentioned as a way to meet one's obligations to ameliorate the extreme needs of hungry people. Yet if we set aside the very real worries about whether any given research project is effective in meeting those needs, for the sake of further argument, it is quite reasonable to presume that philosophical arguments for linking world hunger to moral obligation provide support for agricultural and policy research that contributes to this end.

This reasoning leads us to a key moral hypothesis. If agricultural biotechnology and the development of GM crops does have the potential to contribute to a lessening of hunger and deprivation over the long term, then people have a moral obligation to support the use of these techniques, at least in so far as they are deployed in pursuit of that end. Furthermore, this obligation *overrides* less compelling ethical concerns that may exist concerning GM crops. I will call this the 'Borlaug hypothesis.' In addition to the papers by Norman Borlaug mentioned above, the Borlaug hypothesis has been argued by scientific authors such as Anthony Trewavas (1999) and Florence Wambugu (Ruse and Castle 2002). Philosopher Gregory Pence makes a longer, but still very broad, case for the Borlaug hypothesis in his book, *Designer Genes: Mutant Harvest or Breadbasket of the World?* (2002). Each of these works is notable for the paucity of references to or discussion of published books and articles by critics of biotechnology. Gary Comstock describes how he set aside his own moral qualms about GM crops after becoming convinced that it could help address problems of poverty and hunger (Comstock 2000, 2002). His position thus parallels the Borlaug hypothesis but, unlike these other authors, Comstock does discuss the actual views of critics in some detail. Furthermore, he does not suggest that a critic acts immorally in opposing GM crops.

The empirical claims of the Borlaug hypothesis can certainly be questioned, and it is significant that a large part of the public debate over 'golden rice' has concerned the effectiveness of this application of biotechnology as a strategy for addressing vitamin-A deficiencies in the diet of poor people. In contrast to this debate about empirical effectiveness, the ethical or philosophical elements of this hypothesis appear to be largely secure, especially given the background of thinking that has just been summarized. Although there are many philosophical ways to articulate the exact nature of our personal and political obligations to address issues in world hunger, the voices of people thinking and writing about this issue are virtually unanimous in calling for greater attention to the needs of the hungry. These divergent philosophical rationales converge on a practical imperative to take actions that relieve world hunger, even when these actions require some sacrifice on the part of richer nations. This practical imperative may be plausibly interpreted as supporting agricultural research, including biotechnology, that will help meet the needs of the hungry, now and in the future, just as the Borlaug hypothesis suggests.

The Borlaug hypothesis must be understood as being subject to a number of unspecified but generally non-controversial ethical constraints. Agricultural or food research that involves risky experimentation on human subjects without their consent would not be justified. In a similar spirit, plans for deploying new agricultural technologies must conform to widely shared ethical standards, such as those articulated in the International Declaration of Human Rights. These qualifications indicate that there *is* at least one way in which the Borlaug hypothesis might be challenged on philosophical grounds, even granting that GM technology has the potential to increase or nutritionally enhance the food supplies available to poor people: One may question whether agricultural biotechnology is the *most appropriate* response to hunger and malnutrition. 'Most appropriate' can be understood as a requirement intended to encourage those hunger relief strategies that are compatible with a broad array of development goals, including the growth of participatory democracy or addressing the neediest people first. I will accept this interpretation without further argument, and submit that anyone who interprets the Borlaug hypothesis to justify the suspension of these widely accepted moral constraints on development practice must surely produce an argument to indicate why.

'Most appropriate' might also be interpreted as advocating only the most optimal use of scarce resources. Hunger is a multidimensional problem, and not one that can be addressed solely in terms of increasing agricultural productivity or the nutritional quality of crops. Determining whether biotechnology, which addresses only these two dimensions of hunger, is the optimal use of resources available to combat hunger, plunges the discussion into empirical matters again, for it suggests that one must assess each strategy available for addressing hunger and compare the likely impact of each in order to determine the optimal way to pursue this end. Some critics fault biotechnology (and hence might also wish to challenge the Borlaug hypothesis) on just such grounds. This is, I take it, the key premise of Devinder Sharma's argument (2003), for example, though Sharma builds on this premise in ways that make his total argument mimic some of the concerns noted in the penultimate section of this chapter. The question of whether biotechnology *can* achieve its objective was set aside 'for the sake of argument' in the above discussion because its relevance to any practical evaluation of biotechnology notwithstanding, it is not relevant to the philosophical underpinnings of the Borlaug hypothesis. Questions about whether biotechnology is the *most efficient* way to address hunger also fall into this category. I will not pursue that line of thinking in the remainder of this chapter.

THE CASE AGAINST AGRICULTURAL BIOTECHNOLOGY

Arguments against the use of recombinant DNA to introduce genetic novelty into food crops are also quite diverse and complex. Empirical research suggests that products of agricultural biotechnology have been most successfully resisted in countries where there is reduced confidence in government regulation of food safety and environmental impact (Gaskell et al. 2002). This does not, however, prove that concerns about government regulation or risks from agricultural biotechnology form the intellectual grounds on which opponents of biotechnology base their arguments, and in fact a number of analyses suggest that the core issues giving rise to concern about GMOs are ethical in nature (Sparks et al. 1994; Frewer et al. 1997; Durant et al. 1998; Gaskell and Bauer 2001; Priest 2001). Any summary analysis of these concerns is likely to be controversial in its own right (what follows, for example, gives short shrift to certain trade-related concerns) but most arguments can be classified into one of five main groups.

- The first group of arguments includes disagreements over the appropriate philo-sophical parameters for addressing technologically induced risks.
- Second is a concern that agricultural biotechnology is incompatible with social justice.
- Third, there are arguments to the effect that biotechnology is unnatural.

- Fourth, there are arguments that stress the importance of personal autonomy with respect to food choice.
- Finally, there are aretaic objections that focus on the moral character of the people and groups supporting biotechnology.

I will review each category with as much brevity as possible.

The main rhetorical vehicle in the debate over risk has been the precautionary principle, or alternatively, the precautionary approach. Stated succinctly, the precautionary principle holds that uncertain risks should be given great, perhaps dominant, weight in environmental and food safety decision-making. Uncertain risks are defined in contrast to known risks, which are in turn understood as risks for which both hazard and exposure can be estimated with a high degree of confidence. Perhaps the best overall resource on the conceptual basis for the precautionary principle is Joel Ticknor and Carolyn Raffensperger's 1999 book: *Protecting Public Health and the Environment: Implementing the Precautionary Principle*. This book presents the precautionary principle in a number of theoretical guises, ranging from respecting others to minimizing type-II statistical errors, but this volume does not discuss GM crops. Michael Ruse and David Castle (2002) include what is intended to be a representative discussion of the precautionary principle in their anthology of articles on the GM debate. The paper by Florence Dagicour entitled 'Protecting the environment: from nucleons to nucleotides,' analogizes biotechnology to 'bad actor' chemical and nuclear technologies, but other papers in the volume by Indur Goklany and by Henry Miller and Gregory Conko are critical of the precautionary approach as it is generally understood by its advocates.

However, one anecdote may convey what paragraphs of summary and analytical discussion would not. At a 1999 symposium on GMOs, an officer of France's food safety agency was challenged to explain why they were applying the precautionary principle to GMOs but not to unpasteurized cheese. The answer was, 'We *know* that's dangerous.' Because risks from unpasteurized cheese are known, the precautionary principle does not apply. In contrast, risks may be classified as uncertain when exposure mechanisms for inducing hazards are not understood, because empirical data on the frequency of hazards is lacking or because analysts may have overlooked a novel hazard that they had no basis to expect, the so-called 'unknown unknown.' Critics of the precautionary principle have pointed out that some elements of precaution have long been incorporated into conventional approaches to risk analysis and are, in fact, reflected in regulatory decisions that have approved the release of GMOs. Other elements, such as the concern for unknown unknowns, are ubiquitous and provide no basis for viewing risks associated with GMOs as less certain than risks from conventional foods (Van den Belt 2003).

More sophisticated philosophical defenses of the precautionary approach in decision-making concerning GM crops are cognizant of these difficulties. One approach is to interpret reference to the precautionary principle as a call for steady and evolutionary development of more sophisticated scientific tools for assessing risks, and for regulators to apply burdens of proof that take evidence for risk very seriously, even when that evidence is not wholly convincing (Cranor 2003). Whether current regulatory practice for foods reflects such a burden of proof is controversial. An alternative philosophical interpretation of the precautionary approach calls for a broadening of the terms in which new technologies are evaluated (Korthals 2004). Here, the focus actually has less to do with uncertain risks and more to do with the inclusion of considerations that arise in connection with the four remaining categories of ethical concern. It is to these categories that we now turn.

Arguments stressing social justice build upon three prior critiques of agricultural research. The Green Revolution was criticized for tending to benefit relatively better-off farmers at the expense of poorer ones, even if the beneficiaries are still poor by Western standards (Dahlberg 1979). The 'technological treadmill' identified by agricultural economist Willard Cochrane suggests that yield-enhancing agricultural technologies generally produce temporary benefits for early adopters at the expense of late adopters, who can eventually lose their farms entirely, fueling the trend toward fewer and larger farms (Cochrane 1979). These two arguments suggest that the benefits of agricultural research are inconsistent with the goals of distributive justice, though both arguments neglect the benefits that increased yields have for consumers when there are adjustments in the price of food. The third critique accuses developed-world agricultural researchers of 'biopiracy,' when they collect germplasm developed by poor farmers and use it to develop certified or patented crop varieties (Juma 1989).

All three arguments were extended to agricultural biotechnology in part simply because it was, in the 1980s, the latest thing in agricultural research. Shiva (1995, 2000) was particularly influential in developing this critique. Arguments on social justice have also been a particular focus of reports developed by the UK Nuffield Council on Bioethics (1998, 2003). The biopiracy argument was particularly pertinent in virtue of the way that recombinant DNA techniques for isolating, identifying, and trans-ferring genes introduced new ways in which intellectual property rights (IPRs) could be claimed on genetic resources (Magnus 2002). Prior to the advent of this technology, IPRs could be applied to crop varieties, and the most common form of legal protection under the US Plant Variety Protection Act recognized farmers' rights to save seed for future use. With biotechnology came patents on specific genes, multiplying the ways in which IPRs could be claimed and potentially limiting farmers' rights to save seed and interbreed purchased seed with local varieties (Burk 2002).

The above is, of course, only a cursory discussion of the extensive literature that has appeared on biotechnology and social justice. Criticisms in print by 1996 have been more exhaustively discussed in my book *Food Biotechnology in Ethical Perspective* (Thompson 1997), while more recent overviews have been under-taken by Jonathan Robinson (1999) and Maarten Chrispeels (2000). Furthermore, any effort to either integrate GM crops into the portfolio of poor farmers (or, for that matter, to exclude them) will itself have costs and distributive effects on well-being. The picture becomes very complex. Yet, while all these arguments from social justice make important moral points about the design and implemen-tation of agricultural research that is intended to help the poor, what they mostly establish are conditions that agricultural biotechnology would need to meet in order to attain legitimacy, rather than unilateral arguments against any use of biotechnology whatsoever. As such, the 'social justice' critique does not directly enjoin the Borlaug hypothesis at all. Instead, it stipulates side-constraints that any development initiative would have to meet in order to be justly applied to help the poor.

A third class of arguments concern whether GM crops are unnatural. It is clear that some people feel that they are, and Prince Charles' well known statements about genetically engineered food crops provide an excellent example of one way to arrive at this judgment. Prince Charles' radio address is reprinted in Ruse and Castle (2002), and an editorial 'My 10 fears for GM food' appeared in the 1 June 1999 edition of *The Daily Mail*. Another type of argument owes a debt to a perspective in medical ethics that is associated with Leon Kass (1997) and stresses the simple repugnance that many feel in response to genetically engineered foods (Chadwick 2000; Midgley 2000). It is also possible to argue that GM plants are unnatural on metaphysical grounds (Bockmühl 2001). These arguments are definitely the minority view among academically trained philosophers, however, who point out that our ideas of what is and what is not natural undergo a remarkable amount of change over time. Critics of the view that biotechnology is 'unnatural' argue that it is difficult to maintain any clear conception of 'naturalness' that can be both supported by scientific conceptions of nature and yield clean ethical principles for thinking one way about GM crops while thinking differently about the products of traditional plant breeding (Reiss and Straughn 1996; Rollin 1996; Comstock 1998, 2000; Sagoff 2001; Pence 2002).

I have recently argued that there is a different way to conceptualize the 'unnatural' critique of agricultural biotechnology and that philosophers' tendency to set aside these arguments reflects a way of thinking conditioned by problems in medical, rather than agricultural, ethics (Thompson 2003a). But because I do not believe that my own analysis provides the basis for a strong argument against biotechnology, I will not pursue those arguments here. I have also argued (and here I think many philosophers would agree) that even if concerns about the naturalness of GM crops do not provide convincing arguments for social policies that would ban or discriminate against them, such concerns do indeed provide individuals all the reason they need to avoid them as a matter of personal practice. Put another way, one should not be required to produce a risk assessment to justify one's personal preference for acting on religious or aesthetic values, personal beliefs about what is or is not natural, or even idiosyncratic views on what constitutes wholesome food (Thompson 2002). Even if we do not agree with these personal judgments, we should respect an individual's right to make dietary choices that conform to his or her personal vision of what is natural. This point leads to the fourth class of arguments.

Arguments in the fourth class of ethical concerns note that individual consumers may have a number of personal values that are incompatible with eating foods from GMOs. Mainstreaming GM crops into commodity production and processing could have the effect of making it impossible for people to act on the basis of such values when consuming food. The ethical significance of this possibility is to compromise individuals' ability to lead lives that conform to their freely chosen religious, political, and personal values. The fact that foods enter one's body and are traditional carriers of cultural and religious tradition suggests that such compromise is a significant challenge to personal autonomy. The policy implications point toward discussions of labeling, costs of segregating GMOs from non-GMOs, and the distribution of costs from doing so (Jackson, 2000). Ethical debate concerns the legitimacy and weight that should be given to such dietary concerns. Klaus Leisinger (2000) echoes the Borlaug hypothesis in arguing that we should not 'entangle' these concerns with those that focus on the potential for helping the poor.

Some commentators see the personal autonomy issues associated with labeling and consumer consent as a surrogate for a more systematic divide in which the 'pro-biotech' viewpoint tends to reduce all ethical issues to a cost–benefit calculus, treating all issues as resolvable in terms of the impact on total social utility (see Caplan and Magnus's chapter in Ruse and Castle 2002). This way of thinking implies that greater social utility offsets compromise of personal autonomy, suggesting that a greater net social benefit justifies activities that violate individual rights. Here, the issue comes to a head in manner that reproduces the two-century-long philosophical debate between utilitarian and neo-Kantian moral theory. From the neo-Kantian or rights perspective, the utilitarians exhibit a lack of concern for personal autonomy that manifests itself as willingness to treat individuals and their rights as 'means' that can be sacrificed to pursue socially justifiable 'ends.' Although I am unaware of philosophers who take a classically utilitarian view of the food choice issue, the utilitarian viewpoint on labeling and choice is frequently taken by people who do not even seem to be aware that they are doing so (see, for example, Vogt 1999).

While neo-Kantians and utilitarians debate over the foundations of morality, other philosophers might argue that even though sometimes we do indeed find it necessary to sacrifice individuals and their rights for more compelling social ends, the problem with the utilitarians lies in the way that they seem wholly untroubled by this kind of sacrifice. Optimizing arguments make it so easy to override individual rights that we begin to question the moral character of people who rely on them too readily (or exclusively). Shouldn't one at least regard the sacrifice of autonomy or rights as tragic and regrettable (see Bernard Williams' contributions to Smart and Williams 1973)? This kind of argument spills over into the final category, aretaic objections to GMOs. The word 'aretaic' is from the Greek *arete*, meaning excellence or virtue. The thrust of these concerns is to suggest either that the use of rDNA technologies is contrary to virtue, or that those who have developed and promoted GMOs have engaged in behavior that is contrary to virtue. Aretaic objections to food biotechnology are evident in Brewster Kneen's 2002 article 'A naturalist looks at agricultural biotechnology,' and such arguments are nicely analyzed by Ronald Sandler (2004), who includes further citations to aretaic arguments.

Lack of virtue is sometimes associated with the 'reductionism' of those who develop and promote biotechnology. 'Reductionism' may refer to philosophies of science that interpret life processes as wholly reducible to physics and chemistry, to worldviews or practices that seem to regard life, nature, and even other people as lacking any spiritual dimension or sanctity, or to the belief that the subjectivity of values makes discussion of them a waste of time. Evidence for poor character might also be seen in unrelenting pursuit of personal gain at the expense of others' rights or ideals of the public good, or in a tendency to misrepresent opponents and to treat their objections simply as obstacles to be set aside through whatever means. Neglect of social justice and consumer autonomy might well be interpreted as a sign of weak moral character. The 'reductionism' theme has been an important element of Vandana Shiva's critique, especially in an essay, 'Beyond reductionism,' in a relatively early collection that she edited with Ingunn Moser (1995). The 'reductionism-is-vice' theme has been continued forcefully in a book by Finn Bowring (2003). Articles in the Ruse and Castle (2002) collection also discuss key points relevant to moral character and the role of ethics in the debate over biotechnology (see especially the contributions of Ambuj Sagar, Arthur Daemmrich and Mona Ashiya, 'The tragedy of the commoners: Biotechnology and its publics,' and Marc Saner, 'Real and metaphorical moral limits in the biotech debate').

For many critics who advance aretaic criticisms, the weak moral character of the 'pro-biotech' camp provides a reason to be especially cautious in one's dealings with them. If those who develop and promote GMOs are not to be trusted because they have poor moral character, then it is rational to be wary of these products, to see them as risky. A mutually reinforcing feedback loop begins to develop, where lack of attention to key ethical issues is seen as evidence of poor moral character, and poor moral character is seen as evidence for risk (see Thompson 1997). This evidence does not derive from facts about GMOs or their fate in the environment or the human body, but from facts about the danger that we associate with people who fail to treat others with respect, or who displace serious moral issues with strategic or manipulative argumentation. One can see this way of thinking in action in an article on risk assessment by Sheldon Krimsky (2002). More broadly, the idea that risk and trust are closely correlated is now fairly well established in risk studies. Douglas Powell and William Leiss (1997) provide a philosophically sophisticated treatment of issues relating to risk perception, political participation, and trust. Ironically, the book has a chapter on GM food that was published with a note indicating that the text was felt to be unduly accepting of the pro-GM point of view by the graduate research assistants who helped Powell and Leiss with the research.

As this feedback loop becomes established, the precautionary principle can now be applied to the 'uncertain risks' associated with GMOs in virtue of their shady associations. Such risks do not become better known by producing a conventional risk assessment. They can only be addressed when advocates for the technology desist from conduct that is seen as contrary to moral excellence and re-establish a basis for trust through honest and respectful dealings. This feedback loop allows a form of translation to cut across these five argument forms, so that moral concerns may be interpreted as risks, and the failure to address risks is interpreted as a moral problem. I have long argued that this feedback loop lies at the heart of much public resistance to GMOs, and that it explains the unpredictability, self-righteousness, and explosiveness of opponents' behavior. I also believe that although I do not find myself to be sorely tempted by the translations that generate this feedback, it is perfectly rational for someone having less 'insider' access to the agricultural sciences than I have to react in this way.

CONNECTING THE DOTS

Given a strong presumptive argument favoring agricultural biotechnology on the grounds that it can play a role in addressing world hunger, do the arguments against it provide any basis for overturning that presumption? This question can be put in other ways. Are these ethical concerns about agricultural biotechnology overridden or countered by biotechnology's capacity to address problems of world hunger? Do people who advance these concerns have a morally based reason to stifle their qualms and accept agricultural biotechnology because of its potential to address world hunger? Does a positive evaluation of agricultural biotechnology's potential to address hunger entail a rejection of the arguments against it? While each way of framing the question suggests a different set of nuances, the substantive issues raised by all of them can be addressed by working systematically through each of the five main anti-GM arguments and examining how biotechnology's potential to address global hunger and malnutrition provides a response to them.

Biotechnology's potential to relieve world hunger provides a very strong response to the most typical interpretations of the precautionary principle. Gary Comstock (2002) has produced a very persuasive demonstration of the way that broad interpretations of the precautionary principle produce self-contradictory policy prescriptions in the domain of agriculture and food. Even laying aside these problems, the compelling needs of the world's hungry people must certainly override the views of those who see uncertain risk and little personal benefit to biotechnology. If one accepts the empirical assumptions of the Borlaug hypothesis (i.e., that biotechnology is an important weapon against hunger), it is difficult to see how speculative concerns arising from uncertainty could outweigh its ethical force. If, on the other hand, the point of noting uncertainties is to question whether biotechnology actually does have any capacity to help the needy, then the argument drifts into matters on which moral philosophers are wise to remain silent (at least for a few more paragraphs).

One might think that arguments from social justice would provide the most potent source of opposition to the Borlaug hypothesis. On the contrary, however, arguments from social justice stipulate a series of norms to which *any* socially just form of agricultural technology must conform. As such, these arguments spell out some of the constraints that have been previously characterized as 'widely accepted,' and apply them more specifically to situations relevant to agricultural technology. As previously noted, these arguments *do not* provide a basis for unilateral opposition to GM crops or foods, but do so only to the extent that these technologies are implemented in an autocratic manner that sacrifices the interests of many of the people that development assistance policies are intended to help. As such, concerns arising from social justice are not only compatible with the Borlaug hypothesis, but represent precisely the conditions under which any ethical acceptable interpretation of the Borlaug hypothesis would have to be implemented. Thus, social justice does not so much represent an ethical or philosophical challenge to agricultural biotechnology as it does a set of criteria that biotechnology must meet *in fact*. Whether any given project attempting to use biotechnology to aid the poor does in fact meet these tests is an important, indeed vital, question, yet there is little to dispute philosophically on this point.

Objections raising questions about biotechnology's naturalness or about its consistency with personal autonomy can also be dispensed with fairly quickly, if not altogether cleanly. Clearly, someone who feels that GM crops are unnatural, irreligious, or repugnant may oppose their use to aid the poor. Yet if one is inclined to regard these concerns as relevant largely to the extent that they represent legitimate personal values that deserve protection, the key issue will be whether people holding these values are given adequate opportunity to act upon them. This question points toward two distinct ethical problem sets. One concerns relatively wealthy people who purchase food in industrial food systems. Does their insistence on labels, segregation of GM and non-GM grain and the like impose an ethically unacceptable burden on the poor? This is, of course, a more specific form of the general question that is the central topic of this chapter. At this juncture in the analysis, it is fair to say that if the repercussions of insisting on one's values include the starvation and malnourishment of others, the answer must certainly be 'Yes.' Although it is important for liberal societies to give their citizens wide latitude for adopting and living out life values, and although life values relating to food may be a particularly significant subset of those life values that are protected by liberty of conscience, the evil that is being endured by the hungry is greater still. Protecting the religious and personal liberties of one group does not justify action or policy that causes others to starve. Of course, simply asserting that policies protecting liberty of conscience cause such dire harms does not make it so. Following this line of questioning to the bitter end would require some hard debate about the nature of international commodity markets and their capacity to deliver non-GM crops to those who want them without unduly harming the poor.

The second problem set concerns poor people who are being helped through the development of these GM crops. Have they been given adequate opportunity to apply their own values in deciding whether to adopt or eat GM crops? While it is immanently plausible to believe that concerns about 'naturalness' or 'repugnance' mean little to a hungry person, to simply assume that this is the case fails to treat the recipients of aid with the respect they deserve. As such, there is a genuine need to introduce GM crops intended to benefit the hungry in a manner that both elicits relevant values and that gives the intended beneficiaries an opportunity to accept or reject the largesse of the international agricultural research system. This is not a simple task, to be sure, for it must be done in a manner that does not in itself cause suspicion about the safety of biotechnology or the intentions of donors.

It is reasonable to suspect that there are unresolved ethical issues lurking here. Technically trained experts in biotechnology often express the view that their products will be eagerly adopted by the intended beneficiaries, while there is strong evidence to the contrary in the form of local resistance to biotechnology. However, even this initial description of the task implies that the argument has shifted strongly in the direction of the procedural norms that developers of GM crops must follow, much as with respect to arguments referring to social justice. As such, the problems arising in connection with intended beneficiaries' views on the naturalness of biotechnology, as well as with respect to the autonomy with which they are able to express and act on their own values, do not contradict the Borlaug hypothesis. Instead they represent side-constraints that apply to all applications of agricultural research that are intended to feed the hungry, including those involving biotechnology.

To summarize thus far, I have defended the Borlaug hypothesis against those who express ethical concerns expressed in connection with the precautionary principle and in connection with the right of relatively wealthy people to make food choices that conform to their cultural values, including views on whether GM crops are 'natural.' However, I have noted that in both cases my defense depends upon resolving empirical questions in a manner that favors the optimistic assumptions of the Borlaug hypothesis. I have argued that concerns for social justice and for the autonomy of intended beneficiaries of GM crops are better interpreted as 'side-constraints' that do not overturn or override the Borlaug hypothesis's commitment to biotechnology, but instead limit the set of ethically acceptable strategies for implementing any agricultural research program, including those involving biotechnology. What, then, are we to say about the last group of ethical concerns?

VIRTUE ETHICS AND THE PROBABILITY OF SUCCESS

Does the Borlaug hypothesis provide a reason to overlook or sublimate concerns about the moral character of those who advocate GM crops? Anyone who is inclined to think about the ethics of world hunger in outcome-oriented terms is likely to answer this question in the affirmative. That is, if getting the hungry fed is what matters at the end of the day, then it is difficult to see why weak moral character in the people doing the feeding should contravene an otherwise successful effort. This kind of reasoning is especially relevant to a number of questions involving charitable assistance or aid. Suppose someone advocates the giving of aid not because of any feeling of moral responsibility or desire to help the needy, but because they want to be admired by others in their circle of friends, or because they want a tax deduction, or because they work for a company that will benefit economically from the aid program. These are all cases where the person advocating assistance acts from less than virtuous motives, yet in none of these cases would the defective moral character of the advocate provide a powerful argument against the aid program that is advocated. What matters here is whether the aid program can be justified on its own merits, and if the moral case for extending aid has already been made (as is the case with the Borlaug hypothesis), this justification turns upon the probability that the desired outcome will actually occur.

Any estimate of this probability must be based upon the available evidence and will involve a number of wholly empirical questions, but some of the important questions are not wholly empirical concerns, and these are questions concerning which evidence to consider and to whom that evidence is available. People such as Borlaug himself have a lifetime of experience in developing new crops to address hunger, and will base their estimate of the probability of success on that experience. In addition, there are technical studies on the effectiveness of past agricultural research in addressing hunger, and these studies can be extrapolated to the case of GM crops. This extrapolation is not itself a technical exercise, however, and requires both a firm understanding of the theory and data on which these studies rely and an ability to determine whether limitations in the studies do or do not make them a good basis for estimating the probability that GM crops will have similar success. In either case, then, there are elements of personal judgment that cannot be eliminated from the probability assessment. Furthermore, people who are in a position to exercise this kind of personal judgment are almost certain to be personally involved in agricultural research or development assistance at some level. For the sake of brevity, I will call such people 'insiders.'

What kind of evidence is available to 'outsiders,' to people for whom the above-mentioned types of evidence are distinctly unavailable? Basically, their evidence that GM crops will help the hungry takes the form of insider testimony. How would a rational individual evaluate this kind of evidence? The question that rational people will ask themselves is, 'Should I believe what the insiders say?' Here, the moral character of the insiders is relevant. Lacking any independent knowledge of whether agricultural research, especially research involving GM crops, will or will not help the hungry, a rational person will take the motives, interests, and any other evidence bearing on the character of the insiders into account when making an assessment of whether they are to be believed. The Borlaug hypothesis differs from many ordinary cases in which we are inclined to ignore the motives or character of those who advocate for aid because, unless we are ourselves insiders, the primary judgment we are making concerns whether or not to believe what the insiders say.

Now, the distinction between insiders and outsiders has admittedly been drawn rather broadly, but many readers of this chapter are undoubtedly comfortable in thinking of themselves as insiders, as I am myself. It is these readers for whom the remainder of the chapter is primarily written, and from them I must ask for a special effort to put oneself in the position of someone who knows nothing about agricultural science or the individuals and organizations that pursue it. For someone like this, the evidence that GM crops will help address hunger consists wholly in terms of direct insider testimony (for example, the articles and interviews in which Borlaug or others advocate biotechnology) and journalists' accounts that are themselves based on insider testimony. If the outsider who evaluates these reports believes that the insiders are knowledgeable, forthright, and reasonably well intentioned, they are likely to believe what the insiders say. Furthermore, the person we are imagining is likely to be much more capable of assessing evidence on whether the insiders are forthright and well intentioned than on whether they are knowledgeable. Seeing that insiders possess PhDs and professorships may be the only evidence an outsider has about the state of their knowledge, but an outsider can bring a wealth of information to bear on whether they are forthright and well intentioned. Some of the key issues are fairly obvious. Are insiders disinterested advocates, or do they stand to gain either financially or in prestige if biotechnology is pursued? How are insiders linked to the biotechnology industry? Finding out that insiders' work is often funded by industry, that their universities are seeking patents for which some them, at least, will reap financial rewards, or that private firms have a contractual right to commercialize public-sector research might provide a reason to question the motives of insiders. Yet none of these things would prove that insiders were either less than forthright or ill intentioned.

In fact, some less obvious issues may be more decisive. Have insiders paid careful attention to matters that have been described above as side-constraints? Have they been attentive to social justice? Have they taken pains to ensure that the intended beneficiaries of their research are truly participating in a fully informed and fully empowered way? Are they attentive to ethical, legal, and cultural concerns when they advocate for biotechnology? Given the fact that there are conflicting points of view being expressed with regard to these issues, an outsider might consider whether the insiders are dealing with this controversy in a thorough and respectful manner. That is, do the advocates of GM crops show evidence of having listened to the arguments of their detractors? Do they make responses that are on point and that either rebut their opponents' claims or explain why they are not relevant? Alternatively, do they show little evidence of having taken their opponents seriously? Do they either ignore the arguments altogether or do they caricature and distort arguments in a manner that misses the point, making the concern seem silly? In short, are insiders committed to a serious discussion and resolution of contested issues, or do they deal with them as strategic obstacles to be overcome by whatever means necessary? Of course, these questions lie at the heart of aretaic concerns. Hence we cannot conclude that the Borlaug hypothesis *overrides* aretaic concerns, but rather that questions about the virtue of insiders are critical to assessing the probability that biotechnology will actually help the poor, at least in so far as that assessment is based upon evidence that is accessible to the general public at large.

THE ETHICAL BOTTOM LINE

As a matter of philosophy, I have argued that despite the initial plausibility and limited validity of the claim that duties to aid the hungry through agricultural research override the concerns of biotechnology's detractors, an ethically defensible interpretation demands that some of the detractors' concerns act as side-constraints on the way agricultural research can be implemented, while others, specifically aretaic concerns, actually provide evidence that biotechnology *will not* help the poor. The nature of this evidence is positional, however. Those inside the agricultural research/development assistance establishment have access to other evidence suggesting just the opposite. But the Borlaug hypothesis is not directed to insiders. The intended audience is not other agricultural researchers, but instead thoughtful people who might be persuaded to moderate their qualms about biotechnology in light of its capacity to feed the poor. But if the issue is to be decided on the basis of publicly available information, the virtue of insiders itself becomes a relevant datum. Because I consider myself to be an insider, I find myself in the ironic position of concluding that although I personally believe that biotechnology can be very useful in meeting the needs of the hungry irrespective of the researchers' virtue, it would be irrational for an outsider (that is for a member of the general public) to neglect virtue in assessing the ethical case for and against GM crops.

What can we say about the virtue of agricultural biotechnology insiders? That is, is this just a case where the public is making a tragic mistake? Or alternatively, have research insiders actually failed to perform many of the duties that would make a fair-minded outsider see them as forthright and well intentioned? As with most cases where one attempts to assess the virtue of a group, the record is mixed. On one hand, there are many agricultural scientists who are thoughtful, who have been attentive to issues, and who have given useful service to the public's understanding of the debate. Ethical issues are discussed in many agricultural science courses, scientists have participated in public forums and there are a number of publications by biotechnology insiders that at least attempt to weigh the pros and cons in a deliberative fashion. On the other hand, we insiders know that there are many researchers who are either dismissive or who are too busy to pay much attention to the debate. There are also a few who seem to act on truly disreputable motives.

My personal, anecdotal assessment is that the truly virtuous are roughly offset by the truly disreputable, leaving the field to the dismissive and busy. This tips the balance toward a less than favorable assessment of insiders' virtue when they are viewed as a group. Even among those who take up the pen and write in favor of biotechnology, very few display any evidence of having actually read any of their opponents' views. Citations to opponents' views are even rarer, and patient attempts to restate and fairly represent opponents' positions before launching into the pro-biotech agenda are the rarest of all. As such, I conclude that if there is blame to be distributed for the hostility that even benevolent applications of agricultural biotechnology now face, a large share of that blame must be shouldered by the agricultural research community itself. An outside observer of this debate who voices skepticism about GM crops cannot be held morally responsible for the unfulfilled promise of biotechnology as a response to world hunger. This does not exclude the possibility that some critics might have spread deliberate falsehoods or engaged in behavior that was strategically calculated to bias the public against biotechnology in much the same way that industry public-relations campaigns have been calculated to bias the public in its favor. Such critics could be found morally culpable. But those critics who have expressed honest concerns and have been disappointed when research insiders do not respond in a deliberative and forthright manner cannot be similarly blamed.

Lest any stray outsiders be confused by my argument, this conclusion is *not* an anti-biotechnology conclusion. Recombinant techniques for developing new crops *should be* deployed in the fight against hunger, and ordinary citizens not only *should* support this deployment, but should seek ways to ensure that the industrial world's taste for non-GM crops does not preclude the use of biotechnology to help the hungry. 'Outsiders' interested in further elaboration of my own views on the various questions in the debate over agricultural biotechnology will be better served by other recent publications (Thompson 2003b, 2003c, 2003d) than the current chapter. My point here, however, is that given the current state of the debate it is quite rational for someone who lacks extensive personal, face-to-face contact with the plant scientists, molecular geneticists, entomologists, and other agricultural scientists who actually develop these crops to be very skeptical of these recommendations. Thus these insiders *should* be more active in the public deliberation on biotechnology, and more respectful of their opponents' point of view. This is not to say that they must agree, but they ought, at a minimum, to be capable of restating the positions of their opponents in a manner that they accept as an accurate characterization of the key points. Telling the doubtful to pipe down because we are busy helping the poor is *not* a respectful response. Insiders should then be willing to state clearly *why* they do not accept an argument, and they should be willing to listen carefully to any further reply that opponents care to make, replying themselves once again, if necessary. That is what virtue in the realm of public discourse demands (Habermas 1990, 1993).

I cannot say whether more virtuous future conduct on the part of agricultural research insiders will be effective in restoring the public's confidence. The pattern of inference that begins by noting agricultural research insiders' lack of seriousness in responding to critics, moves from there to question their virtue, and from there to question whether biotechnology will really help the poor can be generalized. Devinder Sharma (2003) begins with a different starting observation – noting that biotechnology was initially developed for the pursuit of profit – then moves on to question researchers' virtue and then whether GM crops can address hunger. Lennart Sjöberg (2004) notes the first point (lack of serious response to critics) and then concludes that people are justified in taking biotechnology to be risky, a pattern of reasoning that was described as 'poisoning the wells,' by Annette Baier (1986). Baier's point is that although such arguments do not establish their conclusion deductively, they are inductively valid. When people observe conduct that is commonly enough associated with a given outcome, they infer that the outcome is a reasonable possibility, one that must be taken into account. Only the gradual accumulation of contrary indicators can tip the balance in the opposite direction.

There is a real possibility that the wells have been poisoned for agricultural biotechnology and that only time can repair the damage. Only the gradual accumulation of positive indicators will reverse the inference that biotechnology will not help the poor, is risky or contrary to justice. The ongoing toll of world hunger makes this observation tragic, and I can only hope that I am wrong. It is possible that an aggressive public-relations campaign might turn the tide of public opinion, but from an ethics perspective this kind of response looks very much like the dismissive and manipulative kind of behavior that has been the root of the problem all along. At a minimum, however, it would appear that agricultural research institutions have a responsibility to entrust the defense of their activities to people who are less busy and dismissive than the majority of their scientific staff, and more substantive and ethically sophisticated than the public-relations officials to whom it often falls by default.

In conclusion, the Borlaug hypothesis fails. Given the mixed record of agricultural insiders' willingness to engage thoughtful and serious criticisms with equally thoughtful responses, and to show that key side-constraints are in fact being observed, one *should not* moderate one's qualms about biotechnology simply because Norman Borlaug, Paul Thompson, or any other single individual in the agricultural research establishment says that it will help address world hunger. In other contexts, I will continue to assert that GM crops are valid tools for addressing world hunger, but I will not assert that this is a sufficient reason to stifle one's doubts, to silence one's questions, or to end one's political opposition to them.

REFERENCES

Aiken, W. and H. LaFollette, eds, 1977. *World Hunger and Moral Obligation*. Englewood Cliffs, NJ: Prentice-Hall.

Baier, A., 1986. Poisoning the Wells. In: MacLean, D., ed. *Values at Risk*. Totowa, NJ: Rowman and Allenheld, pp. 49–74.

Bauer, M.W. and G. Gaskell. 2002. *Biotechnology: The Making of a Global Controversy*. Cambridge, UK: Cambridge U. Press.

Bockmühl, J., 2001. A Goethean view of plants: Unconventional approaches. In: Heaf, D. and J. Wirz, eds. *Intrinsic Value and Integrity of Plants in the Context of Genetic Engineering*. Llanystumdwy, UK: International Forum for Genetic Engineering, pp. 26–31.

Borlaug, N., 2001. Ending world hunger: The promise of biotechnology and the threat of antiscience zealotry. *Plant Physiology* 124: 487–490.

Bowring, F., 2003. *Science, Seeds and Cyborgs: Biotechnology and the Appropriation of Life*. London: Verso Press.

Brown, P. and H. Shue, eds, 1977. *Food Policy: The Responsibility of the U.S. in the Life and Death Choices*. New York: Free Press.

Burk, D.L., 2002. Lex genetica: The law and ethics of programming biological code. *Ethics and Information Technology* 4: 109–121.

Chadwick, R., 2000. Novel, natural, nutritious: Towards a philosophy of food. *Proceedings of the Aristotelian Society* 2000: 193–208.

Chrispeels, M.J., 2000. Biotechnology and the poor *Plant Physiology* 124: 3–6.

Cochrane, W., 1979. *The Development of American Agriculture: A Historical Analysis*. Minneapolis, USA: University of Minnesota Press.

Comstock, G., 1998. Is it unnatural to genetically engineer plants? *Weed Science* 46: 647–651.

Comstock, G., 2000. *Vexing Nature: On the Ethical Case Against Agricultural Biotechnology*. Boston, MA: Kluwer Academic Publishers.

Comstock, G., 2002. *Ethics and Genetically Modified Foods* [available at http://scope.educ.washington.edu/gmfood/commentary/show.php?author=Comstock].

Cranor, C.F., 2003. How should society approach the real and potential risks posed by new technologies? *Plant Physiology* 133: 3–9.

Dahlberg, K.A., 1979. *Beyond the Green Revolution: The Ecology and Politics of Global Agricultural Development.* New York: Plenum Press.

Durant, J., M.W. Bauer and G. Gaskell, eds, 1998. *Biotechnology in the Public Sphere.* London: The Science Museum.

Frewer, L.J., R. Shepherd and P. Sparks, 1997. Public concerns in the United Kingdom about general and specific aspects of genetic engineering: Risk, benefit and ethics *Science, Technology and Human Values* 22: 98–124.

Gaskell, G. and M.W. Bauer, eds, 2001. *Biotechnology: The Years of Controversy.* London: The Science Museum.

Gaskell, G., P.B. Thompson and N. Allum, 2002. Worlds apart? Public opinion in Europe and the USA. In: Bauer, M.W. and G. Gaskell, eds. *Biotechnology: The Making of a Global Controversy.* Cambridge, UK: Cambridge University Press, pp. 351–375.

Habermas, J., 1990. *Moral Consciousness and Communicative Action.* Cambridge, MA: The MIT Press.

Habermas, J., 1993. *Justifications and Applications.* Cambridge, MA: The MIT Press.

Jackson, D. 2000. Labeling products of biotechnology: Towards communication and consent. *Journal of Agricultural and Environmental Ethics* 12: 319–330.

Juma, C., 1989. *The Gene Hunters: Biotechnology and the Scramble for Seeds.* London: Zed Books.

Kass, L., 1997. The Wisdom of Repugnance. *New Republic* 2 June: 17–26.

Kneen, B., 2002. A naturalist looks at agricultural biotechnology. In: Bailey, B. and M. Lappé, eds. *Engineering the Farm: Ethical and Social Aspects of Agricultural Biotechnology.* Washington, DC: Island Press, pp. 45–60.

Krimsky, S., 2002. Risk assessment and regulation of bioengineered food products. *International Journal of Biotechnology* 2: 31–238.

Korthals, M., 2004. Ethics of differences in risk perception and views on food safety. *Food Protection Trends* 24(7): 30–35.

Leisinger, K.M., 2000. Ethical challenges of agricultural biotechnology for developing countries. In: Persley, G.J. and M.M. Cantin, eds. *Agricultural Biotechnology and the Poor.* Washington, DC: CGIAR.

Lucas, G.R. and T.W. Ogletree, 1976. *Lifeboat Ethics: The Moral Dilemmas of World Hunger.* New York: Harper and Row.

Magnus, D., 2002. Intellectual property and agricultural biotechnology: Bioprospecting or biopiracy? In: Magnus, D. and G. McGee, eds. *Who Owns Life?* Amherst, NY: Prometheus Books, pp. 265–276.

Midgley, M., 2000. Biotechnology and monstrosity. *The Hastings Center Report* 30(5): 7–15.

Miller, R.W., 2004. Beneficence, duty and distance *Philosophy and Public Affairs* 32: 357–383.

Nuffield Council on Bioethics, 1998. Genetically modified crops: The ethical and social issues [available at http://www.nuffieldbioethics.org, accessed 31 May 2005].

Nuffield Council on Bioethics, 2003. The use of genetically modified crops in developing countries [available at http://www.nuffieldbioethics.org, accessed 31 May 2005].

O'Neill, O., 1986. *Faces of Hunger.* London: Allen and Unwin.

Pence, G., 2002. *Designer Genes: Mutant Harvest or Breadbasket of the World?* Lanham, MD: Rowman and Littlefield.

Pinstrup-Andersen, P. and E. Schiøler, 2000. *Seeds of Contention: World Hunger and the Global Controversy Over GM Crops.* Baltimore, MA: Johns Hopkins University Press.

Pogge, T., 2002. *World Poverty and Human Rights: Cosmopolitan Responsibilities and Reforms,* Cambridge, UK: Blackwell Publishers.

Powell, D. and W. Leiss, 1997. *Mad Cows And Mother's Milk : The Perils Of Poor Risk Communication.* Montreal, Canada: McGill-Queens University Press.

Priest, S. 2001. *A Grain of Truth,* Lanham, MD: Rowman and Littlefield.

Reiss, M.J. and R. Straughn, 1996. *Improving Nature: The Science and Ethics of Genetic Engineering.* Cambridge, UK: Cambridge University Press.

Robinson, J., 1999. Ethics and transgenic crops: A review. *Electronic Journal of Biotechnology* 2: 71–81.

Rollin, B., 1996. *The Frankenstein Syndrome*. Cambridge, UK: Cambridge University Press.

Ruse, M. and D. Castle, eds, 2002. *Genetically Modified Foods: Debating Biotechnology*. Amherst, NY: Prometheus Press.

Sagoff, M., 2001. Biotechnology and the natural. *Philosophy and Public Policy Quarterly* 21: 1–5.

Sandler, R., 2004. An aretaic objection to agricultural biotechnology. *Journal of Agricultural and Environmental Ethics* 17: 301–317.

Sharma, D., 2003. *GM Food and Hunger: A View from the South*. New Delhi: Forum for Biotechnology and Food Security.

Shiva, V., 2000. *Stolen Harvest: The Hijacking of the Global Food Supply*. Cambridge, MA: South End Press.

Shiva, V. and I. Moser, eds, 1995. *Biopolitics: A Feminist Reader on Biotechnology*. London: Zed Books.

Shue, H., 1980. *Basic Rights*. Princeton, NJ: Princeton University Press.

Singer, P., 1972. Famine, affluence and morality *Philosophy and Public Affairs* 1: 229–248.

Sjöberg, L., 2004. Principles of risk perception applied to gene technology. *EMBO Reports* 5: S47–S51.

Smart, J.C.C. and B. Williams, 1973. *Utilitarianism: For and Against*. Cambridge, UK: Cambridge University Press.

Sparks, P., R. Shepherd and L. Frewer, 1994. Gene technology, food production and public opinion: A UK study. *Agriculture and Human Values* 11: 19–28.

Thompson, P.B., 1992. *The Ethics of Aid and Trade*, Cambridge, UK: Cambridge University Press.

Thompson, P.B., 1997. *Food Biotechnology in Ethical Perspective*. London: Chapman and Hall.

Thompson, P.B., 2002. Why food biotechnology needs an opt out. In: Bailey, B. and M. Lappé, eds. *Engineering the Farm: Ethical and Social Aspects of Agricultural Biotechnology*. Washington, DC: Island Press, pp. 27–44.

Thompson, P.B., 2003a. Unnatural farming and the debate over genetic manipulation. In: Gehring, V.V., ed. *Genetic Prospects: Essays on Biotechnology, Ethics and Public Policy*. Lanham, MD: Rowman and Littlefield, pp. 27–40.

Thompson, P.B., 2003b. The environmental ethics case for crop biotechnology: Putting science back into environmental practice. In: Light, A. and A. de-Shalit, eds. *Moral and Political Reasoning in Environmental Practice*. Cambridge, MA: The MIT Press, pp. 187–217.

Thompson, P.B., 2003c. Cultural integrity, globalization, and technical change: Further thoughts on GMOs in the food supply. In: Herscock, P.D., M. Stepaniants and R. Ames, eds. *Technology and Cultural Value on the Edge of the Third Millennium*. Honolulu: University of Hawaii Press, pp. 222–235.

Thompson, P.B., 2003d. Value judgments and risk comparisons: The case of genetically engineered crops. *Plant Physiology* 132: 10–16.

Ticknor, J. and C. Raffensperger, eds, 1999. *Protecting Public Health and the Environment: Implementing the Precautionary Principle*. Washington, DC: Island Press.

Trewavas, A., 1999. Much food, many problems. *Nature* 17: 231–232.

Unger, P., 1996. *Living High and Letting Die: Our Illusion of Innocence*. Oxford: Oxford University Press.

Van den Belt, H., 2003. Debating the precautionary principle: 'Guilty until proven innocent' or 'innocent until proven guilty'? *Plant Physiology* 132: 1122–1126.

Vogt, D.U., 1999. *Food Biotechnology in the United States: Science Regulation, and Issues*. Washington, DC: Congressional Research Service, Order Code RL30198.

REFORMING AGRICULTURAL TRADE:
NOT JUST FOR THE WEALTHY COUNTRIES

INTRODUCTION

At the most basic level of ethical behavior, individuals have an obligation to attend to the needs of others. As ethicist Peter Singer argues:

> if it is within our power to prevent something bad from happening, without thereby sacrificing anything of comparable moral importance, we ought, morally, to do it (Singer 1972, p. 231).

This dictum might be fairly easy to follow when it comes to direct individual actions, but when it comes to policy-making, and especially to international policy-making, the consequences of actions are not clearly defined, nor are the relationships between actions and consequences well understood.

For example, efforts to end global hunger have long revolved around financial aid and food donations. This foreign charity was grounded in the ethical obligation felt by people in wealthy countries to improve the well-being of people in poor countries. Food aid also had a certain appeal. For taxpayers and for farmers, it was easy to compare food aid to direct individual acts of charity. While ethical obligations normally involve some sacrifice, foreign aid, whether in cash or in kind, allowed richer countries to provide assistance to poor countries without requiring any substantial sacrifice by taxpayers. On the contrary, in-kind aid (like direct food aid) enabled farmers in rich countries to benefit from their own charity by creating an outlet for 'surplus' commodities. Unfortunately, the appeal of direct food aid did not match the result. Although short-term emergency food aid has its place, there are few, if any, indicators that demonstrate long-term benefits from charitable food aid. In this instance, actions that satisfy an individual sense of morality can be counterproductive.

In addition to the ethical imperatives to help the less fortunate, some ethical constructs rely on the notion of self-interest (enlightened or otherwise). This encompasses arguments that the poor, with higher birthrates and few incentives to safeguard natural resources, are a strain on the world's ecosystems. (Notwithstanding, of course, the fact that the rich consume much more of the world's natural resources than do the poor.) Some also argue that wealthy countries have a stake in economic development as a means to stem unpopular or unsustainable immigration. Business and farm leaders in developed countries argue that economic development is essential to the creation of an increased demand for food and agricultural products.

P. Pinstrup-Andersen and P. Sandøe (eds.), Ethics, Hunger and Globalization: In Search of Appropriate Policies, 237–262.

More recently, some have been promoting economic development as a tool to combat terrorism, which they view as being rooted in the hopelessness of poverty.

In the last 20 years or so, the ethical duty to aid the less fortunate and the various self-interested rationales have been supplemented by the more complex concept of a 'negative duty to dismantle unjust structures and to halt injurious action' (Crocker, 2002). Unlike the positive duties of aiding those less fortunate than oneself or the ethical rationales of enlightened self-interest, dismantling unjust structures and halting injurious actions can impose real costs (at least in the short term, and at a political as well as an economic level) on rich countries, and on some individuals in poor countries as well.

However, the difficulty lies in understanding just what constitutes unjust structures and injurious actions. For example, the agricultural subsidies that have been at the center of the Doha trade negotiations benefit some net-food-importing countries by keeping food prices lower than they would otherwise be, while harming those developing countries that attempt to compete with subsidized products. High tariffs on sugar in the EU benefit those countries that have preferential access to the European market, but damage those countries that must compete in a very artificial world sugar market. In fact, according to many analysts, the very food aid that was motivated by one ethical construct often falls into the category of 'injurious actions,' which need to be halted by another ethical construct (Crocker 2002). Even worse, food aid reassures citizens that they are easing the suffering of the poor, on the one hand, while at the same time their tax dollars and government policies are making it more difficult for the poor to escape poverty.

The ethical obligation to halt injurious actions complemented emerging economic analysis demonstrating that the economic policies of the wealthy nations were indeed imposing a demonstrable cost on poorer countries, and that the potential benefits from trade dwarfed the small, and declining, levels of foreign aid. These two complementary understandings formed some of the basis for the Uruguay Round Agreement, in which countries began to restrain domestic agricultural policies that distorted world trade. Setting aside for the moment whether the actual Uruguay Round reforms were effective at disciplining agricultural trade, the philosophical and economic underpinnings of the Uruguay Round's disciplines on domestic agricultural policies marked a sharp departure from the GATT's disciplines on border measures.

Coincident with these emerging views on the duties of various actors in the international policy arena is an evolving understanding of the objectives of economic growth. The basic doctrine of liberal economics – that maximizing incomes is an end in itself regardless of the impact on the poor – has been almost completely repudiated in recent years. In a tribute to Friedrich Hayek in the *Financial Times* (21 September 2004), Nobel Laureate Amartya Sen reminded readers that even Hayek, whom many consider to be the father of liberal economic theory, insisted that any institution, including the market, be judged by its role in advancing human liberty and freedom, not just in generating more income. In place of this utilitarian construct is a more complex notion of development that balances the goal of increasing economic growth with other goals, such as alleviating poverty, hunger, and malnutrition.

In other writings, Amartya Sen remarked that development should be understood not only as economic growth but as the expansion of a people's 'valuable capabilities and functionings'; including lifespan, nutrition, literacy, and opportunity to develop creativity (Sen 1984, p. 497). If ethical development strives to overcome economic and social deprivation then there must be sustained economic growth for the poor – not just for society as a whole. Therefore economic growth cannot be viewed as an end in itself. Alleviating poverty, and thereby improving people's capabilities and functions, must be the ultimate goal of economic development. It should be recognized, however, that there is a strong but not perfect correlation between a country's per capita income and its ranking on the Human Development Index, which measures countries' performance in relation to health, education, and income (WTO 2003). In fact, the only developing countries to deviate from this trend are in Sub-Saharan Africa, where the AIDS epidemic has undermined not only the countries' health but also their economic growth. One could well argue that the USA also deviates from the trend, with the world's highest per capita income yet higher rates of infant mortality than less well-off developed countries.

The Millennium Development Goals, adopted in September 2000 by a wide cross-section of the world's leaders, illustrate this emerging consensus on the inter-connectedness between economic growth and poverty alleviation. Not only do these goals reflect the notion of a direct ethical obligation to aid the hungry and malnourished in developing countries, they also reflect the ethical obligation to dismantle unjust structures. There are two goals that are directly relevant to the topic at hand:

Goal One: Eradicate extreme poverty and hunger
- *Target 1:* Halve the proportion of people whose income is less than a dollar a day.
- *Target 2:* Halve the proportion of people who suffer from malnutrition and hunger.

Goal Eight: Build a global partnership for development
- *Target 12:* Develop further an open trading and financial system that is rule-based, predictable, and non-discriminatory. This includes a commitment to good governance, development, and poverty reduction – both nationally and internationally.
- *Target 13:* Address the least-developed countries' special needs, including tariff- and quota-free access for their exports and more generous official development assistance for countries committed to poverty reduction.

The launch of the Doha Development Round, which pre-dated the Millennium Development Goals, made the link between the domestic and trade policies of the developed countries and the deleterious effect those policies have on developing countries explicit. But, over the three years of agricultural negotiations, the obligation to dismantle unjust structures and to halt injurious actions in the developed world has been extended to include unjust and injurious policies and institutions that are maintained by the developing countries themselves. (At one level, of course, this rationale is driven by the not-so-enlightened self-interest described above. Farmers in wealthy countries have argued they will only dismantle their trade-distorting policies in exchange for access to developing-country markets.)

While some view this demand as unjust – developed countries asking developing countries to do that which they cannot do – it is nevertheless true that some developing countries have maintained policies that are detrimental to the poorest people in those societies. To use another's injurious policies to justify the continuation of one's own injurious policies may be good negotiating strategy, but it is not sound policy or sound ethics. For development economists, it is clear that removing the trade-distorting and deleterious policies of the OECD countries will be of little value if the developing countries themselves do not also tackle their own deleterious policies.

While there is general agreement about the benefits of OECD trade reforms on developing countries, there is still much debate in development circles about the benefits of a 'more open, rule-based, non-discriminatory trading system' for the least-developed countries in particular, and specifically on the poorest citizens in those countries. Also, there is even more disagreement about the benefits of domestic and trade policy reform by developing countries themselves.

This chapter argues that removing the trade-distorting policies of rich and poor countries alike, and creating a more open, rules-based, non-discriminatory trade regime in agriculture is essential to meeting the Millennium Development Goals of halving the percentage of people whose incomes are less than a dollar a day, and halving the percentage of people who suffer from hunger and malnutrition. Placing the burden of trade reforms solely on the wealthy countries risks perpetuating policies in developing countries that harm the poorest citizens in those countries.

But the benefits from a more open agricultural trade system to the world's poorest citizens are not automatic. The tide of economic growth generated by trade can lift some boats faster than others. It is therefore not enough to reduce agricultural subsidies and trade barriers in developed countries. It is not enough to reduce trade barriers in developing countries. A more open global trade regime must be accompanied by strong domestic policy measures: Even a perfect trade system cannot compensate for weak national policies. A more open global trade regime must also be accompanied by flanking measures in developing countries that protect the poor during the transition.

OPEN ECONOMIES AND ECONOMIC GROWTH

Most economists agree that countries that are open to trade grow faster than those that are closed to trade. Trade allows countries to specialize in activities where they have a comparative advantage. Trade expands the market facing local producers, allowing them to take advantage of economies of scale. Trade also expands consumers' purchasing power and raises their real incomes. Trade encourages countries to use their resources more efficiently, which is vital to economic growth.

Equally important in the modern economy, openness to international trade is closely linked to investment (both foreign and domestic), which is in turn linked to economic growth. Openness to trade also strengthens the financial services sector, which can mobilize resources for local and foreign direct investment. The WTO's 2003 World Trade Report illustrates the high correlation between income growth, investment, and trade in fast and slow growing countries since 1960 (Table 14.1). In fact, there are no examples of countries where growth has taken off that have not opened their economies to some extent (Berg and Krueger 2002).

There is strong evidence that open trade regimes (and, more generally, open economies) are associated with higher rates of economic growth. Over the last 50 years, open economies grew 3.5% annually, while closed economies grew at less than 1% annually (Berg and Krueger 2002). Over time, the differential impact these two growth rates have on the level of incomes is astonishing: At a 1% growth rate, it takes 62 years for incomes to double; at 3.5%, incomes will increase 16 times in 62 years. So, even a small annual increase in growth rates due to trade policy can have dramatic effects.

By itself, economic growth is not sufficient to alleviate poverty, but without economic growth, efforts to reduce poverty will be unsuccessful. If trade liberalization leads to more rapid growth, will the conditions of the poor improve? The evidence collected for 80 developing countries, studied over the past 40 years, says in general, 'Yes.' This cross-country data demonstrates that the income of the poorest 20% of the population in developing countries increased by a dollar for every dollar increase in per capita GDP (Dollar and Kraay 2004; Berg and Krueger 2002). For the poorest fifth of the population, incomes grow in direct proportion with overall economic growth (Dollar and Kraay 2004). The World Bank has calculated that a 1% increase in real per capita income reduced poverty by 2% (Cline 2004). In countries with fairly even income distributions, the impact of economic growth on poverty reduction is higher; in countries with unequal income distributions, the impact tends to be lower.

TABLE 14.1 Sources of economic growth (1960–2000) (as a percentage)

	1960–1973		1973–1985		1985–2000	
	Fast growers	Slow growers	Fast growers	Slow growers	Fast growers	Slow growers
Per capita income growth	5	1	3	−1	3	0
Share of investment/ GDP	24	11	21	14	18	12
Ratio of trade/GDP	63	44	72	58	79	64

Source: World Trade Report (WTO 2003).

THE ROLE OF AGRICULTURE IN POVERTY ALLEVIATION

Growth in the agricultural sector has a particularly important role to play in poverty alleviation. First, there is the direct impact of agricultural growth on farm incomes, which accounts for a large share of the GDP in developing countries. Second, there are the rural-economy linkages, such as more jobs in agriculture-related industries, more jobs in the non-farm sector as farmers spend higher incomes; and improvements in nutrition, health, and education as incomes improve. The so-called 'multiplier effect' of rural income is high: an additional dollar of income in the rural sector generates an additional $3 in rural income through increased demand for rural goods and services (IFPRI 2003). Third, there are national impacts, including lower prices for food and raw materials to the urban poor, increased savings, and reduced food imports/reduced foreign exchange costs.

For developing countries, understanding the role of agriculture in reducing poverty could not be more important. Half the world's population lives on less than $2 per day and half of those live on less than $1 a day, but in the poorest of these countries in South Asia and Sub-Saharan Africa, over three-quarters of the population are living on less than $2 a day (Table 14.2). The poor overwhelmingly live in rural areas.

On average, 60% of the population in developing countries is rural. In the poorest countries of Sub-Saharan Africa and South Asia, the percentage of the population living in rural areas approaches 70% (FAO 2003). On average, 55% of each developing countries' labor force is employed in agriculture. But, again, in the poorest countries of Sub-Saharan Africa and South Asia close to 60% of the population is employed in farming. On average, the share of agriculture in developing countries' total gross domestic product is only 14%. But for the poorest countries, over 25% of their country's GDP comes from agriculture.

Countries that are highly dependent on agriculture tend to have higher rates of malnutrition and hunger (Figure 14.1). Countries that derive more than one-third of their national income from agriculture and where over 70% of the population is employed in agriculture have malnutrition rates over 35%. Countries that are heavily dependent on agriculture also have higher rates of food insecurity.

TABLE 14.2 Proportion of population living on less
than US$2 per day, 2001

Region	Proportion (%)
East Asia/Pacific	47.4
South Asia	77.2
Eastern Europe/Central Asia	19.7
Latin America/Caribbean	24.5
Middle East/North Africa	23.2
Sub-Saharan Africa	76.6

Source: World Development Indicators (World Bank 2005).

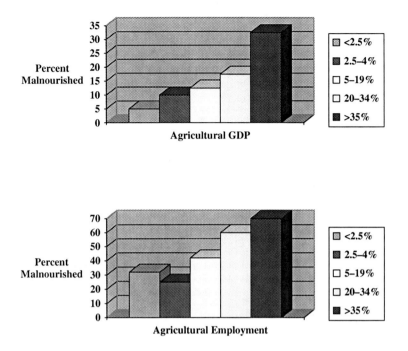

Figure 14.1 Higher agriculture GDP and employment associated with higher malnutrition

In the first place, people who are food-insecure lack the purchasing power to access the food supply. In order to solve the problem of food insecurity we need to solve the problem of poverty in rural areas. Second, the agricultural sector in most developing countries is under-performing relative to its potential. Agriculture is not contributing as much as it should to rural family income, national income, or the balance of payments relative to its potential. Despite the argument that increased productivity can only hurt subsistence farmers by driving prices down, studies that examine the sectoral effect of agricultural growth and development on poverty overwhelmingly conclude that increased agricultural productivity provides an initial platform for economic development (Mellor 1999). There are in fact only five ways that a smallholder can increase family income:

1. Get hold of more land and grow more of what they have been growing
2. Increase the production per hectare of what they are growing
3. Grow a higher value per hectare crop or higher-value products
4. Supplement income from the farm through non-farm employment
5. Migrate out of agriculture to find higher-paid employment, usually in urban areas.

These last two options have become the trend in many developing countries that have succeeded in raising levels of income, but seldom without tremendous levels of urban crime, pollution, and all the accompanying problems of very large cities resulting from excessive out-migration from agriculture. The point being that it is important to have the proper 'enabling' environment so that these factors that can increase family income for impoverished farmers can be activated without grave consequences. We talk about our objective being poverty reduction, but when you follow the money, the priority is not in solving the problem of poverty where the bulk of it resides, in rural areas. Most developing countries have been under-investing in the basic 'Green Box' measures; investments in rural roads, telecommunications, electrification, education, and healthcare in rural areas. Investments in research and development to raise productivity in agriculture, investments in market inspection and quality control systems, know-how in marketing food exports and so on need to be initiated and/or further advanced. There has been an under-investment in all of these by the countries' own governments, under-investment through official development assistance, and under-investment through borrowings from the World Bank and the regional development banks. All of these institutions have significantly reduced their investments in agricultural development in basic Green Box measures over the last 20 years. Without these types of investments and commitments it is very difficult, if not impossible, to be successful in agricultural development or non-agricultural development.

The main conclusion to be drawn from this argument is that an increase in the productivity per hectare or the growing of higher value per hectare crops must be incorporated into a plan for development to permit the rural families of developing countries to earn a higher income and remain on the farm until conditions improve. Poor farmers directly benefit from productivity gains. First, many are also net purchasers of food. Higher productivity enables them to reduce their food purchases. By producing more on their own land, expanding their production, or earning higher wage rates on someone else's land, poor farmers can benefit from higher yields. (Many more people of rural communities who are not directly engaged in agricultural activities also benefit from the off-farm employment that depends to a large extent on agriculture.) Thus, the increased productivity and growth of agriculture as a primary industry has the potential to generate employment, income, and growth for the entire rural economy. In addition, it will be illustrated that developing-country producers also stand to gain from the higher prices generated by more open trade and decreased protectionism in developed countries.

As for those that remain in subsistence farming, the demand for staple crops (rice, maize, and millet) is relatively unresponsive to price changes as well as to increases in per capita income. These crops make up the lion's share of low-income consumers' food purchases. As supply increases from higher yields, prices drop, thereby disproportionately benefiting poor consumers who devote the largest share of their income to the purchase of staple grains. For many consumers, lower prices frees up funds for purchases of other goods and services, creating additional, and more diversified, economic demand.

If an open trade regime is an important precondition for economic growth, if robust economic growth is the only way to lift large numbers of people out of poverty, and if agricultural growth is particularly effective at alleviating poverty in developing countries, then it might logically follow that more open agricultural trade regimes will alleviate poverty. While there is widespread agreement that developed-country trade reforms will benefit most developing countries, there is no consensus on whether developing countries themselves will benefit from their own trade reforms.

THE ROLE OF DEVELOPED-COUNTRY TRADE REFORMS

Most economic studies demonstrate that the biggest beneficiaries from OECD liberalization are the OECD countries themselves, but developing countries also stand to gain (Figure 14.2). An OECD analysis estimates that complete multilateral trade reforms generate an additional US$40 billion in additional income for developing countries. (Note that the various studies cited take as their assumption full multilateral liberalization. It is difficult to imagine that the reforms emerging from the Doha Development Round will approach full liberalization. Nonetheless, these studies indicate the direction and magnitude of the benefits of reform.)

Another study, released by the International Food Policy Research Institute (IFPRI 2003) just prior to the Cancun Ministerial, showed significant gains to developing countries from the complete elimination of trade-distorting subsidies and tariff barriers in developed countries. The global benefit to all developing countries was US$23.4 billion (Table 14.3). Latin American and Asian countries stood to gain the most, but even Sub-Saharan Africa gained almost US$2 billion in additional income.

A more recent study, released by the Center for Global Development, suggests that global free trade could reduce poverty by 540 million people, or 20%. Almost half of these gains would come from agricultural trade reforms (Table 14.4).

Similarly, a recent World Bank report by Hertel and Winters (2005) clarifies the importance of agricultural trade liberalization versus liberalization of other sectors. In that analysis, reform of farm policies contributes 40% of the gain from total liberalization of all countries in all, even though agricultural trade represents only 4% of global merchandise trade (Table 14.5).

These studies consistently find that for developing countries, agriculture is by far the most important sector to liberalize, and that at least one-half and up to

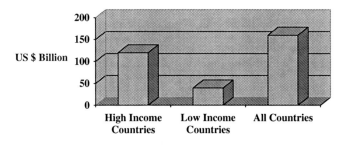

Figure 14.2 Potential annual welfare gains from agricultural trade liberalization

TABLE 14.3 Annual increased income to primary agriculture and agro-industrial production (increase in millions of US dollars)

Changes in agricultural trade policies by impact on:	USA only	EU only	Japan/Korea only	All industrialized countries
Sub-Saharan Africa	455	1,290	150	1,945
Asia	2,186	2,099	2,346	6,624
Latin America and the Caribbean	2,896	4,480	607	8,258
Other developing countries	1,148	5,069	339	6,659
All developing countries	6,684	12,936	3442	23,486

Source: IFPRI (2003).

two-thirds of the potential gains for developing countries come from removing protection against their goods in OECD markets.

While much of the rhetoric surrounding the WTO negotiations has focused on 'reducing the US$1 billion a day in subsidies' that wealthy countries provide their farmers, the reality is that for most developing countries and for most products, removing OECD tariffs and other border measures is more important than removing OECD domestic subsidies. Studies by the OECD and the IMF support this conclusion: The impact of OECD tariffs on developing countries is much worse than the impact of OECD subsidies. For example, an OECD study predicts that removing OECD tariffs would boost developing country incomes by

TABLE 14.4 Global free trade could reduce poverty by 20%

Region	Millions of poor	Reduction in poverty (millions of people)	Reduction in poverty (%)
Asia	2,021	459	23
Latin America	148	15	10
Europe (Central/East)	92	3	4
Middle East/North Africa	88	15	17
Sub-Saharan Africa	393	47	12
Total	2,743	540	20

Source: Cline (2004).

TABLE 14.5 Regional contributions to economic welfare gains from completely removing trade barriers on agriculture and all sectors, post-Uruguay Round (in 1995 billion USD)

	Agricultural liberalization alone			All sectors
Liberalizing region	OECD	Developing Countries	OECD + Developing Countries	OECD + Developing Countries
Benefiting region				
OECD	110.5	11.2	121.7	146.2
Developing Countries	11.6	31.4	43.0	108.1
OECD + Developing Countries	122.1	42.6	164.7	254.3

Source: Anderson et al. (2001).

US$12.5 billion. Removing subsidies, on the other hand, has a mixed effect on developing countries: By raising world market prices, net food importers are hurt, while there is little increase in the prices of the kinds of commodities that these countries tend to export. An IMF study predicts that removing all policy distortions would increase the price of seven out of ten commodities by less than 4%, with large increases for the other three: milk (24%), refined sugar (8%), and sheep meat (22%) (Tokarick, 2003). Removal of production and input subsidies alone increases prices by less than 2% (Table 14.6) Another study comparing the impact of a 50% reduction in tariffs versus a 50% reduction in trade-distorting domestic support illustrated that a tariff cut raised developing countries' income by US$2.3 billion, while a 50% reduction in domestic subsidies reduced developing countries' incomes by US$273 million, mainly because of higher food prices for net food importers (Hoekman et al. 2002).

TABLE 14.6 Changes in world prices of selected commodities (percentage change from baseline in 2015)

Commodities/Policies	Removal of all subsidies and border protection	Removal of border protection only
Paddy rice	6	4
Wheat	12	2
Horticultural products	0	0
Oilseeds	8	1
Refined sugar	9	8
Meat (bovine)	10	2
Dairy products	8	6

Source: Beghin et al. (2002).

However, in an important caveat, the least-developed countries (LDCs) stand to gain more from the reduction in subsidies than from the reduction in tariffs. OECD subsidies depress world market prices for these products, thereby lowering (potential) export earnings for these countries. Nearly one-fifth of the products grown and potentially exported by the LDCs are highly subsidized by at least one OECD member country, compared with 4% of exports by other 'more developed' developing countries. And, for some very poor countries, the number is even higher. For example, approximately 60–80% of the exports of poor countries such as Benin, Burkina Faso, Chad, Malawi, Mali, Rwanda, Sudan, Tanzania, Uganda, and Zimbabwe are produced and subsidized by one or more wealthier countries. These products are mostly grown in countries with high rates of poverty, and high rates of agricultural employment (Table 14.7). This means that reducing OECD trade-distorting subsidies in these commodities can have a particularly positive effect on poor people (Cline, 2004). On the other hand, OECD countries subsidize 9% of LDC imports, but only 4% of the imports by other 'more developed' developing countries. These LDCs tend to benefit (at least in the short run) from subsidized food imports.

While these numbers reflect the aggregate impacts of trade reform on developing countries, whether or not reducing trade-distorting subsidies or reducing tariffs benefits the poorest developing countries, and the poorest farmers within those countries, depends on the composition of their agricultural production. For example, 90% of Africa's exports are in 10 commodities – cocoa, coffee, cotton, tobacco, sugar, tea, palm oil, rubber, bananas, and peanuts (Beierle and Diaz-Bonilla 2003). Reducing distortions in sugar, peanuts, and cotton – which are highly protected in OECD markets – would benefit African exporters. African smallholders, who have to compete with subsidized food grain imports, would also benefit from removing

TABLE 14.7 Poverty intensity of principal developing country agricultural exports to the world, 2000 (percent)

Subsidized commodities	Poverty incidence of producers in developing countries[*]
Wheat	16
Rice	47
Maize	32
Sugar	31
Coffee	44
Cocoa	51
Cotton	50
Tobacco	35
Oilseeds	27

Source: Cline, 2004.

[*] This number represents the share of poor people in developing countries that produce these commodities.

trade-distorting OECD subsidies. But for some of these commodities (i.e., coffee, tea, rubber, bananas), opening markets by reducing tariffs, increasing tariff quotas, reducing tariff escalation, and improving tariff administration will be more important than subsidy reductions.

Most studies predict that commodity prices will rise following multilateral liberalization anywhere from 5% to 15% on average, but this increase is likely to be a one-time event that will not reverse the long-term decline in commodity prices. Prices are expected to increase more steeply for food products that net-food-importing developing countries import than for the commodities they export, because these products tend to be heavily subsidized in OECD countries. However, assuming that liberalization takes place over a number of years, and that liberalization is partial rather than complete, any increase in prices due to liberalization will be more than swamped by normal changes in supply and demand and by exchange rate movements (Anderson 2002). However, the short-term impact of higher prices on urban consumers implies that these countries may need transitional help from international donors if their overall food import bill climbs steeply.

In general, this study and others indicate that, for most countries and most products, the removal of OECD tariffs and other border measures is more important than the removal of OECD domestic subsidies. Reducing tariffs generates significantly higher benefits in these studies than lowering subsidies; in part because both developed and developing countries rely on tariffs, while only developed countries use subsidies. Even though OECD countries have far higher subsidies than developing countries, the reverse is true in regard to tariffs. Therefore, developing countries benefit more from reducing their own tariffs than from OECD liberalization, because high tariffs raise food prices to consumers.

THE ROLE OF DEVELOPING-COUNTRY TRADE REFORMS

While much of the WTO debate has focused on the benefits to developing countries of lower OECD subsidies, the fact that 40% of developing countries' agricultural exports find their way to other developing countries shows that there could be benefits in reducing barriers to trade between developing countries (Cline, 2004). Gains from trade reform typically accrue to the liberalizing region. For example, 90% of the gains from OECD liberalization go to the high-income countries themselves. Similarly, three-quarters of the gain to developing countries comes from liberalizing their own trade measures.

Trade reform in developed countries implies reducing trade-distorting subsidies to farmers and opening markets to imported goods. But, unlike developed countries, which have the financial wherewithal to provide subsidies, developing countries rely almost exclusively on tariffs to protect their domestic markets. Few developing countries have the financial resources to offer direct subsidies to their farmers. Many developing countries import food on world markets, and benefit (at least in the short term) from subsidized commodity prices. Many developing countries cite their heavy dependence on agriculture, the vulnerability of their small farmers to subsidized imports, and the lack of alternative means to support their agricultural sectors, as arguments against their own trade reform.

Developing countries often argue that they need import barriers to protect domestic subsistence farmers from subsidized imports and to provide food security. Despite the intuitive appeal of such arguments, the proportion of malnourished people and underweight children tends to be lower in countries where agricultural trade is large relative to agricultural production. Trade reduces variability in consumption, because countries are not dependent only on their own (often unpredictable) production levels (Beierle and Diaz-Bonilla, 2003; IFPRI, 2003). Poor access to and integration with international markets actually limits the ability of countries with widespread hunger to import enough food to compensate for domestic production shortfalls. Of course, levels of hunger and poverty differ widely, even between countries with very similar levels of agricultural trade. This indicates that the impact of agricultural trade on food security is mediated by other factors, such as access to markets and infrastructure (Figure 14.3). This highlights the fact that trade reform must be accompanied by other policy reforms and investments to maximize its positive contribution to food security.

Lower tariff barriers – in both developed and developing country markets – can help countries diversify their agricultural base by expanding market access and offering potential new markets. Countries with more diverse agricultural sectors also tend to be more food-secure. Countries that depend on a single agricultural export are characterized by high prevalence of undernourishment (36%), and a relatively high probability that consumption will fall below 95% of trend (22%) (see Table 14.8). In part, reliance on a single commodity leads to instability in export earnings and employment, which worsens food security. Countries that are most dependent on a single commodity have by far the highest probability that their food consumption will fall below 95% of their needs. Countries whose agricultural sectors are more diversified have lower probabilities of such variation. Dependency

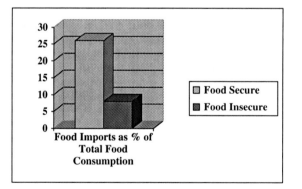

Figure 14.3 Food trade and food security
Source: FAO (2003).

TABLE 14.8 Food insecurity highest among countries that depend on a single commodity

	Per capita food consumption	Incidence of under-nourishment	Probability of consumption shortfall
Single commodity dependent exporters	2, 314	36%	22%
Non-commodity dependent countries	2, 285	22%	15%
China	2, 972	9%	1%
India	2, 493	24%	8%
All low-income, food-deficit countries	2, 317	19%	16%

Source: Pingali and Stringer (2003).

on a single commodity (sugar, coffee) is a particular challenge for several countries in Latin and South America. Ironically, again a misplaced sense of obligation – in this case compensation for past injuries during colonialism – that informs some developed-country preference schemes has actually exacerbated food insecurity in many developing countries by creating dependency on a single commodity.

Agricultural trade liberalization (reducing tariffs) in developing countries is likely to improve the conditions of the poor because tariffs hurt the poor the most, as they act as a tax on consumption. A study of tariff reduction in Sub-Saharan Africa indicates that lowering average tariffs on all products from 40% to 10% caused a real income loss of 35% among urban employers and a 40% loss from urban workers in protected industries; but a gain of 20% for rural farmers. Since in most developing countries, rural farmers far outnumber urban workers, reducing tariffs has an overall positive effect. (This does not mean, however, that the impact on the urban workers should be ignored. Policy measures to offset the impact of higher food prices would need to be implemented.)

Finally, trade measures are not a good way to help subsistence farmers and to enhance food security. Tariffs and border measures make farmers and landowners better off in terms of access to local food and potentially higher incomes, but they are still worse off because of higher prices and limited access to imported food in times of domestic shortfall (Table 14.9). So, to the extent that farmers or landowners also purchase food – domestic or imported – they would be worse off. Targeted social measures and investments in rural infrastructure (both so-called Green Box policies permitted without constraint under the WTO) are the only two measures that enhance food security for farmers and landowners without undermining the food security of society as a whole.

TABLE 14.9 Net effects of targeted policy measures on farmers/landowners and society

	Landowners or farmers			
	Economic access		Physical access	
Policy	Income effect	Price effect	Access to domestic food	Access to imported food
Import restrictions	Better	Worse	Better	Worse
Domestic subsidies	Better	None	Better	None
Target social security	Better for poor	None	None	None
Rural infrastructure	Better	Better	Better	Better

	Others in society			
	Economic access		Physical access	
Policy	Income effect	Price effect	Access to domestic food	Access to imported food
Import restrictions	Worse	Worse	Better	Worse
Domestic subsidies	Worse	None	Better	None
Target social security	Better for Poor	None	None	None
Rural infrastructure	Worse	Better	Better	Better

Another concern often cited with respect to reducing trade barriers in developing counties is the potential effect on developing-country tax revenues. In many developing countries, tariff revenues comprise a significant share of government resources. Twenty-five developing countries derive 30% of their total tax revenue from tariffs, according to an IMF study by Bannister and Thugge (2001) Critics argue that lowering these tariffs may deprive governments of much-needed funds.

There are several fallacies with this argument:

- Most developing countries maintain very high bound tariffs (which would be the base for any WTO tariff cuts) but impose relatively low applied tariffs. Reducing bound tariffs, which are not in fact being imposed, would have no effect on tariff revenue.
- On products where bound and applied tariffs are high, reducing them would expand import volumes (and tariff revenues), potentially canceling out the reduction in tariff levels.
- High tariffs may drive some trade underground into the 'black' or 'gray' market, where it is not taxed at all. Lowering tariffs may move some trade from the 'informal' to the formal sector.

Some policy-makers argue that, while trade liberalization may be good for the economy, some sectors may not be able to withstand the competition. In a variation on the 'infant industry' argument, policy-makers advocate 'protecting' these sectors from competition until they are stronger. There are several problems with this line of reasoning. First, it is impossible for governments to identify, in advance, which sectors should be protected and which can ultimately survive. Second, and more compelling, protection begets protection once the political forces are lined up to lobby and support it. As experience in the USA, Japan, and Europe has proved, it is difficult to dismantle protections and subsidies once political forces have captured them. Third, protection also breeds sanctioned and unsanctioned corruption, as protected companies lobby to retain their benefits, to the detriment of taxpayers and consumers.

Foregoing liberalization altogether or simply postponing it in those sectors that may have a greater impact on the poor is not the solution, either. The evidence suggests that in the long run, this would hurt the poor further by perpetuating slow growth and distorting incentives for investment and innovation in the economy. In any case, trade policy is not a very transparent or effective tool to use to maintain incomes. There are better policy alternatives, even in developing countries, to help maintain poor people's incomes. Moreover, even in developing countries, adjustment costs are not usually large in relation to the entire economy – and are usually small relative to the benefits.

Alternatively, policy-makers may argue to postpone liberalization until a better time. This may be appropriate for a country in the midst of a recession, when the pain of adjustment is likely to be magnified and the impacts on the least fortunate more difficult to ameliorate. However, there is a difference between trade liberalization with a long adjustment period (such as that provided by 'Special and Differential Treatment' under the WTO) and postponing liberalization altogether. Interestingly, once firms and farmers recognize that liberalization is inevitable, they ask for liberalization to move faster than scheduled, even when trade agreements envision long time-frames.

There is also a downside to long transition periods: Elected governments may be tempted to push back necessary reforms and adjustments to the next election and perhaps to another party, leaving the protected sector further and further behind. Then the needed reforms would look too large and too painful to be politically palatable. Finally, some developing countries argue that they should not reduce their border measures unless and until developed countries reduce their subsidies. In negotiations, this is certainly good strategy. But, as economic policy, it does not hold water. Trade-oriented economies prospered more in the 1990s, relative to closed economies, even though they each faced the same external trade policy environment.

THE RELATIONSHIPS BETWEEN TRADE REFORM, ECONOMIC GROWTH, AND POVERTY

Economic analysis indicates that trade reforms by developed and developing countries are likely to be, on the whole, beneficial for developing countries, and for the poor in developing countries. As noted earlier, there is nothing about trade-derived growth that increases or decreases income inequality. The impact of any economic growth, regardless of its source, depends on the initial holdings of the factors of production, the flexibility of the economy, and flanking and accommodating policy measures.

However, if income inequality does increase at the same time as growth occurs, it does not necessarily mean that the poor are absolutely worse off. In other words, there is a difference between poverty alleviation and income distribution, and there is a difference between absolute and relative poverty. A policy can alleviate poverty, but not necessarily improve income distribution. China's recent growth is often cited as a classic example. There is no question that economic growth has raised many Chinese people out of poverty, but it is also true that income distribution has worsened. Increasing inequity in income distribution can have serious consequences that need to be anticipated and addressed. For example, such inequality often spurs unsustainable rural–urban migration.

But it is not the case that inequitable income distribution always leads to increased absolute poverty. Poor people may be relatively worse off, but absolutely better off as a result of economic growth. For example, in Bangladesh, trade liberalization led to an increase in income inequality but a reduction in the percentage of people living below the poverty line, from 28% to 25%. Similarly, in Chile, income inequality increased while Chile was opening its markets to international trade, but the proportion of people living in poverty fell from 17% to 6% in the space of 16 years (WTO 2003).

The case of East Asia is similar. In the mid-1970s, six of every ten people in East Asia lived in extreme poverty. Today, fewer than two in ten live in extreme poverty. The absolute number of people living on less than a dollar a day in the region has fallen from 720 million to 278 million. Average incomes have grown by 5% annually, resulting in a doubling of per capita income every 14 years. This growth was mostly associated with rising exports, which drove the demand for goods in labor-intensive manufacturing and generated foreign exchange.

The structure of the economy, the pre-existing policy biases, and the implementation of trade reforms will determine the effect of economic growth (and by implication) trade-generated economic growth, on income inequality and on the alleviation of poverty. For example, in East Asia, pro-urban policies used low procurement prices to subsidize food for urban consumers. Price reforms that moved toward more realistic valuations raised prices to farmers and urban consumers. In Central and Eastern Europe and the former Soviet Union, agricultural prices had been supported at above 'market' levels, and inputs were heavily subsidized. Therefore, price liberalization in those countries caused substantial declines in the agricultural terms of trade – and improved (lower) prices for urban consumers. China's WTO reforms will result in falling prices for some commodities. However, China's agricultural policy reforms were accompanied by reforms in other arenas (and hopefully by reduced tariffs and quotas in textiles) that will allow for a smoother transition to a more open trade regime (Anderson 2002).

Property rights reform has given strong income and asset control to producers in Asia and Central Europe. For example, in East Asia, governments deliberately provided incentives to farmers through property rights reform. At the same time, governments also restructured farms to more efficient sizes. In Central Europe, reforms gave land back to farmers who had lost it during collectivization. By contrast, land reforms in the former Soviet Union have been more gradual, and less effective.

The emergence of institutions of exchange is crucial to the success of trade reforms. For example, the countries of the former Soviet Union, by rapidly removing the centrally planned institutions of exchange before market structures were in place, created widespread, short-term disruptions in agricultural production. The East Asian economies gradually replaced the planned economy with a more market-oriented system, beginning instead by gradually raising the prices paid to farmers for their crops.

The experience of these 'transition economies' varied depending on whether they pursued a gradual or a rapid approach to land reform and privatization of markets. In addition, it is important to note that neither full privatization of property rights nor fully private markets were necessary in either Asia or Central Europe, as long as the rights were perceived as strong and enduring and the hybrid markets reflected a real market.

Initial land distribution and economic structure influences the impact of trade liberalization on the different groups in society. In Latin America, for example, the hugely uneven distribution of land, capital, and education have skewed income growth in favor of those with land. This uneven distribution of land and social capital has been exacerbated by growth policies (trade and others) that have favored large landholders and more highly educated labor. As a result, declining growth rates in South America, coupled with uneven land distribution, have particularly hurt the poor. Exports have grown slowly (due to global economic slowdown). And, while agriculture should have played a bigger role in these countries' economic growth strategies, it has generally been ignored or discriminated against in Latin America. (Generally, trade protectionism in Latin America has hurt agriculture by taxing exports, by raising the price of manufactured inputs, and by maintaining an overvalued currency that damages exports.)

In Africa, where there are huge disparities between urban and rural areas left over from colonial times, trade reforms that boosted export crops reversed rural decline in some countries. Where these crops were grown by smallholders, the impact on rural welfare was positive. But the benefits were lower than they might have been, because many countries waited to make reforms until the situation was fairly desperate. Government services had deteriorated and external debt had increased. Countries that succeeded usually did so after prolonged civil strife, when citizens were eager for some change, and under charismatic leadership that was able to lead countries through difficult transitions.

There is another, less discussed, benefit from trade reforms in developing countries. In recent years, improved governance has become a centerpiece of national development strategies. The role of open trade regimes in improving governance is often overlooked. One of the biggest challenges for developing countries is pervasive corruption (Figure 14.4). Corruption is driven by rent-seeking

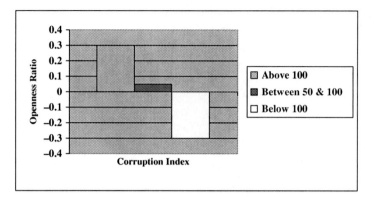

Figure 14.4 Openness and corruption
Source: World Trade Report (WTO 2003).

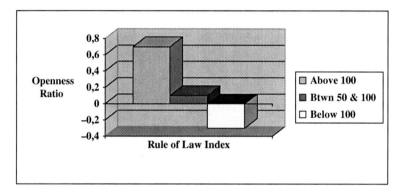

Figure 14.5 Openness and the rule of law
Source: World Trade Report (WTO 2003).

behavior. When trade barriers are high, or where import and export quotas are in place, merchants resort to bribery to subvert high tariffs or to buy import and export licenses. Generally, corruption favors the rich and well-connected, who have the means and access to bribe government officials, and it hurts the poor, who are often its victims (Berg and Krueger 2002). There is also a strong correlation between openness to trade and the rule of law (Figure 14.5).

THE VITAL IMPORTANCE OF FLANKING MEASURES

Trade promotes economic growth because it serves as a conduit for new ideas, new technology, and competition, which drive innovation and increase productivity. If markets are missing or do not function properly, shifts in relative prices (i.e., from tariff or subsidy cuts) will not lead to a shift of production, jobs, and investment, as the economic theory assumes. Similarly, the lack of good roads, ports, telecommunications, and marketing infrastructure can hamper a country's ability to participate in and benefit from international trade. Some of these conditions are inherited from geography; some are the result of inadequate or misguided investments.

Generally, to be effective, open trade must be part of a constellation of policies that are pro-growth and pro-poor: market orientation, strong competition, macroeconomic stability, legal and institutional frameworks, transparency, predictability, and a better investment climate. The common thread behind these reforms is creating flexibility in markets – land, labor, and capital – that allows countries to grow. For example, entry rates of firms into liberalized sectors of the economy are 20% higher than into closed sectors of the economy, leading to higher job creation (Berg and Krueger 2002). Open trade is also associated with higher foreign and domestic investment in an economy. Attracting domestic and foreign investment in the agricultural sector (both upstream and downstream) is particularly important, because as development occurs small and subsistence farmers must move out of agriculture and into off-farm employment.

The flexibility of labor markets is critical to how trade liberalization will affect poverty. If labor markets prevent firms from adjusting their workforce, most of the adjustment to trade will come in the form of changes in wages to already employed workers. If workers can move from one sector to another, or if there is a minimum wage in place, then the adjustment will come in the form of changes in employment.

In the rural areas of most developing countries, the labor market is unskilled but very flexible and highly responsive to changes in wage rates. For the rural poor, adjustments to trade will take place largely through changes in employment. Reforms that turn the terms of trade against agriculture will lead to higher unemployment in rural areas, with the burden falling on the poor. If trade liberalization improves the agricultural terms of trade, then the likely result will be higher employment, benefiting the poor.

For example, the aforementioned reforms in East Asia improved the terms of trade for farmers, while reforms in Central Europe turned the terms of trade against farmers. As a result, agricultural output rose in Asia, whereas it fell in Central Europe, with predictable consequences for the rural sector. (It should be pointed out that in neither East Asia, nor in Central Europe did initial agricultural prices or input prices reflect the market. The direction of reforms in both sets of countries moved the market toward a more 'rational' allocation of resources in the rural sector. In the long term, the economy and society will be better off, but in the short term, the very real transition costs cannot be ignored.)

However, in some developing countries, employment and industrial policies aimed at maintaining employment have created rigid markets that do just the opposite. For example, in India, there are 749 products that are reserved for small-scale firms. Other tax exemptions and production subsidies also favor small-scale producers. These policies prevent firms from growing and ultimately from competing in the export market. While in the short term, such regulations may keep excess labor employed (in fact, Indian firms say they have 17% more labor than they need), over the longer term these regulations inhibit economic growth and employment generation (Pursell, cited in World Bank 2002).

Another factor determining how an economy weathers trade liberalization depends on how widely the rest of the economy is liberalized. Transition costs are lower when liberalization occurs across a wide swath of the economy. This also points toward staging of market reforms. For example, if monopolies dominate a sector (particularly agricultural suppliers or purchasers), or if price controls limit adjustment, or if labor markets are inflexible, removing these constraints widen the domain of trade and ease adjustments. For example, it costs nearly half of India's per capita GDP to start a new business, compared to 13% in Chile and China. And, due to bureaucracy, it takes nearly three times longer to clear goods through customs than in the average OECD country. These rigidities amplify transition costs. When New Zealand decided to liberalize its markets in the early 1980s, it decided to liberalize across the board, which facilitated the adjustments that were bound to arise by increasing the flexibility in the economy.

For poor people to benefit from liberalization, they have to be able to participate in markets. Reforms that enhance their ability to participate in the formal market will ease the transition to liberalization. Where markets have been liberalized without accompanying policy reforms and investments (such as improved roads, improved communications, marketing infrastructure), the impact on food security and poverty has been detrimental. A few examples illustrate the importance of these measures.

In the early 1990s, Mozambique removed a ban on raw cashew exports, which was originally imposed to guarantee a source of raw nuts to its local processing industry and to prevent a drop in exports of processed nuts. As a result, a million cashew farmers received higher prices for the nuts in the domestic market. But, at least half the higher prices received for exports of these nuts went to traders, and not to farmers, so there was no increase in production in response to the higher prices. At the same time, Mozambique's nut-processing industry lost its guaranteed supply of raw nuts, and was forced to shut down processing plants and lay off 7,000 workers (FAO 2003).

In Zambia, before liberalization, maize producers benefited from subsidies to the mining sector, which lowered the price of fertilizer. A State buyer further subsidized small farmers. When these subsidies were removed, and the para-State privatized, larger farmers close to international markets saw few changes, but small farmers in remote areas were left without a formal market for their maize.

In Vietnam, trade liberalization was accompanied by tax reductions, land reforms, and marketing reforms that allowed farmers to benefit from increased sales to the market. As Vietnam made these investments, it began to phase out domestic subsidies and reduce border protection against imports. An aggressive program of targeted rural investments accompanied these reforms. During this liberalization, Vietnam's overall economy grew at 7% annually, agricultural output grew by 6%, and the proportion of undernourished people fell from 27% to 19% of the population. Vietnam moved from being a net importer of food to a net exporter (FAO 2003).

Similarly, in Zimbabwe, before liberalization of the cotton sector, the government was the single buyer of cotton from farmers, offering low prices to subsidized textile firms. Facing lower prices, commercial farmers diversified into other crops (tobacco, horticulture) but smaller farmers who could not diversify suffered. Internal liberalization eliminated price controls and privatized the marketing board. The result was higher cotton prices and competition among the three principal buyers. Poorer farmers benefited through increased market opportunities, as well as better extension and services. As a result, agricultural employment rose by 40%, with production of traditional and non-traditional crops increasing.

Policy reforms can decrease employment in the short run, but in general, changes in employment caused by trade liberalization are small relative to the overall size of the economy and the natural dynamics of the labor market. But, for some countries that rely heavily on one sector and do not have flexible economies, the transition can be difficult. Even though there are long-term and economy-wide benefits to trade liberalization, there may be short-term disruptions and economic shocks which may be hard for the poor to endure.

Once a government decides to undertake a reform, the focus should be on easing the impact of reforms on the losers – either through education, retraining, or income assistance. Government policy should also focus on helping those who will be able to compete in the new environment to take advantage of new opportunities. Even though trade on balance has a positive impact on growth, and therefore on poverty alleviation, developing countries should pursue trade liberalization with a pro-poor strategy. In other words, they should focus on liberalizing those sectors that will absorb non-skilled labor from rural areas, as agriculture becomes more competitive. The focus should be on trade liberalization that will enhance economic sectors that have the potential to employ people in deprived areas. Trade liberalization must be complemented by policies to improve education, rural roads, communications, etc., so that liberalization can be positive for people living in rural areas, not just in urban centers or favored areas. These underlying issues need to be addressed if trade (or any growth) is to reach the poorest; or the reforms and liberalization need to be directed toward smallholders, and landless and unskilled labor.

BUT THE POOR IN DEVELOPING COUNTRIES DON'T BENEFIT EQUALLY

All policies create winners and losers. Continuing the *status quo* simply maintains the current cast of winners and losers. Too often in developing countries, the winners from current policies are not the poor living in rural areas. Policy reforms (whether in trade or in other arenas) simply create a different set of winners and losers.

Notwithstanding the overall positive analyses of the impact of trade liberalization on developing countries as a group, there are significant variations by country, commodity, and different sectors within developing countries. Most analysts combine all but the largest developing countries into regional groupings, so it is difficult to determine the precise impacts on individual countries. Even those studies that show long-term or eventual gains for rural households or for the poor do not focus on the costs imposed during the transition from one regime to another. It is even more difficult to evaluate the impact on different types of producers within different countries, such as smallholders and subsistence farmers. Also, economic models cannot evaluate how trade policies will affect poverty among different households, or among women and children within households.

Allen Winters (2002) has proposed a useful set of questions that policy-makers should ask when they consider trade reforms:

1. Will the effects of changed border prices be passed through the economy? If not, the effects –positive or negative – on poverty will be muted.
2. Is reform likely to destroy or create markets? Will it allow poor consumers to obtain new goods?
3. Are reforms likely to affect different household members – women, children – differently?
4. Will spillovers be concentrated on areas/activities that are relevant to the poor?
5. What factors – land, labor, and capital – are used in what sectors? How responsive is the supply of those factors to changes in prices?
6. Will reform reduce or increase government revenue? By how much?
7. Will reforms allow people to combine their domestic and international activities, or will it require them to switch from one to another?
8. Does the reform depend on or affect the ability of poor people to assume risks?
9. Will reforms cause major shocks for certain regions within the country?
10. Will transitional unemployment be concentrated among the poor?

Although trade liberalization is often blamed for increasing poverty in developing countries, the links between trade liberalization and poverty are more complex. Clearly, more open trade regimes lead to higher rates of economic growth, and without economic growth any effort to alleviate poverty, hunger, and malnutrition will be unproductive. But, without accompanying national policies in education, health, land reforms, micro-credit, infrastructure, and governance, economic growth (whether derived from trade or other sources) is much less likely to alleviate poverty, hunger, and malnutrition in the poorest developing countries.

CONCLUSIONS

The imperative to dismantle unjust structures and to halt injurious actions is enshrined in the Millennium Development Goals, and in the goals of the Doha Development Round. This imperative has been primarily directed at the OECD countries that maintain high levels of agricultural subsidies and protection against many commodities that are vital to the economic well-being of developing countries. The OECD countries must reduce their trade barriers, reduce and reform their domestic subsidies; but, as this chapter makes clear, the OECD reforms must be accompanied by trade policy reforms in the developing countries as well.

Open trade is one of the strongest forces for economic development and growth. Developing countries and civil society groups who oppose these trade reforms in order to 'protect' subsistence farmers are doing these farmers a disservice. Developing countries and civil society are correct in the narrow view that markets cannot solve every problem, and that there is a role for government and for public policies. As the Doha negotiators get down to business, their energies would be better used in ensuring that developing countries begin to prepare for a more open trade regime by enacting policies that promote overall economic growth and that promote agricultural development. Their energies would be better spent convincing the population (taxpayers and consumers) in developed countries of the need for agricultural trade reform, and in convincing the multilateral aid agencies to help developing countries invest in public goods and public policies to ensure that trade policy reforms are pro-poor.

It is clear from an examination of the evidence that trade reform, by itself, does not exacerbate poverty in developing countries. Rather, the failure of trade reforms to alleviate poverty lies in the underlying economic structures, adverse domestic policies, and the lack of strong flanking measures. To ensure that trade reform is pro-poor, the key is not to seek additional exemptions from trade disciplines for developing countries, which will only be met with counter-demands for other exemptions by developed countries, but to ensure that the WTO agreement is strong and effective in disciplining subsidies and reducing barriers to trade by all countries.

Open trade is a key determinant of economic growth, and economic growth is the only path to poverty alleviation. This is equally true in agriculture as in other sectors of the economy. In most cases, trade reforms in agriculture will benefit the poor in developing countries. In cases where the impact of trade reforms is ambiguous or negative, the answer is not to postpone trade reform. Rather, trade reforms must be accompanied by flanking policies that make needed investments or that provide needed compensation, so that trade-led growth can benefit the poor.

REFERENCES

Anderson, K. 2002. Agricultural Trade Reform and Poverty Reduction in Developing Countries, Discussion Paper No. 0234, CIES, School of Econom ics, Adelaide University

Anderson, K., B. Dimaranan, J. Francois, T. Hertel, B. Hoekman and W. Martin. 2001. The Cost of Rich (and Poor) Country Protection to Developing Countries', *Journal of African Economies* 10(3): 227–57.

Bannister, G.J. and K. Thugge, 2001. *International Trade and Poverty Alleviation*. IMF Working Paper WP/01/54. Washington, DC: International Monetary Fund.

Beghin, J., D. Roland-Holst and D. Van der Mensbrugghe, eds, 2002. *Trade and the Environment in General Equilibrium: Evidence from Developing Economies*. Staff General Research Papers 4090, Iowa State University, Department of Economics.

Beierle, T.C. and E. Diaz-Bonilla, 2003. The impact of agricultural trade liberalization on the rural poor: An overview. Paper prepared for Resources for the Future workshop. November.

Berg, A. and A. Krueger, 2002. Trade, growth and poverty: A selective survey. Paper presented at the World Bank's Annual Bank Conference on Development Economics, Washington, DC, 29–30 April.

Crocker, D.A. 2002. Development Ethics and Globalization. Philosophical Topics, 30, 2, Issue on Global Inequalities, 9–28.

Cline, W. R. 2004 *Trade Policy and Global Poverty.* Washington, DC: Institute for International Economics.

Dollar, D. and Aart Kraay. 2004. "Trade, Growth, and Poverty." *Economic Journal* 114(493): F22–49.

FAO [Food and Agriculture Organization of the United Nations], 2003. *The State of Food Insecurity in the World, 2003*. Rome: FAO.

Hertel, T.W. and L.A. Winters, eds. 2005. "Putting Development Back Into the Doha Agenda: Poverty Impacts of a WTO Agreement, New York: Oxford University Press. World Bank.

Hoekman, B., F. Ng and M. Olarreaga, 2002. Reducing agricultural tariffs versus domestic support: What's more important for developing countries? Paper prepared for IATRC Meeting, June.

IFPRI [International Food Policy Research Institute], 2003. *How Much Does it Hurt? The Impact of Agricultural Trade Policies on Developing Countries*. Washington, DC: IFPRI.

Mellor, J.W., 1999. Faster, more equitable growth: The relation between growth in agriculture and poverty reduction. *Agricultural Policy Development Project Research Report No. 4*. Cambridge, MA: ABT Associates.

Pingali, P. and R. Stringer, 2003. *Food Security and Agriculture in the Low Income Food Deficit Countries: 10 Years After the Uruguay Round*. Paper presented at the IATRC International Conference, 'Agricultural Policy Reform and the WTO: Where are we Heading?' Capri, Italy, 23–26 June.

Sen, A., 1984. *Resources, Values and Development*. Oxford: Blackwell.

Sen, A., 2004. An enduring insight into the purpose of prosperity. *Financial Times*, 21 September.

Singer, P., 1972. Famine, Affluence, and Morality. *Philosophy and Public Affairs* 1(3): 229–243.

Tokarick, S. "Measuring the Impact of Distortions in Agricultural Trade in Partial and General Equilibrium." IMF Working Paper 03/110, 2003.

Winters, A.L., 2002. Trade and poverty: Is there a connection? Paper prepared for WTO.

World Bank, 2002. What should India do to leverage trade for growth? Unattributed Paper.

World Bank. 2005. World Development Indicators. Washington, DC.

WTO, 2003. *World Trade Report*. Geneva: World Trade Organization.

AGRICULTURAL SUBSIDY AND TRADE POLICIES

INTRODUCTION

Were those high duties and prohibitions taken away all at once, cheaper foreign goods of the same kind might be poured so fast into the home market as to deprive all at once many thousands of our people of their ordinary employment and means of subsistence. The disorder which this occasioned might no doubt be very considerable (*Wealth of Nations*: Adam Smith 1776).

More than 200 years ago, the main architect of the free-trade paradigm had visualized the disastrous fallout from an uneven trade regime. The consequences of ignoring that warning has been that rapid economic growth has failed to translate the benefits to those who suffer from hunger and live in squalid poverty.

Ten years after the World Trade Organization (WTO) came into existence, and some 20 years after the holy grail of economic liberalization for more open markets and less government intervention in the developing world, based on the idea that economies must grow if poor people are to reap the benefits of globalization, the tragedy is that the process of economic liberalization may already have set poor communities back a generation (Christian Aid 2004). Nowhere has the negative impact been felt more severely than in agriculture – the first line of defense against poverty. The role of agriculture is central to poverty eradication and the removal of hunger and is fundamental to sustainable development; thereby ensuring global peace and political stability.

As an overview, Mark Malloch Brown, administrator of the UN Development Programme (UNDP), decried the faulty economic prescription being doled out for reducing global economic inequalities. On the release of the *Human Development Report 2003* (HDR 2003), he stated:

> In the so-called great decade, a very significant hard core of countries ended further behind with more poor people.

Explaining the socio-economic debacle, he said that 54 countries, almost half of them in Africa, were poorer than in the 1990s, and some will not meet the development goals for 50 years. The UNDP had earlier pointed out that before globalization became the buzzword, the richest one-fifth of the world's population in 1960 were 30 times better off than the poorest one-fifth. By 1997, this figure had increased to 74 times.

P. Pinstrup-Andersen and P. Sandøe (eds.), Ethics, Hunger and Globalization: In Search of Appropriate Policies, 263–279.
© 2007 *Springer*.

The impact on farming communities has been even more pronounced – the past decade saw rural livelihoods collapsing in the developing countries, leading to more unemployment and more migration from the rural to the urban areas. Poverty and hunger multiplied, thereby leading to further marginalization of the rural communities. Although many economists have now begun to concede that the relationship between economic liberalization and growth is uncertain at best (Winters 2000), the fact remains that the world hasn't learned any meaningful lesson from the unethical dichotomy that prevails at the economic and policy planning level.

A year after the launch of the HDR 2003, the WTO reached what was hailed by some as a historic framework agreement in 2004 that unfortunately deepens the dark abyss leading to further marginalization of the developing economies. The July Framework, as it is called, is being promoted as a 'common vision' for boosting the global economy without first addressing trade policies that worsen income inequalities. It is being projected as the 'road map' for furthering the Doha Development Agenda, which had suffered a setback after the failed Cancun Ministerial in September 2003.

In reality, the July Framework does nothing to reduce the continuing crisis of food insecurity in some of the developing countries already wilting under the compound impact of the Agreement on Agriculture (AoA) (Sharma 2004). This comes at a time when the World Food Summit and Millennium Development Goals for removing hunger are far from being realized.

JULY FRAMEWORK: FAULTY FRAME, RUDE REALITY

Although the WTO Director General, Dr. Supachai Panitchpakdi, calls the July Framework a historic development, the fact remains that the rich and industrialized countries have successfully managed to hoodwink the developing country negotiators. Defying ethical and human rights perspectives, they have gone back more than satisfied with the empty promise of reducing contentious monumental agricultural subsidies, but in reality getting a legal stamp of approval from the developing countries that allows them to increase subsidies.

Let us first understand the political ramifications. Agricultural subsidies had been (and will remain) the bone of contention in the ongoing trade negotiations. It is because of the disagreement on the reduction of agricultural subsidies (to the tune of US$ 320 billion annually) that the developed countries refuse to budge, thereby even allowing the collapse of the WTO Cancun Ministerial in September 2003.

It is accepted that any move to significantly cut agricultural subsidies will be politically suicidal for the rich countries, even more so in an election year. US President George Bush would have never stepped into the election fray after agreeing to chop subsidies for his farmers. European nations, especially France, Germany, and the Nordic countries, would have been faced with political turmoil within a day or two of the July Framework being agreed if it had meant any drastic cut in subsidies.

No political reaction in any of the developed countries is a clear enough indication that the rich countries have managed to protect their subsidies.

The devil is in the detail. Paragraph 7 of the Framework for Establishing Modalities in Agriculture (31 July final draft) says:

> As the first installment of the overall cut, in the first year and throughout the implementation period, the sum of all trade-distorting support will not exceed 80 per cent of the sum of Final Bound Total AMS (Aggregate Measurement of Support) plus permitted *de minimis* plus the Blue Box at the level determined in paragraph 15.

And in paragraph 15, it adds:

> In cases where a Member has placed an exceptionally large percentage of its trade-distorting support in the Blue Box, some flexibility will be provided on a basis to be agreed to ensure that such a Member is not called upon to make a wholly disproportionate cut.

Reading this together means that, first, all the efforts made by developing countries to see that the trade-distorting Blue Box is removed has not only been nullified, but in fact, it institutionalizes the Blue Box. This allows the developed countries to shift a large chunk of its agricultural subsidies to the Blue Box. In other words, the advantage that the developing countries hoped to gain with the termination of the Peace Clause on 31 December 2003 (under which the developing countries could not challenge agricultural subsidies in the rich countries) was overshadowed by the potential negative effects of the expanded Blue Box. They will now be confronted by an equally detrimental Blue Box.

The Framework actually provides a cushion to the USA and EU to raise farm subsidies from the existing level. If you read the draft carefully, it becomes obvious that the first installment of a cut in subsidies by 20% is not based on the present level of subsidies but on a much higher level that has been now authorized based on the three components – the final bound total AMS, plus permitted *de minimis*, plus the Blue Box. For the EU, this should come to €101.6 billion, and after applying the first cut, the subsidies that can be retained will be €81.3 billion.

If we were to add all the components as specified in the WTO Framework, the EU subsidies at present will total (including the under-notified coupled support) around €78.1 billion, which is far less than what it is supposed to reduce. In other words, the EU gets enough leverage to increase its subsidies. No wonder the so-called phase-out of agricultural subsidies has not snowballed into a political crisis in any of the European countries.

Furthermore, the EU has Blue Box subsidies to the tune of €22.3 billion. This is a huge amount, and therefore the Framework states:

> In cases where a Member has placed an exceptionally large percentage
> of its trade-distorting support in the Blue Box, some flexibility will be
> provided on a basis to be agreed to ensure that such a Member is not
> called upon to make a wholly disproportionate cut.

The EU, therefore, has nothing to worry about in cutting the Blue Box
subsidies.

The USA, on the other hand, is wanting to shift the cyclic payments (part of the
US$180 billion for 10 years) that it has provided to farmers under the notorious
Farm Bill 2002 (70% of this amount is to be spent in the first three years) to
the Blue Box. Since the WTO will now specify the historical period from which the
Blue Box implementation will begin, it means that the USA can now protect
the yearly installment of its counter-cyclic payments to farmers. In the case of
cotton subsidies, where the USA provides a daily support of US$10.7 million to its
25,000 cotton growers, and where the ruling of the WTO Dispute Panel has gone
against the USA cotton subsidies, the WTO has not yet ruled.

'Special and differential (S&D) treatment' was a measure that was originally
carved out for the developing countries, given their varying levels of development,
and therefore these countries needed to be given some concessions in implementation. However, in reality, these S&D measures were actually used only by the
developed countries. Instead of dispensing with these measures, the Framework
legitimizes its application for the rich countries. The only redeeming feature is that
the developing countries have been promised that a special safeguard mechanism
will be established.

The question of market access assumes importance in the light of the special
and differential treatment, special safeguard measures, and the domestic support
(including Green Box subsidies) remaining intact in the developed countries. Using
a tiered formula, the developed countries have managed to seek overall tariff
reductions from bound rates and intends that 'substantial improvements in market
access will be achieved for all products.' The only defense that the developing
countries have been allowed is to place some of their important agricultural products
into the 'special product' category. But the fact is that the developing countries
have already opened up their markets by phasing-out or removing the quantitative
restrictions or lowering the tariffs.

Thus, there is no justification for the developing countries to rejoice. The fact is
that the developed countries have also been allowed the provision to put some of
their products in the category of 'sensitive,' which means that they can designate
some crucial commodities as sensitive and thereby deny market access. For instance,
the USA, the EU, Japan, and Canada maintain tariff peaks of 350–900% on food
products such as sugar, rice, dairy products, meat, fruits, vegetables, and fish, which
could be brought under the category of 'sensitive,' and some 25–40 of the sensitive
tariff lines under the tariff rate quota could – after further negotiation – easily be
protected under this category.

Why did the developing countries concede to this agreement within five days
of negotiations? Let us take a peek at what transpired behind the scenes through

arm-twisting, coercion, and allurement (read bribery). The leader of the G-20 group of developing countries, Brazil, was among a number of developing countries that was thrown sugar-coated bait just a week before the negotiations had entered the decisive phase. On 23 July, the USA announced its sugar quota allocation for 40 countries. This system allows these countries to export a fixed quota to the USA at a lower tariff rate. The largest recipients were the Dominican Republic (185,335 metric tons) followed by Brazil (152,691 t), the Philippines (142,160 t), Australia (87,402 t), Guatemala (50,546 t), and Argentina (45,281 t).

International NGOs have reported that the EU had withdrawn aid to Kenya, the most vocal of the African countries. It may be recalled that Kenya was the country that had staged a walkout at Cancun, thereby leading to the collapse of the WTO Ministerial. This time EU withdrew US$60.2 million aid to Kenya on 21 July under the pretext of 'bad governance.' UK Trade Minister Patricia Hewitt has already gone on record stating that Britain was using its influence to persuade developing countries. Obviously, free terror does not operate on ethics and morality. Nor is it directed towards the humanitarian objective of fighting hunger and malnutrition.

For the farmers and agribusiness in North America, Europe, and the Pacific, it will be business as usual. Rich countries subsidize agribusiness by allowing them to buy very cheaply, with the government then making up some of the difference with direct payment to farmers. Since much of the subsidy is capitalized into land values, the major beneficiaries are the landowners, including large ones such as Ted Turner and David Rockefeller (Csaki 2003). The richest man in the UK, the Duke of Westminster, who owns about 55,000 ha of farm estates, receives an average subsidy of £300,000 as direct payments, and in addition gets £350,000 per year for the 1,200 dairy cows he owns (Barnet 2001). It is likely that the British Royal Family is also among the large recipients.

It certainly is an unequal world, and perhaps the most debasing and demeaning of all the world's inequalities is the manner in which the cattle in the rich countries are pampered at the cost of several hundred million farmers in the developing world. When I first compared the life of the Western cow with that of the developing-world farmer (Sharma 2002), I didn't realize that this would offend the sensibilities of at least some of the economists and policy-makers. It has now been estimated that the EU provides a daily subsidy, of US$2.7 per cow, and Japan provides three times more, at US$8, whereas the bulk of India's people live on less than US$2 a day.[1]

Irrespective of the stark inequalities, the new agreement throws a stronger protective ring around the domestic producers in the richest trading bloc – the Organisation for Economic Cooperation and Development (OECD). Unmindful of the negative consequences inflicted with impunity, the rich countries continue to protect their own agriculture with massive subsidies (estimated to be in range of US$320 billion a year) and other protectionist measures. The resulting impact is two-fold for the developing countries – it greatly restricts the access for developing-country farmers to Western markets and at the same time inundates the domestic markets with cheaper agricultural imports, thereby driving out the small farmers from their meager land-holdings.

Toward Food Insecurity

First, let us get a glimpse of the extent of exploitation that the WTO agreement and the policies of developed countries have inflicted on the poor and vulnerable ever since the international trade agreement was signed in January 1995. In the Philippines, agricultural export earnings were expected to increase by billions of pesos a year after 1994, generating 500,000 additional jobs a year in the Philippines. Instead, traditional exports such as coconut, abaca, and sugar have lost markets. Maize production suffered significant negative growth between 1994 and 2000 partly because of cheaper subsidized grains. With incomes falling, the agricultural sector had lost an estimated 710,000 jobs, and another 2 million by the year 2000 Pascual and Gilpo 2001). While this may not all be due to the Uruguay Round, it may be hypothesized that a large share of it is.

Trade liberalization has already exposed developing-country farmers to ruinous competition, driving down prices, undermining rural wages, and exacerbating unemployment. In the Philippines, opening up of the maize market in 1997 reduced corn prices by one-third. At that time, US corn-growers were receiving US$20,000 a year on average in subsidies, while Filipino farmers in Mindanao had average income levels of US$365 (Oxfam International 2002). Between 1993 and 2000, cheap maize imports from the USA into Mexico increased 18 times, leading to accelerated migration from rural areas to urban centers. This was a result of inappropriate agricultural policies in Mexico, resulting in domestic maize deficits, and availability of US maize at prices below the cost of production.

Haiti has been forced to import highly subsidized rice (imports total 312,006 t) from the USA by the World Bank/IMF.[2] The negative impact was also felt in Sub-Saharan Africa, where Ethiopia and Uganda reported huge losses in export revenues. In 2000/01, Uganda exported roughly the same volume, but it earned the country US$110 million, a steep drop from the US$433 million that it notched up five years earlier in 1994/95.[3] Ethiopia reported that export revenues had dropped from US$257 million to US$149 million between 1999 and 2000. Ironically, in January 2002, the EU and USAID warned of increased poverty and food insecurity in Ethiopia, not realizing that much of the reason was the very low international prices resulting in part from OECD export subsidies.

In 2001, the 25,000 US cotton-growers received roughly US$3.9 billion in subsidy payments, for producing a cotton crop that was worth only US$3 billion at world market prices. These subsidies are more than the entire gross domestic product of several African countries and three times the amount the USA spends on aid to half a billion Africans living in poverty. In 2002, export subsidies by a number of exporting countries, including China, the EU, and the USA, to the tune of 73% of the world cotton production, destroyed millions of livelihoods in West-African countries (Benin, Burkina Faso, Mali, and Chad).

Kenya is another victim of the cotton subsidies. Studies have shown that by 1995, Kenya's cotton production had plummeted to 20,000 bales per year from a peak of 70,000 bales being produced some 10 years earlier. Government record shows that while in the mid-1980s there were more than 200,000 small-scale cotton farmers, there were fewer than 140,000 in 2000 (Ikiara and Ndirangu 2000). Employment in the Kenyan textile industry also dropped, from 120,000 to 85,000. In Ghana, the tomato-canning industry was first wiped out by internal reforms pushed through by the World Bank/IMF, and then 24,077 tons of cheaper tomato paste was dumped from southern Germany.[4]

In the dairy sector, EU-subsidized exports have hit the dairy industry in many developing countries including Brazil, Jamaica, and India. In 1999/2000, India imported over 130,000 tons of the EU's highly subsidized skimmed milk powder. This was the result of €5 million export subsidies that were provided, approximately 10,000 times the annual income of a small-scale milk producer (Oxfam 2002). Butter export subsidy paid by the EU, for instance, is currently at a five-year high and butter export refunds have risen to an equivalent of 60% of the EU market price. Consequently, butter oil import into India has grown at an average rate of 7.7% annually. This trend has already had a dampening effect on the price of *ghee* in the domestic market. Ironically, India is the biggest producer of milk in the world, and does not provide any subsidy for the dairy sector.

Indonesia was rated among the top-10 exporters of rice before the WTO came into effect. Three years later, in 1998, Indonesia had emerged as the world's largest importer of rice. Rice imports in Sri Lanka have doubled between 1985 and 1998. In India, the biggest producer of vegetables in the world, the import of vegetables has almost doubled in just one year – from Rs 92.8 million in 2001/02 to Rs 171 million in 2002/03 (Mishra 2003). Far away in Peru, food imports increased dramatically in the wake of liberalization. Food imports now account for 40% of the total national food consumption. Wheat imports doubled in the 1990s, imports of maize overtook domestic production, and milk imports rose three times in the first half of the previous decade, playing havoc with the livelihood of Peruvian farmers (Oxfam International 2002). Increased food imports may be caused by many factors and are not necessarily bad. The problem is that much of the imported food is available at prices below the cost of production in the exporting countries because of subsidies. This makes it virtually impossible for farmers in the importing countries to compete.

It may look shocking, but this is merely a peek into the destruction wrought by the agreement on agriculture. Every day, thousands of farmers and rural people in the developing world – with little or no land and inadequate livelihoods – constituting a reservoir of frustration and disaffection, trudge to the cities, their abject poverty contrasting vividly with the affluence of the urban centers. These are the victims – in fact, the first generation of the affected – of the 'great trade robbery.' These are the hapless sufferers, who are being fed a daily dose of promises – an increase in poverty in the short-run is a price that has to be paid for long-term economic growth.

Surging food imports have hit farm incomes and had severe employment effects in many developing countries. Unable to compete with cheap food imports, and in the absence of any adequate protection measures, income and livelihood losses have hurt women and poor farmers the most. The complete impact on human lives – women and children in particular – and the resulting loss in livelihood security, and thereby the accelerated march toward hunger and destitution, cannot easily be quantified. But unless the social and environmental costs of globalization are first computed, it is futile to treat the economic growth as a touchstone of development.

Through a variety of instruments, the rich countries have maintained a large degree of protectionism in agriculture. Trade policies have remained highly discriminatory against the developing-country farmers. Such is the extent of protection that even the benevolence that the OECD exhibits through development aid to all countries – totaling US$52 billion – is dwarfed by the monumental agricultural subsidies of US$320 billion that these countries provided to their own agriculture in 2001.[5] In reality, rich countries effectively use development aid to convince the domestic audiences of their generosity towards human suffering, in essence using aid as the human face for 'ambitious' one-way trade – from the OECD to the rest of the world.

The colorful row of boxes – Green Box, Blue Box, and Amber Box – have come in handy for the rich countries to protect their subsidies to agriculture, and at the same time dump their surpluses all over the world. Considering that the world commodity prices are far from adequate anywhere to provide them with a living, these subsidies are actually the cause of excessive supplies in the world markets, and thus result in low prevailing world markets. Still further, the USA is permitted under AoA to provide US$363 million in export subsidies for wheat and wheat flour, and the EU can limit it to US$1.4 billion a year.[6] At the same time, the USA annually incurs US$478 million under its Export Enhancement Program (EEP). While the July Framework calls for the elimination of these measures, no agreement has been reached on the timetable.

With the availability of all such subsidies, agribusiness companies find it much easier and economical to export. Export credits, used primarily by the USA, and not counted as export subsidies, doubled in just one year to reach US$5.9 billion in 1998 (IATP 2003). The export subsidies and credits are cornered by the food-exporting companies. In the USA, for instance, more than 80% of the corn exports are handled by three firms: Cargill, ADM, and Zen Noh. The level of dumping by the USA alone hovers around 40% for wheat, 30% for soybeans, 25–30% for corn, and 57% for cotton (IATP 2003). Furthermore, each ton of wheat and sugar that the UK sells on international market is priced 40–60% lower than the cost of production (ActionAid 2002).

The shocking level of food dumping and its little-understood but horrendous impact on the farming sector in the developing countries is the result of clever manipulations at the WTO. The USA and the EU were successful in ensuring that some subsidies – including direct payments – have little or no impact on production levels and so have little or no impact on trade. Using sophisticated models and taking advantage of the un-preparedness of the developing-country negotiators, they devised a complicated set of rules that designated only Amber Box subsidies as 'trade-distorting' subsidies that needed to be cut. As it turned out, these were the type of subsidies that the poor countries were also using.

On the other hand, Green Box and Blue Box subsidies categorize the farm support that only the rich countries were providing, and which the developing countries are not in a position to afford. Subsequently, in July 2002, the USA proposed significant cuts in 'trade-distorting' domestic support for all products and trade partners, with a ceiling of 5% of the value of agricultural production for industrial countries and 10% for developing countries. This proposal did not become reality and the USA did not make any major cuts in its farm subsidy support (as is evident from the July Framework agreement). On the contrary, the US Farm Security and Rural Investment Act 2002, which provides for US$180 billion in subsidies to agriculture for the next 10 years, with more than one-third coming in the first three years (Dhar 2002).

New EU Common Agricultural Policy (CAP) reform proposals that were announced prior to the Cancun WTO Ministerial have also shown no attempt to make radical changes in reduction commitments. Moving on US lines, it has shifted most of the Blue Box subsidies to Green Box. European agriculture will continue to be subsidized to the tune of €43 billion for another decade, and that amount will increase further when the new members join in. Like a magician, both the USA and the EU have managed to juggle the farm support from one box to another without making any significant commitments. This magical trick is now being used to create an illusion of sincerity of the rich towards 'free' trade.

CAP Reforms

Probably drawing inspiration from the influential work of Nobel Laureate Amartya Sen, the EU is using the same principles to reform its notorious Common Agricultural Policy (CAP). While Sen's entitlement theory focuses on the socio-economic relationship with food, the CAP reforms uses the entitlement approach to protect the massive agricultural support it doles out to its minuscule farming population.

The CAP reforms initiated in 2003, with implementation slated to begin from 2005, will keep agricultural subsidies constant as a percentage of the national incomes for the EU countries. The overall level of subsidization of Europe's farm producers will not change. The amount of subsidy that a farmer receives in the reference period 2000–2002 becomes his personal entitlement. For the next 10 years, until 2013, farmers are entitled to receive the same amount of subsidy. All that he must do is to ensure that he keeps the land, and if he sells or rents a part of the land to another tiller, an equal proportion of subsidy also goes to the new cultivator.

The WTO will have little, if any, control over taming these subsidies. Decoupling the subsidies from production to single farm payments means that the EU is justified in shifting the subsidies from the Blue Box to the Green Box. Further to ensure that the EU doesn't have to make any drastic reduction commitments in Blue Box subsidies, the July Framework explicitly states:

> In cases where a Member has placed an exceptionally large percentage of its trade-distorting support in the Blue Box, some flexibility will be provided on a basis to be agreed to ensure that such a Member is not called upon to make a wholly disproportionate cut.

As if this is not enough, the EU has received another waiver to keep the subsidies intact. Spelling out the criteria for direct payments to farmers, Article 14 of the Framework for Establishing Modalities in Agriculture (Annex A) of the July Framework agreement states:

> Any new criteria to be agreed will not have the perverse effect of undoing ongoing reforms.

Thanks to the wisdom and analytical skill of the EU negotiators at the WTO, Europe's CAP reforms have for all practical purposes become sacrosanct.

Before we try to understand the implications of CAP reform on developing-country agriculture, it is important to see what it means to small farmers in Europe. In 1999, 56% of all EU agricultural expenditure was in the form of direct payment to farmers. Like elsewhere, it is the big industrial farms that continue to receive the bulk of the direct payments. As few as 2.2% of the 4.5 million farms in Europe receive 40% of the total payments (Ribbe 2002). This small but influential group of farmers receives more than €50,000 every year. For reasons that remain unexplained by proponents of free-market economy, these 2.2% of the farmers will continue to receive the same level of direct payments year after year till 2013 (Ribbe 2002). Interestingly, the EU Commission proposal to cap the direct payments at €300,000 in single farm payments every year met with such stiff opposition that it had to be withdrawn. The opposition came from a mere 2,000 farmers (0.04% of all farms – mostly large), the majority (1,260) of them in East Germany, who receive more than the stipulated ceiling.

For the small farmers, the direct support does not exceed €5,000 a year. Such farmers constitute 78.6% of the European farm-holdings. While the subsidy entitlements of small farmers may be justified considering the socio-economic context they are farming in, it is obvious that a handful of rich farmers in Europe are holding the global trade negotiations on agriculture to ransom. These farms are located in prosperous areas, and depending upon the industrial lobby whose commercial interests are paramount, the political lobbying becomes intense.

Take the case of maize. It never got any price support but continues to attract a large chunk of the agricultural subsidies. It now attracts the highest price support among cereals, €475 per hectare compared with €323 for wheat. The reason for this is that maize is the crop that benefits the industry the most. Approximately, €1600 million is distributed as direct payments to maize growers mainly in three countries – Germany, Italy, and France. At the same time, direct payments are also provided to consolidate diplomatic control over the developing countries through the supply of improved livestock breeds. France, for instance, supplies purebred rabbits for breeding purposes to the Caribbean (and also to India), subsidizing each rabbit to the tune of €60.

The subsidy benefit does not percolate down to all farmers. It is so designed that it benefits the sector where the EU countries have more commercial interests. The direct payments are therefore loaded in favor of beef and veal, whereas poultry and pig-meat does not receive the same level of support. Take beef, for example;

the EU policy encouraged dairy farmers to also rear a bull to become eligible for subsidy. Why bulls? Because the government was protecting the interests of the slaughterhouses. In other words, it was a subsidy to the slaughterhouses. Under the reforms, a dairy farmer is no longer expected to slaughter a bull to claim subsidy but instead can maintain the grassland under cultivation.

Huge subsidies also go to 'milk and milk products.' The bulk of the milk subsidies have so far gone to the milk retailers for producing skimmed milk powder and products such as ice-cream. The reforms will reduce the intervention prices, thereby lowering the domestic prices for milk and milk products. This will result in a lower production of skimmed milk powder but the world prices are not expected to make any appreciable jump. For the dairy farmer, the subsidy will move from the number of cows he keeps to the area under grassland. The overall milk quota will, however, remain stagnant till 2013 and therefore the reforms process is unlikely to have any meaningful impact on international trade.

For the majority of the farmers, the CAP reform does not provide any cut under the planned 'modulation' that reduces direct payments to foster rural development. For the remainder, the direct payments have to be cut in an arithmetic proportion by a nominal 3% in 2005, 4% in 2006 and 5% in the following years (Windfur 2004). Two-third of Europe's farmers will therefore continue to receive the same subsidy entitlement of €5000 every year during the period of the reform. The resulting distribution of funds among the member countries will therefore differ based on their farm structure and composition. In Germany, for instance, 61.7% of farmers receive less than €5,000. In Portugal, this exemption will benefit 96% of the farmers (as they received less than €5,000 in 2002) (Ribbe 2002).

Behind the complexities of the CAP structure and the reform process, the real intention is only to pacify the growing anger of the taxpayers. With mounting outrage, taxpayers have begun to ask uncomfortable questions about the necessity to maintain farm support. The entire exercise in the name of reform is to make certain adjustments that hoodwink the taxpayers to believe that farming is multifunctional and also performs the important role of environmental protection. The subsidies are therefore being shifted from production to environmental protection. In reality, the EU Commission is not making any meaningful change in the farming systems to make them more sustainable and environmentally safe.

The direct payments are not linked to environmental protection. Payments are made without any consideration of the environment relevance of these crops, mainly in arable lands which are under intensive and industrial farm practices. Except for a small set of 'rural development' measures that will bring in an additional diversion of €1.2 billion every year, the entire focus of European farming remains highly skewed and unsustainable. In fact, given the groundwater contamination and the destruction of soil structure and fertility, Europe's agriculture tops the global chart in having the most environmentally unfavorable and highly unsustainable farming systems.

No wonder the EU's support for environmental programs is increasing. In 1998/99, the EU made available €4,965 million under various environmental programs, which increased to €5,458 the next year. Environment subsidies alone are more than seven times what the Indian farm sector gets as State support. The EU makes the highest provision for the environmental protection program, followed by Japan, Switzerland, and the USA (Wiggerthale 2004). Interestingly, a significant proportion of these subsidies (especially in Germany) are provided under the MEKA programs. Talking to German farmers, it becomes apparent that these subsidies are in reality a bonus payment. Farmers are not even sure of the purpose of these subsidies and are utilizing them to write-off expenses under other heads.[7] In short, it is additional income-support that is being doled out to farmers.

Whatever the impact of CAP reforms on domestic agriculture in Europe may be, the fact remains that the entire exercise is to reinforce the protective ring around European agriculture. Whether these subsidies are socially and environmentally justified is a matter of internal debate for the EU member nations, but when such highly subsidized agriculture is linked to international trade, it results in glaring inequalities in the trade regime, negatively impacting the farmers in the developing world. EU agriculture subsidies (including the environmental subsidies) provide a cushion for European farmers which keeps them insulated from the volatility of the commodity markets. Whether the international prices fall or rise, European farm income remains largely unaffected.

Protecting OECD Agriculture

As if the massive subsidies are not enough, developed countries have used high tariffs to successfully block imports from developing countries. Thirty-eight rich countries have used special safeguards (SSG) to restrict imports from developing countries. Developed countries took advantage of this flexibility by reserving the right to use the SSG for a large number of products: Canada reserves the right to use SSG for 150 tariff lines, the EU for 539 tariff lines, Japan for 121 tariff lines, the USA for 189 tariff lines, and Switzerland for 961 tariff lines. On the other hand, only 22 developing countries can make use of SSG.

Interestingly, there is talk of phasing-out the SSG provisions in the next 5–7 years. By that time, the developing countries would have been forced to open up their markets still further with devastating results. The markets of the developed countries will, however, remain protected for the next seven years.

At the same time, these countries have managed to fulfill the technical requirements for tariff cuts under AoA without any meaningful reductions. Technically speaking, the reductions in tariff cuts are in place, but in reality they have defied the letter and spirit of the agreement. Although the USA, the EU, Japan, and Canada maintain tariff peaks of 350–900% on food products such as sugar, rice, dairy products, meat, fruits, vegetables, and fish (Shirotori 2000), the thrust of the ongoing negotiations remain on gradually forcing an opening of the developing-country markets to more subsidized exports. The USA has offered a *quid pro quo* to cut its subsidies in exchange for market access.

The USA has thus adopted an aggressive posture. After ensuring that the developing countries are made to conform to the WTO obligations of phasing-out or lifting of quantitative restrictions that allow easy penetration of the American farm commodities and the processed products, it is now preparing for the final assault. The new policy is directed at the 600 million 'new consumers' in Asia and Southeast Asia and another 400 million in Latin America and Central America. It also meets 'eye to eye' with the EU's Common Agricultural Policy. And in this 'clash of civilizations' the battle is primarily between the developed and the developing countries, between industrial agriculture and food security, between value-added functional foods and growing hunger.

The hypocrisy of the developed countries has been echoed by the former World Bank Chief Economist Nicholas Stern, who, while traveling through India recently, denounced subsidies paid by rich countries to their farmers as 'sin ... on a very big scale' but warned India against any attempts to resist opening its markets.

> Developing countries must remove their trade barriers regardless of what is happening in the developed countries.

No wonder, while the negotiation continues and the developing countries are kept busy with diversionary tactics like 'special products,' agricultural exports from the OECD countries continue to rise. Between 1970 and 2000, France increased its share from 5.7% to 8.1%, Germany from 2.6% to 5.9% and the UK from 2.7% to 4.1%.[8]

LESSONS FROM THE COTTON CONUNDRUM

Just before the Cancun Ministerial, President Toure of Mali co-authored a letter to the *New York Times* condemning the cotton subsidies in the USA that have been devastating for West-African countries – Burkina Faso, Mali, Chad, and Benin. His colleague, President Compaore of Burkina Faso, spoke to the Trade Negotiating Committee of the WTO in June. They voiced their concern at the way direct financial assistance by a number of exporting countries, including the USA, the EU, and China, to the tune of 73% of the world cotton production, destroyed millions of livelihoods in West-African countries. As a result, African cotton producers realize only 60% of their costs, although their cost of production is less than half of that incurred in the developed countries.

Unrelenting, the WTO had delivered its verdict. The text of the Draft of the failed Cancun Ministerial said:

> The Director-General is instructed to consult with the relevant international organizations including the Bretton Woods Institutions, the Food and Agriculture Organization and the International Trade Centre to effectively direct existing programs and resources towards diversification of the economies where cotton accounts for major share of their GDP.

In simple words, there is nothing wrong with the highly subsidized cotton farming in the USA, the EU, and China – the fault rests with millions of small and marginal farmers in West-Africa. Cancun Ministerial had instructed (the Draft obviously remains rejected with Cancun's failure) the WTO Director General, the FAO, and the World Bank/IMF to make available adequate investments for suitable programs that enable these farmers to diversify from cotton to other crops. This was also reiterated under the WTO July Framework.

The WTO says the West-African farmers should stop growing cotton.

The lesson for the rest of the world is crystal clear. The developing world should stop growing crops that are being negatively impacted by the monumental subsidies that the rich and industrialized countries provide. For the G-20, which created a lot of noise and dust over the US$311 billion in farm subsidies that the richest trading bloc – the OECD – provides for its agriculture; the writing is on the wall. The process to shift the production of staple foods and major commercial commodities to the OECD had in fact begun much earlier. WTO is merely legitimizing the new farming system approach.

The World Bank/IMF has, under the Structural Adjustment Programs (SAP), very clearly tied up credit with crop diversification. It continues to force developing countries to shift from staple foods (crucial for food security needs) to cash crops that meet the luxury requirements of the Western countries. It has therefore been forcing developing countries to dismantle State support to food procurement, to withdraw price support to farmers, to dismantle food procurement, and to relax land ceiling laws, enabling corporate producers to move into agriculture. Farmers need to be left at the mercy of the market forces. Since they are 'inefficient' producers, they need to be replaced by the industry.

The same prescription for farming has never been suggested for the rich and industrialized countries. Let us be very clear – one part of the world that needs to go in for immediate crop diversification is the industrial world. These are the countries that produce mounting surpluses of wheat, rice, corn, soybean, sugar beet, cotton, all too often under environmentally unsound conditions, leading to an ecological catastrophe. These are the countries that inflict double the damage – first destroying the land by highly intensive crop practices, polluting the groundwater, contaminating the environment, and then receiving massive subsidies to keep these unsustainable practices artificially viable. These are the countries that are faced with the tragic consequences of massive farm displacements, and are in the grip of food calamities arising from industrial farming.

If the WTO has its way, and the developing countries fail to understand the prevailing politics that drive the agriculture trade agenda, the world will soon have two kinds of agriculture system – the rich countries will produce staple foods for the world's 6-billion-plus people, and developing countries will grow cash crops such tomato, cut flowers, peas, sunflower, strawberries, and vegetables. The dollars that developing countries earn from exporting these crops will eventually be used to buy food grains from the developed nations – in reality, back to the days of 'ship-to-mouth' existence.

Take the case of Central America. The debt crisis that inflicted the Central American countries in the 1980s was very conveniently used as the right opportunity to shift the cropping pattern to non-traditional exports. Aided and abetted by the US Agency for International Development (USAID), farmers were enticed by the illusion of greener pastures in the developed world. They shifted to crops like melons, strawberries, cauliflower, broccoli, and squash that were shipped to the supermarkets, mainly in he USA. In turn, these Central-American countries disbanded cultivation of staple crops like corn and bean, and have now become major importers and that too from the USA.

In India, which only three decades back emerged from the shadows of massive food imports, the strategy is the same. The World Bank/IMF have forced successive governments to adopt policies that force farmers to abandon staple crops like wheat, rice, and coarse cereals, and diversify into cash crops. Punjab, the country's food bowl, is presently engaged in a desperate effort to shift from a wheat–rice cropping pattern to cultivating cut flowers and the like. Andhra Pradesh, in southern India, has already embarked on a misplaced rural development vision that aims at industrial agriculture at the cost of its millions of small and marginal farmers. As if this alone is not enough, biotechnology companies are having State largesse and prime real estate doled out to them so as to encourage corporate farming.[9] Developed country agriculture has so far enjoyed a unique 'special and differential' treatment that was actually intended for the developing and least-developed countries. The impregnable wall that has been built since the days of the Uruguay Round is not so easy to negotiate. For millions of toiling farmers in the majority of the world, the failure of Seattle and the Cancun Ministerial does not signal the end of the unequal and unjust trade regime. It is merely one stop in their long and arduous battle to retain control over their own food security needs, to protect their own livelihoods, and to move toward a sustainable farming model that survives on equity and justice.

Tragically, the suicide of the Korean farmer Lee Kyung-hae at Cancun typifies the devastation that the WTO has wrought on farming communities all over the world. Not listening to the voice of the marginalized and the poor, the majority of them actively involved with farming, will not only be suicidal but can be catastrophic for the powers that be. The message from Lee's sacrifice is loud and clear. Not listening to the growing discontent and frustration that prevails on the farm front, exacerbated through the trade reforms, will only lead to the usurping of the human rights of the poor including the threat it poses to the right to food and livelihood.

A true reform in agriculture is only possible when the global community accepts the guiding principles of ethics in trade and justice, when it ensures that food for all is an international obligation. It can only be achieved when the need for national food sovereignty becomes the cornerstone of the agricultural trade negotiations. It can only be put into practice when the developed and the developing countries refrain from a battle of food supremacy to reorient efforts to bring equality, justice, and human compassion in addressing the mankind's biggest scourge – chronic hunger and acute malnutrition.

Easing the transition to more open and ethical global markets has to begin by a radical restructuring of the agriculture in North America and the European Union. The way to move forward in a manner that not only minimizes the negative impact of the OECD agricultural subsidies but also addresses the inter-related ethical problems of widespread absolute poverty, skewed and worsening relative income distribution, and the massive humanitarian task of removing hunger and malnutrition has to be based on the following three planks:

- *National Food Sovereignty:* Every country should have the right to protect its agriculture, and thereby the livelihood security of its farming community. Production systems based on efficiency that do not include energy consumption (and refuse to examine the resulting social and environmental costs) in the final analysis have to be discarded. Since the OEDC agriculture is environmentally devastating, ecologically unsound, and economically unviable, the global focus should be to reduce agricultural production in the North under a phase-out program. At the same time, developing countries will need support to move towards food self-sufficiency.

- *Restoration of Quantitative Restrictions:* Developing countries should be allowed to restore quantitative restrictions and tariffs. In fact, the removal of subsidies should be linked with the removal of quantitative restrictions. Since the agricultural subsidies (including the *income support* being granted under the Green Box) are not being phased-out, the developing countries need an immediate protection from the flood of cheap imports. This alone will provide the much needed ethical balance to exploitation in the name of trade and development by adequately safeguarding developing countries' agriculture and food security.

- *Multilateral Agreement Against Hunger:* Since international trade has no relation to removing hunger and malnutrition, and has in fact been responsible for worsening the crisis, the international community needs to strive for a Multi-lateral Agreement Against Hunger. This should be based on the guiding principle of the right to food and should form the basis for all future negotiations. Such a multilateral agreement would ensure that countries will have the right to take adequate safeguard measures if their commitment towards the WTO obligations leads to more hunger and poverty.

NOTES

[1] UNDP (2003).
[2] FAO (2004).
[3] Based on data from ICO, covering the periods October 1994–September 1995 and July 2000–June 2001.
[4] FAO (2004).
[5] OECD (2003). *Indicator Tables 12 and 15*. Development Assistance Committee.
[6] UNDP (2003).
[7] Based on personal interviews during a field trip of some southern German farms, 5–7 September 2004.
[8] UNDP 2003
[9] From reports appearing in *BioSpectrum*, a monthly magazine for the biotechnology industry published from Bangalore.

REFERENCES

ActionAid, 2002. *Farmgate: The Developmental Impact of Agricultural Subsidies.* August.

Barnet, A., 2001. Revealed: How Britain's richest man takes a £3 million tax hand-out. *The Observer*, 20 May.

Christian Aid, 2004. *Taking Liberties: Poor People, Free Trade and Trade Justice.* Christian Aid.

Csaki, C., 2003. The right to food and OECD and developing country trade policy reform. Paper presented at the International Conference on the Right to Food and the Cost of Hunger, Rome, 20–21 June.

Dhar, B., 2002. Subsidising U.S. farmers under AoA. *Economic Times* 9 August.

IATP, 2003. *United States Dumping on World Agricultural Markets.* WTO Cancun Series Paper No. 1.

Ikiara, M.M. and L.K. Ndirangu, 2000, *Developing a Revival Strategy for the Kenyan Cotton-Textile Industry: A Value Chain Approach.* KIPPRA Working Paper No. 8. Kenya Institute for Public Policy Research, August.

Mishra, S., 2003. Foreign fruits and vegetables imports at what cost? *Hindustan Times* July 1.

Oxfam, 2002. *Milking the CAP.* Oxfam Briefing Paper 34.

Oxfam International, 2002. *Rigged Rules and Double Standards.* Oxfam.

Pascual, F. and A. Gilpo, 2001. *WTO and Philippine Agriculture: Seven Years of Unbridled Trade Liberalization and Misery for Small Farmers.* Quezon City, The Philippines: Integrated Rural Development Foundation.

Ribbe, L., 2002. *Observations on the Environmental Compatibility of the EU Agricultural Budget: A Study.* Euronatur and AbL, Germany.

Sharma, D., 2002. From the bovine to the ridiculous. *Ecologist* 32(3).

Sharma, D., 2004. WTO framework: Faulty frame, rude shock. *Hindu Business Line* 5 August. Chennai, India.

Shirotori, M., 2000. *WTO Negotiations on Agriculture: The 13th special Session on Agriculture – Market Access: Chairman's Oral Summary.* UNCTAD, 6 September, Geneva.

Smith, A., 1776. *Wealth of Nations*, Book 4, Chapter 2.

Wiggerthale, M., 2004. *EU Agri-environmental Policies in the Context of the WTO.* Germanwatch.

Windfur, M., 2004. Assessment of the EU-CAP reform on agriculture in developing countries. Presentation at the Workshop on *WTO Agricultural Negotiations and Nature Conservation: Towards Sustainable Rural Development*, Geneva, 7 September.

Winters, A., 2000. *Trade Policy and Poverty: What are the Links?* Centre for Economic Policy, UK.

JULIE A. CASWELL AND CHRISTIAN FRIIS BACH

FOOD SAFETY STANDARDS IN RICH
AND POOR COUNTRIES

INTRODUCTION

Increased food safety has long been associated with higher income. Consumers and governments can afford to focus more on reducing food-borne safety risks once basic quantity needs for foods have been met or are in the process of being met. This would suggest that policies focused on increasing income are the surest path to improving food safety in all countries, which they probably are. However, several questions arise regarding this simple proposition:

- In a world economy with increasing levels of trade in food, how does demand for food safety in rich countries affect the level of exports, income, and food safety in poor countries?
- Can food safety regulations be designed to meet the food safety demands of consumers in rich countries and, at the same time, further the interests of both consumers and producers in poor countries?

In recent years, several important analyses have been published on the impact of food safety and food safety standards on low-income countries (see, e.g., Unnevehr and Hirschhorn 1999; Henson et al. 2000b; Unnevehr 2003; Jaffee and Henson 2004). These conceptual and empirical studies yield insights into what is currently occurring internationally on the food safety front and also make recommendations regarding what should occur. Here we turn this body of evidence toward answering the question of whether globalization and economic policies can be guided by ethical considerations to achieve the World Food Summit Goal and the Millennium Development Goal on Hunger.

Several important ethical issues arise from the increasing demand for food safety and other quality attributes in rich countries, the disparity in domestic food standards between rich and poor countries, and the need for poor countries to generate income by exporting food products to rich countries (Unnevehr 2002). These issues revolve around:

1. The degree of obligation that rich countries and consumers have to consider poor countries when making food standards decisions
2. The responsibility of poor countries to consider and weigh the food safety and economic risks associated with food safety
3. The roles of governments and consumers in assuring an increase in the health of poor citizens around the world through improvements in the safety of the foods they eat.

281

P. Pinstrup-Andersen and P. Sandøe (eds.), Ethics, Hunger and Globalization: In Search of Appropriate Policies, 281–304.
© 2007 *Springer.*

We begin by briefly looking at the development of food safety concerns and food standards, and then turn to the issue of international regulation. Thereafter, we look at the effects on exports from poor countries and on their food standards. Finally, before we conclude, we look at potential solutions in terms of harmonization, changes in domestic policy approaches, and capacity-building efforts.

THE IMPORTANCE OF FOOD SAFETY

The production of safe food is important because of the public health burden that results from the consumption of unsafe foods. Reliable worldwide data on the incidence of food-borne illness, and the total impact generated, are not available. However, the World Health Organization (WHO) believes the health burden from poor food safety is very significant and is placing an emphasis on reducing this burden (WHO 2002a, 2002b). Better, but by no means perfect, data are available in more developed countries. For example, in the USA, the latest estimate is that food-borne diseases annually cause approximately 76 million illnesses, 325,000 hospitalizations, and 5,000 deaths (Mead et al. 1999). Of these, known pathogens account for an estimated 14 million illnesses, 60,000 hospitalizations, and 1,800 deaths.

In terms of risk ranking, this burden is smaller than for other health risks, but these numbers suggest a significant public health and economic burden from food-borne illness. Moreover, food safety is generally underprovided in markets relative to what is a social optimum, because of market failures. For example, consumers and governments may under demand food safety because of a lack on information about the incidence and impacts of food-borne illness. For the same reason, consumers may not seek out and reward producers with better safety records.

Although food safety is not at the top of a risk ranking for public health, the demand for food safety has nonetheless been rising, largely due to increasing incomes and access to more information (Krissoff et al. 2002; Buzby 2003; Caswell 2006). Overall demand for food is income-inelastic: Food consumption rises more slowly than income does. However, as incomes rise, consumers demand products of higher quality, including more safety and freshness, as well as better tracking of attributes such as production and marketing practices (e.g., organic, fair trade). At the same time, food safety crises, such as BSE in the EU and outbreaks associated with *E. coli* O157:H7 in the USA, raise the demand for increased government regulation of food safety.

Both of the demand factors (higher income and better information) are weak in poor countries, especially among the poorest segments of society. As a result, governments, companies, producers, and consumers have probably very significantly underinvested in the provision of food safety in poor countries relative to the public health burden it poses.

Improving food safety in poor countries increases the welfare of citizens in two ways. First there is the direct effect of better health and the increased productivity associated with a higher level of safety for domestically consumed products. Second, higher food safety levels for exported products can serve to establish and/or maintain access to markets that are important generators of income. This higher income, in turn, allows for the consumption of more and safer foods, indirectly improving public health through an income effect. This dual role is crucial to the ethical questions regarding the use of food safety standards by rich and poor countries.

THE EVOLUTION OF FOOD STANDARDS

Food safety and other quality standards in rich countries have been growing progressively more stringent and are being extended into additional areas of regulation (Henson et al. 1999; Blandford et al. 2002). Food safety standards are criteria set for products to be sold in markets. While technically they may set maximums or minimums, they are overwhelmingly framed as minimum standards. These standards may be focused on content attributes of the finished product (e.g., pathogen counts below a specific level), the process under which the product was produced (e.g., requirements for use of Hazard Analysis Critical Control Points (HACCP) systems), or the information required to be delivered to the consumer with the product. Standards may be public (set by governmental regulatory agencies) or private (set by companies).

There has been a concerted movement, led by the Codex Alimentarius Commission (Codex), to encourage countries to focus their regulatory decision-making in the food area on improving public health through the use of risk analysis principles (Caswell 2003a). Under these principles, countries conduct risk assessments to evaluate the degree of risk posed by a food safety hazard, apply risk management principles to identify effective regulatory measures to address the risk, and use risk communication to make the process transparent. The value of standardizing decision-making under the risk analysis framework is that it leads countries to formally justify their decisions based on a set approach to analysis. This standardization can frequently highlight inconsistencies in regulatory approaches; for example, a too stringent or lax approach to mitigating a particular risk.

The regulatory trend toward more stringent regulation is prominent in rich countries (Jaffee and Henson 2004). In addition, private standards are increasing in these same markets, as retailers and food service operators set stricter requirements for their suppliers, and processors pass those requirements back to producers (see, e.g., Golan et al. 2004). In some markets and submarkets, private standards lead public standards. Public and private standards combine to set the product quality requirements that exporting countries must meet to enter markets and gain share.

In many countries, HACCP has been increasingly embraced as a regulatory framework to improve food safety. Its advantages are that it places the responsibility for controlling the safety of food products squarely on producers and employs a scientific approach to hazard identification and control. HACCP is essentially a process standard that requires companies to analyze how hazards such as food-borne pathogens may enter the product, establish effective control points for those hazards, and monitor and update their systems to assure high levels of food safety.

HACCP is nearly always combined with an underlying code of Good Manufacturing Practices that specifies further standards for operation. These process standards may be combined with performance standards that specify acceptable levels of content attributes in food products. The performance standards function as a check on the effectiveness of the process controls.

HACCP and other new systems require greater documentation in terms of record keeping, certification, and/or traceability. Traceability is defined as the ability to follow the movement of a food through specified stage(s) of processing, production, and distribution. Due in large part to the BSE crisis, regulatory standards for traceability are currently most developed for products of animal origin (Souza-Monteiro and Caswell 2004). However, the EU is on a track requiring traceability for all food products. From a public health perspective, traceability offers the ability to track problem food products back to their source and to also track products forward for recall purposes. More generally, traceability is an element in overall quality assurance programs and can be used to track multiple food attributes based on product content and processing. Traceability is an example of the direction in which food safety standards are evolving.

A recent study of traceability systems in major beef exporting and importing countries of the world shows the development of dual traceability systems (Table 16.1). The EU and Japan are leading with mandatory traceability that reaches across several levels in the chain of distribution, focuses on safety and origin of animals and beef products, and is precise in its ability to pinpoint problems. Major exporting countries such as Australia, Argentina, and Brazil are following rapidly behind with mandatory traceability, but only for export. These systems are being put in place in order to maintain access to important importing country markets. Traceability offers an additional example of how increasing standards work out to the comparative advantage of some exporting countries while marginalizing others.

Adoption of HACCP and traceability are examples of a larger phenomenon of the effects of higher food safety standards in rich countries on poor countries. There is significant evidence that food distribution systems in many medium- and some low-income countries are evolving in directions that will standardize food further and likely contribute to increased food safety (see, e.g., Reardon and Berdegue 2002; Weatherspoon and Reardon 2003). As a general proposition, the evidence does not suggest either a definite negative or positive effect of higher food safety standards in rich countries on poor countries. It does suggest a trickle-down situation, where changes among the rich flow down through the system to affect the poor.

INTERNATIONAL REGULATION OF FOOD STANDARDS

Imposing some discipline on food safety regulation has become a focus of international trade agreements as traditional barriers to trade such as tariffs and quotas have been controlled (Josling et al. 2004). Regulatory programs pose what are referred to as non-tariff barriers to trade. The concern is that these standards will be used to cloak discrimination against imported products.

TABLE 16.1 Comparison of country-level beef traceability systems in terms of depth, breadth, and precision[a]

Country	System type[b]	Depth[c] Feed producers to retail	Retail to farm	Farm to abattoir	Abattoir to retail	Abattoir to export ports	Abattoir to import ports	Breadth[c] Safety and origin	Safety, origin, animal welfare, feed and others	Precision[c] Individual animals to their place of birth	Groups of animals to place of birth	Integrity Verification[c] DNA	Other
EU	B	P	X	X	X			X	P	X	X	P	X
Japan	B	P	X	X	X			X		X		X	
Australia	ME			X			X	X	P	X		P	
Brazil	ME			X				X	X		X	P	X
Argentina	ME			X		X		X			X		
Canada	M			X		X		X			X		
USA	V	P	P	P	P			P		P			

[a] Golan et al. (2004) define breadth as the amount of information recorded by the system, depth as how far backward and forward traceability is maintained, and precision as the ability of the system to pinpoint the original source of a problem.

[b] M = mandatory, V = voluntary, B = both mandatory and voluntary, ME = mandatory for export.

[c] X = characteristic of present system, P = potential characteristic of system.

Source: Souza-Monteiro and Caswell (2004).

It is a challenge to sort out potentially discriminatory regulations in an era when the volume and stringency of food safety regulation is increasing. The main mechanism for doing so is the Agreement on the Application of Sanitary and Phytosanitary Measures (SPS Agreement) under the auspices of the World Trade Organization (WTO). The SPS Agreement has been in force since January 1995. It recognizes the right of a country to set the appropriate level of risk (i.e., level of protection) it wishes to achieve. However, if that standard is stricter than that set by Codex, the international food standards body, and the standard is challenged, the country must be able to support its choice based on a scientific risk assessment. In addition, the risk management options (i.e., regulations and enforcement regimes) chosen should be clearly linked to achieving the targeted level of protection, be proportional to the targeted goal, be as least trade-restrictive as possible, and apply national treatment under which the same standards are applied to domestic and imported products.

The SPS Agreement has been reasonably effective in disciplining food safety regulations that act as illegitimate non-tariff barriers to trade. This has occurred partly through the dispute process but also through its support for the use of Codex standards, its encouragement of the recognition of equivalence, and the transparency it has added to the process. Under the Agreement, countries are required to notify changes in their SPS regulations to the SPS Committee. This forum has allowed other countries to informally question and challenge standards and has led to better country-level decision-making (Roberts et al. 2001; Roberts 2004).

While food safety standards are the focus here, it should not be forgotten that an array of additional standards affect international trade in food products (Roberts et al. 2001). In the WTO framework, these fall under the Agreement on Technical Barriers to Trade (TBT Agreement) for regulations such as most labeling and the Agreement on Trade-Related Aspects on Intellectual Property Rights (TRIPS Agreement) for regulations such as labels indicating geographical origin. Market access in international trade is affected by a combination of government and private standards that apply to all aspects of food quality.

EFFECTS ON EXPORTS FROM POOR COUNTRIES

The effect of food safety standards on exports from poor countries is difficult to assess quantitatively. The value of food exports from Asia and Latin America has increased in recent years, raising the stakes for food safety standards, while the food exports from Africa and from the group of least-developed countries have remained almost constant over the past decades (see Table 16.2). As a percentage of the world, total food exports from developing countries – and especially from the poorer ones – has fallen behind.

Assessing the effect of food safety standards on the volume of exports requires answering a 'What if' question: What would the volume and value of trade from poor countries have been in the absence of (excessively strict) standards in rich countries? To date the analysis to effectively answer this comprehensive question has not been completed, although several case studies and overall reviews are available.

TABLE 16.2 Exports of food and animals

	1980	1990	2000	2003
Value (US$1,000)				
Asia	17.342.550	27.143.108	39.255.359	47.706.443
Africa	10.631.709	8.257.095	9.109.959	11.970.762
LAC	26.761.793	27.499.893	36.066.672	43.190.801
LDCs	4.797.833	2.256.543	3.484.229	3.069.002
Developed countries	113.235.918	162.093.653	200.086.370	255.391.771
World	165.390.547	222.391.640	280.859.585	353.796.507
% of world total				
Asia	10	12	14	13
Africa	6	4	3	3
LAC	16	12	13	12
LDCs	3	1	1	1
Developed countries	68	73	71	72
World	100	100	100	100

Source: FAOSTAT data, February 2005, See http://faostat.fao.org/.

The issue is complex because formal and informal trade barriers interact. For the richer developing countries, the main obstacles to trade may be found within the formal trade barriers and the persistence of agricultural subsidies in rich countries. Indeed a number of studies have found quite significant trade and welfare effects in developing countries following agricultural reforms in rich countries (Anderson 2004). These effects may dwarf the potential negative impacts of higher food safety standards. However, as the numbers in Table 16.2 indicate, the main obstacles for the poorer developing countries – for whom market access is generally better than for the richer ones – may be found in supply side-constraints including lack of production capacity and capacity to meet the food safety standards of the rich countries. This also indicates that the impact of food safety standards is likely to grow as rich countries reform their agricultural policies over time and may be tempted to regain market advantage through the strategic use of food safety standards.

Effects of Food Safety Standards on Overall Exports

The strengthening of food standards in rich countries implies that exporting countries, particularly poor ones, can experience restricted or no access to rich-country food markets because of an inability to be competitive in meeting the food standards of these countries. Exporting countries also face sudden cutoffs of market access when problems arise (Henson et al. 2000a; Calvin et al. 2002). All countries are subject to this risk, as is evident in the breakdown of the North American beef market in 2003/2004 with the discovery of a BSE case in Canada and another in the USA (Caswell and Sparling 2005). However, poor countries are more vulnerable to such cutoffs because a significant portion of their export income frequently comes from agricultural and food exports (Unnevehr and Hirschhorn 1999). As such they have been hit hard by total loss of markets in cases where food safety problems have emerged (Henson et al. 2000a; Calvin et al. 2002).

Higher standards can become a critical obstacle for developing countries' ability to export for two reasons: the developing countries are not able to meet the standards or they are able to meet them but cannot prove it due to a lack of control systems, laboratories, and staff. However, as noted above, it is difficult to judge how large this problem is as the evidence often stems from a number of more or less well-researched case studies.

Researchers at the World Bank undertook the most widely quoted – and criticized – studies. They claimed that the EU standards on aflatoxin, when compared with the adoption of the less stringent internationally recommended Codex standards, only saved about one life in the EU but meant that African countries would lose about US$670 million a year in export revenues (Otsuki et al. 2001; Wilson and Otsuki 2001). Similar studies were carried out regarding pesticides and bananas (Wilson and Otsuki 2002). Subsequent analysis by Jaffee and Henson (2004) questions the size of the estimated trade impacts as a result of EU aflatoxin standards, finding them likely to be in the hundreds of thousands, rather than hundreds of millions, of dollars.

The Kenyan fish industry experienced repeated disruption in its ability to export to the EU during the 1990s, each resulting in large economic impacts (Abila 2003). In 1997, Spain and Italy banned fish imports, claiming that *Salmonella* was present. In 1998, the EU banned imports of chilled fish products from Lake Victoria after a report of a cholera outbreak in Kenya and neighboring countries. Finally, imports stopped in 1999 due to the alleged use of pesticides in Lake Victoria. The latter ban lasted for over 10 months and had severe economic implications in both Kenya and Tanzania, where 4,000 people where suspended from work, apart from the impact on small-scale fishermen (Musonda and Mbowe 2001).

A study carried out in six countries – Jamaica, Kenya, Malaysia, Mauritius, Namibia, and Uganda – found that they all had problems with health standards, especially because rich countries often introduced standards that were much stricter than the international standards (Gujadhur 2002). The EU, for instance, has special standards for slaughterhouses, and Norway has strict standards for the control of *Salmonella*. Moreover, standards change all the time and are difficult to see through. This makes it very difficult, if not impossible, for companies to penetrate new markets and maintain existing ones. This is important for large firms with large numbers of employees as well as for small and medium-sized companies.

High and fast-changing standards may also make it impossible for small-scale farmers to participate in markets. Exporters of camel-milk cheese from Mauritania, sourced from poor nomad milk producers, ran into numerous problems in the EU – effectively squeezing them out. Catfish producers in Vietnam have had similar difficulties in accessing the US market (World Bank 2003).

In Kenya the participation of smallholders in the export of fresh fruit and vegetables has decreased during the 1990s, after a period of success in the 1970s

TABLE 16.3 Smallholder participation in exports from Kenya (% of exports)

	Fresh fruit	Fresh vegetables	Fresh fruit & vegetables	Cut flowers	Fresh horticulture
Mid-1980s to early 1990s					
Jaffee (1999)			50%		
Kimenye (1995)	70%	80%		10%	
Harris (1992)			75%		
Late 1990s					
Jensen (2004)	50%	50%	50%	5%	30%

Source: Jensen (2004).

and the 1980s (see Table 16.3). This has happened as food safety requirements have become stricter and more detailed in major markets for Kenyan fresh produce exports. These problems have been deepened significantly by the increased demand for traceability (Jensen 2004). New and even more demanding requirements may follow from the regulation on genetically modified organisms.

Another study argues that most of the phytosanitary standards applied by the EU in the area of fruit and vegetables can be justified and do not constitute disguised barriers to trade (Grethe and Tangermann 1999). One important exception could be the EU ban on citrus imports originating from production areas infected with citrus cancer or certain fungus diseases. Before the ban was implemented, Italy and Greece kept their markets closed for citrus from third countries, whereas citrus could be imported by other Member States, including Spain and Portugal, even from countries where the diseases prevailed. Apparently this caused no problems, so the union-wide ban does seem partly unjustified.

Finally, a detailed study from India shows a wide range of problems related to health and environmental standards and labeling requirements for a broad range of products – from agricultural products to cloth and electronics (Chaturvedi and Nagpal 2003). For some sectors, the increasing standards were reported to impose considerable cost disadvantages.

A more general indication of the importance of food standards on import flows stems from an analysis of import detentions and import alerts by the US Food and Drug Administration. For example, Caswell and Wang (2001) report the number of detentions and the number of different products detained for Asian imports into the USA. In 1995, the FDA executed a total of 5,030 import detentions of Asian products, covering 631 different foods. Japan had the smallest share of detentions (4.2%), while the newly industrialized countries of Hong Kong, Korea, Singapore, and Taiwan accounted for the next largest share (19.9%). Asian developing countries accounted for the largest share (75.9%) of all detentions, with China alone accounting for 26% of the total Asian detentions. Unfortunately, these are count data and do not reflect the value of detained products relative to the value of imports. Caswell and Wang (2001) have estimated a very rough estimate of relative detention rates that shows the number of detentions per US$1 million in imports is at least twice as high for the newly industrialized and developing countries than for Japan. They conclude that food products from Asia face significant challenges in entering the USA.

Another indication of the extent to which food standards act as disguised barriers to trade can be found in the number of formal and informal disputes related to the SPS Agreement at the WTO (see Box 16.1). Out of the 20 formal disputes taken to the dispute settlement system, only three come from developing countries and no African LDC has made a formal dispute (see Appendix for details). Rather than reflecting the actual problems that developing countries have with increasing food standards, this probably reflects the difficulties they have in utilizing the dispute settlement system. When it comes to informal disputes – that is, issues raised in the SPS Committee – developing countries' complaints take up a much larger share.

Redistribution Between Poor Countries

A major source of the impact of higher standards in rich countries on poor countries may not result from a significant blocking of exports from them as a whole. Rather, a redistribution of export activity among the poor countries themselves may be the larger effect, with countries that can meet the standards gaining market share while others lose it. Thus the impact of such regulations among poorer countries may be not so much to reduce trade but to redistribute export market share to those who are able to meet the standards from those who are not (Zaibet 2000; Wang et al. 2002; Jaffee and Henson 2004).

HACCP and other higher food safety standards require investments in infrastructure and human capital that may be difficult to attain by some companies and in some countries. Evidence of this can be found in a study of the impact of HACCP requirements for seafood processing in the USA (Sun 2002; Wang et al. 2002). HACCP was required for domestic and imported products as of December 1997. A case study of the impact of this regulation on imports showed there was an increase

Box 16.1 Formal and informal disputes at the WTO invoking the SPS Agreement

Formal (Dispute Settlement Body):
- 20 formal complaints, three from developing countries
- No African LDCs have made a formal complaint
- Developing countries have been successful in challenging developed countries under other agreements

Informal (SPS Committee):
- 183 specific trade concerns raised during 1995–2003
- 40% of issues raised are about developing countries' market access
- Issues mainly raised by a handful of countries primarily developing country members of the Cairns Group

Source: Jensen (2004).

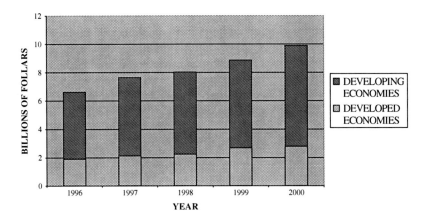

Figure 16.1 US imports of fish products from developed and developing economies
Source: Sun (2002).

in total imports in the years immediately after the requirement was implemented for both developing and developed countries (Figure 16.1).

Further econometric analysis has related changes in export volume to the USA for 32 countries, individually, to the country's geographic location in the world, whether it was a developed or developing economy, and HACCP becoming required. No evidence was found of interactions of the effect on export volume between HACCP and geographical location or HACCP and development status. For example, after HACCP was required by the USA, some developing countries gained export volume to the USA and some lost volume. The size of the export industry was a better predictor of the HACCP effect than was the country's development status. This study provides preliminary evidence of the possibility that higher standards will have differential effects on poor countries – helping those with industries that can attain sufficient size and quality assurance levels and hurting others who cannot.

A fairly broad and deep set of analyses of the actual market effects of higher standards and enforcement regimes in rich countries on exports from developing economies is now developing (see Jaffee and Henson (2004) for a summary). An important question in this work is whether the impacts of such standards will be unevenly experienced among poor countries, with the emergence of clear winners and losers.

EFFECTS ON FOOD STANDARDS IN POOR COUNTRIES

Less analysis has been done on the impact of stronger food standards in rich countries on food safety levels in developing countries. A potentially beneficial effect of higher food standards in rich countries could be a spillover effect to poor country consumers, resulting in beneficial health impacts. The question is whether there is a direct effect on public health through an eventual trading up to stricter standards for domestic production in poorer countries, and/or whether there is a significant indirect effect through higher income levels.

The central ethical question for poor countries is whether to expend scarce resources on improving domestic or export food safety levels or both. This is a complex question because of the dual roles of food safety in improving the welfare of citizens in poor countries. Improvements in domestic food safety levels have direct benefits in terms of better health and higher productivity. Investments in export infrastructure, such as establishment of competent authorities and export certification, are expected to generate indirect health benefits through higher income. There may be some or significant spillover of knowledge gained in the export market to the domestic market that would create additional indirect benefits. Some countries, such as Vietnam, have made a commitment to moving forward on both domestic and export food safety at the same time. In countries that do not have viable export markets for food, this trade-off between direct and indirect effects is not present and the only issue is whether it is worthwhile, on a relative basis, to invest more in producing food safety.

In general, differentiated quality systems, including those based on safety, exist for every good and service in every country of the world. Dual standards and markets for food products have developed in poor countries due to the need to meet rich-country standards for exports and because resources are not available to attain the same standards domestically. In fact, these markets may be more than dual, with a separate set of standards for export to medium- or other low-income countries and with specific standards developing for particular private retail outlets. It is interesting to note that under the WTO dual standards are not permitted for domestically produced and imported products but there is, no doubt sensibly, no such restriction on dual standards for domestic and exported products.

Spillover Effects are Weak

One study on potential spillover effects was done on the adoption of HACCP standards in Brazil (Donovan et al. 2001). A common response to HACCP requirements for exporting to rich countries has been the development of explicit or implicit dual systems in poorer exporting countries. The earliest adoption of HACCP requirements in the USA and EU was for fishery products. In Brazil the federal government adopted HACCP as the standard for all fisheries plants in 1993. However, by 1999, HACCP adoption was still ongoing among the 322 plants in the country and was required only for exporters. HACCP adoption was heavily concentrated among plants that were on the export roll, with nearly 40% of these plants having approved plans and another 5% being in the process of becoming approved (Table 16.4). In contrast, less than 10% of the plants that were not on the export roll had an approved plan, while another 2% were in the process of approval.

The Brazilian case study focused on the effect of stricter foreign regulations on food safety levels in developing countries. The study concluded that the direct impact in Brazil at the time of the study had been negligible or non-existent. HACCP

TABLE 16.4 HACCP compliance by Brazilian fishery plants

	Total		On Export Roll		Not on Export Roll	
	No.	%[a]	No.	%[a]	No.	%[a]
Plants with Approved HACCP Plan	71	22.0	54	38.6	17	9.3
Plants with Submitted but Not Approved HACCP Plan	11	3.4	7	5.0	4	2.2
Plants without Submitted HACCP Plan	240	74.5	79	56.4	161	88.5
Total Plants	322	100.0	140	100.0	182	100.0

[a]Column percentage.
Source: Donovan et al. (2001).

adoption was believed to be producing safer fishery products but those products were almost exclusively sold in the export market. Brazilian consumers did not have direct access to products produced under HACCP systems. However, a trading up within Brazil could occur over the longer term as the government and companies apply HACCP to the domestic market. The study did not evaluate the indirect effect of higher export income on access to safer foods by Brazilians. However, a core concern is whether it is ethical for improved food safety approaches not to reach poor consumers directly but only through the trickle-down effect of higher income.

NATIONAL AND INTERNATIONAL SOLUTIONS

The potential negative effects on developing countries' exports and the possible lack of positive impacts on domestic food safety standards in these countries call for international and national measures. In the following, we look at attempts to harmonize standards, integrate concerns into the domestic policy procedures of rich countries, and build food safety capacity in developing countries.

Harmonizing Standards

While Codex guidance and WTO disciplines have resulted in some standardization of regulatory practice across the world, and some accountability for national-level decision-makers, full harmonization of standards is proving to be an elusive goal. Such harmonization does not appear to be necessary for trade in food products, since such trade has grown robustly without it. It may well be that the benefits of harmonization, even if it is possible, are not worth the cost. This is particularly true because standards change frequently, making harmonization a constant rather than a one-time process. However, to avoid a plethora of different standards and regulations, some degree of international harmonization is desirable where possible. Here international mechanisms and domestic efforts can become mutually supportive.

Generally, international standards can be brought into the WTO in different ways. One model is to write international standards and regulations directly into the WTO agreements. This was the strategy when the basic international patent regulations agreed upon in the World Intellectual Property Organization (WIPO) were written into the Uruguay Round Agreement. This approach has created a very rigid, inflexible system, where international negotiations on intellectual property rights are undertaken in both the WTO and WIPO without a clear division of work. Moreover, the WTO is often accused of not having the necessary expertise to host and facilitate the discussions.

Another approach is the model used in the SPS and TBT Agreements of the WTO. These agreements have, as a clearly stated objective, to ensure that

> measures are not applied in a manner that would constitute a means of arbitrary or unjustifiable discrimination between members where the same conditions prevail or a disguised restriction on international trade (World Trade Organization 1994).

But instead of defining relevant rules and regulations, the WTO states that members shall, in general, base their standards and measures on international standards, guidelines, or recommendations, *where they exist*. The SPS Agreement makes specific reference to the FAO/WHO Codex Alimentarius Commission for food; the International Animal Health Organization (Office International des Epizooties) for animal health; and the FAO's Secretariat of the International Plant Protection Convention for plant health. Governments can add any other international organizations or agreements whose membership is open to all WTO members. These standards are recognized within the WTO framework as legitimate in that if a country applies them it cannot be challenged on the basis of the standard it sets. If a member wishes to introduce a higher level of protection than agreed upon in international organizations, it should be based on a scientific justification and use a least trade-restrictive measure.

Internationally negotiated standards and regulations are thus in reality given priority over WTO free trade regulations. If a country introduces a standard in line with the standards developed in the international agencies, they cannot be challenged based on the standard in the WTO dispute settlement system. This creates an automatic tendency and desire to harmonize standards (Bach 1999; Jensen 2002). Moreover, both the SPS and the TBT Agreements specifically refer to the desire and obligation to encourage and take part in the development of international standards and conformity assessment systems.

The advantage of this model is that negotiations on standards are passed on to organizations that have both the professional insight and the most suitable working methods to deal with the specific issues in question. International standards and rules may gradually become the basis on which international trade takes place. This approach would ensure more dynamism in the development of international regulations and standards. It would also ensure that the poorest countries and farmers of the world face a far more homogeneous set of regulations and standards. Partly as a result of the link with the WTO framework, Codex now plays a key role in providing consensus guidance to governments on good regulatory practices and in developing a broad range of food standards. Codex has become the major worldwide player in establishing the risk analysis approach as the criterion for judging the soundness of standard-setting at the national and international levels.

Codex has been criticized for being too responsive to the interests of rich countries and not responsive enough to those of the poor. This imbalance is being slowly addressed but the result may be a stymieing of the standard-setting process itself as it becomes more difficult to craft compromise standards that suit rich and poor countries' needs alike. Clearly there are limits to the pursuit of harmonization of standards between countries. Risks, benefits, and costs may vary widely across countries due to differences in production, marketing, and consumption. The use of the concept of equivalence, the pursuit of similar risk protection outcomes even if attained through different means, may be a more productive approach (Unnevehr and Roberts 2004). A more proactive approach to negotiating standards and equivalence recognition is needed from exporting and importing countries alike (Jaffee and Henson 2004).

At the WTO, a major ethical issue is whether the structure of the agreement provides adequate fora or incentives for the consideration of the effects of rich-country standards on poor countries. As noted above, the notification process in the SPS Committee provides a discussion venue but there is no requirement that countries respond to critiques of their proposed regulations. The dispute process offers a final recourse for countries adversely affected by the food safety regulations of other countries. To date this process has been dominated by rich-country challenges to each other's regulations, as poorer countries are less able to afford this activity. Although there have been some dispute settlement cases related to standards (e.g., the sardine, asbestos, and hormone cases), it is still too early to say whether the WTO rules will provide an adequate level of protection against standards being used as disguised barriers to trade.

Changes in Domestic Policy Approaches

Consumers in rich countries demand increased levels of food safety indirectly through pressure for higher regulatory standards and directly through purchases in the market place. A core ethical question is whether these consumers have a responsibility to consider the effects of their demand patterns on the welfare of the citizens of poor countries. The response may be different for indirect and direct demand for food safety.

In their indirect demand, consumers as an unorganized group are not likely to consider impacts outside the country when they place demands on their governments for stricter regulations. Consumer advocacy groups, as well as food companies, may be aware of and take consideration of such effects. Ultimately, however, the responsibility to consider them is in the hands of government officials, who must weigh up an array of issues when choosing risk management strategies.

In markets, consumers frequently directly demand quality levels above and beyond the minimums set by government regulations. This demand reflects an ability to pay for safety, or perceived safety, that is associated with higher income levels. While it may be possible to convince these consumers to curb their demand for food safety in order to improve the welfare of others (in other words, food safety for a small planet), experience suggests that harnessing this demand could have a much bigger effect. For example, in a manner directly analogous to the fair trade movement, consumers could demand that companies obtain certification that producers and processors in poor countries had been fairly compensated for the additional effort required to produce higher levels of food safety. In addition, these demands could include certification that companies have made investments in the public health of exporting communities, for example through local water sanitation systems. This could then lead companies to incorporate public health into their paradigms of sustainability.

The central ethical issue arising from the standard-setting process in rich countries is whether the effect of those decisions on others should be considered. In particular, is it the responsibility, for example, of the USA, the EU, or Japan to consider the impact of a new standard on the welfare of citizens of poor countries around the world? If so, how and to what degree? Such consideration could be of a qualitative or quantitative nature.

In government regulatory agencies, it is the job of risk managers to look at the trade-offs associated with different choices of standards and enforcement approaches. Cost-effectiveness and benefit–cost analyses are means to quantify the trade-offs. Cost-effectiveness focuses on the risk reductions achieved (e.g., lower incidence of illness or death) relative to the monetary cost, while benefit–cost analysis focuses on the monetary benefits (e.g., avoidance of loss of productivity and healthcare costs) of a policy choice relative to its monetary costs. The use of such analyses as a means of evaluating policy has met with varying levels of acceptance in different countries. Benefit–cost evaluations are not widely conducted in countries around the world for evaluating the domestic impacts of policies. Their use is most comprehensive in the USA, where they is required as a part of the regulatory decision-making process for major regulations. Such analyses are not required to justify a regulation under the SPS Agreement of the WTO.

To our knowledge, in the USA there are no cost-effectiveness or benefit–cost analyses that take into consideration anything other than the domestic benefits and costs of a food safety regulation. The impact elsewhere in the world is not considered, while the relative burden of new regulations on small and medium enterprises within the country is routinely given extensive attention in the USA and the EU.

The previously mentioned study of new harmonized aflatoxin standards in the EU and their impacts on Africa is a rare exception where an attempt has been made to evaluate the distribution of benefits and costs across parts of the world (Otsuki et al. 2001). That this type of analysis is rare starkly illustrates the degree to which rich-country standard-making does not take into consideration effects elsewhere in the world. Subsequent analysis by Jaffee and Henson (2004) suggests that the impacts in Africa were much smaller than originally estimated in this particular case. However, it is likely that if similar analysis were applied to other rich-country regulations, several would be identified that generate negligible benefits at home and much larger offsetting costs abroad.

Part of the costs abroad may result from the diverting of government resources in poor countries away from improving domestic food safety in favor of investing in meeting rich-country standards for exports. The discussion of trade-offs has been joined most actively in regard to biotechnology but deserves to be conducted in regard to the much broader scope of safety and quality regulation.

Strengthening Capacity-Building Efforts

As full harmonization is an elusive goal, poor countries can expect to continue to face diverse and increasingly stringent food safety requirements for exports to rich countries. Empirical evidence shows that responding to this shift has been costly for poor countries, particularly when the higher standards require significant investments in infrastructure (e.g., Cato and Dos Santos 2000; Zugarramurdi et al. 2000). Moreover, there has up until recently been little to no support for any type of special or differential treatment for poor countries with regard to meeting standards.

Rich countries not only have higher standards; they also have more comprehensive and effective enforcement mechanisms (Caswell 2003b). As the imported share of their food supplies has increased, they have devoted additional resources to inspecting and monitoring the safety of food produced in other countries. To the extent that product content (performance) standards are used, this enforcement can take place through inspection at the border. However, when standards are process-based, such as HACCP, monitoring of the production facilities in exporting countries is required. Importing countries may directly inspect and certify plants in other countries or may require exporting countries to provide a regulatory structure (i.e., a competent authority) that the importer deems to be sufficient to carry out inspection and certification. The latter approach actually exports part of the cost of regulation to the governments of exporting countries. This cost may be significant for poor countries whose internal systems do not currently meet the standards to be judged competent. Thus, a clear result of high standards in rich countries is the development of dual safety systems in lower-income, exporting countries. This has a cost.

The negative impact of higher standards for developing countries can be moderated through investment in capacity-building efforts. The impact of increasing health and environmental standards could be eased if developing countries received the necessary economic and technical assistance to allow them to meet higher standards and regulations. However, to date, support for technical assistance is high but the commitment of resources to accomplish it is not.

There is some disagreement on how severe the lack of capacity is and on how large the costs are. Some evidence suggests that most food safety-related problems that developing-country exporters encounter are not that difficult to solve. Most detentions of developing-country food products seem to involve labeling violations or very basic problems of food hygiene – and thus of quality assurance (World Bank 2003). Here simple training for farmers and processors can go a long way in ensuring compliance with most food safety standards.

Other evidence suggests that there may be considerable costs related to the imposition of still more stringent environmental and health standards by foreign States and of private standards by large retail outlets (Chaturvedi and Nagpal 2003). The private-sector standards can make it difficult or even impossible for both large- and small-scale producers to participate. Here transparency and notification procedures are critical.

Research at the plant level in developing countries has shown the types of costs that must be incurred to comply with HACCP requirements. For example, Maldonado et al. (2004) surveyed 92 Federal Inspection Type (TIF) meat processing plants on their experience with HACCP adoption. Figure 16.2 shows the major cost categories for HACCP adoption and how actual costs compared with those expected. In all categories, a significant proportion of the companies found the costs of adoption to be higher than expected. Since TIF plants are the most technically progressive in Mexico, it can be expected that costs for smaller operators would exceed expectations to an even larger degree.

In these circumstances, it is important to create international mechanisms to provide market information and analysis about product requirements and to strengthen capacity-building initiatives. Moreover, it is important to start the process of removing duplicative testing and certification requirements among different public and private standards. These efforts could ease the access of developing countries to export markets.

The WTO has taken a step forward with its recent decision on special treatment within the SPS Agreement (World Trade Organization 2004). This decision strengthens the commitments of importing countries to provide an opportunity for exporting developing countries to seek revisions or ask for technical assistance when new or revised measures affecting imports are proposed or introduced. If complaints are raised, it can lead to revision of the new or proposed measure for imports from all WTO members, the provision of technical assistance to exporting developing countries to help them meet new requirements, and/or special treatment for exports from developing countries, such as a longer period for adjustment. This new mechanism can alleviate some of the negative impacts of stricter safety standards for developing countries.

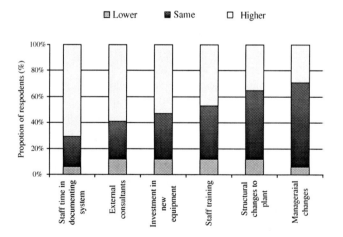

Figure 16.2 Comparison of actual with expected costs of implementing HACCP
Source: Maldonado et al. (2004).

FOOD STANDARDS, SAFETY, AND POVERTY

Access to safe food is very unequal around the world, as is access to every other good and service. The values and ethics of high-income countries are propelling them toward requiring that increasingly safer products be offered to their citizens. At the same time, consumers in those countries are using their buying power to demand safer and more highly differentiated products. Combined with the global sourcing of food products, producers in rich and poor countries alike are being required to produce to these higher food safety standards. Are the values and ethics in rich countries regarding their own food safety levels in conflict with goals of eradicating poverty, hunger, malnutrition, and exposure to unsafe foods in low-income countries?

The answer appears to be no and yes. The establishment of higher standards in rich countries results in the further development of dual food safety systems in exporting countries, especially in low-income countries. Such systems may have positive impacts in exporting countries that can make the investment necessary to participate in higher-safety, presumably higher-value markets in rich countries. Higher export earnings will support income growth and may increase the ability of poorer citizens to buy higher quantities and qualities of foods. At the same time, the building of governmental and private-sector capacity in the export sector may create positive spillovers to more efficient production of food safety for the domestic sector as the country trades up.

The congruence of the food safety goals of rich countries and the aspirations of poor countries holds only if the exporter is fairly compensated for the effort and investment needed to produce higher safety levels. This may be partially assured through the development of private market mechanisms akin to the fair trade movement, where consumers demand that companies certify fair compensation, and could be extended to reward companies that invest in public health, particularly food and water safety, in exporting communities. It may also be partially assured through domestic and international policy requirements, such as the recent decision in the WTO on special treatment within the SPS Agreement. Of course this trickle-down food safety will not benefit poor countries that cannot effectively participate in export markets.

If the trickle-down effect is not sufficiently large, timely, or evenly distributed among the poor countries of the world, there is a conflict of the values and ethics in rich countries regarding their own food safety with the goals of eradicating poverty, hunger, malnutrition, and exposure to unsafe foods in low-income countries. Richer countries and consumers must recognize that the size of the impact of an increase in standards in rich countries on food safety in poor countries through a trickle-down effect will likely be relatively small, slow, and unevenly distributed compared with the impact of direct investment in improved safety in these countries.

Based on ability to pay, we are, as a world, buying fairly marginal improvements in food safety in richer countries at the same cost that we could buy large increases in food safety in poor countries. To the extent that governments and consumers in rich countries ignore the impacts of their demands for food safety improvements on the welfare of producers and consumers in poor countries, there is a definite conflict in values and goals. Taking these effects into consideration in national-level benefit and cost calculations, even in a rough manner, would help to avoid situations where very small welfare gains in rich countries are attained at the cost of significant welfare losses or lack of progress on food safety issues in poor countries.

Escalating standards in rich countries skew the food safety effort of governments and companies in poor countries toward the export sector. Again, this does not necessarily result in a decline in the welfare of the citizens in poor countries if export income is sufficiently large. However, a desirable outcome involves more balanced investment in improving export and domestic food safety. The continuously higher food standards in rich countries can add to an even more skewed international income distribution as the poorest developing countries, and the poorest producers within all developing countries, are squeezed out of the international market place.

There is an important role for a shared vision of moral rights and duties to be brought to play in international discussions and action on food safety. There is no likelihood that rich countries will end their march toward increasingly higher standards for food products; nor should they. We will not have harmonized food safety standards across the world, because food safety is closely linked to income and ability to buy. However, there should be increased efforts to seek at least a minimum degree of international harmonization where possible and the institutional mechanisms for doing so could be strengthened. Moreover, there is ample scope for rich countries to be more cognizant of the extra-national effects of their food safety choices. More analyses, for example cost–benefit analysis with a global scope, should be done to shed a strong light on the nature and magnitude of these trade-offs. There is also ample scope for a larger investment by rich countries in improving food safety and in building capacity in poor countries. Approaches that balance the improvement of domestic food safety and export development in poor countries are being, and can be further developed, by countries and our international institutions. The private market, through companies and consumers, can take a stronger role in considering the ethics of food safety in their production and consumption decisions.

There are smart strategies to follow if we decide that we wish to minimize the potentially negative impact of higher food standards on the exports and income of poor countries, and if we decide that the trickle-down approach to improving food safety in poor countries is not enough. We must consider the ethics of our approaches to food safety if we are to achieve the Millennium Development Goals on hunger, health, and poverty.

APPENDIX

Formal WTO disputes invoking the SPS Agreement
[a] Disputes recorded between 1 January 1995 and April 2002.
Source: WTO (2004): http://www.wto.org/english/tratop_e/sps_e/sps_agreement_cbt_e/c5s2p1_e.htm

DS Number[a]	Parties and nature of complaint	Comments
WT/DS3	US complaint against Korea's inspection procedures for fresh fruits	Pending
WT/DS41	US complaint against Korea's inspection procedures for fresh fruits	Pending
WT/DS5	US complaint against Korea's shelf-life requirements for frozen processed meats and other products	Mutually agreed solution
WT/DS18	Canada's complaint against Australia's import restrictions on fresh, chilled or frozen salmon	Awaiting confirmation of settlement
WT/DS21	US complaint against Australia's import restrictions on fresh, chilled or frozen salmon	Mutually agreed solution
WT/DS20	Canada's complaint against Korea's restrictions on treatment methods for bottled water	Mutually agreed solution
WT/DS26	US complaint against EC's import prohibition on imports of meat treated with growth-promoting hormones	Retaliation
WT/DS48	Canada's complaint against EC's import prohibition on imports of meat treated with growth-promoting hormones	Retaliation
WT/DS76	US complaint against Japan's "varietal testing" requirement for fresh fruits	Agreed solution
WT/DS96	EC complaint against India's quantitative restrictions on agricultural and other products	Mutually agreed solution
WT/DS100	EC complaint against US restrictions on poultry imports	Pending
WT/DS133	Swiss complaint against Slovakia's BSE-related restrictions on cattle and meat	Pending
WT/DS134	India's complaint against EC restrictions on rice imports	Pending
WT/DS135	Canada's complaint against EC (French) measures affecting asbestos	Decided
WT/DS137	Canada's complaint against EC restrictions due to pine wood nematodes	Pending
WT/DS144	Canada's complaint against US state restrictions (South Dakota, etc) on movement of Canadian trucks carrying live animals and grains	Pending
WT/DS203	US complaint against Mexico on measures affecting trade in live swine	Pending
WT/DS205	Thai complaint against Egypt's GMO-related prohibition on imports of canned tuna with soybean oil	Pending
WT/DS237	Ecuadorian complaint against Turkey's import requirements for fresh fruit, especially bananas	Pending
WT/DS245	US complaint against Japan's restrictions on apples due to fire blight	Pending

REFERENCES

Abila, R., 2003. Case Study: Kenyan Fish Exports. In: Unnevehr, L. ed. *Food Safety in Food Security and Food Trade*. Focus 10, Brief 8. Washington, DC: International Food Policy Research Institute [available at http://www.ifpri.org/2020/focus/focus10/focus10_08.pdf].

Anderson, K., 2004. Agriculture, developing countries, and the WTO's Millennium Round. In: Ingco, M.D. and L.A. Winters, eds. *Agriculture and the New Trade Agenda from a Development Perspective*. Cambridge and New York: Cambridge University Press.

Bach, C.F., 1999. *The Global EU*. Copenhagen: New Europe and Mellemfolkeligt Samvirke [available at www.friisbach.dk/theglobaleu].

Blandford, D., J.-C. Bureau, L. Fulponi and S. Henson, 2002. Potential Implications of animal welfare concerns and public policies in industrialized countries for international trade. In: Krissoff, B., M. Bohman and J.A. Caswell, eds. *Global Food Trade and Consumer Demand for Quality*. New York: Kluwer Academic/Plenum Publishers, pp. 77–99.

Buzby, J., ed., 2003. *International Trade and Food Safety: Economic Theory and Case Studies*. Washington, DC: United States Department of Agriculture, Agricultural Economic Report No. 828.

Calvin, L., W. Foster, L. Solorzano, J.D. Mooney, L. Flores and V. Barrios, 2002. Response to a food safety problem in produce: a case study of a *Cyclosporiasis* outbreak. In: In: Krissoff, B., M. Bohman and J.A. Caswell, eds. *Global Food Trade and Consumer Demand for Quality*. New York: Kluwer Academic/Plenum Publishers, pp. 101–127.

Caswell, J.A., 2003a. Food safety standards and regulation. In: Unnevehr, L., ed. *Collection of Policy Briefs: Food Safety in Food Security and Food Trade*. Washington, DC: International Food Policy Research Institute (IFPRI).

Caswell, J.A., 2003b. International food inspection. In: *Encyclopedia of Life Support Systems*, Article 5.18.3.5. Paris, France: United Nations Educational, Scientific, and Cultural Organization (UNESCO).

Caswell, J.A., 2006. Food safety. In: Vaidya, A., *Globalization: The Encyclopedia of Trade, Labor, and Politics*. Santa Barbara, CA: ABC-CLIO Publishers.

Caswell, J.A. and D. Sparling, 2005. Risk management in the integrated NAFTA market: Lessons from the case of BSE. In: Huff, K.M., K.D. Meilke, R.D. Knutson, R.F. Ochoa, J. Rude and A. Yunez-Naude, eds. *North American Agrifood Market Integration: Situation and Perspectives*, Proceedings of the First Annual North American Agrifood Market Integration Workshop. College Station, Texas: Texas A & M University, pp. 141–172.

Caswell, J.A. and J. Wang, 2001. Quantifying regulatory barriers to Asian–U.S. Food Trade. *Journal of Agribusiness* 19(2):121–128.

Cato, J.C. and C.A.L. Dos Santos, 2000. Costs to upgrade the Bangladesh frozen shrimp processing sector to adequate technical and sanitary standards. In: Unnevehr, L.J., ed. *The Economics of HACCP*. St. Paul, MN: Eagan Press, pp. 385–401.

Chaturvedi, S. and G. Nagpal, 2003. *WTO and Product-Related Environmental Standards: Emerging Issues and Policy Options*. EPW Special Article [available at http://www.epw.org.in/showArticles.php?root=2003&leaf=01&filename=5341&filetype=html].

Donovan, J.A., J.A. Caswell and E. Salay, 2001. The effect of stricter foreign regulations on food safety levels in developing countries: A study of Brazil. *Review of Agricultural Economics* 23(1):163–175.

Golan, E., B. Krissoff, F. Kuchler, K. Nelson, G. Price and L. Calvin, 2004. *Traceability in the U.S. Food Supply: Economic Theory and Industry Studies*. Economic Research Service, U.S. Department of Agriculture, Agricultural Economic Report No. 830, March.

Grethe, H. and S. Tangermann, 1999. The EU import regime for fresh fruit and vegetables after implementation of the results of the Uruguay Round. Paper prepared for the Commodities and Trade Division, FAO Economic and Social Department [available at http://wwwuser.gwdg.de/~uaao/disbeit/fuv.pdf].

Gujadhur, S.K., 2002. *Technical Assistance for SPS Measures: Protect Health, Not Trade*. International Trade Forum: Issue 3/2002 [available at http://www.tradeforum.org/news/fullstory.php/aid/460/Technical_Assistance_for_SPS_Measures:_Protect_].

Henson, S., R. Loader, R. Bennett, G. Harper and A. Swinbank, 1999. *Possible Implications for Developing Countries of Higher Standards of Farm Animal Welfare in the European Union*. Reading,

UK: Department of Agricultural and Food Economics, The University of Reading.

Henson, S., A.-M. Brouder and W. Mitullah, 2000a. Food safety requirements and food exports from developing countries: The case of fish exports from Kenya to the European Union. *American Journal of Agricultural Economics* 82(5): 1159–1169.

Henson, S., R. Loader, A. Swinbank, M. Bredahl and N. Lux, 2000b. *Impact of Sanitary and Phytosanitary Measures on Developing Countries*. Reading, UK: Department of Agricultural and Food Economics, The University of Reading.

Jaffee, S. and S. Henson, 2004. *Standards and Agro-Food Exports from Developing Countries: Rebalancing the Debate*. World Bank Policy Research Working Paper 3348, June.

Jensen, M.F., 2002. *Reviewing the SPS Agreement: A Developing Country Perspective*. Working Paper 01/2001. Fødevareøkonomisk Institut.

Jensen, M.F., 2004. *Food Safety Requirements and Smallholders: A Case Study of Kenyan Fresh Produce Exports*. PhD thesis, Royal Veterinary and Agricultural University, Copenhagen, Denmark.

Josling, T., D. Roberts and D. Orden, 2004. *Food Regulation and Trade: Toward a Safe and Open Global System*. Washington, DC: Institute for International Economics.

Krissoff, B., M. Bohman and J.A. Caswell, eds., 2002. *Global Food Trade and Consumer Demand for Quality*. New York: Kluwer Academic/Plenum Publishers.

Maldonado, E.S., S.J. Henson, J.A. Caswell, L.A. Leos, P.A. Martinez, G. Aranda and J.A. Cadena, 2004. Cost–benefit analysis of HACCP implementation in the Mexican meat industry. *Food Control* 16(4): 375–381.

Mead, P.S., L. Slutsker, V. Dietz, L.F. McCaig, J.S. Bresee, C. Shapiro, P.M. Griffin and R.V. Tauxe, 1999. Food-related illness and death in the United States. *Emerging Infectious Diseases* 5 (5, Sept–Oct) [available at http://www.cdc.gov/ncidod/eid/vol5no5/mead.htm].

Musonda, F. and W. Mbowe, 2001. *The Impact of Implementing SPS and TBT Agreements: The Case of Fish Exports to the European Union by Tanzania*. ESRF.

Otsuki, T., J.S. Wilson and M. Sewadeh, 2001. Saving two in a billion: Quantifying the trade effect of European food safety standards on African exports. *Food Policy* 26(5): 495–514.

Reardon, T. and J.A. Berdegue, 2002. The rapid rise of supermarkets in Latin America: Challenges and opportunities for development. *Development Policy Review* 20(4): 371–388.

Roberts, D., 2004. The multilateral governance framework for sanitary and phytosanitary regulations: Challenges and prospects. Prepared for World Bank Training Seminar on Standards and Trade, 27–28 January, Washington, DC.

Roberts, D., L. Unnevehr, J.A. Caswell, I. Sheldon, J. Wilson, T. Otsuki and D. Orden, 2001. The role of product attributes in the agricultural negotiations. Commissioned Paper No. 19 presented at the International Agricultural Trade Research Consortium (IATRC) Conference on *Agriculture in the WTO*, Washington, DC, May [available at http://agecon.lib.umn.edu/cgi-bin/pdf_view.pl?paperid=3022].

Souza-Monteiro, D.M. and J.A. Caswell, 2004. *The Economics of Implementing Traceability in Beef Supply Chains: Trends in Major Producing and Trading Countries*. Working Paper 2004–06, Department of Resource Economics, University of Massachusetts Amherst [available at http://www.umass.edu/resec/workingpapers/index.html].

Sun, Y., 2002. *Implications of Food Safety for Trade between Developing and Developed Countries*. MS thesis.

Unnevehr, L., 2002. LDC Food exports and food safety standards in high income countries: What role for the public sector in overcoming barriers to trade? In: Krissoff, B., M. Bohman and J.A. Caswell, eds. *Global Food Trade and Consumer Demand for Quality*. New York: Kluwer Academic/Plenum Publishers, pp. 63–73.

Unnevehr, L., ed., 2003. *Food Safety in Food Security and Food Trade*. Washington, DC: International Food Policy Research Institute (IFPRI).

Unnevehr, L. and N. Hirschhorn, 1999. *Food Safety Issues in the Developing World*. World Bank Technical Paper No. 469. Washington, DC: World Bank.

Unnevehr, L. and D. Roberts, 2004. Food safety and quality: Regulations, trade and the WTO. In: Anania, G., M.E. Bohman, C.A. Carter and A.F. McCalla, eds. *Agricultural Policy Reform and the WTO: Where Are We Heading?* Cheltenham, UK and Northampton, MA: Edward Elgar, pp. 512–530.

Wang, X., Y. Sun and J.A. Caswell, 2002. Random coefficient model of the effect of mandating hazard analysis critical control points (HACCP): A pilot study. Paper presented at the Midwest SAS User Group Conference, Indianapolis, Indiana, October.

Weatherspoon, D.D. and T. Reardon, 2003. The rise of supermarkets in Africa: Implications for agrifood systems and the rural poor. *Development Policy Review* 21(3): 1–16.

WHO [World Health Organization], 2002a. *Food Safety and Foodborne Illness.* Fact Sheet No. 237. Revised January 2002 [available at http://www.who.int/mediacentre/factsheets/fs237/en/].

WHO [World Health Organization], 2002b. *WHO Global Strategy for Food Safety: Safer Food for Better Health* [available at http://www.who.int/fsf/Documents/fos_strategy_en.pdf].

Wilson, J.S. and T. Otsuki, 2001. *Global Trade and Food Safety: Winners and Losers in a Fragmented System.* Policy Research Working Paper No. WPS2689, World Bank.

Wilson, J.S. and T. Otsuki, 2002. *To Spray or Not to Spray? Pesticides, Banana Exports, and Food Safety.* Policy Research Working Paper No. WPS2805, World Bank.

World Bank, 2003. *Global Economic Prospects 2004.* Chapter 3. Washington, DC: World Bank [available at http://www.worldbank.org/prospects/gep2004/chapter3.pdf].

World Trade Organization, 1994. *Agreement on the Application of Sanitary and Phytosanitary Measures* [available at http://www.wto.org/english/docs_e/legal_e/15sps_01_e.htm] and *Agreement on Technical Barriers to Trade* [available at http://www.wto.org/english/docs_e/legal_e/17-tbt_e.htm].

World Trade Organization, 2004. *Final OK for SPS Special Treatment Decision* [available at http://www.wto.org/english/news_e/news04_e/sps_27_28_oct04_e.htm].

Zaibet, L., 2000. Compliance to HACCP and competitiveness of Oman fish processing. *International Food and Agribusiness Management Review* 3: 311–321.

Zugarramurdi, A., M.A. Parin, L. Gadaleta and H.M. Lupin, 2000. The economics of HACCP application in Argentine fish products. In: Unnevehr, L., ed. *The Economics of HACCP: Costs and Benefits.* St. Paul, MN: Eagan Press, pp. 403–412.

PETER SANDØE, KARSTEN KLINT JENSEN
AND PER PINSTRUP-ANDERSEN

CONCLUDING REFLECTIONS ON THE ROLE OF ETHICS

INTRODUCTION

Attempts to bring the word 'ethics' into discussions about poverty and hunger typically give rise to one of the following two reactions: 'Yes, of course, it is all about ethics,' or 'Oh no! Please, no more rhetoric – we need action.'

Concerning the first reaction it is fair to say that, for more than half a century initiatives have, in the name of ethics, been taken by individuals, organizations, and governments to try to alleviate or prevent poverty and hunger in the less-developed parts of the world. The key ethical message has been that those who have much more than they need to sustain a decent life have a moral duty to help those who, without assistance, are bound to suffer and die prematurely. This message has served as the more or less unquestioned background of initiatives to set up programs and policies.

However, although the motivation has been ethical, ethics has not been much discussed in relation to development. The obstacles to carrying through the initiatives have been assumed to be of either a technical or a political nature. The technical issues have been to find the most efficient policies and mechanisms to alleviate and prevent poverty and hunger in developing countries. The political issues have been about motivation. Specifically, here, we mean the willingness of governments and private organizations in the rich part of the world to contribute funding to development projects; the willingness of governments and international organizations to handle trade issues in a way that supports, or at least does no harm to, developing countries; and the willingness of developing-world governments to govern in ways that further, or at least do not hinder, policies and mechanisms designed to alleviate poverty.

The second reaction has to do with what Jonsson, in Chapter 7, refers to as the 'rhetoric/action gap.' Ethical statements are seen as rhetoric: fine words diverting attention away from inaction (cf. Pinstrup-Andersen in Chapter 2). What is wanted now is more action and less talk. Eye-catching ethical language has been inserted into the preambles of an endless number of declarations and plans to indicate good intentions. And this, of course, gives rise to impatience.

In the past, therefore, ethics has not really been put to work in relation to the fight against poverty and hunger. However, this now seems to be changing. Ethics increasingly seems to be a genuine issue in discussions both about the goals of development and about the means by which to achieve those goals.

There is a growing awareness that tough ethical discussions need to be held, for example, about whether the goal is simply to alleviate hunger and poverty or a

305

P. Pinstrup-Andersen and P. Sandøe (eds.), Ethics, Hunger and Globalization: In Search of Appropriate Policies, 305–321.
© 2007 *Springer.*

much wider one involving democratic empowerment of those who today are not only poor and hungry but also lack the basic ability to govern their own lives. And there need to be, to take another example, discussions about the relationships between the goal of ending hunger and the goal of achieving (more) sustainable development.

Regarding the means, there is a growing awareness that the tools applied in encouraging positive development are not always just tools but may also embody ethical assumptions. For example, nowadays neo-classical economics is seen as part and parcel of a utilitarian line of thinking that needs to be discussed in ethical terms. These changes are clearly reflected in the chapters of this book.

In this concluding chapter we try to bring together some lines of thought emerging from the previous chapters. We begin, in the next section, by trying to pinpoint some of the factors that have led to the growing focus on ethics in relation to development and the fight against poverty and hunger. In the third section we try to clarify the different meanings of the kinds of 'ethics' at play in the discussion of ethics and development. In the fourth section we give an overview of the academic discussion of the principles of rightness and fairness. This presentation can hopefully serve as an introduction for those readers who are not already familiar with the attempts made by philosophers to theorize about ethics. Readers who are already familiar with ethical theory may want to skip this section. In the fifth section we indicate ways in which academic ethics is relevant to practical issues raised by development. One conclusion of this discussion is that academic ethics helps to make the ethical concerns at play, and the kinds of priorities and trade-offs that have to be made, more transparent. However, it cannot in itself create consensus about which ethical concerns are relevant and the relative importance of these concerns. Therefore, in the penultimate section, we discuss the sources on which a consensus over ethical assumptions might be based, and we point to international law as a starting point for building an ethical vision that is shared around the globe. Finally, in last section, we make some suggestions about how ethical thinking could be used to further global dialogue about development – a dialogue which, ideally, will not only create a better mutual understanding but will also speed up the process of reaching decent minimum goals of development.

WHY IS INTEREST IN ETHICS GROWING?

Over the last three decades, the subject of ethics has attracted growing interest from corporations, NGOs, governments, and international organizations. This is not just because moral standards have been going up. Rather, it is in many ways a sign of crisis.

This crisis is rooted in the following six factors:

1. The breakdown of traditional hierarchies and value systems that arrived in the Western world with the so-called youth revolution in the late 1960s.

2. The decline in technological optimism and trust in science – something which makes it obvious that difficult priorities must be set when we try to solve the problems of this world.

3. New scientific and technological developments, notably gene technology, creating ethical challenges which are not easily dealt with by existing values, norms and visions.

4. Economic stagnation combined with increased international competition. This has made it especially clear to governments in the rich world that there is a limit to tax revenues and a need for priorities in the spending of taxpayers' money.

5. Growing awareness of environmental problems that call for new solutions and which challenge traditional anthropocentric ethical values, norms, and visions.

6. Globalization. We have become more aware of the fact that other people have different values and do not necessarily share our norms and visions; also, globalization in itself creates new ethical challenges.

Each of these factors is clearly relevant to discussions about development and the fight against poverty.

(i) During the last three decades there has been a shift in the ethical values at play in the relationship between rich and poor countries. On the one hand, the rich countries are required to treat the poor countries as equals who, in turn, are seen not just as recipients of help but as active agents capable of determining their own future. On the other hand, demands are placed on poor countries, notably in the area of human rights.

(ii) It was an article of faith in previous strategies that modern biological science would play a key role in the fight against poverty. It was assumed that modern plant breeding, combined with other technologies, could be used to improve agricultural productivity in the developing world. However, in the aftermath of the Green Revolution, which was a great success on its own terms, growing skepticism about the solutions offered by agricultural science has developed. Again, analyses and policy advice regarding development based on neo-classical economics are increasingly met with moral objections (see Jonsson, Chapter 7, and von Braun and Mengistu, Chapter 11, who discuss some of these objections). There is also growing agreement that the assumptions underlying economics must be discussed in ethical terms.

(iii) Gene technology is in many ways a potent and obvious tool for trying to boost agricultural productivity. However, in many parts of the Western world, and also to some extent in the developing world, there is widespread skepticism about GM foods.

(iv) Together with the decline in technological optimism, there has been a growing awareness of the fact that the economic resources made available to fight poverty and malnutrition in the developing world are bound to be limited. Since, at the same time, the problems seem to be growing, there is increasing awareness of the need to set priorities in helping people in the developing world.

(v) Clearly, there may be conflicts between the short-term aim of providing food to the poor to prevent starvation and malnutrition and the long-term aim of preserving biodiversity and the environment. To deal with this, many organizations involved in development have had to change their strategies.

(vi) Within the international community, there is a growing awareness of the need both to respect the values and world views of different cultures and to abide by universal declarations on human rights, protection of biodiversity, and the like. It is also true that globalization creates new problems. For example, food standards defined in the rich countries may have a serious impact on agricultural production in the poor countries.

To tackle these issues, more ethical input is called for. However, several different concepts fall under the heading of 'ethics.' It is important to distinguish between these different notions of ethics.

WHAT IS MEANT BY 'ETHICS'?

As humans we act, and what we do affects ourselves, other people, the natural world, and indeed what, more generally, we think of as sacred. Therefore, everything we do has, in a way, ethical significance. However, we also formulate norms and visions of how we ought to behave toward ourselves, toward other people, toward our God or gods, and toward nature. The development of these norms and visions is a central part of culture and civilization. Traditionally, this development has taken place within religious movements and institutions. Historically, States have often backed ethical norms with State sanctions; violation of the norms has been punished.

With the development of culture and the evolution of more liberal societies, ethical norms and visions have been subjected to philosophical scrutiny. Different schools of ethical thought have developed, such as utilitarianism, rights theories, and virtue ethics. In modern times, philosophers have also tried to analyze and understand the role and status of ethics; and here they have made comparisons with the main branches of science. It has been concluded that ethical questions about what we ought to do and how we ought to live cannot be answered by means similar to those by which scientific questions are answered. However, philosophers disagree about the extent to which ethical questions can be the subject of rational discussion, and about the extent to which such discussions may lead to convergence on universally accepted ethical principles.

During the twentieth century, ethical norms were also studied within sociology, anthropology, and other branches of social science. Whereas moral philosophers and other, more applied, ethicists typically study ethics with the aim of improving our ethical norms and our ethical thinking, social scientists want to describe and compare existing norms, and examine their role in human life.

With these points in mind, it is possible to distinguish between four topics falling under the general heading of 'ethics':

1. *The ethics of a person or a group of persons:* Values underlying the ways in which a person or group of persons treat themselves, others, the sacred, and nature.
2. *Empirical ethics:* The study by social science of the values that people live by, of their stated values, norms, and visions, and of the role of these values, norms, and visions in social groups and societies.
3. *Stated ethical norms and visions:* Traditionally these norms and visions can be found in religious texts, but they may also be found in secular documents, such as ethico-legal declarations.
4. *Critical ethics:* The attempt to understand, criticize, improve, and systematize existing ethical values, norms, and visions.

Clearly (1), (2), and (3) will be relevant in any attempt to discuss the ethics of development and the fight against poverty. They may deliver insights and starting points for discussion. This would, however, leave a need for structure and analysis. Here (4) is a key element.

The main input to critical ethics comes from the academic study of ethical theory. This can be quite hard to penetrate for an outsider. In the next section we will therefore try to give a brief and simple overview. However, we would also like to stress at the outset that, if it is to be relevant in the context of development, academic ethics needs to be merely *part* of a wider interdisciplinary discussion of the value assumptions underpinning explicit statements of the means and goals of development.

AN OVERVIEW OF THE ACADEMIC STUDY OF ETHICAL THEORY

Outside the academic world, it is natural to meet ethics in the form of concerns and considerations that appear to enter with some force into the deliberations about how to act in a given situation. Where development is the issue at hand, the *concerns* might be about hunger, poverty, the exhaustion or destruction of natural resources, decreasing biodiversity, and so on. The *considerations*, on the other hand, might be equity or fairness, increasing welfare, respect for rights, individual autonomy, democracy, protection of nature, and sustainable development.

The main aim of academic ethics is that of critically understanding, improving, and systematizing ethical values, norms, and visions. The critical nature of its methods and investigations leads to serious disagreement about its arguments and results. There is not even agreement as to what are the most fundamental questions.

Still, it is possible to describe certain schools of thought that have evolved over time, effectively as competing research programs. An ethical theory, as such a program can be called, should, in principle, provide a precise interpretation of ethical concerns, and a determination of their relative weight in decision-making.

In modern times, the dominant task for ethical theories has been to answer the question: Which act (or acts), in a range of alternatives, is (or are) *morally right* in a given situation? An ethical theory is, accordingly, a systematic account of all the relevant ethical considerations and a determination of how these considerations combine to dictate an overall judgment as to which act is right.

Theories of the right act are often divided into *teleological* (consequentialist) theories and *deontological* (non-teleological, non-consequentialist) theories. There is some disagreement about how this distinction should be drawn (Vallentyne 1987), but we suggest the following rough division. Teleological theories claim that the right act is determined exclusively by considerations about the *good*, whereas deontological theories deny this claim. A teleological theory thus builds on or implies a theory of the good. A theory of the good tells us how to determine the relative value of outcomes (consequences) of an act.

Utilitarianism is the best-known teleological ethical theory (classical sources are Bentham (1789), Mill (1861), and Sidgwick (1874); a modern statement is that of Smart (1973)). It claims that the right act is the act that maximizes total welfare. Thus its underlying theory of the good claims that the best outcome is the outcome with the greatest total of welfare. This theory of the good is *individualistic*, because it claims that the overall good is an increasing function of what is good for individuals (individual welfare) and nothing else. Other teleological theories (e.g., Temkin 1993) would allow for non-individualistic values, i.e., values or ideals whose fulfillment is considered good even though nobody thereby gets a better life. Equality, cultural integrity, the nation, and autonomy are examples of such non-individualistic values. (Note, however, that these values could also be interpreted individualistically.)

Among individualistic theories, utilitarianism claims that it is *total* welfare that counts. Other individualistic teleological theories would claim that the *distribution* of welfare also counts. Thus, (individualistic) *egalitarians* claim that the more equally a quantity of welfare is distributed, the better (Sen 1973); and *prioritarians* claim that benefiting people matters more, the worse-off these people are (Parfit 1997). It is an empirical question to what extent the theories in practice will prescribe different policies. In Chapter 10, for example, Thorbecke argues that more equality – at least up to a certain point – may actually be an efficient means for the creation of a greater total welfare.

Utilitarianism and other individualistic teleological theories must incorporate a theory of welfare: What makes one life better than another or ensures that it contains more welfare? Here several theories have been proposed. Most prominent are perfectionism (the good life consists in realizing the essential aspects of human nature, see Hurka 1993), hedonism (the good life consists in the greatest balance of pleasure over pain, see Bentham 1789), preference satisfaction theory (the good life is the highest possible level of preference satisfaction, see Griffin 1986) and various religious theories (in which, roughly speaking, the good life consists in living in accordance with one's religion).

An influential add-on to these classical theories of the good life is Amartya Sen's theory of 'entitlements' or 'capabilities,' according to which a good life is not defined by the outcome but by the ability to control one's own life (Sen 1981, 1985). This view is explicitly endorsed by Eide in Chapter 6 in the context of a human-rights approach to the fight against hunger, by Jonsson in Chapter 7, by Arnold in Chapter 9, and by Tutwiler and Straub in Chapter 14. The fact that the theme of 'empowerment' of the poor is found throughout the chapters of this book is clearly a sign of the deep and lasting influence of Sen's ideas.

Teleological theories set up a common goal for all of us: maximizing the good (however defined). Deontological theories claim that some ethical considerations work in another way. Marinoff, in Chapter 3, mentions rule-based morality 'epito-mized by the Ten Commandments in the Judeo-Christian tradition and the Eight-Fold Way in Buddhism.' A more sophisticated example is side-constraint theory (see Nozick 1974). This claims that certain specified acts are wrong. A side-constraint cannot be outweighed by considerations of the good. An example is the Kantian view that we should not use other persons exclusively as means in pursuit of our goals – not even in pursuit of the overall good, however defined (Kant 1959).

Pinstrup-Andersen, in Chapter 2, mentions among other examples the case of successful fight against poverty in China and Vietnam at the cost of violations of political rights. According to influential deontological theories of the kind here discussed, these violations – despite their beneficial effects – are not justified. Others with a more utilitarian approach, like Aziz in Chapter 8, point to the development of China and Vietnam as examples to be followed by others.

Another class of deontological theories are *contractualist*. They claim, roughly, that the right act in a given set of circumstances is the act that rational and equal agents can agree on under certain more or less idealized conditions. Contrac-tualist theorists differ as to what the relevant conditions are. Some theories (e.g., Gauthier 1986) attach weight to the idea that ethics should appeal to self-interest only. Others (e.g., Rawls 1972) emphasize the idea that agreement should be unbiased and unforced. All involve an attempt to define conditions of agreement that ensure the right kind of impartiality.

An important, and in some ways separate, question here concerns the way in which *States* ought to act. *Liberals* like Rawls and Nozick claim, roughly, that the State should be neutral between competing conceptions of the good life; it should not prescribe how citizens ought to live, as long as their way of life does not harm others. *Communitarians*, on the other hand, claim that the State ought to promote values inherent in the local, historically evolved community and its culture. The State, therefore, need not be neutral between competing conceptions of the good life (see MacIntyre 1981).

A complication for ethical theories concerns uncertainty. If there is uncertainty about what exactly the outcome of an act will be, there will be a risk of unintended consequences. Ethical theories have disappointingly little to say about uncertainty. However, very roughly, the teleological tradition would want to take probabilities into account when valuing acts with uncertain outcomes (see Harsanyi 1955); the side-constraint tradition would like to maintain that a given *act* is either right or wrong, regardless of its possible unintended consequences (see Nozick 1974); and the contractualist tradition would seek rational agreement about how to deal with the uncertainty in question (see Rawls 1972).

Another task for ethical theories is to say which traits of character each of us ought to cultivate. These traits are often called *virtues*. Many ethical theorists consider this question a secondary one. They believe that the answer should be derived from the answer to the primary question about the right act, and hence, in effect, that virtues are traits of character that lead a person to perform the right act in any circumstances. However, following classical and medieval traditions, a significant number of theorists (e.g., MacIntyre 1981) argue that this puts the cart before the horse: Instead of exploring virtue by working back from right action, we should tackle virtue directly and *then* try to shed light on right action by asking, in any given situation, what the virtuous agent would do. (Marinoff, in Chapter 3, seems to support this line of thought.) By focusing on the virtues, moreover, it is possible to tackle the thorny issue of motivation. Normally, when we accept that it would be (say) wrong to lie, we act accordingly (in this case, refrain from lying). But why? Virtue theory has a ready answer to this question, since to possess a virtue is by definition to be motivated in a certain way.

A final task is to answer the question: What must be taken into account in ethical deliberation? Traditionally, ethical theories have been anthropocentric. They have concentrated on human needs and interests. However, even this claim raises difficult problems of demarcation. Especially relevant to economic development is the issue of whether future generations matter as much, right now, as we, the present generation, do. In reality we tend to think not, but is that a defensible bias?

Animal ethicists and environmental ethicists have challenged the anthropocentric view. One line of argument, called *extensionism*, points out that features we would refer to, to explain our moral concern for humans – complexity, vitality, the capacity to feel pain, and so on – are shared by sentient animals (Singer 1975; Regan 1983). Some environmental ethicists (e.g., Taylor 1986) have extended this argument to plants (focusing, obviously, on features other than pain). Another line of argument, often called *holism*, claims that both anthropocentric ethics and extensionism represent an individualistic conception of nature. But if we reflect on the value of nature, we see that we value ecosystems or landscapes as interdependent wholes (Callicott 1980; Rolston 1988). A third line of argument, *deep ecology*, claims that if we reflect on ourselves, and on the way in which we are intertwined with other life-forms, we shall eventually develop a new understanding of 'self' that involves recognizing other life-forms on equal terms as being part of our own flourishing (Næss 1973).

Let us conclude this section by summarizing some important distinctions. Ethical considerations can be divided into two different types. One concerns the way in which we compare the outcomes of action. Should our objective be one of, as it were, 'totalist' benevolence (utilitarian in nature), or should benevolence be disciplined by equality or fairness? Again, should we be anthropocentric or should we focus on nature for its own sake? The other type of ethical consideration introduces constraints on the pursuit of the first objective. These constraints include respect for persons and their right to autonomy, self-determination, and political participation. These constraints demand that the overall objective is pursued only through acts that are acceptable in that they do not violate rights or other standards of conduct. (For a complementary description of the theories presented in this section, see Thompson in Chapter 13.)

THE RELEVANCE OF THE ACADEMIC ETHICAL DEBATE

From the perspective of someone actively involved in development, academic debate about subjects such as food security, developing-world aid, and the like, may appear disappointingly abstract. However, the importance of academic ethics lies in its willingness to draw distinctions, make progress on hard questions, and clarify conflicting lines of argument. Academic ethics does not, when done well, turn away from real issues; it is an attempt to think clearly about problems that most of us would recognize that we need to address.

The goal of increasing food security and alleviating poverty is a case in point. Discussions of the ethical principles underlying this goal often take the 'right to adequate food' as their point of departure. Since this right is part of the Universal Declaration of Human Rights, it is widely recognized, legally as well as politically. However, from an academic perspective, the implications and basis of the right to food are well worth exploring.

It is common to distinguish between negative and positive rights. A positive right obliges another person to *do* something to, or for, the holder of the right (e.g., pay a bill), whereas a negative right obliges others to *refrain from doing* something to the right-holder (e.g., steal his property). In connection with food security, the right to demand that others refrain from taking food to which you are entitled is a negative right. By contrast, the right of poor people with no access to food to be provided with food is a positive right.

The libertarian tradition (e.g., Nozick 1974) has argued that there is a big difference between the status of negative and positive rights. Negative rights protect people against harmful acts of other individuals, organizations, and governments to which they have not consented. This protection is a matter of respect for persons, i.e., not treating them exclusively as means in the pursuit of goals; and this respect should be backed up by legal sanctions. Governments are entitled to use force to stop one person from violating another's negative rights.

Positive rights, on the other hand, imply a duty that something (e.g., food) is provided for others. But who has this duty and how is it to be fulfilled? Suppose a government were to use tax money to provide food for the poor. According to the libertarian tradition, this would violate the taxpayer's negative right not to have others taking resources to which he (the taxpayer) is entitled without his consent. The upshot is that positive rights (if they deserve that title at all) must be respected on a voluntary basis, not by the use of force.

Where could the duty to respect positive rights derive justification? One answer to this question is given by utilitarianism. Utilitarianism prescribes universal benevolence. It claims that the only right-making feature of an act is its tendency to increase the sum total of welfare in the universe. This implies a duty to use resources most efficiently with respect to the objective of maximizing total welfare: Each individual, organization, or government should allocate resources so as to produce the most welfare. However, resources normally provide diminishing marginal benefits: Roughly speaking, well-off people tend to derive less benefit from them than less well-off people do. And typically, this means that, up to a point, the good is most effectively maximized when rich people's resources are transferred to poor people.

It ought to be apparent that, unless people are in general philanthropic in outlook, the utilitarian objective of universal benevolence will come into conflict with the libertarian ideal of respect for persons. One may very well produce higher total welfare by transferring resources from the rich to the poor; but without people's consent, that transfer will violate the rights of the rich. The utilitarian attitude here is that respecting people's rights involves a cost in the sense that people will be worse off than they might have been.

Both Eide in Chapter 6 and Jonsson in Chapter 7 focus on the distinction between positive and negative rights, and they are highly critical of past liberal policies which have tended to downplay the positive rights. However, they do not seem to endorse positive rights at the cost of political rights; rather they seem to favor a focus on fairness, where political rights are not to be traded off against positive rights. Aziz, in Chapter 8, on the other hand, seems to have much more teleological approach. His focus is on outcomes and the reduction of poverty; for him political rights are secondary.

Fairness has been a key concept in the critique of the utilitarian ideal of efficient use of resources with respect to welfare. One line of thought (*prioritarianism*) claims that we have a duty to benefit the worse-off simply because they are worse-off and not just to the extent that they derive a higher marginal benefit than others (Parfit 1997). In point of fact, some very badly off persons might be very costly to benefit. The utilitarian, seeing that these people are inefficient recipients of resources, would recommend diverting resources away from them. The prioritarian would agree about the inefficiency, but would say that we nevertheless have a special duty to assist the least well-off. For cases of development policy in which this kind of dilemma surfaces, see Chapter 2 by Pinstrup-Andersen.

In *egalitarian* thought, fairness is again emphasized. Here, though, it is taken to require that each of us has an equal share of resources (Dworkin 1981) or at least a certain a minimum level of basic resources (Rawls 1972). This minimum might include the bases of self respect; the right to decide about one's own life, and the right to participate in political decisions.

A third criticism of the utilitarian objective of universal benevolence is that it is too demanding (Williams 1973). For instance, it appears to demand that people in developed countries give up most of their wealth for the sake of the developing countries and future generations. Doing that would seriously prevent richer people from pursuing their own goals in life and, hence, it is claimed, threaten their integrity. There are two sorts of utilitarian answer to this criticism. One is short: the fact that benevolence is demanding does not make it mistaken (Smart 1973).

The other involves a refinement of the utilitarian calculation: It is probably a psychological fact that, in practice, people are only able to provide help for others to a certain extent, while still maintaining a good life for themselves. Hence, if the demands of benevolence are unlimited, they risk being counterproductive. So efficiency is probably best achieved by modest demands: There are good utilitarian reasons to respect the integrity of donors' lives (Parfit 1984).

Another important concept in recent discussions about development is that of *sustainability*. However, this widely used concept is seldom precisely defined, and its clarification involves making up one's own mind about a range of difficult questions. A starting point is to define sustainable agricultural practice as a practice that can be continued in perpetuity. However, as economists would point out, the likelihood of substitution of goods (e.g., due to technological development) makes it irrelevant to consider continuing the *same* practice in the future. But if we are to compare the sustainability of evolving practices, sustainability has to be measured in a more sophisticated way.

Here, *Our Common Future* (World Commission on Environment and Development 1990) deploys a useful measure; namely that the present generation's need-satisfaction does not compromise the need-satisfaction of future generations. Some economists have tried to state this more precisely as the view that economic development should be constrained by the condition that natural resources do not *decrease* over time. However, in this form, the measure still raises several questions.

- *First*, at present we do not know what substitutions will be possible in the future. This uncertainty clearly leads to uncertainty about what the no-decrease measure of sustainability requires. Some authors distinguish between optimistic and pessimistic views on possibilities of substitution, the latter leading to stricter requirements than the former.

- *Second*, on either reading, this measure of sustainability implicitly assumes that each generation will contain the same number of people. But this assumption is extremely unlikely to be correct. However, if generations differ in size, it is not clear what conclusions we should draw concerning sustainability: Should each generation have the same stock of natural resources, or should each individual have the same stock? (On the difficult issue of population ethics, see Broome 2004).

- *Third*, again on either reading, the measure takes a rather rigid view of equality between generations. It might well be doubted that this rigid view is tenable. At the opposite extreme is the utilitarian measure of maximizing the total of welfare in all generations. This allows for the case in which some generations get less than others if this will increase the overall total. A middle position would allow some trade-offs between equality and the overall total of welfare (Broome 1992).

- *Fourth*, many environmental ethicists would protest that the ideal of sustainability builds on an anthropocentric view of nature: it directs us to protect nature merely because it provides natural resources for the satisfaction of human needs. But nature should be valued not just instrumentally as a resource for human welfare, the protest goes; it should also be valued for its own sake. Thus, for instance, certain areas should be left alone and allowed to develop flora and fauna on their own terms, instead of being used for human purposes.

The ideal of protecting natural biodiversity raises a similar problem. From an anthropocentric point of view, biological diversity is valuable because it represents a valuable resource – for instance, for future developments in agriculture. But from an environmental ethicist's view, we should also value the evolved diversity for its own sake.

WHOSE POINT OF VIEW?

Academic discussion of ethical issues may help to clarify ethical concerns and the kinds of priority and trade-off that have to be made. However, it cannot in itself create consensus over which ethical concerns are relevant, and over the relative importance of these concerns. Moral philosophers subscribing to specific schools of ethical thought would be willing to set out answers to the question of which consensus is desirable; but they would offer *different* answers, depending on their theoretical views, and so obviously this cannot be the right way to proceed in the face of the serious disagreements described above.

If academics cannot be relied upon to reach agreement over what is right or wrong, how will the experts who undertake the ethical review move toward any kind of consensus? One answer is that the experts should refer to the shared culture of those nations and organizations that are involved. However, this answer seems to run into an objection from cultural relativism, which is that, since ethics is based on culture, and since culture varies from place to place, there is no single, correct ethical perspective but a number of conflicting perspectives, each connected with a more or less distinctive cultural tradition.

Clearly different cultures do indeed have different values, but this objection involves two further ideas.

1. The values in different cultures define ethical perspectives that are in conflict with each other.
2. If different cultures define conflicting ethical perspectives, there is no way in which it is possible to find common global ethical standards.

These ideas are intuitively plausible, but both can be questioned.

Regarding the first claim, it is certainly true that in India and China, and in the Christian, Buddhist, Islamic, and Jewish traditions, ethical thinking and ethical practice have developed in different ways. However, this is not to say that the world's great ethical traditions are in conflict. Of course, one can find examples of conflict. For example, the focus on individual autonomy in some forms of Christianity may be in conflict with more collective forms of thinking found in some forms of traditional Chinese philosophy. (For other examples, see Gilbert in Chapter 5.) On the other hand, if one takes a closer look at the main ethical traditions, it soon becomes clear that *within* each there are tensions and conflicts that are often as serious as those between the traditions. For example, within the Christian tradition one finds both very hierarchical and highly egalitarian views about the duties and meritorious characteristics of the individual person. If ethical thinking is pervaded with tension, as indeed it is, the lines of conflict are not necessarily to be drawn between different cultures. And, as becomes clear from Gilbert's comprehensive review, in Chapter 5, of the ways in which the main religions view hunger and social injustice, religious outlooks seem to have a great deal in common when it comes to concern for poor, starving, people and the criticism of greed and excessive wealth.

Regarding the second claim, it is worth noting that, in point of fact, some kind of system has evolved by means of which the world community is able to define ethical standards that are broadly viewed as binding on everyone. The system has grown out of international law and incorporates a number of conventions and declarations which are widely seen as having ethical significance. For example, after World War II, conventions about the use of human subjects in biomedical research grew out of the trials of the leaders of the defeated Nazi regime. These are widely recognized as having ethical significance. Thus, today, a biomedical program in which human subjects are involved without informed consent can be said to violate not only international law but also recognized ethical principles. In Chapter 6, Eide gives a very compelling description of the way in which the right to food and to be free of hunger is written into an impressive body of international law. However, it is also argued by Jonsson in Chapter 7 that, within the world of development, the human rights framework has met with resistance or less than whole-hearted acceptance.

Some may argue that the international law approach is just the 'power of the strongest' in disguise. Strong, influential nations band together and impose international law on the rest of the world; and among the different parts of international law they pick and choose those that they wish to elevate to the status of ethical principles.

Three points deserve to be made about this view.

1. In reality no nation is in a position to dictate the content of international law. The very Western nations that were instrumental in setting up the relevant systems of international law are themselves sometimes bound by laws they do not like.
2. What is the alternative? It is widely recognized that in an age of globalization it is necessary to operate with a shared ethical vision and binding minimum ethical standards of conduct. There is no obvious alternative to the present system of trying to reach a common understanding through argument, with all its imperfections.
3. Parts of international law protect religious and ethical differences. Likewise, the ethical framework of international collaboration ought to accept and respect cultural differences as far as this is compatible with key ethical principles and concerns.

Of course, it should not be denied that within the human rights approach to development there are some real tensions to be found – particularly as presented above between those who focus mainly on positive rights and those who see negative rights as being of greater importance. However, the main problem does not seem to be that we disagree about the ethical importance of helping and empowering the hundreds of millions who suffer from poverty and hunger. The main problems are about lack of motivation.

MOTIVATION AND THE ROLE OF ETHICS

Marshall, in Chapter 4, and Gilbert, in Chapter 5, point to the role of religion and religious institutions. As mentioned above, there seems to be considerable common ground in the various religious outlooks; and each religion can be a powerful motivating force. This notwithstanding, Gilbert warns of the limitations of a religious approach which is, in the main, based on compassion and charity:

> ...compassion is no longer enough, if it ever was enough. Charity without justice... is like rearranging deckchairs on the *Titanic*.

In Chapter 13, Thompson makes a similar observation about the way philosophers have conceptualized our obligations to the poor. He points out, for example, that in his seminal paper of 1972, Peter Singer often equates those obligations with the making of donations to famine relief.

As made clear by several of the contributions in this book, famine relief is only useful in very exceptional circumstances. The main task is not to give food to the poor but to organize things so that the poor will be able to feed themselves and achieve development through production and trade with the rest of the world. However, then the relation between those in need of help and those who can provide help becomes much less direct than it is in the case of famine relief. And this may affect motivation.

Most normal people will be strongly motivated to help if they are confronted with a fellow human in need – as Singer reminds us with the example of the drowning child. For a number of reasons, they may be much less motivated when faced with facts about the hundreds of millions of poor and hungry people in the developing world who are affected by policies on which the individual citizen has only a marginal influence. One reason for this lack of motivation is that it is not obvious who is responsible for what. (Why *me*? Why *my* government?) Another reason is the feeling of powerlessness. (What difference can *I* make?)

In Chapter 3, Marinoff gives a very clear description of a problem of coordination which may also negatively affect motivation. On any decent analysis, a number of factors are responsible for poverty: lack of willingness to give in wealthy countries, trade barriers set up by the more prosperous countries, a shortage of sound economic policies in poor countries, corruption and lack of political freedom in those countries – to mention just a few of the more important factors (cf. Pinstrup-Andersen in Chapter 2, Aziz in Chapter 8, Arnold in Chapter 9, Tutweiler and Straub in Chapter 14, and Sharma in Chapter 15). To bring about real change it will be necessary to deal with several of these factors. This means that there is a need for coordinated action between several actors. But a need for coordination may also be an opportunity to shift responsibility. And indeed this opportunity seems to have been seized on by many actors, often with significant public appeal.

It may add to the feeling that many people have of not being part of the issue of fighting poverty, and that those who are involved in drafting policies present the issues as being merely technical and thereby leave out the moral issues to which ordinary citizens attach significance. In Chapter 11, von Braun and Mengistu describe how

> ... the lack of ethical perspective in food and agricultural policies results partly from the neglect of ethics in mainstream economic theory...

and they go on to explain the way in which this neglect has, in some cases, prevented policy-makers from being aware of important perspectives – for example, about

> ... human motivations such as 'goodwill,' 'duty,' 'altruism,' and 'loyalty' as well as the role of many social institutions, such as community groups, cooperatives, and faith-based organizations, in influencing behavior.

Other things may contribute to the development of a feeling of alienation among ordinary citizens: Thompson argues in Chapter 13 that those who promote GM crops for the developing world have, in one important respect, failed. Even though he personally agrees that GM crops should be used to solve problems in developing countries, Thompson thinks that, in the debate, the pro-GM lobby has simply failed to understand and address a number of concerns put forward by the skeptics. Thus members of the lobby have displayed lack of respect for others and weakened a good cause:

> Telling the doubtful to pipe down because we are busy helping the poor is *not* a respectful response.

Similar points about lack of lack of care in debates, not only about GM crops, but also about animal welfare and about food safety, are made by Sandøe and Madsen in Chapter 12 and Caswell and Bach in Chapter 16.

In short, these obstacles to motivation present a formidable challenge. We know that much can be done with current knowledge, technologies, and economic resources. The more wealthy population groups, whether they live in high- or low-income countries, could do much to improve the situation for the very poor without sacrificing anything of equivalent moral value. In fact, it is plausible to suppose that, ultimately, both the very poor and the more wealthy stand to gain here. The only thing lacking is motivation.

Of course, ethics is not a magic formula that can generate motivation by itself; but an increased focus on ethics may make a difference. First, bringing out the ethical assumptions underlying different policy options may help to bring the issue of development back into the domain of public discussion – with the help, perhaps, of rock-stars and other celebrities. Secondly, it may be helpful to bring the concerns and values of 'outsiders' into the discussions of scientists and policy-makers. The latter may find that they have something to learn, and the widening of the forum may promote a more respectful discussion of ways in which development can be combined with other goals that matter to people around the world.

In Chapter 11, von Braun and Mengistu consider ways of institutionalizing ethics within the institutions working in development. We find their ideas interesting, but we warn against the danger of introducing ethics as one more discipline on top of the others, or as one more department placed next to others. The focus on ethics should be another way of doing things rather than another thing to do. It ought to mean greater transparency about value issues, greater openness to, and respect for, the values and perspectives of others, and greater willingness to acknowledge the local character of one's own value commitments.

The most important challenge before us is that of integrating ethical considerations into economic and political deliberation and action. We propose that analyses, plans, strategies, and other activities intended to facilitate action incorporate not only economic and social reflection, but also an ethical perspective as well. The explicit inclusion of an ethical perspective would show a willingness to ventilate and discuss value issues.

Also it is extremely important to let ethics move, rather than stand in the way of, action. We therefore propose that international activities in the coming years, including summits and other conferences, should prioritize implementation and action. Analyses should be undertaken, where they are, to explain why action is not following words at the national level. The findings of such analyses ought to be presented and discussed at national and international meetings. The central purpose of these meetings would be to promote action, rather than to set new goals or to develop new strategies and plans.

Ethics may have a role to play in the coordinating of action and the sharing of responsibility. Respectful discussion, leading to recognition of each others' values, may result in shared goals. Those shared goals will, we hope and trust, open the door to coordinated action.

REFERENCES

Bentham, J., 1789. *The Principles of Morals and Legislation*. New York: Hafner.
Broome, J., 1992. *Counting the Cost of Global Warming*. Isle of Harris: The White Horse Press.
Broome, J., 2004. *Weighing Lives*. Oxford: Oxford University Press.
Callicott, J.B., 1980. Animal liberation: A triangular affair. *Environmental Ethics* 2: 311–338.
Dworkin, R., 1981. What is equality? *Philosophy and Public Affairs* 10: 185–246, 283–345.
Gauthier, D., 1986. *Morals by Agreement*. Oxford: Oxford University Press.
Griffin, J., 1986. *Well-Being: Its Meaning, Measurement and Moral Importance*. Oxford: Clarendon Press.
Harsanyi, J., 1955. Cardinal welfare, individualistic ethics, and interpersonal comparisons of utility. *Journal of Political Economy* 63: 309–321.
Hurka, T., 1993. *Perfectionism*. Oxford: Oxford University Press.
Kant, I., 1959. *Foundations of the Metaphysics of Morals*. Translated by Lewis White Beck. Indianapolis: Bobbs-Merrill.

MacIntyre, A., 1981. *After Virtue*. London: Duckworth.

Mill, J.S., 1861. *Utilitarianism*. Reprinted in Mill, J. S. *Utilitarianism, On Liberty, Considerations on Representative Government*. London: J. M. Dent 1996: 1–67.

Nozick, R., 1974. *Anarchy, State, and Utopia*. Oxford: Blackwell.

Næss, A., 1973. The shallow and the deep, long range ecology movement: A summary. *Inquiry* 16: 95–96.

Parfit, D., 1984. *Reasons and Persons*. Oxford: Clarendon Press.

Parfit, D., 1997. Equality or Priority? *Ratio* 10: 202–221.

Rawls, J., 1972. *A Theory of Justice*. Cambridge, MA: Harvard University Press.

Regan, T., 1983. *The Case for Animal Rights*. London: Routledge and Kegan Paul.

Rolston, H., 1988. *Environmental Ethics*. Philadelphia: Temple University Press.

Sen, A., 1973. *On Economic Inequality*. Oxford: Clarendon Press.

Sen, A., 1981. *Poverty and Famines: An Essay on Entitlements and Deprivation*. Oxford: Clarendon Press.

Sen, A., 1985. *Commodities and Capabilities*. Amsterdam: North-Holland.

Sidgwick, H., 1874. *The Methods of Ethics*.

Singer, P., 1972. Famine, affluence and morality. *Philosophy and Public Affairs* 1: 229–248.

Singer, P., 1975. *Animal Liberation: A New Ethics for Our Treatment of Animals*. New York: New York Review and Random House.

Smart, J.J.C., 1973. An outline of a system of utilitarian ethics. In: Smart, J.J.C. and B. Williams, eds. *Utilitarianism: For and Against*. Cambridge, UK: Cambridge University Press.

Taylor, P., 1986. *Respect for Nature*. Princeton University Press.

Temkin, L,S., 1993. *Inequality*. Oxford: Oxford University Press.

Vallentyne, P., 1987. The teleological/deontological distinction. *Journal of Value Inquiry* 21: 21–32.

Williams, B., 1973. A critique of utilitarianism. In: Smart, J.J.C. and B. Williams, eds. *Utilitarianism: For and Against*. Cambridge, UK: Cambridge University Press.

World Commission on Environment and Development, 1990. *Our Common Future*. Oxford: Oxford University Press.

INDEX

Academic ethics, 2, 13, 306, 310–313
Advocacy, 160–161
Africa, 16, 55, 111, 131, 149, 176
    affect of GM debate on, 211
    Green Revolution, 67
    rejection of GM crops, 201
    weakness of rural economy, 154, 155
Agreement on the application of Sanitary and
    Phytosanitary Measures (SPS agreement),
    286, 289
Agricultural biotechnology, *see* Genetically
    modified crops, Biotechnology
Agricultural research, 218–223, 229
Agricultural subsidies, 29, 39, 63, 134–135, 253,
    263–278
    Amber Box, 270
    Blue Box, 265–266, 270–271
    in dairy sector, 269
    Green Box, 266, 270–271
    negative impact on developing world, 29, 238,
        240, 245–249, 260, 263–278
    in rice, 268–269
    victims of, 268–269
Agricultural trade liberalization, 11, 188, 241,
    251–260; *see also* Tariff reduction
    negative impact on developing countries,
        239–240, 268–270
    and poverty alleviation, 242–245
    versus liberalization of other sectors, 245–246
Agricultural trade reform
    in developed countries, 154, 245–249
    of developing countries, 154–155, 249–260
Altruistic behavior, 185
American Bill of Rights, 45
Analects, 77
Animal and environment ethics
    extensionism, 312
Animal production in developed countries,
    203, 204
    animal welfare, 203–204
        regulation by governments, 204

Animal rights, 206
    versus human rights, 206
Animal welfare, 203–204
    regulation of, 204
    western standards, 205
Animal Welfare Imperialism
    case against, 203–207, 212
Annan, Kofi, 67, 120–121
Argentina
    GM crops, 209–210, 215
Aristotle, 111
Arnold, Tom, 8–9, 12, 149
Asia, 16, 111, 242
Assadourian, Erik, 90
Association for Social Economics
    (ASE), 186
Atlas of Global Inequality, 72
Aziz, Sartaj, 7–8, 131, 314

Banik, Dan, 96
Basic needs, 116
Becker, G.S., 173
    economic theory of crime, 173
Behavior
    competitive, 167
    cooperative, 167
Benefit-cost analysis, in choice of food safety
    standards, 296
Bentham, J., 41, 310
Berger, John, 83
Billionaires, 83
Biopiracy, 222
Biotechnology, 10–11, 170, 201, 207–213; *see
    also* Genetically modified crops
Bloom, Alfred, 76
Bodhisattva, 76
Borlaug, Norman, 23
    Borlaug hypothesis, 219–220, 223–233
    in defence of GM crops, 216, 229
Borlaug hypothesis, 219–220, 223–233
Brazil, 22, 25, 176, 267

The International Library of Environmental, Agricultural and Food Ethics

springer.com

Printed in the United States
84906LV00002B/1-30/A